Roman Alcester Series

Volume 1

ROMAN ALCESTER:
SOUTHERN EXTRAMURAL AREA
1964–1966 Excavations

PART 1: STRATIGRAPHY AND STRUCTURES

Roman Alcester Series

Volume 1

ROMAN ALCESTER:
SOUTHERN EXTRAMURAL AREA
1964–1966 Excavations

PART 1: STRATIGRAPHY AND STRUCTURES

edited by Christine Mahany

with contributions by
M S Alabaster, E Allnut, Paul Booth,
S Cracknell, J Evans, C M Mahany,
G McDonnell, R S Langley,
and C Wingfield

CBA Research Report 96
Council for British Archaeology
1994

Published 1994 by the Council for British Archaeology
Bowes Morrell House, 111 Walmgate, York YO1 2UA

British Library Cataloguing in Publication Data
A catalogue record for this book is available from the British Library

ISSN 0141 7819

ISBN 1 872414 41 9

Typeset from authors' discs by Archetype, Stow-on-the-Wold

Printed by Adpower Advertising, Halifax

The publishers acknowledge with gratitude a grant from
English Heritage towards the publication of this report.

Front cover Constantinian milestone found on site G
Back cover Headstud brooch from site E

Contents

List of illustrations

List of tables

Tables in microfiche

List of plates

6 Site E I, phase VI, structures EH, EI, EJ, with phase III and IV enclosure trenches, E I 10, 36, 19, 43, looking north-west. Scale in 1ft (0.30m) divisions (see also figs 67, 68, 70)

7 Site E, parts of timber buildings at the north end of trench E II, looking south-west. Scale in 1ft (0.30m) divisions

8 Site B IA, phase III, well B IA 25, looking south-west. Scale in 1in (25mm) divisions (see also figs 83–4)

9 Site G IV, phases VI–IX, east wall of structure GE, G IV 15, looking south-west. Scale in 1ft (0.30m) divisions (see also figs 94, 95, 97, 98)

10 Site G IV, phases VI–IX. Milestone in north wall of structure GE, G IV 10, looking south. Scale in 1in (25mm) divisions (see also figs 94, 95, 97, 98)

11 Site M, phase III postholes of the timber pile foundation for the late 4th-century town wall. Scales in 1ft (0.30m) divisions (see also fig 106)

12 Aerial view of the fields to the south of Stratford Road, looking south-west. The south end of Bleachfield Street and the corner of the housing estate built following the 1964–6 excavations can be seen at top right; the river is marked by the line of trees in front of the caravan park and sewage works. The main features visible are ditch A, the road system, and a series of enclosure ditches at right-angles to street A. (Copyright A Baker)

List of microfiche

Foreword and acknowledgements

The excavations here described were directed by C M Mahany and took place between September 1964 and April 1966, mainly on the area known as Birch Abbey, Alcester, Warwickshire, which was to be covered with a housing estate (fig 2). In addition small excavations were undertaken to the west of the High Street, south of the Stratford Road (site L), on the site of the demolished Globe Inn (site O), behind Meeting Lane in an area now known as Tibbet's Close (site M), and west of Churchill House, Henley Street (site N). No archaeological deposits were encountered in sites N and O.

The labour force, which for much of the time included prisoners from Winson Green Prison, was for the most part composed of unpaid volunteers, in the summer of 1965 numbering more than one hundred. A staff of up to twelve was employed at any one time. The excavation was funded by the then Ministry of Public Buildings and Works, and especial thanks are due to the then Inspector, Miss S A Butcher, in whose area of control the site lay. Gratitude to Miss Butcher, former Principal Inspector in charge of post-excavation backlog sites, has increased over the years that the report has been in preparation. Thanks are also due to the governor of Winson Green Prison, and to the many officers and prisoners who worked on the site.

An especial debt is owed to the staff of the excavation, many of whom were at Alcester for the whole period and through two severe winters. They are P A Broxton, C S B Young, J Specht, B Thomas, H Smith, S J Taylor, E Dowman, Mrs A Wacher, P D C Brown (supervisors), T Miles (pottery and finds assistant), Mrs J Taylor (draughtsman), Miss T Martin (conservator).

In addition, I am grateful to the following for their work on the report under the direction of C M Mahany: C S B Young, S J Taylor, R S Langley, E Allnut, F Jay, C Wingfield, M S Alabaster, G Pickin, F Lee, H Roberts, Mrs J Richards, Mrs S Smith, Mrs C Debney, R Clarkson, and S Semmens. Where appropriate, sections of the report appear under the names of certain of the above. The many specialists, whose reports appear under their own names, are owed a particular debt.

Thanks are also due to Messrs Wimpey Limited, for co-operation at all stages of the work and for help in kind. Finally I owe a special debt of gratitude to Dr Graham Webster, for his help and encouragement at all stages of the excavation, and throughout the production of the report.

Extremely grateful thanks are due to the staff of Warwickshire Museum who undertook the final preparation of the text for publication: Stephen Cracknell, Nigel Dodds, Susan Lisk, Helen Maclagan, Stephen Rigby, and Lorraine Webb. Thanks are also due to Mrs Pamela Irving of English Heritage who oversaw the later stages of the project.

Lastly I would like to thank the Council for British Archaeology and their managing editor Christine Pietrowski for publishing the work.

The photographs are by C M Mahany, with the exception of Plate 12 which is by Arnold Baker.

Christine Mahany

Summary of Part 1

The 1964–6 excavations at the Roman small town of Alcester, Warwickshire, were directed by Christine Mahany for the Ministry of Public Buildings and Works. The work was concentrated on the southern extramural area at Birch Abbey, where a housing estate was due to be constructed, and there were also two investigations of the town defences (sites K and M) and one excavation (site L) in the northern extramural area.

The results are reported in two parts. Part 1, this volume, describes the background to the excavations, and the stratigraphy and structures found on the sites. It also contains a discussion of the structures in their Roman context, and includes a review of work in the town up to December 1989.

The town lies at the confluence of the rivers Alne and Arrow, primarily on river terrace gravel. By 1964, when the excavations started, amateur and latterly university-organized excavations had identified the principal roads, several buildings including substantial stone structures, and the cemeteries, but the location of the town defences was not known. The 1964–6 excavations uncovered, amongst other things, the principal Stratford–Droitwich road, two minor roads, many buildings and enclosures, a substantial ditch, and human burials. There was no evidence of formal planning. Agricultural and industrial functions are suggested for some of the structures. There was successive rebuilding on several sites.

The earliest 1st-century features were only identified in the northern part of the site. Later occupation was most intensive on either side of the main through route. From the late 2nd or early 3rd century onwards a large area in the central part of the site was used for gravel quarrying with the dumping of rubbish in the worked-out pits. In the late 2nd to mid-3rd century a substantial east–west ditch was dug along the base of the river terrace but it was backfilled before the end of the 3rd century. South of the former ditch was a very large timber building: the presence of leather scrap suggests that the manufacture of shoes may have been carried out there. During the 4th century, developments on all parts of the site were complex. Structures included a probable smithy and a building with an unparalleled constructional technique involving stone foundations, multiple posts (some in common pits) and plastered walls. A total of 56 human skeletons were represented on the Birch Abbey site.

The buildings fall into six types: native-type huts and enclosures, timber buildings with horizontal sleeper beams, those with post-in-trench construction, those with individual postholes, buildings incorporating stone foundations, and others which do not fit into any of the categories listed above. No public buildings were certainly identified on the Birch Abbey site but two possible examples from elsewhere in the town are noted.

The evidence from the 1964–6 excavations and from other work in the town is discussed. The settlement may have originated in the context of early Roman military activity although there was no evidence for this from the Birch Abbey sites. Recent work to the south of the town may suggest a diversion of Ryknild Street; within the town the street pattern was irregular although most of the excavated structures in the southern part of the town were related to streets or lay close to a known street line. The defences, which are largely known from more recent work, were first identified by the 1964–6 excavations on site M. They consisted of a bank dating to perhaps the later 2nd century and a stone wall (to which external towers were added) dated on external evidence to the late 4th century. The cemeteries are poorly known. The burials in Birch Abbey seem to be relatively dispersed with the exception of one cluster. A possible market area may lie largely beyond the north edge of the Birch Abbey excavations. One of the most significant results of the excavations is the demonstration of the considerable variety of building types to be found in a Romano-British small town.

A medieval drying kiln is also reported.

Outline of the contents of Part 2

Part 2 contains details of the pottery and other finds, and a synthetic discussion of both the finds and the function of the site. The coarse pottery is presented as a type series with discussions of fabric groups and vessel forms followed by a corpus in which the pottery types are illustrated. Some important pit groups are discussed separately. The microfiche section contains tables giving the number of sherds found in each phase with information on the types of vessels and fabrics encountered. The extensive corpus of samian pottery includes a pit group of 69 vessels with the stamps or signatures of 30 Lezoux potters.

There are also sections on incised graffiti, petrology, *amphorae*, and the size of Severn Valley ware tankards. There is a short section on the post-Roman pottery and a discussion in which the Roman assemblages are compared with more recent finds from the town and elsewhere.

The report continues with details of the non-ceramic finds and contains a synthetic discussion of the excavations taking into account excavations in recent years. There are extensive sections on coins, copper alloy objects, iron objects, bone objects, human bone, and stone objects.

Introduction to Part 1

Where the printed text is amplified in microfiche the location is indicated at the start of the section, for example [M1:A10].

Physical background

Paul Booth

Alcester is situated in west Warwickshire 30km south of Birmingham city centre and 12km west of Stratford-upon-Avon (figs 1, 2). It lies at the confluence of the rivers Alne and Arrow, both of which rise in the higher ground of the Birmingham plateau to the north. From Alcester the river Arrow flows to a confluence with the river Avon 6km south of the town.

The basic geology in the western part of the town and much of the immediate surrounding area is Mercia Mudstone ('Keuper Marl'), producing a gently undulating terrain, but ridges to the west and south-east of Alcester are formed by glacial sands and gravels, and Arden sandstone respectively. The latter is part of the Mercia Mudstone series. Though of relatively poor quality, it was used as a building stone in the Roman town.

The Roman town itself lies primarily on gravel of the first and second terraces to the west of the Arrow, but there are very localized variations in the subsoil throughout the settlement. In the south-eastern part Roman deposits on the gravel are sealed by superficial alluvium. The alluvial flood plains of the Arrow and Alne are generally fairly narrow, but are at about their widest around the eastern and southern sides of Alcester.

The river Arrow was one of the principal physical constraints on settlement, and ultimately it bounded the Roman town on its north-east and east sides, though occupation does not seem to have extended into the flood plain south of the town. Recent work has demonstrated the existence of occupation on the gravels to the south of the river, but its relationship to the rest of the town has yet to be established.

To the west of the defended area, in the northern part of the settlement, the occupied area was restricted by the presence of a marsh which was still extant in the Roman period (fig 2). The marsh may have originated as a water course of the river Arrow which once ran to the west of the medieval and modern town centre, before returning east, perhaps roughly along the line of the modern Stratford Road, to the present course of the river. This water course is likely to have become partly naturally blocked well before the Roman period, but to the west of the town it survived as an open, wet feature much later (Booth 1985, 97). Indeed evidence from site K (**41** on fig 3) suggested that it was at that point still in existence in the medieval period. The land defined by this feature to the west (and originally to the south) and by the course of the river in the Roman period (to the north and east) was thus an island of gravel surrounded by wet or lower-lying ground. This distinct topographical unit was to have an important influence on the later development of the Roman town, being enclosed within defences from perhaps the end of the 2nd century onwards. It subsequently formed the nucleus of the medieval town and is still the centre of the modern settlement, despite extensive 20th-century development to the north of the river Arrow.

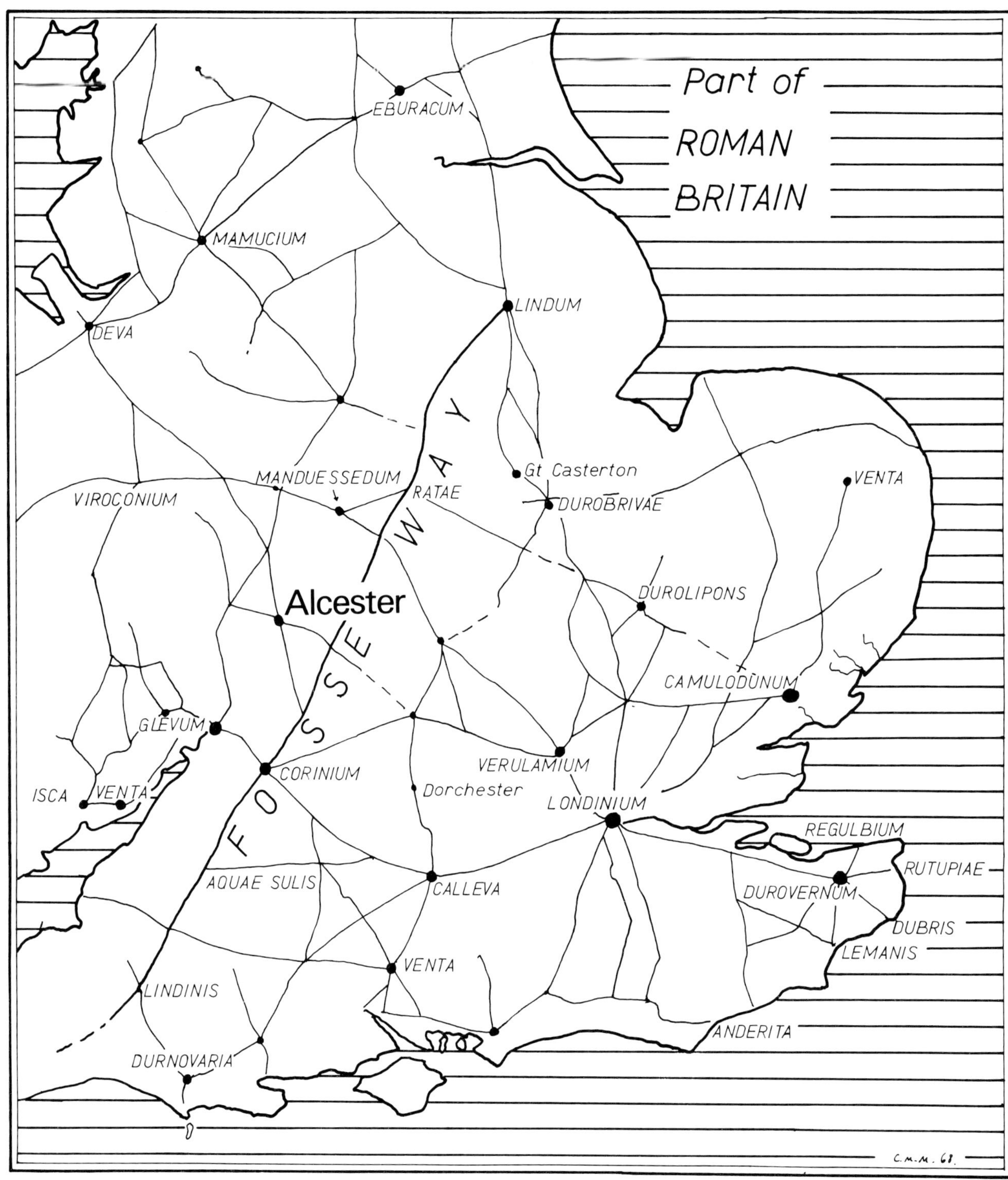

Figure 1 *Location of Alcester in Roman Britain*

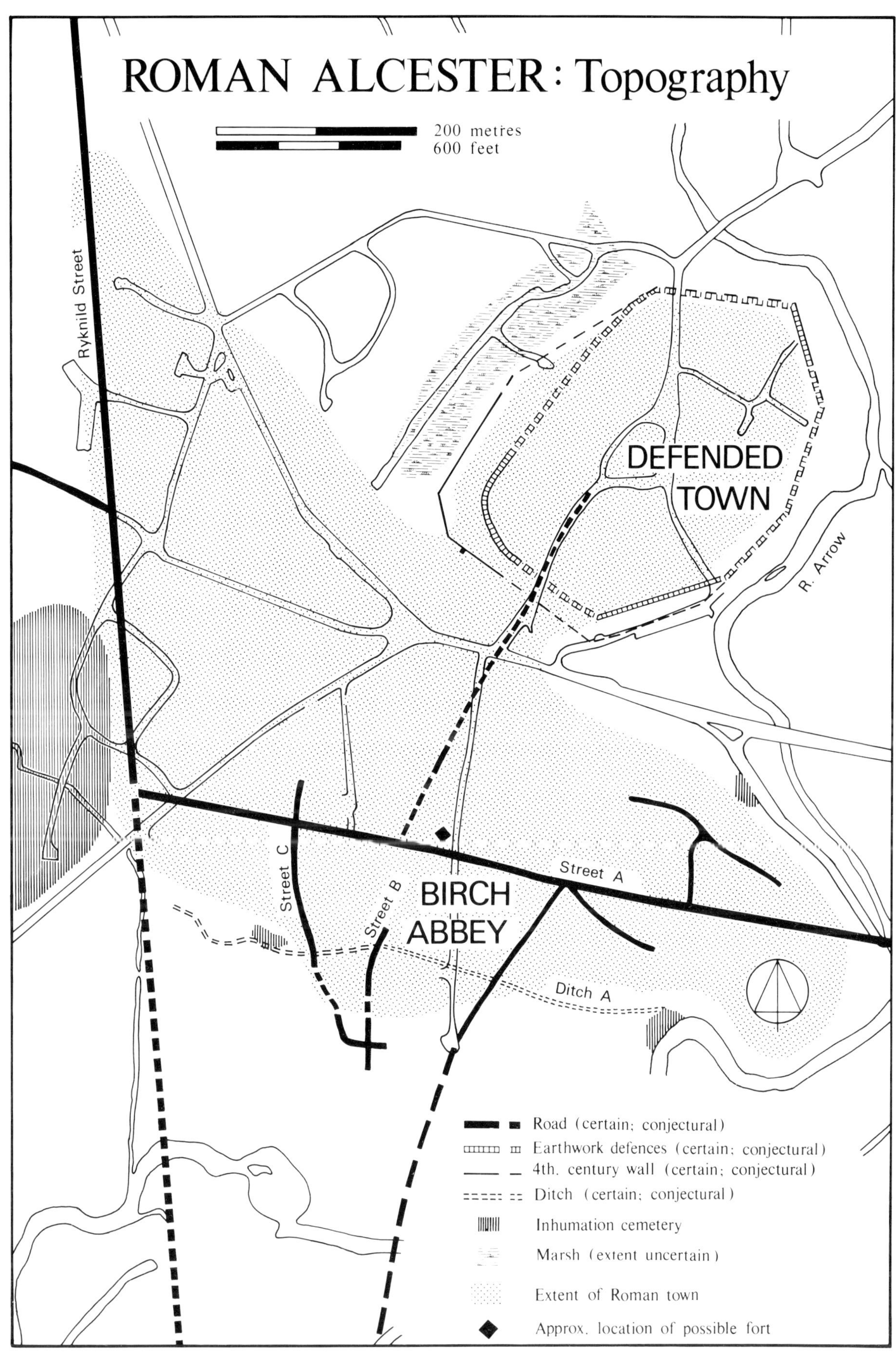

Figure 2   Alcester topography (for modern street names see fig 3)

Archaeological work in Alcester to December 1989 (key to fig 3 sites)

Number (fig 3)	Site name	Excavator	Date	Type of site
1	Butter Street hoard	–	*c* 1638	C
2	Baptist chapel, Meeting Lane	–	*c* 1660	C
3*	Stone coffin on railway	–	1867	C
4	Seggs Lane	–	1913	C
5	Bleachfield St allotments	B W Davis	1920s & 1930s	E
6	Bleachfield St sewage works	B W Davis	1923	S
7	Folley Field	B W Davis	1923 & 1925	E
8	Show Field	B W Davis	1923	E
9	Old Stratford Road burials	B W Davis	1925	W
10	No 1 Meeting Lane	B W Davis	1926 & 1927	E
11	Tibbet's Close	B W Davis	–	E?
12	Priory Road	W Seaby, J Brookes & R Tomlinson	1938 & 1962	E
13	Site A	H V Hughes	1957 & 1960	E
14	Site B	H V Hughes	1957–8	E
15	Site C	H V Hughes	1957–8	E
16	Site D	H V Hughes	1957–8	E
17	Site E	H V Hughes	1957–8	E
18	Site F	H V Hughes	1957–8	E
19	Site G	H V Hughes	1957–8	E
20	Site H	H V Hughes	1957–8	E
21	Site K	H V Hughes	1957–8	E
22	Site M	H V Hughes	1957–8	E
23	Site N	H V Hughes	1957–8	E
24	Site P	H V Hughes	1957–8	E
25*	Site Q	H V Hughes	1957	E
26	Site R	R J Horsfall	1958–9	E
27	Site S ('Dog and Partridge')	R J Horsfall	1960	E
28	Sites T and Tw	H V Hughes	1960–2	E
29	Field 275 burials	H V Hughes	1962	S
30	Birch Abbey (ABA)	R A Tomlinson	1963	E
31	Birch Abbey (ABA)	R A Tomlinson	1964	E
32	Site A	C M Mahany	1964–6	E
33	Site B	C M Mahany	1964–6	E
34	Site C	C M Mahany	1964–6	E
35	Site D	C M Mahany	1964–6	E
36	Site E	C M Mahany	1964–6	E
37	Site F	C M Mahany	1964–6	E
38	Site G	C M Mahany	1964–6	E
39	Site H	C M Mahany	1964–6	E
40	Site J	C M Mahany	1964–6	E
41	Site K	C M Mahany	1964–6	E

Number (fig 3)	Site name	Excavator	Date	Type of site
42	Site L	C M Mahany	1964–6	E
43	Site M	C M Mahany & R A Tomlinson	1964–6	E
44	Gas House Lane	U Place	1967	E
45	Malt Mill Lane	U Place	1967	E
		P Booth	1981	W
46	Caravan park coin hoard	–	1967	C
47	Baromix, Bleachfield St (AL 1)	S J Taylor	1969–72	E
48	Bleachfield St western flood barrier (AL 2)	S J Taylor	1970	E
49	Birch Abbey (AL 3)	S J Taylor	1972	E
50	Bleachfield St eastern flood barrier (AL 4)	S J Taylor	1973	E
51	Malt Mill Lane, sheltered housing	S J Taylor	1973	S
52	Recreation Ground flood barrier	S J Taylor	1973	W
53	Gas House Lane	R G Lamb	1975	E
54*	Ragley Mill	J R Greig, P M Booth & R G Lamb	1975	E
55	Lloyd's Bank	E M Evans	1975	E
56	Acorn House, Evesham Street (AL 17)	G E Saville	1975	E
57	'Explosion site', 1–5 Bleachfield St (AL 25)	P M Booth	1976–7	E
58	Bull's Head Yard (1)	P M Booth	1976	S
59	Pipeline	P M Booth	1977	W
60	Bull's Head Yard (2)	R G Lamb & P M Booth	1976	E
		R G Lamb & P M Booth	1978	S
61	Coulters Garage	P M Booth	1979	S & E
62	22 Hadrian's Walk	P M Booth	1979–80	W
63	'The Fields', Seggs Lane	P M Booth	1979–80	W
64	Baromix extension	P M Booth	1980	W
65*	Grammar School playing field	P M Booth	1980	E
66	30 Birmingham Road	P M Booth	1980	W
67	38 Birmingham Road	P M Booth	1980	W
68	'Burdens', Swan St	P M Booth	1980	W
69	79 Priory Road (AL 7)	D Ford	1977	W
		P M Booth	1981	S
70	Greig Hall	P M Booth	1981	E
71	7 Station Road	P M Booth	1981	W
72	28 Hadrian's Walk	P M Booth	1981	W
73	64a Bleachfield St (AL 9)	P M Booth	1981	E
74	12 Roman Way	P M Booth	1982	W
75	2 Newport Drive	P M Booth	1982	W
76	Market site	P M Booth	1982	S

Number (fig 3)	Site name	Excavator	Date	Type of site
77	Stratford House, Stratford Road (AL 8)	S Cracknell	1982	E
		S Cracknell	1983	W
78	'The Bell', Evesham Street (AL 6)	P M Booth & S Cracknell	1982 & 1983	W
79	30 Evesham St	P M Booth	1983	W
80	34 Evesham St (AL 11)	S Cracknell	1983	E
81	6 Birch Abbey (AL 10)	S Cracknell	1983	E
82	'Skeleton Bend'	B W Davis	1927	C
		H V Hughes	1958	C
		P M Booth	1976–83	C & S
83	Tibbet's Close (AL 12)	S Cracknell	1983	E
84	Royal Oak Passage	P M Booth	1983	W
85	9 Meeting Lane (AL 14)	S Cracknell	1983	E
86	21 Bleachfield St (AL 15)	N White	1984	E
87	Midland Bank (AL 16)	N White	1984	W
88	Gateway supermarket, Moorfield Road (AL 18)	S Cracknell	1986	E
89	18 Bleachfield St (AL 19)	S Cracknell	1986	W
90	Builder's Yard, Bleachfield St (AL 20)	S Cracknell	1987	S
91*	Roebuck Inn field (AL 21)	S Cracknell	1987	E
92	27 High Street (AL 22)	S Cracknell	1987	W
93	Riverside Works, Gas House Lane (AL 23)	M Jones & S Cracknell	1988–9	E
94	11 Meeting Lane (AL 24)	M Jones	1988	E
95	Baromix/Dennisons (AL 28)	S Cracknell	1989	E
96	Hockley Chemicals, Stratford Road (AL 29)	S Cracknell	1989	E

Key to table:
C   Chance find
E   Excavation
W   Watching brief
S   Salvage work
*   Not on figure

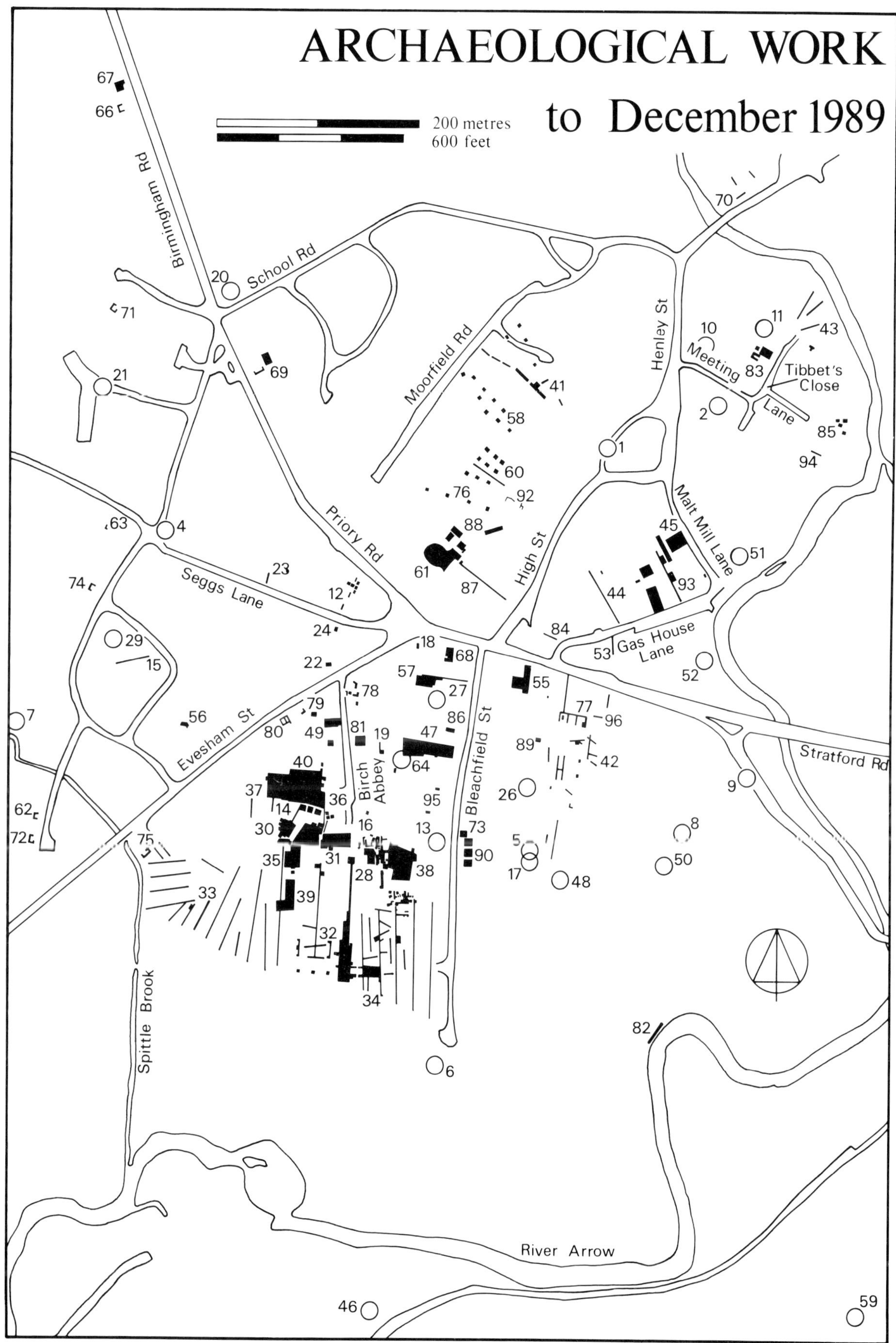

Figure 3   Archaeological work in Alcester to December 1989. The 1964–6 excavations are nos 32–43; the main Birch Abbey sites are also shown on fig 4; site K is 41 on fig 3; site L is 42; site M is 43

Roman Alcester: the state of knowledge in 1964

Paul Booth

There had been quite widespread, if relatively small-scale, archaeological activity in Alcester prior to Mahany's excavations (fig 3). Although some of this work has been summarized before (Booth 1980; Booth & Cracknell 1986), it seems appropriate to present the material in rather more detail here, in order to place the excavations of 1964–6 in context. Almost all of the work described below is unpublished in detail and is likely to remain so in the foreseeable future.

The great antiquity of the town of Alcester was realized at least as long ago as the 16th century, in the writings of John Leland. Indeed it may possibly have been the surviving evidence of Roman buildings which prompted the idea of the association of St Ecgwine with the settlement at a much earlier date, though this association has been shown to date no earlier than the 13th-century version of the life of the saint (Lapidge 1977, 89). William Dugdale (1656, 568), however, was the first of the early writers to record more specific observations about Alcester's Roman remains, although none of these was precisely located. The earliest record of an individual discovery was published in 1671, though the find itself, of a ?4th-century coin hoard, was made in about 1638 (Haverfield 1904, 236; **1** on fig 3). Subsequent writers (see Booth 1980, 2) dealt with visible surface traces which may have related to the Roman town, and the discovery of burials in the southern part of the town (eg *Archaeologia* 17 (1814), 332–3), though the latter were considered at the time and subsequently (Meaney 1964, 257) to be of Anglo-Saxon date.

There are no records of further significant discoveries in the course of the 19th century, so Haverfield's perceptive assessment in the *Victoria County History*, that Alcester 'at any rate during the latter part of the Roman period, was a village or perhaps a tiny town built by the side of the Roman road' (Haverfield 1904, 237) was based entirely on chance finds and the antiquarian observations.

The first specifically archaeological investigations did not take place until 1923. These were carried out by B W Davis, an Alcester needle factory owner. In the period from 1923 almost up to the Second World War Davis, with the assistance of a few friends and sometimes employing workmen, conducted excavations at a variety of sites, mainly in available gardens and allotments, returning to some of these sites repeatedly over a period of several years. He also pieced together information from other sources such as chance discoveries and observation of the digging of trenches for services.

Davis had no archaeological training but was keenly encouraged in his work by John Humphreys, president of the Birmingham Archaeological Society, as it then was, from 1916 to 1932. Humphreys gave Davis much guidance and visited him frequently, though there is no evidence that his ideas of excavation technique and recording were any more advanced than those of Davis. It seems possible that Davis' enthusiasm for archaeology received a serious setback with Humphreys' death in 1937, which may explain why the date of his latest activity is uncertain.

Unfortunately the quality of Davis' excavation and recording was such that detailed reconstruction of his findings is impossible. Short notes on some of his work and finds were published in the *Transactions of the Birmingham Archaeological Society* for 1924 (79), 1927 (288–9) and 1929 (76) and in *A History of Alcester* (Gwinnett 1954) which, while published in 1954, was written considerably earlier and took no account of discoveries after 1926 (*ibid*, 4–9). Many of Davis' notes and relevant diary entries survive, although not in manuscript form, along with copies of some of his extensive correspondence with Humphreys. From these sources it is possible to locate approximately most of Davis' more important excavations and to describe them in outline. This was first attempted by W A Seaby who in 1954 compiled an annotated map of archaeological discoveries in Alcester up to that date. The present writer has carried out the same exercise, with results which differ in some details from those of Seaby, who drew on the diary and notes but does not seem to have used the letters.

Davis' work was important for the understanding of three main aspects of the Roman town; the cemeteries around the south side of the settlement and two significant areas of occupation within it. The first of these was in the allotment areas which overlaid much of the southern part of the Roman town before the mid-1960s, the second was to the north of Meeting Lane, within the area of the medieval town centre and the part of the Roman settlement enclosed by defences (though this was, of course, not known at the time).

Four separate areas of burials can be identified from Davis' notes. Not all, however, were certainly of Roman date. They were, from east to west:

(i) A possible group of four burials found in 1925 beside the old Alcester–Stratford road in an uncertain location perhaps fairly close to the river Arrow north-west of Oversley Bridge (**9** on fig 3).

(ii) A group of three adults and one child in burials apparently aligned north–south, located in the north bank of the river Arrow at the point where this river, having run east–west through the flood plain, turns sharply southwards. This site can be precisely located (**82** on fig 3). It was known to Hughes (1959, 31–2) and was repeatedly visited by the present writer between 1975 and 1982. There can be no doubt that a significant Roman cemetery existed at this point and its continual and continuing erosion remains a matter of concern.

(iii) Two crouched inhumations and a group of skulls and other bones were found at various times between 1923 and 1929 in the beds of the old sewage works to the west of Bleachfield Street on the south side of the town (**6** on fig 3). The site cannot be more closely defined. None of these burials was associated with dating material and it seems quite likely from the account of the circumstances of the discovery that they were of pre-Roman date.

(iv) In 1925 Davis excavated fifteen east–west aligned inhumations and a cremation in Folley Field and Orchard just west of the former railway line on the west side of the town (**7** on fig 3). Three of the inhumations were contained in crude stone cists and one was associated with a coin of Constans. The burials lay some 180m north of the probable find-spot of a stone coffin discovered in 1866 at the time of the construction of the Evesham Road railway bridge. These finds, together with the later exposure of 'over a hundred burials' in an adjacent area to the east (Hughes 1962), suggest the presence of a major late Roman cemetery, perhaps with earlier antecedents.

Davis worked on two areas within the southern part of the Roman town, in the allotments east of Bleachfield Street and around the Old Grammar School in Birch Abbey. The former of these sites, referred to by Davis as 'Blacklands' (a name already in use when Dugdale (1656, 568) was writing), seems to have been situated within the south-east corner of the allotments (**5** on fig 3). This area was partly examined later by Hughes (1958, 15–16) and is of relevance for the excavations of site L. Here Davis found remains of one, and possibly more, substantial stone buildings, probably facing onto the north side of the main east–west road through the Roman settlement. To the west was 'a strong wall of mortared stone blocks with a stone floor inside this to the north. On the south side was a strong gravel path'. The latter, if Davis' orientations can be trusted (there is evidence from elsewhere in his journals that this is not always the case), may have been the road. East of this wall, but perhaps still part of the same building, was a structure which apparently went through several periods of construction. Walls and successive floor layers are referred to, and two hypocausts 'ten yards [9.15m] apart'. Surviving finds include unusual, circular *pilae*, and Davis recorded painted plaster and roof and flue tiles among the finds. Three tiles, bearing the unique stamp TCD (Booth 1980, 4) are known from this site, two of them from Hughes' excavations in the area. These, together with the other evidence, suggest the presence of an important, possibly official or public structure, perhaps a *mansio*. The very limited reference which Davis makes to dating material suggests that the two main construction phases which he noted may both have been of 2nd-century date, but this cannot be certain.

To the east of this site, in Show Field, one of Davis' earliest excavations, in 1923, located 'some Roman wall and building'. Later references mention a stone floor and *tesserae* which seem to have come from the same building. This is not precisely located, however,

within the field, though a note by Davis to the effect that he could trace the course of one of the walls all the way to the gardens in Bleachfield Street may suggest that he was seeing the line of the east–west Roman road and that the building therefore lay close to this road. In 1973, salvage excavation in advance of flood barrier construction in this field revealed part of a substantial structure with large quantities of painted wallplaster (Taylor 1973, 22; **50** on fig 3). This may have lain quite close to, or even possibly have been part of, the building located by Davis.

West of Bleachfield Street Davis excavated in the garden of the Old Grammar School in Birch Abbey (**16** on fig 3), and adjacent to this site ('across the road', ie presumably on the west side of Birch Abbey) he encountered 'a made road of very strong and large gravel, and beside the gravel road . . . an old foundation of stone'. Again a precise location and orientation are lacking, but it seems possible that Davis had found another part of the main east–west road, later sectioned by Hughes, and another stone building lying on its north side, perhaps in the vicinity of the electricity sub-station which was later situated on the west side of Birch Abbey until its removal in advance of house construction in *c* 1966.

Within the area of the medieval town centre Davis carried out further excavations, revealing part of another Roman stone structure. This site was in the garden of no 1 Meeting Lane, on the north side of the lane (**10** on fig 3). As in the 'Blacklands' site there seems to have been evidence of at least two major construction periods, the remains of a stone wall being completely sealed by a concrete floor. In all, four floors seem to have been found, but their relationships are unclear. Painted plaster and *tesserae* were recovered from the site.

Further work in 1926 at the site of an old sawpit produced evidence for another stone building, with fragments of wall, concrete floor, flue tiles, *tesserae* and painted plaster. This site is unlocated, but Seaby placed it near the Meeting Lane site, which is not unlikely. North of here, behind the old police station on the east side of Henley Street (**11** on fig 3), traces of a further (presumably stone) building were encountered, but there is no record of formal excavation here.

The results of Davis' work were incorporated in a brief summary of the area by W A Seaby (1951, 119–20) who also produced the first formal publication of an Alcester site, at no 4 Priory Road (**12** on fig 3), investigated initially by associates of Davis in 1925 and subsequently in 1938 (Seaby 1945). This site produced evidence of a stone building and artefacts of late 1st- to 4th-century date, though the nature and function of the building was not established. In 1954, as mentioned above, Seaby compiled a gazetteer of Alcester finds, principally those of Davis, but this was not published.

In 1956 the archaeology of Alcester was put on a more organized footing with the institution of a campaign principally of problem-oriented excavations organized by the University of Birmingham Department of Extramural Studies and directed by H V Hughes. The objectives of these excavations were to elucidate the problems of the major Roman roads, the town defences, and the nature and date range of the occupation (Hughes 1958 (1960), 10–11). Work on these objectives up to 1960 was reported on by Hughes (1958 (1960); 1959 (1961)) but only brief interim notes (Hughes 1960; 1961; 1962; 1963; 1964) were published on the excavations after that date, which continued until 1964. Work on the full publication was halted by Hughes' untimely death in 1967. From 1960 the main excavation was of a stone building (Hughes' site T; **28** on fig 3) in Birch Abbey, which by 1965 lay immediately west of site G and is discussed in more detail below.

In 1962 this work was supplemented by the Department of Ancient History and Archaeology of the University of Birmingham. Under the direction of R A Tomlinson (now professor) the Department carried out an excavation prior to redevelopment at the Old Cattle Market in Priory Road (**12** on fig 3), immediately adjacent to the site reported on by Seaby (1945), revealing more of the same building and providing an outline of the development of its structural sequence (Hughes 1962).

In the following year the department became involved, alongside Hughes, in excavation in Birch Abbey, in the field to the west of Birch Abbey itself (**30** on fig 3). These excavations, which continued until 1965, were concentrated on another substantial stone building (Hughes 1963). They were ultimately, like Hughes' site T, surrounded by sites D, E, and F, site D I lying between the main part of the University excavation to the west and a further series of trenches to the east (Tomlinson 1964; 1965; **31** on fig 3). Associated trenches, excavated partly by the Leamington and District Research Group, lay northeast of Tomlinson's 1963 site and were eventually incorporated within Mahany's excavations as site P (Place 1964; 1965). The University excavations remain unpublished.

By 1964, therefore, there was considerable evidence for some aspects of the Roman town, though little of this evidence was readily available in published form. The principal known elements of the town plan were the two main roads, Ryknild Street running north–south through the western part of the settlement, and the east–west Stratford to Droitwich road, later called the Salt Way. The routes of both these roads within the environs of the town had been established by excavation by Hughes (1958, 12–17). In addition a road almost parallel to the main east–west road was thought to lie beneath the line of Seggs Lane to the north (Hughes 1958, 15–16). The evidence for this road, recovered in Swan Street (**18** on fig 3), was and remains ambiguous, but it was thought that it might have replaced the main east–west route which had been built over. Further roads in the south-eastern part of the settlement were evident on aerial photographs taken by Arnold Baker in 1957 (Hughes 1958, plate 1).

While the outline of the road network was tolerably clear the location of the defences, if indeed they had existed at all, remained unknown. A mid-18th-century estate map showed in the open fields to the south-east of the town a line which was described as a defensive wall. Hughes' excavations had shown that this was the *agger* of the main east–west road which had probably also been seen by Davis. Other banks at various points around the southern part of the town appeared to be of medieval or later date (Hughes 1958, 11). No further candidates for defensive circuits presented themselves at this time.

The extent of the town was in the southern part defined by the areas of cemetery known from Davis' work and from Hughes' observations, although it is not certain that the significance of the former was fully appreciated. Further north it was clear that there were buildings beneath the medieval and modern town centre, but their relationship to those in 'Blacklands' and Birch Abbey was not clear. Understanding of the influence of topographical constraints on the development of the town grew as work continued, but was not advanced in 1964.

The structural evidence suggested a thriving settlement. In the northern part fragments of possibly at least three or four substantial stone buildings had been seen by Davis. There was no evidence for their form or date, but the presence of painted plaster, hypocaust tiles and, in one case at least, *tesserae*, suggests that they were probably town houses of 3rd- to 4th-century date. In Priory Road the building published by Seaby (1945) was shown in the excavations of 1962 to have had a timber predecessor, though neither the timber nor the stone phase was well understood or closely dated. Further south, stone buildings were still apparently the norm. They included the structure examined by Davis in Show Field and the large building excavated by him and by Hughes in 'Blacklands', the plan of which, however, remains obscure. No plans or notes for Hughes' site E survive. This is all the more regrettable because of the importance of this site not only in structural terms but also for the understanding of the development of the town plan. Hughes' discoveries are described as indicating a building 'not inconsistent with a villa of the "corridor" type' built over the road (1958, 15–16). Much hinges on the exact meaning of the phrase 'over the road'. In site T, to the west of Bleachfield Street, Hughes (1960) observed the same phenomenon in relation to the stone building there. However, it can be shown that this building only impinged marginally on the road, certainly not to the extent of blocking it. While this may have been the case at site E, it cannot be proven on present evidence. The extent to which the road was built over was clearly sufficient for Hughes to consider that it might have gone out of use (Hughes 1958, 16).

Other stone buildings in the area may have occurred just to the north of the latter site (at Hughes' site R; **26** on fig 3) and at the north end of Bleachfield Street (site S; **27** on fig 3), since both sites are marked as the location of buildings on Hughes' published plan (1958, 11). No definite evidence of structural remains on either of these sites has survived (Hughes 1959, 32), but a letter in Warwickshire Museum refers to the discovery of part of a stone column from site S, perhaps implying the existence of a stone structure there. A particular feature of this site was the discovery of a pit containing a very good group of pottery of Hadrianic date.

West of Bleachfield Street the evidence is clearer. Hughes' site T produced a large building with its short axis to the main road but not well aligned on it. This seems to have been in origin an aisled structure, to the east of which was added a corridor and small projecting wings. Some 35m west of this lay one of the buildings excavated by the University of Birmingham. This apparently consisted of ranges of rooms north and south of a courtyard open to the west. The eastern ends of the ranges were joined by a wall, although there was no evidence for further rooms along the east side of the building. The excavation of this building was in part concurrent with Mahany's excavations; it was not, therefore, well known when her work at Alcester commenced. Further west again was the principal building excavated by Tomlinson. This was also roughly aligned with its short axis on the main east–west road. The building, like that excavated in Priory Road in 1962, had a timber-built predecessor, possibly of late 1st-century date, of uncertain form, with both postholes and slots present. The stone building itself was of more than one phase. It was perhaps constructed in the later 3rd century and subsequently underwent considerable internal alterations, presumably at some time in the 4th century. It may have been overlain by a late Roman posthole structure.

The evidence therefore indicated a thriving settlement with a considerable number of stone buildings, of which most were probably of later 3rd- to 4th-century date but at least one (in 'Blacklands') was probably earlier. In some cases these had been preceded by timber structures. Many of the known structures were laid out along the main east–west road through the settlement. The overall date range of occupation was from the late 1st to late 4th century.

Excavations of 1964–6

Christine Mahany

The principal reason for the excavation was the impending destruction of some 5.7ha of the Roman town by a housing estate, in the area known as Birch Abbey, to the south and west of the present, and Roman, nucleus (figs 2–4). Opportunity was also taken to examine other sites, on a much smaller scale, in an attempt to understand the nature and topography of Roman Alcester as a whole. In particular an effort was made to examine the supposed defence circuit, and this was partially successful (see site M).

The Birch Abbey sites (sites A–H and J) were selected as the excavation proceeded. Although some previous work had been done by a variety of individuals and groups, the limits of the occupation of Birch Abbey were unknown, and the grid system of excavation which had without exception been employed gave little clue as to its nature. The initial uncertainty of continued government funding — the

excavation commenced with a grant to employ four labourers and one member of staff for a month — dictated the policy of the first few weeks' work. A series of trial trenches was cut by machine in order to define the main centres of occupation, and then areas were selected for stripping. In the latter cases the topsoil was removed with a Traxcavator, and the subsequent excavation proceeded by hand. The housing development scheme required that work should in general proceed from south to north. The early discovery of timber buildings in a trial trench led to a decision to employ open area excavation leaving few or no baulks. This proved to be a wise decision, given the nature of the deposits, and the preponderance of timber buildings of unusual and unpredictable design, over the more conventional Roman town structures. In all cases the depth of stratification between the topsoil and undisturbed subsoil was scarcely more than 0.6m, sometimes less.

Recording system

Christine Mahany

The separate areas excavated were given site numbers (A, B, C, etc). Individual cuttings within sites were numbered I, II, III, etc. Archaeological deposits, whether features or layers, were numbered serially 1, 2, 3, etc, thus 23 might be a pit, 24 a layer, and 25 a well. Details of features were described in a series of site notebooks for each site. Each site notebook contained a small finds list of material from that site, and these were correlated with a master list, arranged by class of object.

Planning was, for the most part, done by triangulation from grid pegs, at a scale of one inch to two feet (1:24). Very complex or intricate areas were also planned at a scale of one inch to one foot (1:12), and sections were drawn at that scale. The pottery recording system is described in Part 2.

Form of the report

Christine Mahany

The form of the report is, to some extent, dictated by the excavation strategy, which concentrated on five discrete sites within Birch Abbey after exploratory trenching across much of the area. The report analyses the stratigraphy of these main excavations and summarizes the more significant features observed in the exploratory trenches.

Because each of the major areas of excavation was a discrete entity, and because the dating evidence is somewhat tenuous, it is convenient to describe them individually. However, a general chronological introduction combines the evidence from all the excavations to produce a general phase plan. Detailed phase plans of individual sites follow under the site heading. There are also sections on the building types and on the structures and site layout in terms of Roman Alcester as a whole.

The terms cobble surface and pebble surface indicate a laid surface with little or no matrix of sand. Gravel layers and surfaces contain more sand and were not necessarily 'laid' surfaces. Fig 13 gives a key to conventions repeatedly used on site plans.

The printed text summarizes the dating evidence: more details can be found in tables M3–M6 in microfiche. A full analysis of the artefacts can be found in Part 2.

Previously unpublished work on adjacent sites, directed by H V Hughes and R Tomlinson, is occasionally mentioned in this report where it throws light on particular problems. However, the present study does not undertake a systematic evaluation of these excavations.

Cross-references between the printed text and microfiche are indicated in square brackets at the beginning of each section. Table M3 lists the dates of all phases. Table M4 lists all contexts which have been assigned to a structural phase.

The site archive and finds have been deposited in the Warwickshire Museum. A copy of the archive will be deposited in the National Monuments Record.

Description of the excavations

Summary of the Birch Abbey area
Christine Mahany and R S Langley

Birch Abbey (NGR SP087570) lies to the south of the area enclosed by the Roman defences, the area of the modern town (figs 2–4). The site slopes gently from north to south down to the flood plains of the river Arrow. In general there are three distinct zones. In the northern part of the site is a gravel terrace, and this is the area with the highest density of occupation. The central area where the slope was greatest (see contour plan, fig 4) was mainly taken up with large pits. There was further occupation in the southern part of the site, which had as a subsoil a fine clayey silt. This area may have been liable to flooding.

The principal Stratford–Droitwich road, street A, crossed the northern part of the site from east to west. Two minor roads, streets B and C, extended down the slope from north to south (fig 2). There was no evidence of a formal Roman town plan with insulation. There was successive rebuilding on a number of sites within the area; earlier buildings were of timber but many of the late Roman buildings were on stone foundations. Agricultural and industrial functions are suggested for some of these buildings.

First-century material occurred in residual contexts in many parts of the site, and included two Dobunnic coins, but 1st-century features could be identified only at the top of the terrace north of street A (fig 5). In this area, street C was defined by a drainage gully and a metalled surface at an early date. To the west a boundary ditch and later slots may have dated from the Flavian period. Street A was one of the main roads through the town. The interim report on Hughes' site E gives a *terminus post quem* of late 1st century for the road, based on a sherd of rusticated ware (Hughes 1958, 15), although the first evidence for metalling from the present excavations dates to the 4th century.

By the mid to late 1st-century period, occupation was well established on both sides of street C (fig 5). Metalled surfaces were laid over much of the area, associated with a large circular timber building, structure EA, on the east side of the road, and a double-quadrilateral enclosure on the west side. The enclosure was aligned on street A, to the south, but opposed entrances gave on to the east and west sides. The circular building was entered from the north-eastern side. Boundary ditches defined the eastern edge of street C, which turned sharply to the west at the northern end of the site.

In the late 1st to early 2nd century the circular building to the north of street A was reconstructed, structure EB, and the associated boundary ditches marking street C were recut (fig 6). Street C was also resurfaced in this area. In this period occupation had begun to spread to the south. A large but ill-defined timber building, structure DA, lay opposite the circular building, on the south side of street A, and east of street C. To the south of street A, street C was an unmetalled trackway running between ditched enclosures extending over the area above the steepest part of the terrace.

The first indications of settlement at the south end of the site, at the base of the terrace, occurred in this period. Street B was defined by boundary ditches, with an enclosure and further boundary ditches lying to the west.

By the late 2nd to early 3rd century the quadrilateral enclosure at the north end of the site had probably been abandoned. The circular structure opposite was replaced by a long rectangular building, structure EC, set along the eastern edge of street C (fig 7). From this period onwards a large area in the centre of the site, including the edge of the level ground to the north and the steeper part of the terrace to the south, was used for gravel quarrying with dumping of rubbish in the worked-out pits. It is not clear whether these were confined to the areas immediately abutting the roads, principally providing material for road metalling, or whether they covered the greater part of the central zone.

A substantial ditch, ditch A, was dug along the base of the terrace, extending across the Birch Abbey area and east towards the river Arrow (figs 7, 8). The ditch was up to 2m deep and 3m wide and must have been a significant element in the town plan at that time. The ditch followed the contours of the slope in the eastern half of the area but deviated to the south further west. The diversion may have been made to include a pre-existing building or land-holding; in any case no feature was recorded. A bank with postsettings lay on the south side of the ditch for at least part of its length. The early trackway on the line of street C was interrupted where it crossed the ditch, although the later metalled surfaces ran over the filled-in ditch. The ditch either terminated at street B or was crossed by a causeway carrying the road. The ditch was not recorded immediately east of street B but was visible on aerial photographs extending to the east between Bleachfield Street and the river (plate 12). The function of the ditch is unclear. Although it may have marked the southern limit of the town, settlement continued to develop beyond it in the area to the south. At the base of the terrace, the ditches defining street B were recut and boundary ditches were dug in the area to the west of the road. As a physical barrier, the ditch appears only to duplicate the natural boundary formed by the river not far to the south. The presence of a large millstone in trench A XIV and the location of the west end of the ditch close to Spittle Brook might suggest that the ditch was a mill leet. However, there are problems with this interpretation, mainly the apparent interruption of the ditch at Street B and the lack of a significant gradient over the length of the ditch.

North of ditch A a timber building, structure HA, stood on the west side of street C. Street C itself was defined by a ditch on its eastern edge. North of street A, four groups of very small, square, timber buildings (structures FA, ED, EE, EF, EG, EH, EI, EJ), some associated with small enclosures, were set back from both sides of street C (fig 8). Both the small scale of these buildings and their positions on new axes suggest a complete break with what had gone before. The same factors may have lain behind this change and the establishment of ditch A.

On the eastern side of the site a timber building within a ditched enclosure, structure GA, lay to the south of street A. This was set well back from the main road, but may have fronted the western edge of street B. A series of small ill-defined timber buildings, including structure GB, lay on the street A frontage immediately to the north-west.

In the middle to late 3rd century activity increased (fig 9). The main change was the backfilling of ditch A by the levelling of its bank. At the north end of the site a large rectangular building, structure EK, set end-on to the road, replaced one of the small square buildings west of street C, indicating that the road continued to be diverted to the west. In a second period, structure EK was rebuilt on a smaller scale, structure EM, and repairs were carried out to structure EL, now called structure ELA.

The area east of the road formerly occupied by the circular buildings EA, EB and their successors had been permanently abandoned leaving a large empty plot on both street A and street C frontages. It may be speculated that this open space was related to a building outside the excavated area to the east; in any case there was a significant change in the pattern of settlement.

In the late 3rd to early 4th century, south of the former ditch A, a very large timber building, structure AA, lay on the east side of street C (fig 10). This was one of two locations specifically identified with industrial activity. A large quantity of leather scrap was associated with the building and the manufacture of shoes appears to have been carried out there. To the east, a gully marked the eastern edge of street B, and to the north-west an earlier boundary was redefined by a bank and ditch. The latter was the only boundary apart from the street frontages to have been continuously maintained from the Antonine through to the later Roman periods, and appears to have had a particular significance as the northern boundary of the occupation in the southern part of the area. In the north part of the site a large timber building, structure DB, lay along the eastern side of street C, to the south of street A.

North of street A, and west of street C, a large timber building, structure FC, was erected. The axis of the building in this area had reverted to an alignment on street A, and the large scale of the

building contrasted with the earlier building on that site.

During the 4th century, developments in all parts of the site were complex. Their chronological span and the date of ultimate abandonment of the area could not be precisely defined.

In the early to mid-4th century, a rectangular timber structure, DC, lay along the eastern edge of street C. This was the second of the locations associated with industrial activity. Two possible smithing hearths lay within the building and waste pits were grouped around it. At a later date the building was extended to accommodate a third hearth, and a metalled surface was laid on street C, south of street A. North of street A and west of street C a single-aisled timber building, structure FD, may have been built on the same plan as two bays of the earlier structure FC. On the eastern part of the site, a building with a circular or D-shaped ditched enclosure, structure GC, was, like its predecessor, set back from the south side of street A, and was probably aligned on street B which extended outside the excavated area (fig 11). Small buildings lay on the street A frontage to the north-west on GI. Structure GC was of unusual construction, part being defined by stone cill walls and part by clusters of multiple posts, some set in single postpits. South of the line of the former ditch A, a stone-cilled timber building, structure CEA, lay on the E side of street B, succeeded by a similar structure CEB. On the west side a timber building, structure CWA, was replaced by two adjacent buildings, structures CWB and CWC. The plans of these buildings were incompletely recovered. Metalled surfaces were laid over street B.

The large stone buildings excavated by Hughes and Tomlinson may have dated from the late 3rd century onwards, although this is not certain, and they are shown in fig 11 as dating from the early 4th century (Hughes 1960–5; Tomlinson 1965). The three buildings were set at intervals of some 40m, end-on to the south side of street A. The present sites D and G were adjacent to these buildings, and some of the structures described here must be assumed to have been subsidiary to them. This might also imply that earlier buildings in those areas had similar relative status. The building excavated by Hughes at the east end of the area was the largest of the stone structures. It was of at least two phases, an aisled building having been extended by the addition of a corridor with wings projecting eastwards at each end. The northernmost wing may have encroached on street A. West of the winged corridor building, the smaller of the two buildings excavated by Tomlinson may have been a winged building, or two ranges of rooms on opposite sides of a courtyard. The largest of Tomlinson's buildings lay on the opposite side of street C at its junction with street A. The building was of corridor type, but elements of an earlier stone building are evident in the plan. The remains of earlier timber buildings were also discovered.

In the late 4th century, the site of the building within the ditched enclosure, structure GC, was occupied by a rectangular building with slightly bowed sides raised on stone cills and incorporating a row of square posts, structure GE (fig 12). Less substantial buildings lay in the area to the north-west, structures GF, GG, GH, and GJ. Later activity consisted of alteration and reconstruction of these buildings.

The single-aisled building west of street C, structure FD, was repaired, and enclosed by a stone wall forming a square compound, structure FE (fig 12). The enclosure wall was erected later than AD 353. An alternative, though perhaps less likely explanation initially has a free-standing building in the northern 'aisle' replaced by ranges of rooms attached to the stone enclosure walls. In a third period the building was demolished and a stone structure, FF, was erected in the south-eastern corner of the compound. The first evidence for the metalling of street A dated from this period, although it would seem unlikely that the main highway had not been resurfaced at an earlier date, as the minor streets had been. A drainage ditch was dug along the north side of the road, and north of this ditch were two parallel alignments of posts. The possible encroachment on the road by the winged corridor building may have necessitated a diversion of the road on the eastern side of the area, but the exact alignment is uncertain.

Street C extended south across the line of the former ditch A, and metalled surfaces were laid over the backfilled ditch after AD 364. To the north-west, the boundary line noted in earlier periods was maintained with successive gullies, and at the latest stage a stone-walled D-shaped enclosure was built with its straight side against the boundary line. In the centre of the site there was evidence of the dissolution of the long-established street pattern with a possible building, structure DD, lying over street C. Later two buildings raised on stone bosses, structures DE and DF, extended over street C near its junction with street A.

In the 4th century the south-western part of the site was used for burial (figs 107–8).

Phase dates

Frances Lee, Jeremy Evans, and Stephen Cracknell

Table M5 (microfiche M3:A4) lists the coarse pottery forms and their contexts by phase within each site area. The pottery was recorded on a presence/absence basis, on site, with most of it being subsequently discarded. This section is prepared from tables based on the site records. Full details are given in Part 2.

For most sites and phases the dating relies on this pottery. Where it is significant, the pottery forms which date the phase are noted. In some cases the illustrations of the vessels in the pottery report itself show similar examples found in different contexts.

Table M6 (M3:G11) lists all other datable finds from contexts which have been assigned to phases. A discussion of the dating evidence for each site can be found after the stratigraphic descriptions.

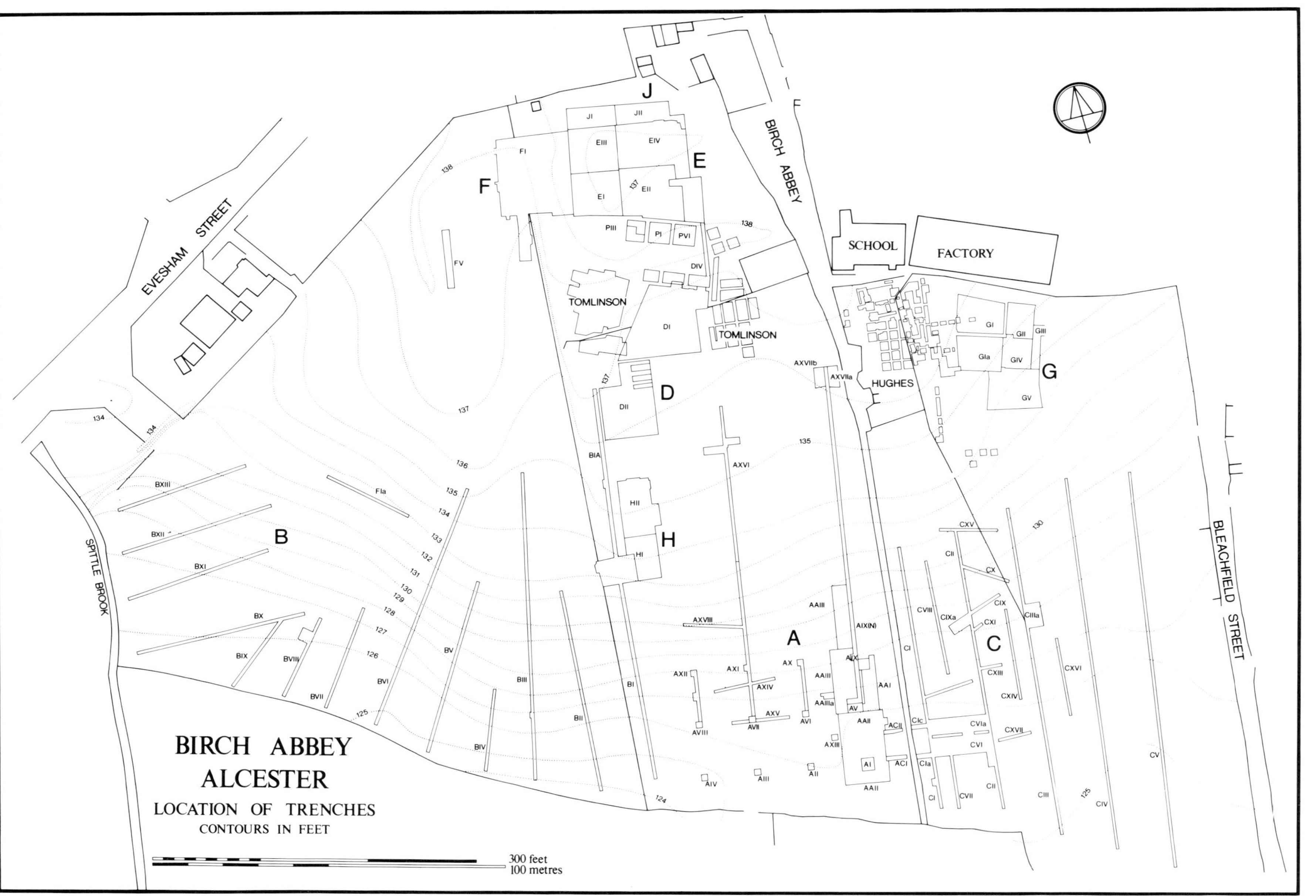

Figure 4 Birch Abbey, location of trenches

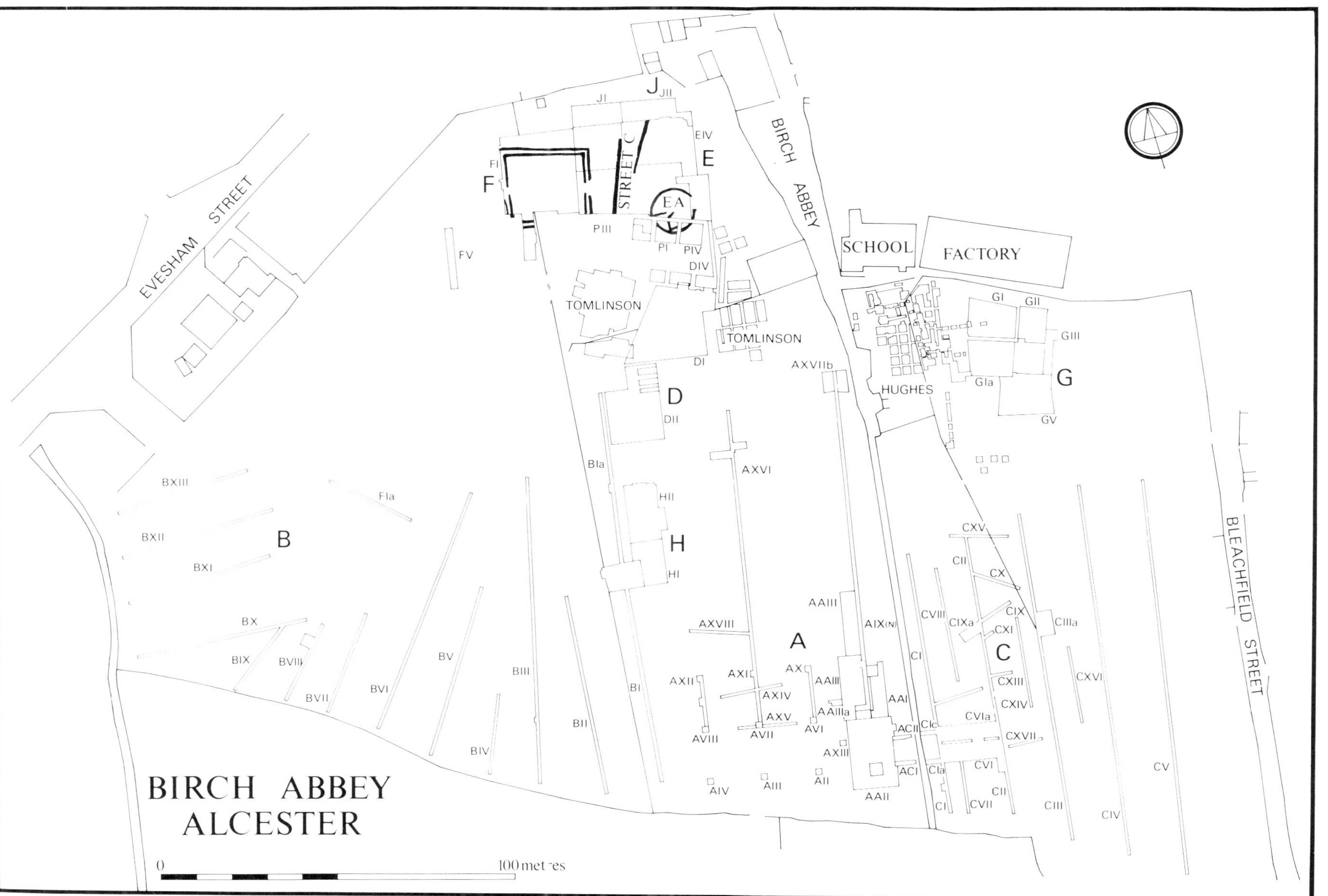

Figure 5   Birch Abbey, mid- to late 1st century

17

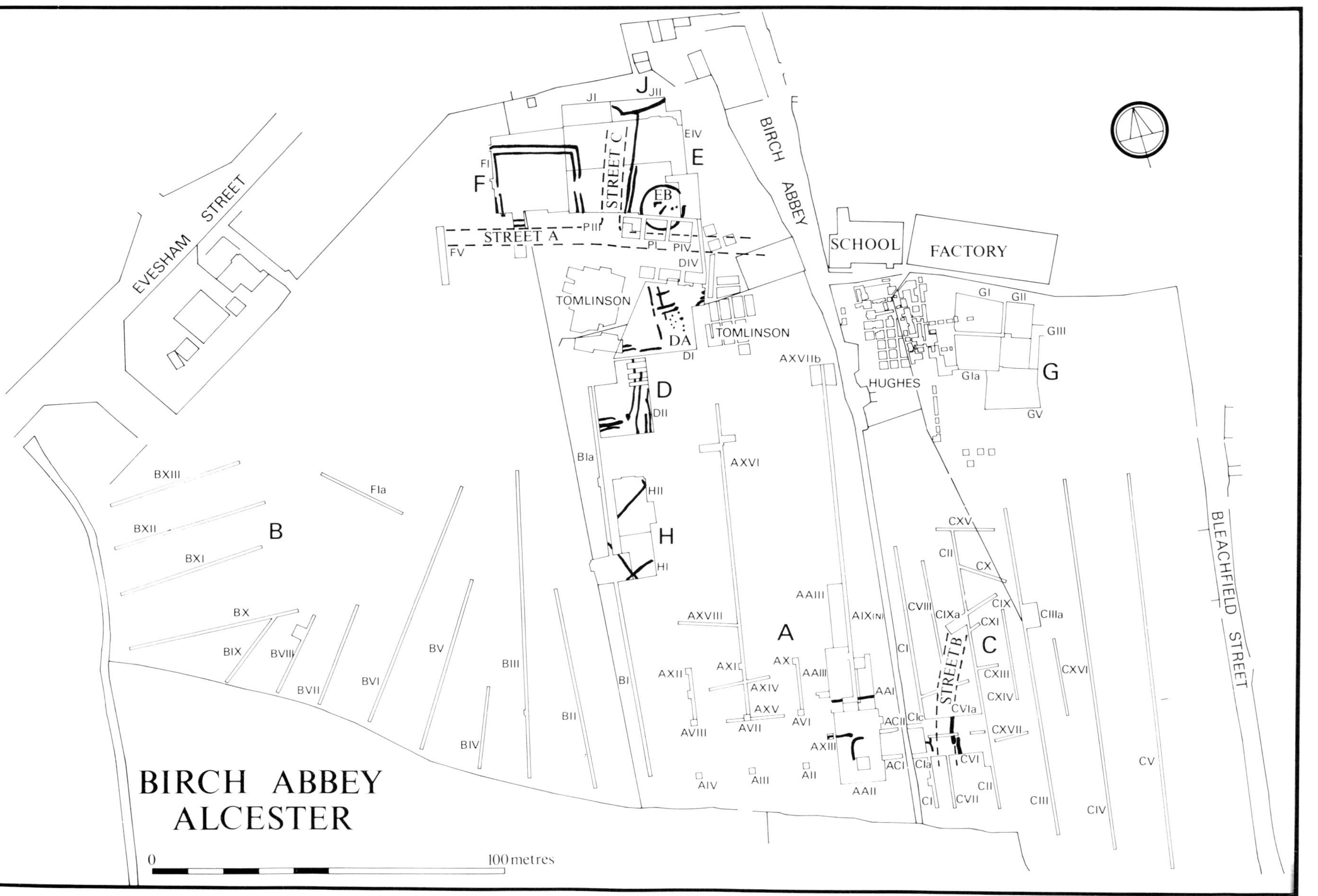

Figure 6   Birch Abbey, late 1st to early 2nd century

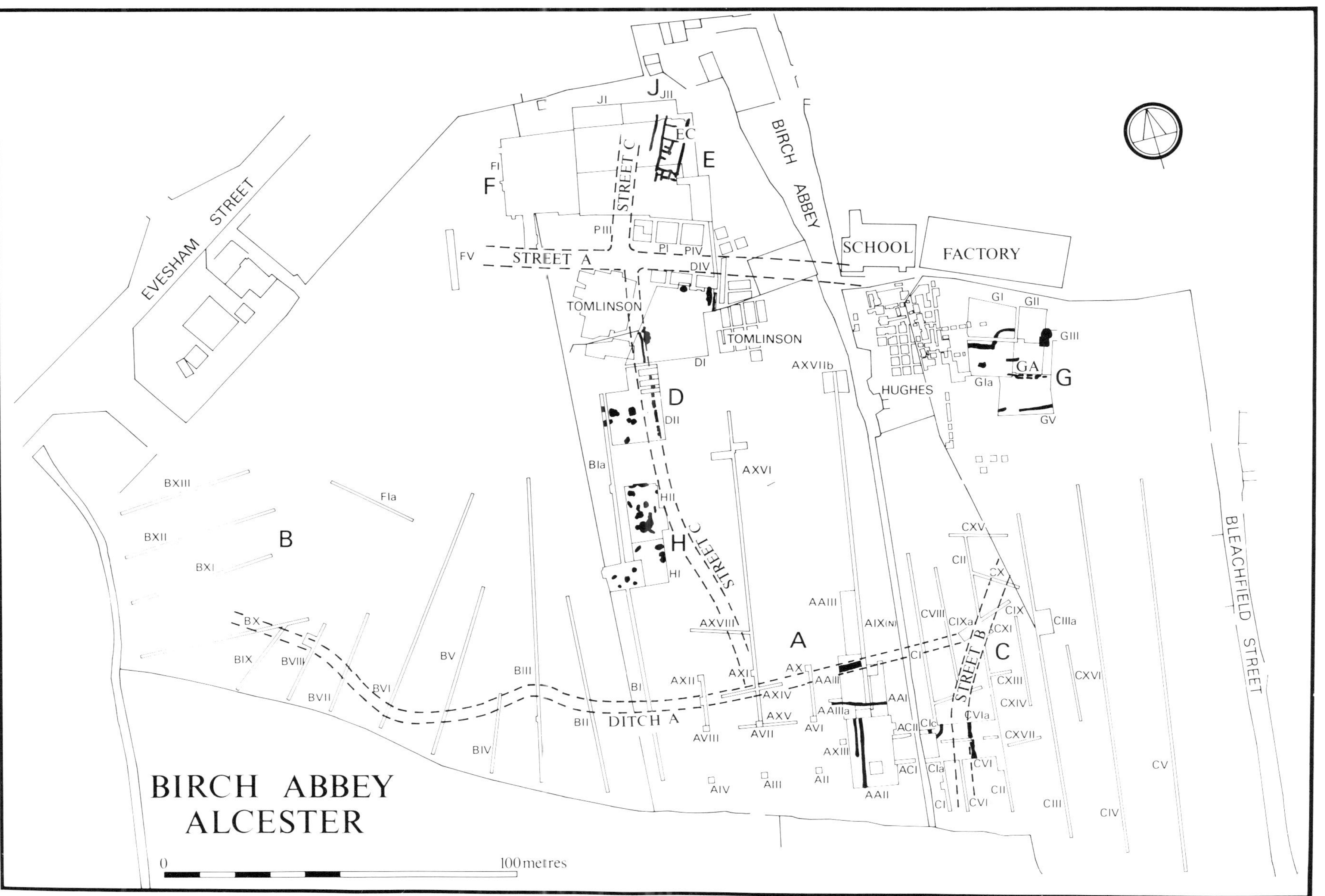

Figure 7 Birch Abbey, late 2nd century

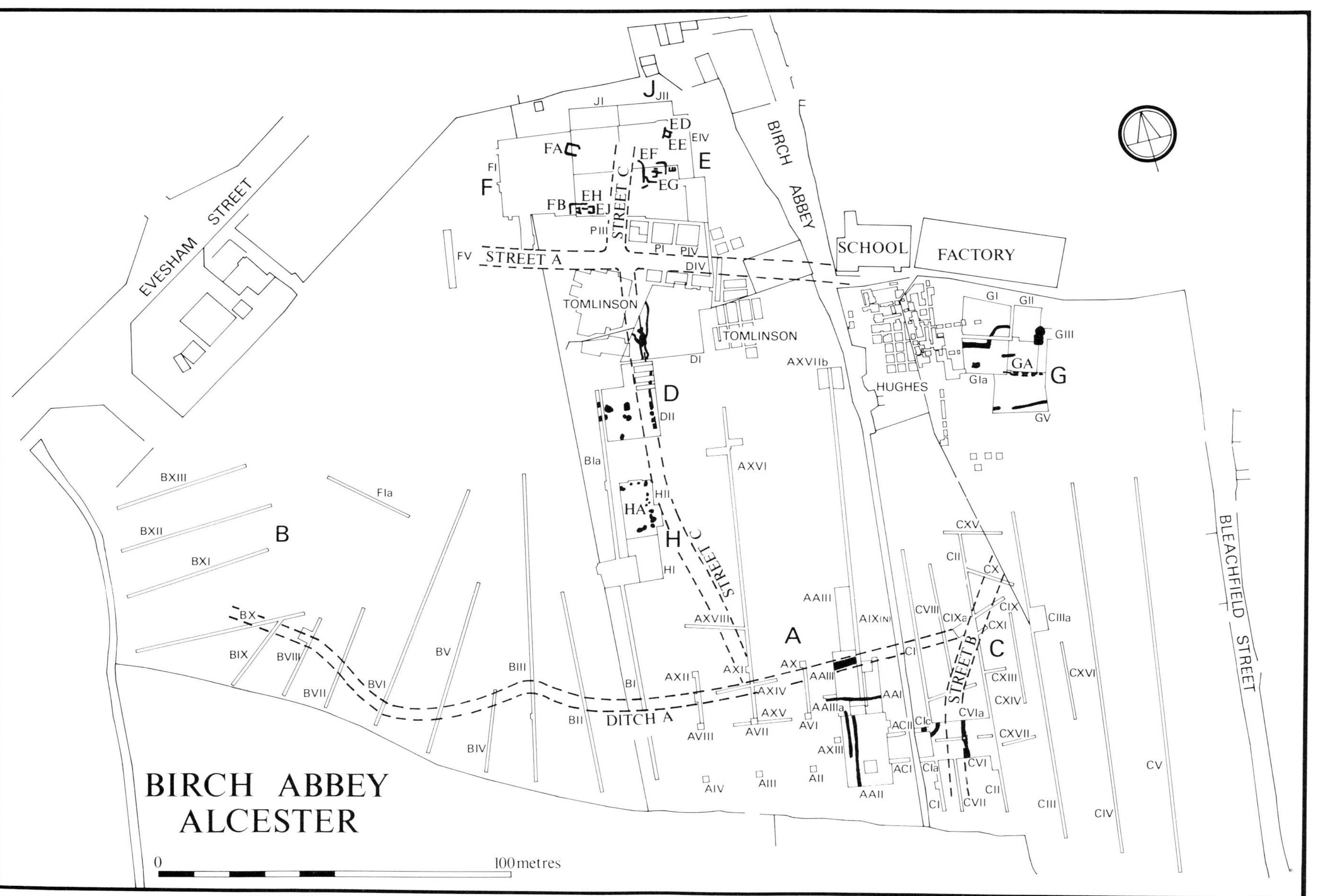

Figure 8 *Birch Abbey, early 3rd century*

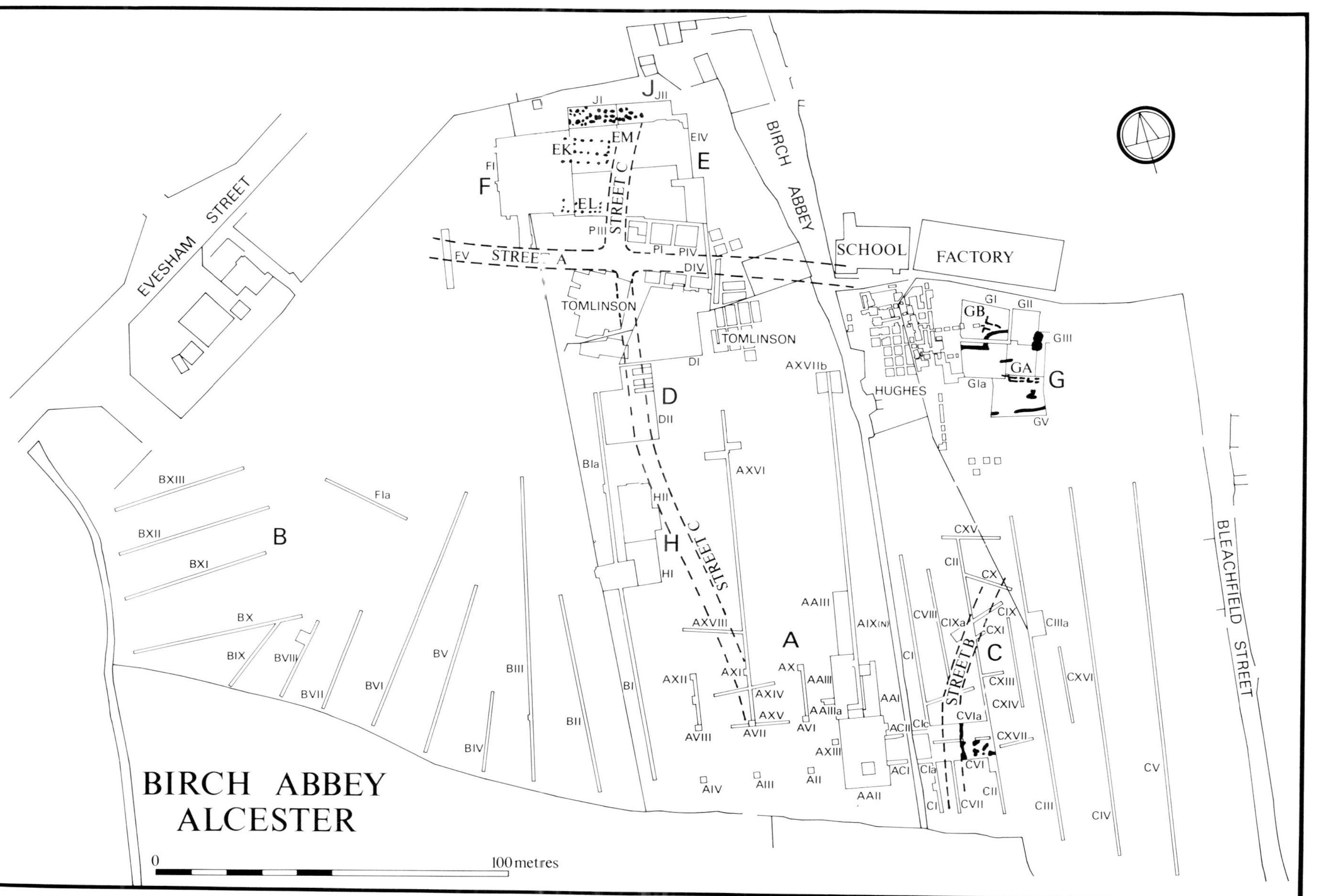

Figure 9 Birch Abbey, 3rd century

21

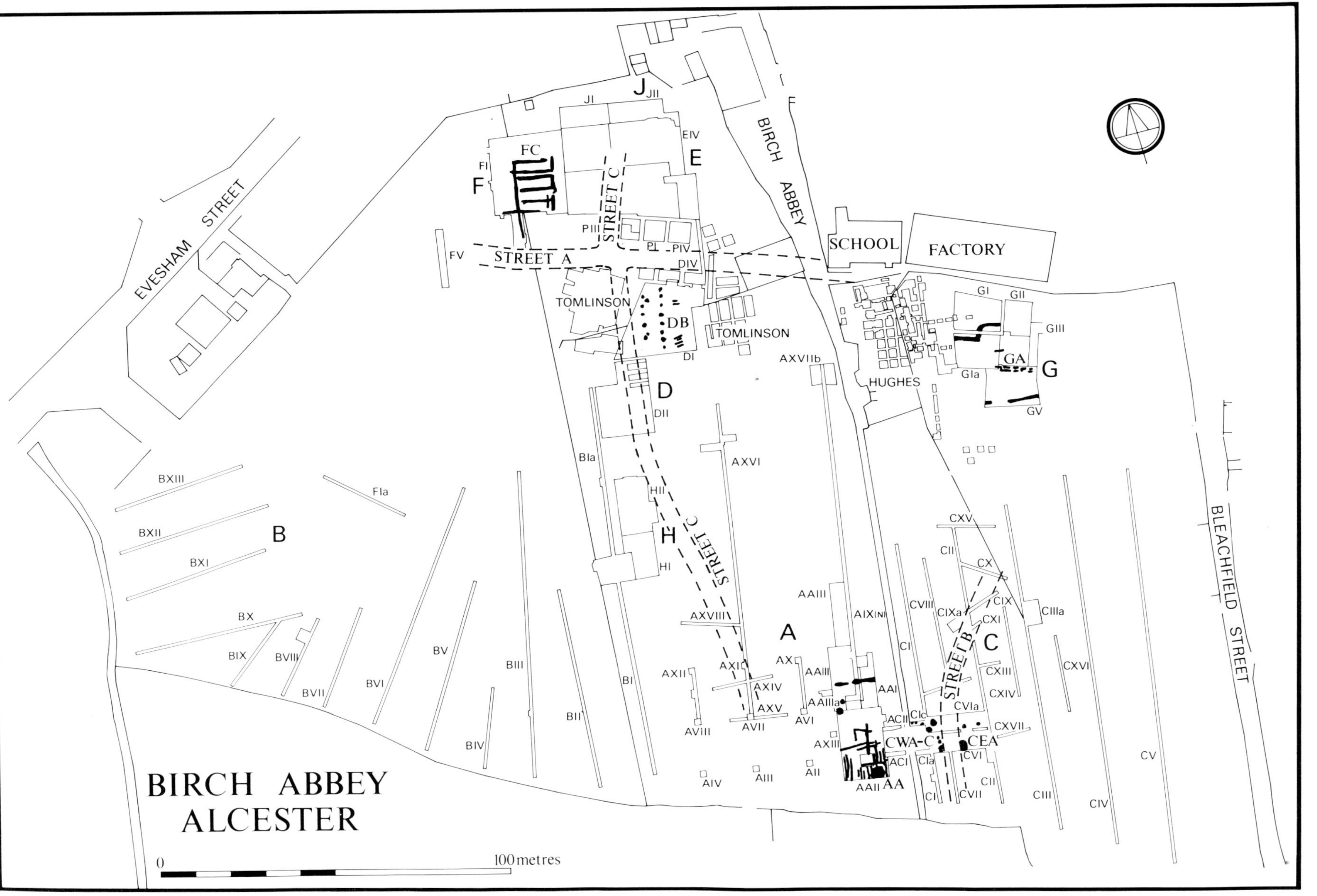

Figure 10   Birch Abbey, late 3rd century to early 4th century

22

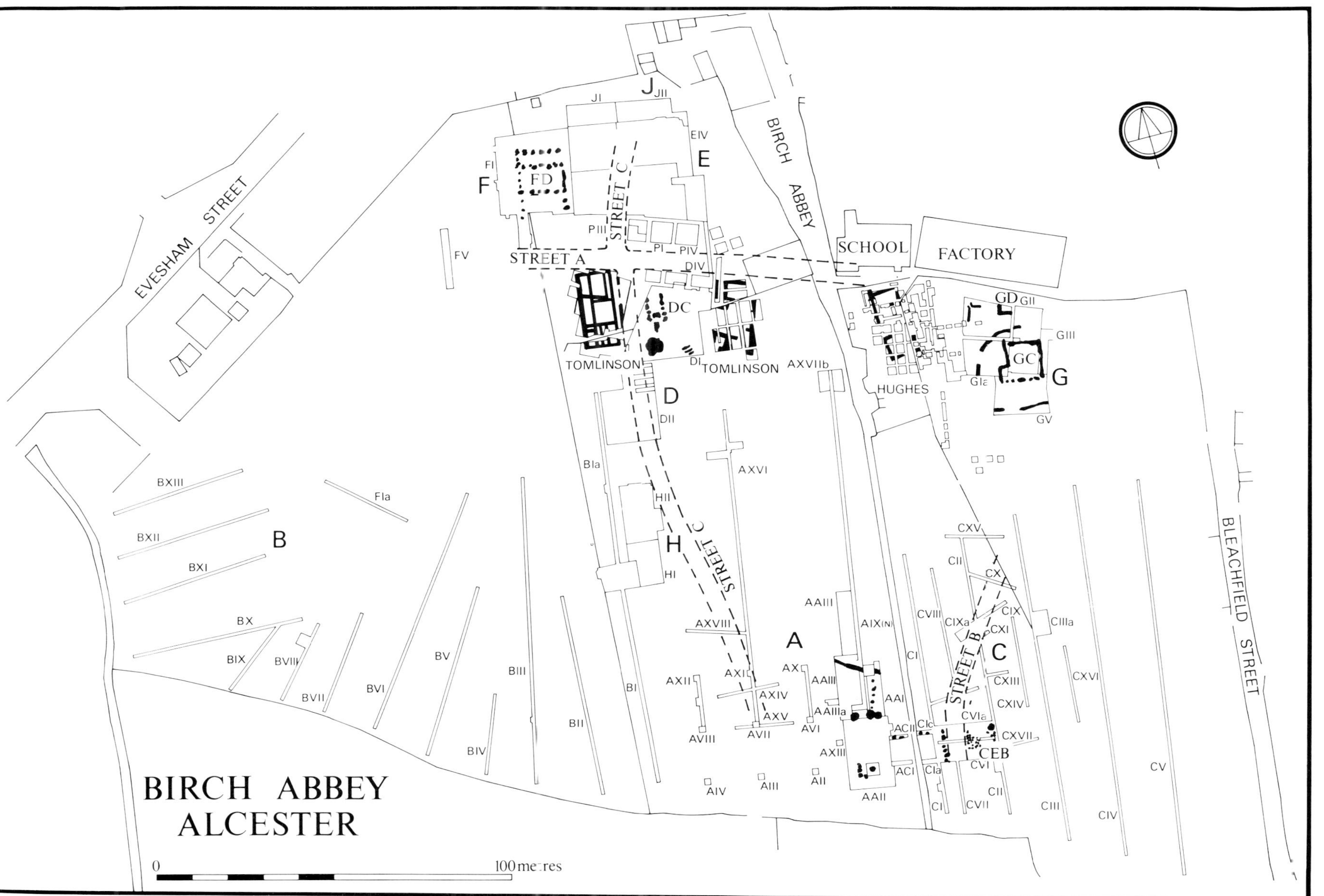

Figure 11 Birch Abbey, early to mid-4th century

23

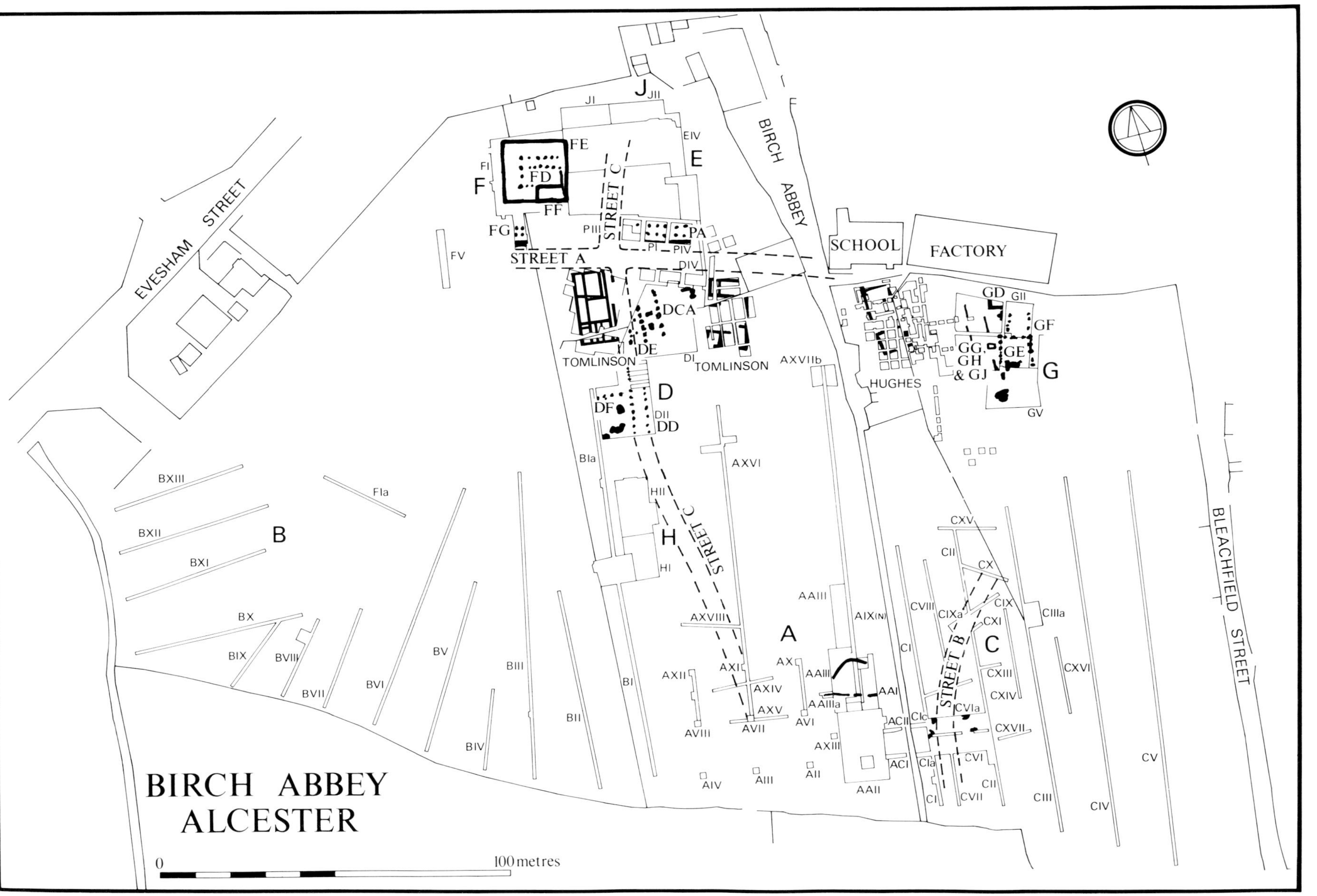

Figure 12 Birch Abbey, late 4th century

24

Sites AA and C

R S Langley with C Wingfield and M S Alabaster

[M1:A12] Two open sites, sites AA and C, were excavated in the south-eastern part of Birch Abbey, divided by the modern lane of that name. These sites were on the edge of the clays at the base of the gravel terrace (fig 3 nos **32, 34**, figs 4, 14, 23; see also fig 13, a general key to repeated conventions on site plans). The area was divided on topographical and strati-graphic grounds into three parts:

Site AA North (trenches A IX, A V, AA I, AA III, AA IIIA);
Site AA South and site C West (trenches AA II, A I, A XIII, AC I, AC II, C VI West, C VIA West, C I, C IA, C IC);
Site C East (trenches C VI East, C VIA East, C II).

The links between the three areas were not always certain, and so in what follows site AA North is described separately from sites AA South and C, although the phases are periods of probably similar date in each area.

The principal features were a road extending north–south dividing the two parts of site C (street B) and a ditch extending east–west through site AA (ditch A). Settlement lay to each side of the road and south of the ditch. The other main features of site A were a hearth in trench A XVII (see plate 1) and human burials (see 'Birch Abbey burials', p 144). Sections of the sites are reproduced in figs 32, 33 (site AA), 37–40 (site C); street B appears in sections of figs 38–41; ditch A appears in figs 32, 34, 37, and 85.

Site AA North

[M1:A12] This site covered some 214sq m (trenches AA I, AA III, A V, A IX and AA IIIA) (fig 3 no **32**, and figs 4, 14). Throughout the Roman period the area was an open space subdivided by ditches and gullies; in particular a boundary extending east–west in the

Plate 1 Site A XVII, hearth, looking south. Scale in 1ft (0.30m) divisions

KEY TO PLANS

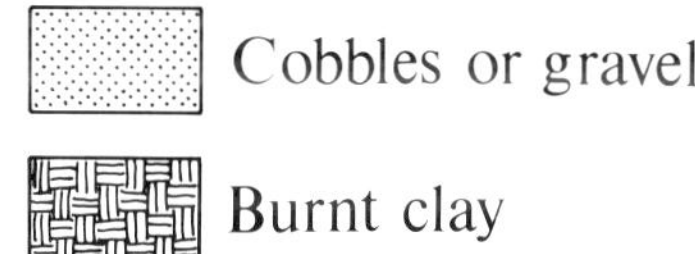

Cobbles or gravel

Burnt clay

Figure 13 General key to plans and sections

Table 1 Site AA North: phases, dates, and main features

Phase		Date
I	east–west gully	late 1st to early 2nd C
II	east–west gully; ditch A; upcast bank and postholes	late 2nd to mid-3rd C
III	loam; east–west ditch; bank and postholes; north–south gully; ditch A fills	later 3rd C
IV	loam	later 3rd C on
V	stake-lined gully; pits	later 3rd C on
VI	loam; gravel surface; pits	late 3rd to early 4th C
VII	ditch; postholes	late 3rd to early 4th C
VIII	east–west gully; graves	early to mid-4th C
IX	D-shaped enclosure	mid-4th C

southern half of the area was continually maintained. Ditch A crossed the northern side of the area.
These features were stratified within horizons of soil
that had washed from the slope to the north.

Phase I (fig 15)

[M1:A12] The first of the series of gullies bounding
the southern third of the area was dug in the late 1st
to early 2nd century. A trackway may have extended
from east to west between this and a parallel
boundary 9m to the south in site AA South.

Phase II (fig 16)

[M1:A13] The boundary gully was recut along its
northern edge. The possible trackway on the south
side had gone out of use and was crossed by gullies
extending north–south through site AA South. Ditch
A extended east–west across the north side of the
area. It followed the base of the gravel terrace
through the whole of the Birch Abbey area to the west
of street B, and can be identified on aerial photographs to the east of Bleachfield Street (plate 12), but
the course of the ditch could not be established
between trench C II and Bleachfield Street. In site
AA the ditch was up to 2m deep and 3m wide with a
characteristic V-shaped profile, sloping gently on the
northern side and steeply on the south side. A bank
of upcast lay on the south side; this was consolidated
with posts set in a random configuration, but had in
places slumped back into the ditch. The bank was
evident only in site A. The boundary gully in the
southern part of the area may have been dug in the
later part of the Antonine period, contemporary with
gullies extending north–south in site AA South.
Ditch A and the associated bank were established in
this phase.

Phase III (fig 17)

[M1:B2] Loam accumulated over the western side of
the area during the later 3rd century; this may
represent the abandonment and contraction of settlement noted in other parts of Birch Abbey during this
period. Ditch A was also filled in at this time. The
boundary line across the southern part of the site was
redefined, after the accumulation of the loam, by a
clay bank with posts set along its crest. On the
western side of the area, a ditch extended to the west
on the south side of the bank. The ditch was 1m deep
and 2.5m wide, with a U-shaped profile. The bank
had partly slumped into the bottom of this ditch. At
the extreme western edge of the area, a gully
extended north from the north side of the bank (not
illustrated).

Phase IV

[M1:B3] Loam accumulated over the area covering
the former ditch A and the ditch and boundary bank
on the south side of the site, and there was no activity
in this area.

Phase V (fig 18)

[M1:B3] In this phase the boundary line on the south
side of the site was again redefined. A shallow trough,
1.5m wide, was dug across the eastern half of the
area. Stakehole settings lay along either edge of
the feature. A number of small pits lay in the area to
the south of the boundary, on the western side of this
area.

Phase VI (fig 19)

[M1:B4] A further deposit of loam accumulated over
the area. This was covered by a gravel surface on the
north-eastern part of the site which, with charcoal
and clay inclusions in the loam on the eastern side of
the area, may indicate occupation to the east of the
excavated area. Three large pits lay on the south side
of the area immediately within the former boundary
line; a number of small pits lay to their north.

Phase VII (fig 20)

[M1:B5] Loam accumulated over the eastern side of
the area; included within it were charcoal, clay, and
mortar flecks, possibly destruction material from a
structure to the east. A line of postholes extended
north–south on the eastern side of the area, immediately north of the former boundary line. It may have
been part of a structure extending over the area to
the east. East of the alignment lay a concentration of
slag and charcoal. At the north end of the area, a
ditch crossed the line of the former ditch A from
north-west to south-east.

Phase VIII (fig 21)

[M1:B5] The boundary on the south side of the area
was again defined by a gully extending east–west.
Immediately to the south of the boundary was the
grave of a man. The decapitated skeleton was aligned
north–south, with the skull laid beyond the feet,
around which were hobnails. A second grave, also
aligned north–south, lay on the northern edge of the
former ditch at the north end of the area. The feet
were also booted in this burial. Both bodies had been
buried in wooden coffins.

Phase IX (fig 22)

[M1:B5] A D-shaped enclosure was defined by rubble
foundations, the straight side lying on the boundary
across the south side of the area, the curved side
extending north and terminating at the north-
eastern corner of the site.

The later phases, from phase IV onwards, are of
uncertain date, from the later 3rd century onwards.
A mid-4th-century date would be appropriate for this
phase.

Site AA North: sites A V, A IX, AA I, AA III, and AA IIIA phase dates

Site AA North was an open area throughout the Roman period, subdivided by a series of ditches and gullies.

The pottery included residual material with well-dated early types appearing throughout the life of the site. Over 50% of the vessels were in local grey wares in a fairly limited range of vessel types, the utilitarian jars and bowls being the most prevalent. During the later phases local grey wares become less important in relation to Black-Burnished ware and Severn Valley ware.

Severn Valley wares account for approximately a quarter of the material on site AA North, increasing in importance from phase VII onwards. The Severn Valley potters produced a greater range of vessels than the local grey ware producers, including flagons, narrow-necked jars, rough cast jars, tankards, cups, beakers, and bowls.

Black-Burnished ware does not appear until phase II, and increases in importance from phase VI onwards illustrating the influence of the Black-Burnished potters up to the end of the occupation at Alcester. It accounts for one-fifth of the total pottery assemblage; the earlier phases contain both cooking pots and bowls while the later phases contain predominantly bowls and dishes.

Shell-gritted wares occur only in the later contexts (phase IX onwards) and are dated to the 4th century.

Colour-coated wares are relatively common from phase VI onwards, and include material produced in the Nene Valley, Oxfordshire, and the South-West. These are all represented by table wares including colour-coated flagons, beakers, and bowls.

Only a handful of white wares are found on site A and are represented by table wares, including cups, bowls, and beakers. The majority appear in phases VI and VII.

There is very little non-ceramic dating evidence.

Phase I: late 1st to early 2nd century

Most of the recorded coarse pottery from this phase has a 1st- to early 2nd-century date range. The latest piece is probably a form R.416, a dish with grooved rim and chamfered base, probably a BB copy from AA III **99A** and there is 2nd-century samian from AA I *49*.

There was a single coin, a Claudian copy (cat no 14).

Phase II: late 2nd to mid-3rd century

During this phase the boundary gully was recut, and ditch A dug.

Much of the material is residual 1st- to early 2nd-century pottery. There are two Hadrianic–Antonine BB copy jars, forms R.172 and R.199, from AA III **73** and *32* respectively, and two BB flanged bowls, B.44 and B.46, from the upcast material of the bank flanking ditch A, context AA III *32*, which were of early to mid-3rd-century date. If all of the above material belongs in the phase then, perhaps, an

Antonine to mid-3rd-century date range might be suggested.

There was no useful non-ceramic dating evidence.

Phase III: later 3rd century

This period may denote the abandonment and contraction of the settlement in this area. Most of the recorded pottery is residual late 1st- to early 2nd-century material, with some Hadrianic–Antonine material. There are three Black-Burnished BB1 flanged bowls (B.44 and B.46) of early to mid-3rd-century date and three obtuse-lattice-decorated jars (B.17, B.20 and B.21). The latest of these, B.21, from AA IIIA 11 is probably late 3rd century.

A mid- to late 3rd-century date might seem to fit this phase. AA I *36* included intrusive material in the form of a medieval sherd.

Other datable items were a 1st-century bronze mirror (cat no 71) and a fragment of a coin (cat no 267) dated AD 337–40, which is presumably intrusive.

Phase IV: later 3rd century on

This was a period of inactivity on the site, and resulted in the in-filling of features. All of the pottery would seem to be residual, the latest piece is an early to mid-3rd-century flanged bowl, B.44.

The datable non-ceramics were residual glass fragments, a bone pin (cat no 26) dated to after AD 200, and two coins (cat nos 101, 126) which provide the date for the phase. The coins date to 270 and 270–3.

Phase V: later 3rd century on

The former boundary line was redefined during this period and a shallow trough dug in the eastern half of the area. The assemblage is essentially the same as in previous phases, with the presence of a substantial number of rusticated jars illustrating the residual nature of the material. The only reasonably contemporary material was a wide-mouthed Severn Valley ware jar, O.136, of 3rd- to 4th-century date, and a 3rd-century Black-Burnished BB1 jar B.20 from AA III 25. A mid-3rd-century or later *mortarium* was found in AA III 25. The two datable non-ceramic finds are also residual.

This phase need not continue beyond the end of the 3rd century.

Phase VI: late 3rd to early 4th century

This phase contained a great deal of residual Hadrianic–Antonine material. The only possible contemporary form recorded is O.358 from AA III *10* of 3rd to 4th-century date. In terms of the coarse pottery, this phase need not continue beyond the end of the 3rd century. There was a single late 3rd-century coin (cat no 163) from AA III *8* dated to AD 287–90.

Phase VII: late 3rd to early 4th century

This phase contained much residual Hadrianic–Antonine material, the only possibly contemporary coarse pottery form recorded is B.21, a late 3rd century BB1 jar. There is a *mortarium* dating to after AD 240 from AA I *18*. AA I 16 contained an intrusive medieval sherd. The dating is provided by the previous phases.

Phase VIII: early to mid-4th century

This phase contained a Black-Burnished BB1 flanged bowl of late 3rd- to mid-4th-century date (B.50) from AA III 11. Perhaps early to mid-4th century.

Phase IX: mid-4th century

This phase contains shell-gritted ware (R.104 and R.111) from AA III **7** and two Black-Burnished BB1 flanged bowls (B.50) from AA III *3* and *7*. Perhaps a mid-4th-century date would be appropriate.

Site AA South and site C

[M1:B6] Site AA South covered an area of 260sq m, comprising trenches AA II, A I, A XIII, AC I, and AC II (fig 3 no **32**, and figs 4, 14). Immediately to the east, beyond a modern road, site C covered some 199sq m, comprising trenches C VI, C VIA, C I, C IA, C IB, C IC, and C II (fig 3 no **34**, and figs 4, 14, 23). Street B extended north–south through the centre of site C, and in one period extended over the rear plot on the western side, in site AA South. The buildings were for the most part identified by their metalled floors and street frontages; they were in other respects fragmentary and ill-defined.

Phase I (figs 15, 24)

[M1:B6 & M1:C2] In the late 1st century and Antonine period, an unmetalled trackway lay on the line of street B. This was defined on the eastern side by two interlocking ditches (ditches C and D), 1.5m wide and over 1m deep. The western side of the trackway was bounded by a gully up to 0.5m wide, which turned sharply to the west and then south, enclosing an area some 22m east–west. The alignment of the northern side of this enclosure was continued to the west by a ditch, 0.6m deep and 1.85m wide. The area between the enclosure and the ditch in sites AA South and C and the boundary gully in the southern part of site AA N may have been a trackway extending to the west.

Phase II (figs 16, 25)

[M1:B6 & M1:C2] By the end of the 2nd century, the interlocking ditches on the eastern side of street B were redefined by a single ditch of similar form. Street B was metalled with a gravel surface before the ditch had fully silted up. This metalling was associated with a ditch on the western side of the road on the northern side of site C. This turned to the south-west in the centre of the area, but its extent to the west, and the significance of the westward turn, are unknown.

In the area to the west, some 24m behind the street frontage, two parallel gullies extended north–south in the late 2nd/early 3rd century. They bisected the area between street B and street C further to the

Table 2   Sites AA South and C: phases, dates, and main features

Phase	AA South and C West	C East	Dating AAs + Cw	Dating Ce
I	enclosure ditch	ditches C & D; trackway	late 1st to 2nd C	late 1st to 2nd C
II	loam; north–south gullies; ditch	ditch B; street B surface I	late 2nd to early 3rd C	late 2nd C
III	cobble surface I; structure AA (joisted building); ditch recut	road silt; roadside gully; subsidence over ditches	3rd C	3rd C
IV	ditch recut fills; subsidence over ditches	cobble surface; structure CEA	later 3rd C on	later 3rd C on
V	deposits in NW area; cobble surface II; structure CWA	road silts; postholes (destruction of structure CEA)	later 3rd on	later 3rd C on
VI	cobble surface III; structures CWB & CWC; pits	street B surface II; drainage gullies	early to mid-4th C	early to mid-4th C
VII	as VI continuing?	street B surface III; loam	early to mid-4th C	early to mid-4th C
VIII	as VI continuing?	cobble surface; structure CEB; street B surface IV or patching	early to mid-4th C on	early to mid-4th C on
VIIIa	as VI continuing?	structure CEB; cobble surface and stone flags	early to mid-4th C on	early to mid-4th C on
IX	robbing and destruction	robbing and destruction	mid-4th C on	mid-4th C on

west. These gullies crossed the line of the presumed east–west trackway of phase I, which must therefore have gone out of use.

Phase III (figs 17, 26)

[M1:B7 & M1:C3] The ditch on the eastern side of street B was replaced by a narrow gully, 500mm wide and 350mm deep. This was cut through the edge of silt that had accumulated over the road in the northern part of the area. On the south side of the area, subsidence over the former roadside ditches was consolidated with clay and gravel. On the north-western side of the area, the ditch on the western side of the road was recut on its original line. On the south-western side, a timber slot lay on the western edge of the road, representing the front of a large building or complex of buildings, structure AA, extending for more than 29m to the west. A cobble floor lay on the front part of the building. To the rear, the building was represented by the impressions made by the joists of a raised floor into clays probably deposited as a levelling layer. These impressions covered the greater part of site AA South, but the full extent and form of the building could not be closely defined. The joists all extended north–south. There were at least four irregular bays on each side of a broad slot forming a spine down the centre of the area. Postholes were set into a slot extending north–south on the eastern edge of site AA South, which may have been the rear of the range of a building fronting street B. The building was associated with a large pit in the south-eastern corner of the area. The pit may have lain open beneath the joisted floor. A quantity of leather cutting scrap preserved in the pit showed that the building, at least in part, had been used as a shoemaking workshop. This industry might have been associated with tanning, but there was no positive evidence for this in the immediate vicinity. Six infant burials found in this area may have been inserted under the floor and a further three occurred in associated pits. This complex may have dated from the 3rd century.

Phase IV (fig 27)

[M1:B11 & M1:C4] On the south-eastern side of the area a structure, CEA, was represented by a cobble floor extending east from street B, associated with two substantial postholes and a stone sleeper wall on the edge of the road. The form and extent of the building further to the east are uncertain. The street frontage lay over the roadside gully of phase III; the cobble floor was bedded on a thick foundation of clay where it lay over the former roadside ditches. Subsidence over the earlier ditches was also made up on the southern edge of the area. The building probably dated from the later 3rd century on.

Phase V (figs 18, 28)

[M1:B11 & M1:C5] Pebbly silt accumulated over the road surface, on the east side covering stones of the sleeper wall of the phase IV structure. On the western side of the road the edge of the silt was covered by the edge of a cobble floor in the southern half of the area, part of structure CWA. This floor was associated with a series of postholes on the street frontages, and others (eg AA II 17, 18, 19) may have formed the rear of the building on the eastern edge of site AA, some 15m behind the street. A cobble surface survived in patches over the area of the phase III joisted building. In the north-western part of site C, a thick deposit of loam had accumulated over the former ditch on the western edge of the street. The upper part of the loam had accumulated around a series of postholes extending on a line at right-angles to the former ditch.

These features were late 3rd century or later.

Phase VI (figs 19, 29)

[M1:B13 & M1:C6] A second surface was laid over street B, and this drained into shallow gullies on each side. The road surface covered the edge of a cobble floor on the western side of the road. In the southern half the cobble floor was contemporary with a line of substantial postholes along the street frontage. Postholes on the eastern edge of site AA, as noted in phase V, may have formed the rear of the building, structure CWC. In the northern half of the area there were two postholes associated with a foundation trench along the street frontage, and a stone cill wall some 15m to the rear in site AA, forming structure CWB. Large postholes lay in the internal area, but this could only be partly excavated and the plan is necessarily incomplete. In the south-western part of site AA, a number of rectangular pits may have been contemporary. One of these included the burial of a bird in a pot (BB5), possibly associated with an adjacent human cremation.

This and succeeding phases may have dated from the early to mid-4th century or later.

Phase VII (fig 20)

[M1:B14 & M1:C6] A third surface was laid over street B. Loam accumulated over the eastern side of the area. The structure of phase VI may have continued to stand on the western side of the road.

Phase VIII (figs 21, 30)

[M1:B14 & M1:C7] A cobble floor was laid over the eastern part of the area. This was associated with a foundation trench lying along the street frontage in the northern part of the area, in which was set a socketed stone, C VIA 50, to retain the door post of structure CEB. The wall may have returned to the east in the centre of the area, but the form and extent of the building to the east are uncertain. The phase VI building on the western side of the road may have continued in use. Repair patches were laid on each edge of the road. In phase VIIIa a paved yard was added to the south side of structure CEB.

Description of the excavations

Phase IX (figs 22, 31)

[M1:B14 & M1:C9] The buildings on both sides of the road were extensively robbed. There was evidence that the building on the western side had been burnt.

Trench C IIIA

A keyhole-shaped medieval drying kiln, which was rebuilt at least once, was found in trench C IIIA (see plate 2).

Site AA South and site C phase dates

Site AA South and site C contained evidence for the presence of buildings either side of street B. The pottery contained a high proportion of residual material, illustrated by the appearance of grey rusticated jars, Malvernian bowls and cooking pots, and London-type ware, found in the later phases on the site.

Local grey wares account for over 57% of the pottery assemblage with Black-Burnished and Severn Valley wares accounting for a further 35%. Fine wares are relatively uncommon, being produced either in the Severn Valley (fabric DW), or in one of the British colour-coats, with only one example of a foreign import, in phase III. White ware occurs in pre-phase V contexts, produced in the Mancetter/Hartshill kilns.

The range of vessel types is fairly conservative. Utilitarian jars and bowls are the predominant forms, with a substantial number of Black-Burnished cooking pots and bowls.

Phase I: late 1st to 2nd century

Approximately two-thirds of the pottery from phase I is accounted for by the local grey wares, with utilitarian jars and bowls the predominant forms.

There is some late 1st- to early 2nd-century material in area AA South but a reasonable quantity of Hadrianic–Antonine types (R.189, R.199, R.204, R.357, and B.39). In site C West there is 2nd-century samian from contexts C VIA 112, Hadrianic–Antonine jars from C VI **32B** (R.173 and R.391) and an Antonine or later Malvernian jar from C VI **32B**. A late 1st-century to Antonine date would seem reasonable for the phase.

In site C East the latest piece (O.386) is a Severn Valley ware bowl from C VI *102* of 2nd-century date with most other pieces being of late 1st- to early 2nd-century date. A late 1st- to 2nd-century date range would seem appropriate.

Phase II: late 2nd to early 3rd century (AA South and C West); late 2nd century (C East)

In site AA South there is a good collection of Hadrianic–Antonine material from AA II 78 and **91**, 2nd- to 3rd-century Severn Valley ware (O.140) from AA II 78 and later 2nd- to 3rd-century Severn Valley ware (O.265) from AA II 78, **79** and **91**. However, the dark loam over the western half of trench AA II

Plate 2 Site C III, medieval drying kiln, looking west. Scale in 1ft (0.30m) and 1in (25mm) divisions

contained intrusive(?) later pieces (R.388 in AA II 78 and **79** and C.37 in AA II 78). In site C West the little material is all residual and of 1st- to early 2nd-century date. The date range of the phase is presumably late 2nd, perhaps to early 3rd century.

In area C East all the recorded samian is 1st-century and much of the coarse pottery is also residual and of 1st- to early 2nd-century date. The latest piece is a Black-Burnished BB1 dish (B.74) with intersecting arc decoration (from C VIA 103), although C VIA *90* contained an intrusive Oxfordshire sherd (C.61) dating to AD 240–400. The pottery does not suggest a date later than the late 2nd century.

Phase III: 3rd century

In site AA South in this phase, amongst a quantity of 1st- and 2nd-century material, are some of 2nd- to 3rd-century Severn Valley wares, together with a 3rd-century piece (O.359) from AA II 13, an earlier 3rd-century Black-Burnished BB1 jar (B.12) from AA II 109, and a shell-tempered storage jar (R.42 from AA II 13) which is unlikely to be earlier than the late 3rd century. There are also two late 3rd-century Black-Burnished BB1 jars (B.21) from AA II 87. The timber structure to the south-west of the site contained an intrusive medieval sherd within its clays (AA II 26). To the rear of the building were the impressions of the joists of the floor, and contained within one, AA II **72A**, was another medieval sherd. In site C West the latest piece is a mid-2nd- to early 3rd-century Severn Valley ware bowl (O.380) from C VI 31. There is a 3rd-century *mortarium* in AA II 13.

The material from this phase would seem to suggest that it spanned the 3rd century.

In site C East the latest piece (R.197) in a small collection is Hadrianic–Antonine, suggesting all the pottery in this phase is residual. None of the other finds is useful in providing a date for the phase.

Phase IV: later 3rd century on

Phase IV represents the recutting of ditch B (ditch 126). No pottery was recorded from site AA South and all that from C West was residual.

In site C East most of the dating material was inconclusive and included much residual 1st- and 2nd-century material, although postpit C VI 43 contained a late 3rd-century Black-Burnished ware jar (B.20). There was also a Crummy type 5 bone pin (cat no 40), which is dated as after AD 250, from C VI **79**.

Phase V: later 3rd century on

There is a significant rise in the proportion of Black-Burnished and Severn Valley wares to local grey ware. The residual nature of the material is emphasized by the quantity of rusticated jars and London-type wares occurring in phase V. The only non-residual piece in site AA South (O.143) was a wide-mouthed Severn Valley ware jar perhaps of later 3rd- to 4th-century date from AA II 29. In site C West there was an everted rimmed shell-tempered ware storage jar (R.42) which is unlikely to date before the later 3rd century from C VIA *107*. There is a *mortarium* dating to after AD 240 from C IA 2. The phase is presumably, therefore, late 3rd century or later.

All the pottery in site C East was residual 1st- and 2nd-century material.

Phase VI: early to mid-4th century

In site AA South 4th-century Nene Valley wares (CW.6 and CW.8) come from AA II **45** and **50** respectively, together with an Oxfordshire ware bowl from AA II **45** (C.54). In site C West there is a later 3rd- to 4th-century Severn Valley ware bowl (O.146) from C VI **12**, a late 3rd-century Black-Burnished BB1 jar (B.21) from C VIA **105**, and a south-western brown slipped ware vessel (C.34) from C VI 12A. This last pot must be mid-4th century or later. Overall an early to mid-4th-century date range seems appropriate for this phase.

In site C East all the material is residual, of 1st- to 3rd-century date.

Phase VII: early to mid-4th century

No ceramics or datable finds are recorded from sites AA South and C West for this phase.

In site C East there are 4th-century Severn Valley wares (O.150 and O.281) and Oxfordshire ware (C.40) from C VI *24* suggesting an early to mid-4th-century date. The gully filled with compact pebbles and the gravel (C VIA *76*) contained a possible medieval sherd.

Phase VIII: early to mid-4th century on

No pottery is recorded from sites AA South and C West in phases VIII and VIIIa. In site C East all the material is residual. The non-ceramics are not helpful, so the date relies on the previous phases.

Phase IX: mid-4th century on

All the pottery from this phase in sites AA South and C West is residual.

In site C East there are 4th-century Severn Valley wares (O.150 and O.281) from C VIA **10** and C VIA *19* together with an Oxfordshire(?) sherd (C.69) from C VIA **10**, a Nene Valley beaker (CW.5) from C VIA 52, and a shell-tempered ware jar (R.111) from C VIA *12*.

A copper alloy bracelet (cat no 33) from C VI *4* is dated as 4th century, as is a glass fragment (GL 102). C VIA *12* contained a coin (cat no 294) dated as AD 346–8 and a copper alloy necklace (cat no 35) dated to the 4th century. C VIA 52 contained a coin of Constantine I, dated 325–6. A mid-4th-century date (or later) would seem reasonable for the material.

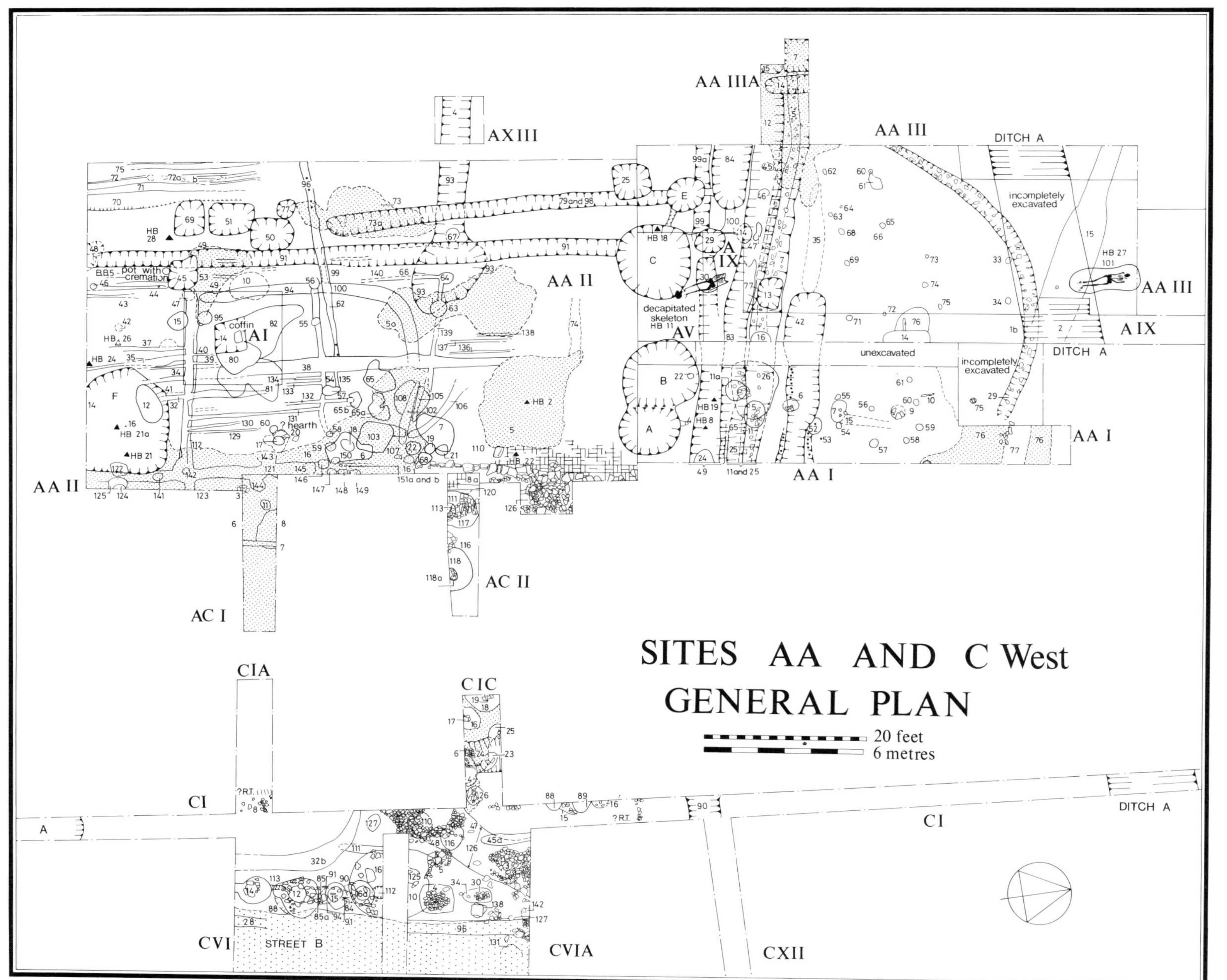

Figure 14 Sites AA and C West, general plan

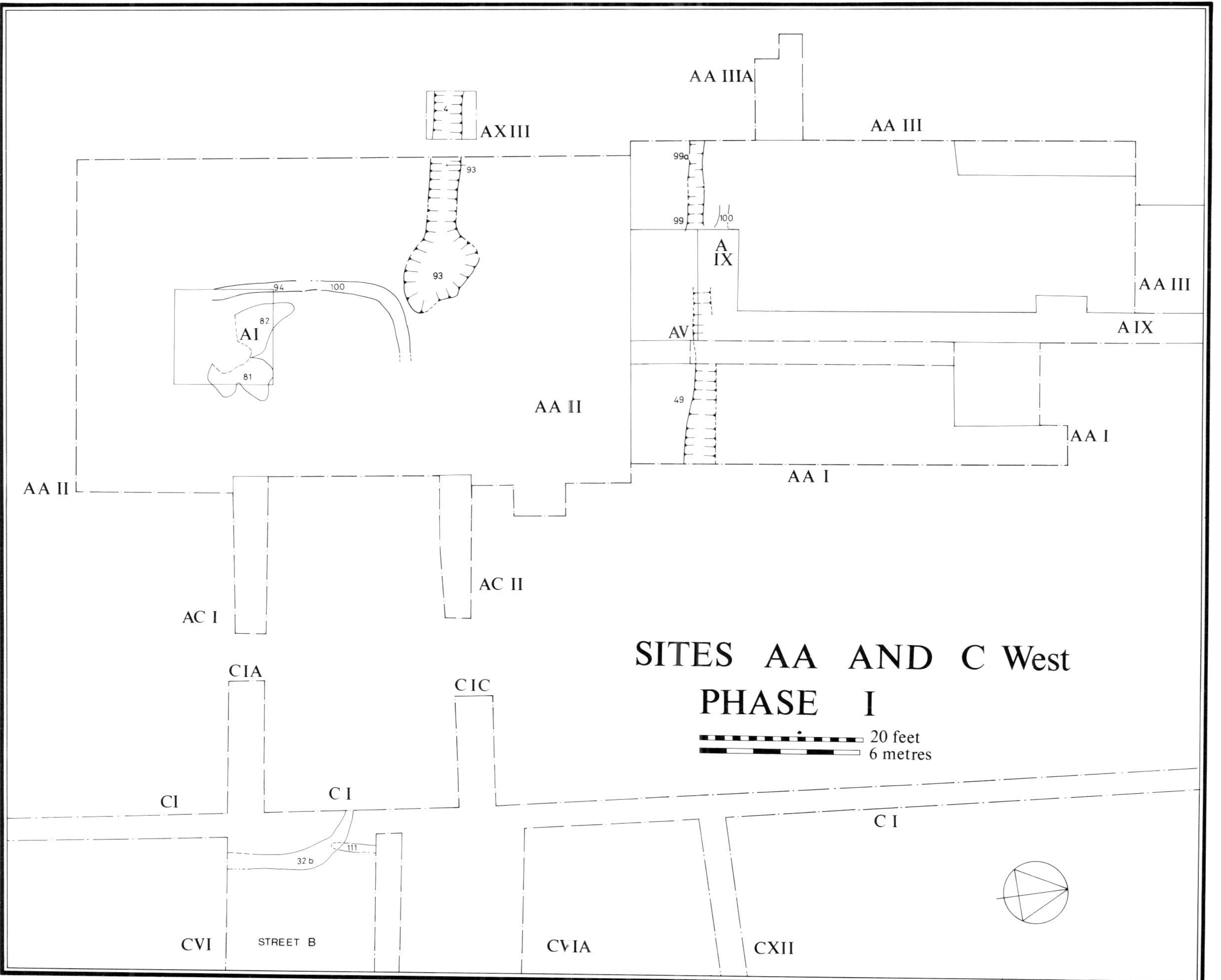

Figure 15 Sites AA and C West, phase I

33

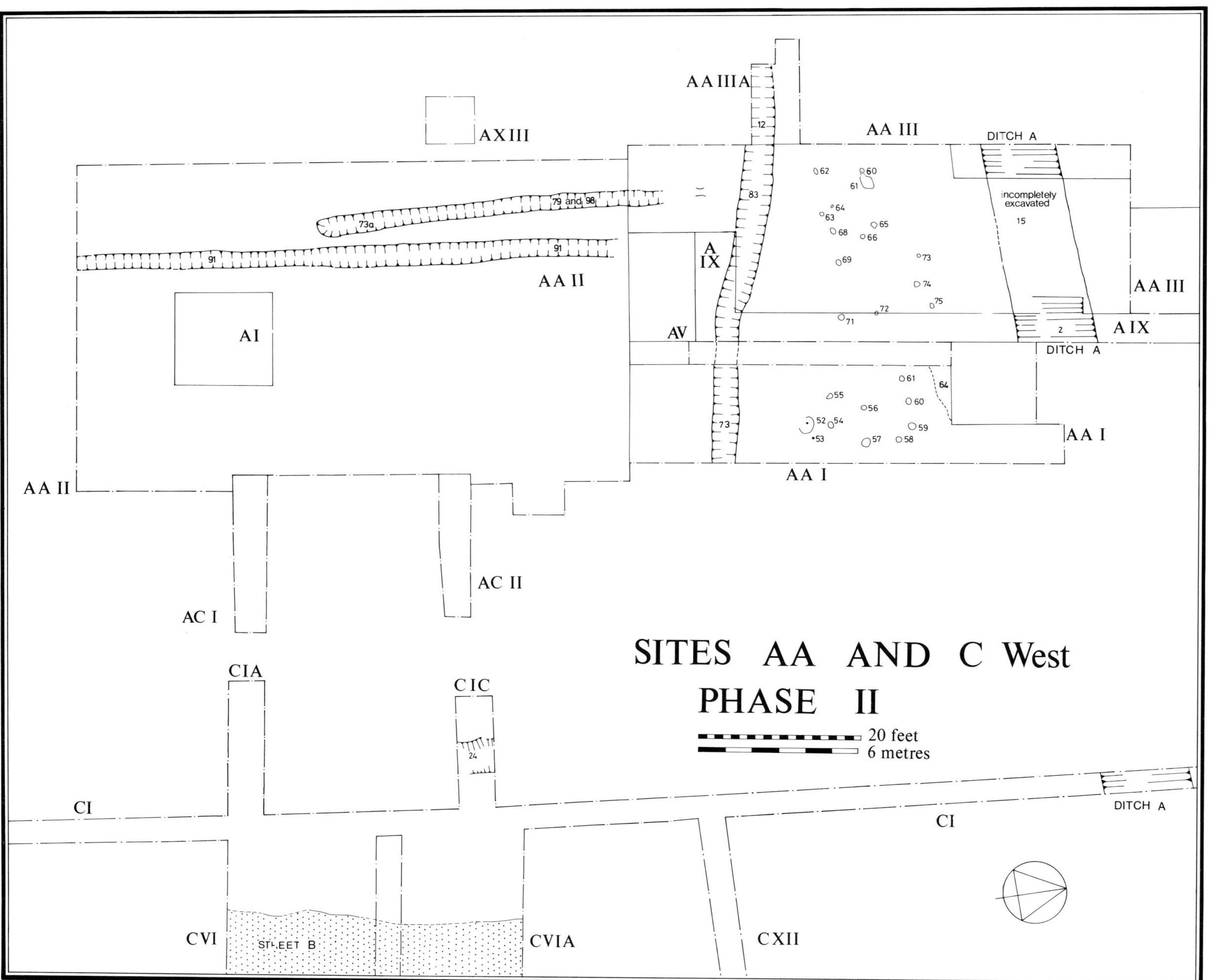

Figure 16 Sites AA and C West, phase II

34

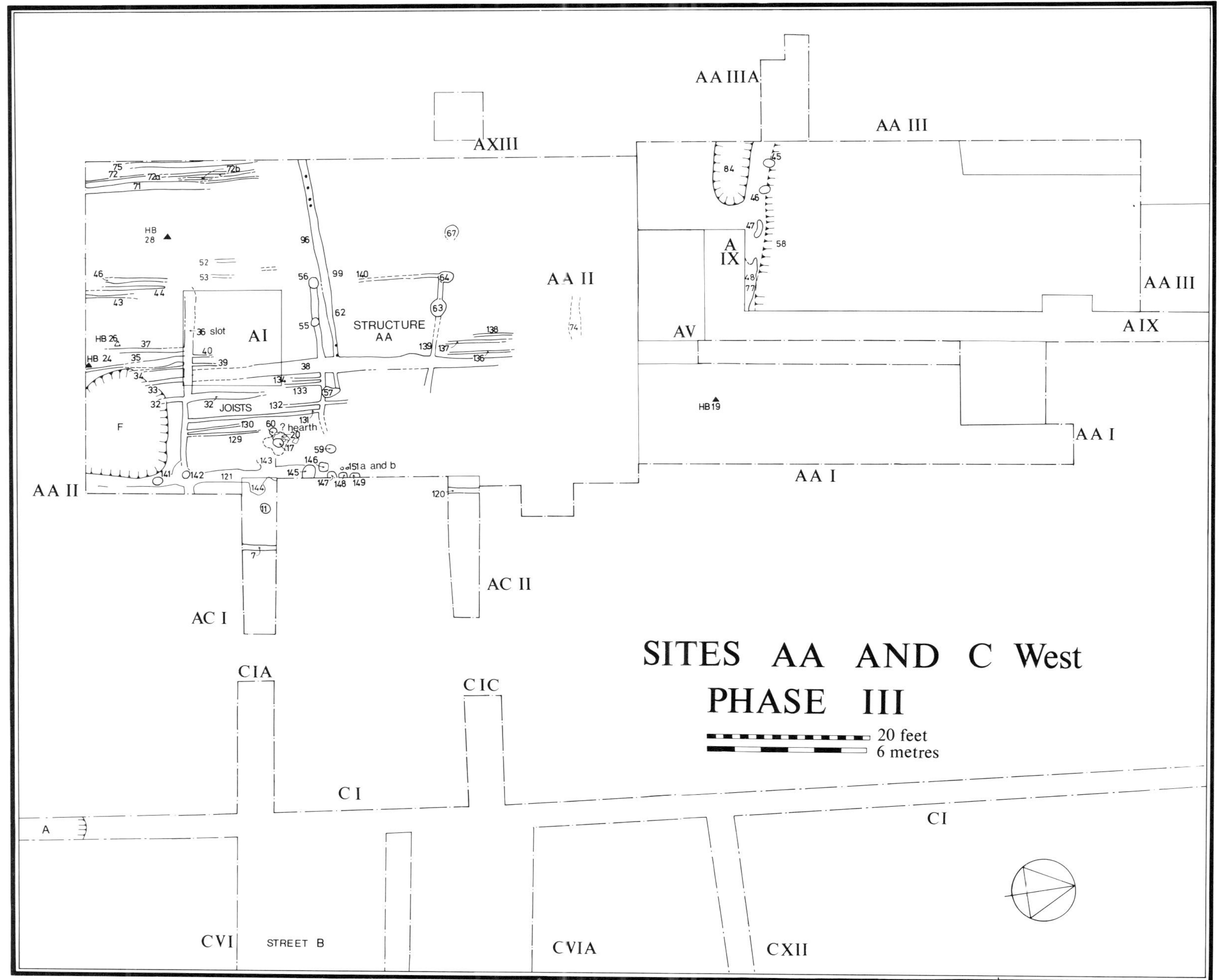

Figure 17 Sites AA and C West, phase III

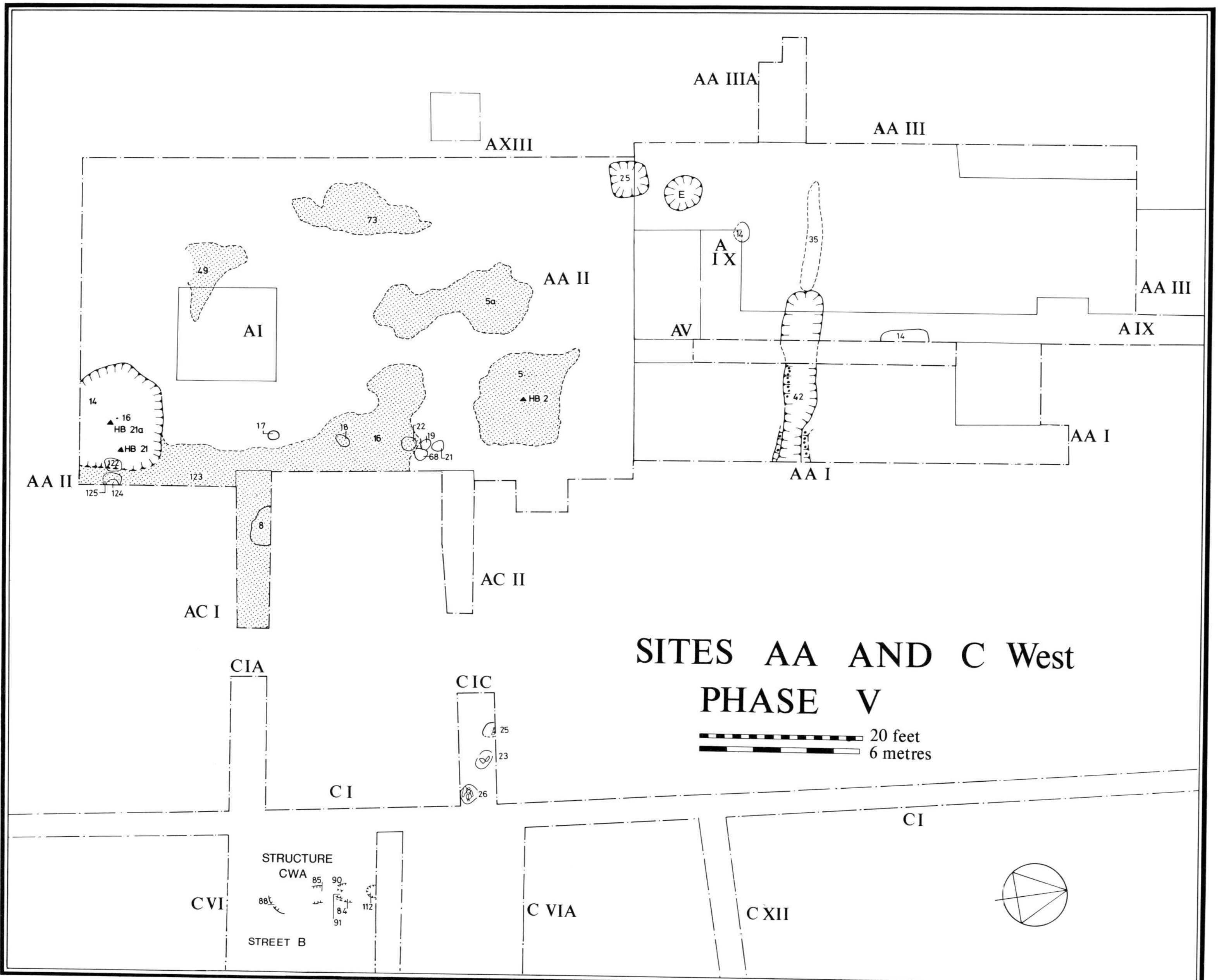

AA IIIA
AA III
AXIII
25
E
35
A IX
AA III
AA II
AV
14
A IX
49
73
5a
AI
5
AA I
HB 2
14
16
HB 21a
17
18
16
22
19
AA I
HB 21
68
21
AA II
123
125 124
8
AC II
AC I
SITES AA AND C West
PHASE V
CIA
CIC
25
23
20 feet
6 metres
CI
26
CI
STRUCTURE
CWA 85 90
88 8.4 112
CVI 91
C VIA
C XII
STREET B

Figure 18 Sites AA
and C West, phase V

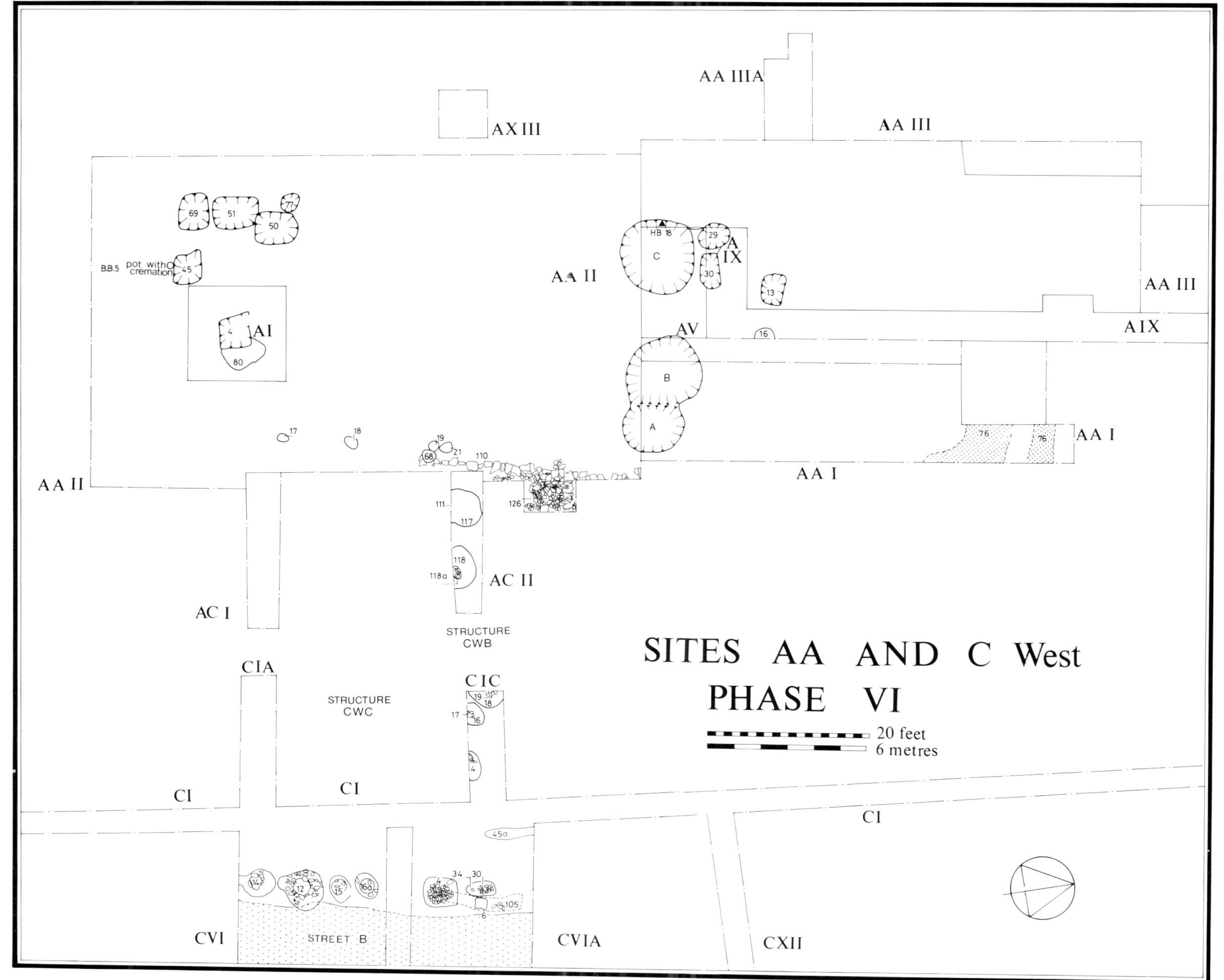

Figure 19 Sites AA and C West, phase VI

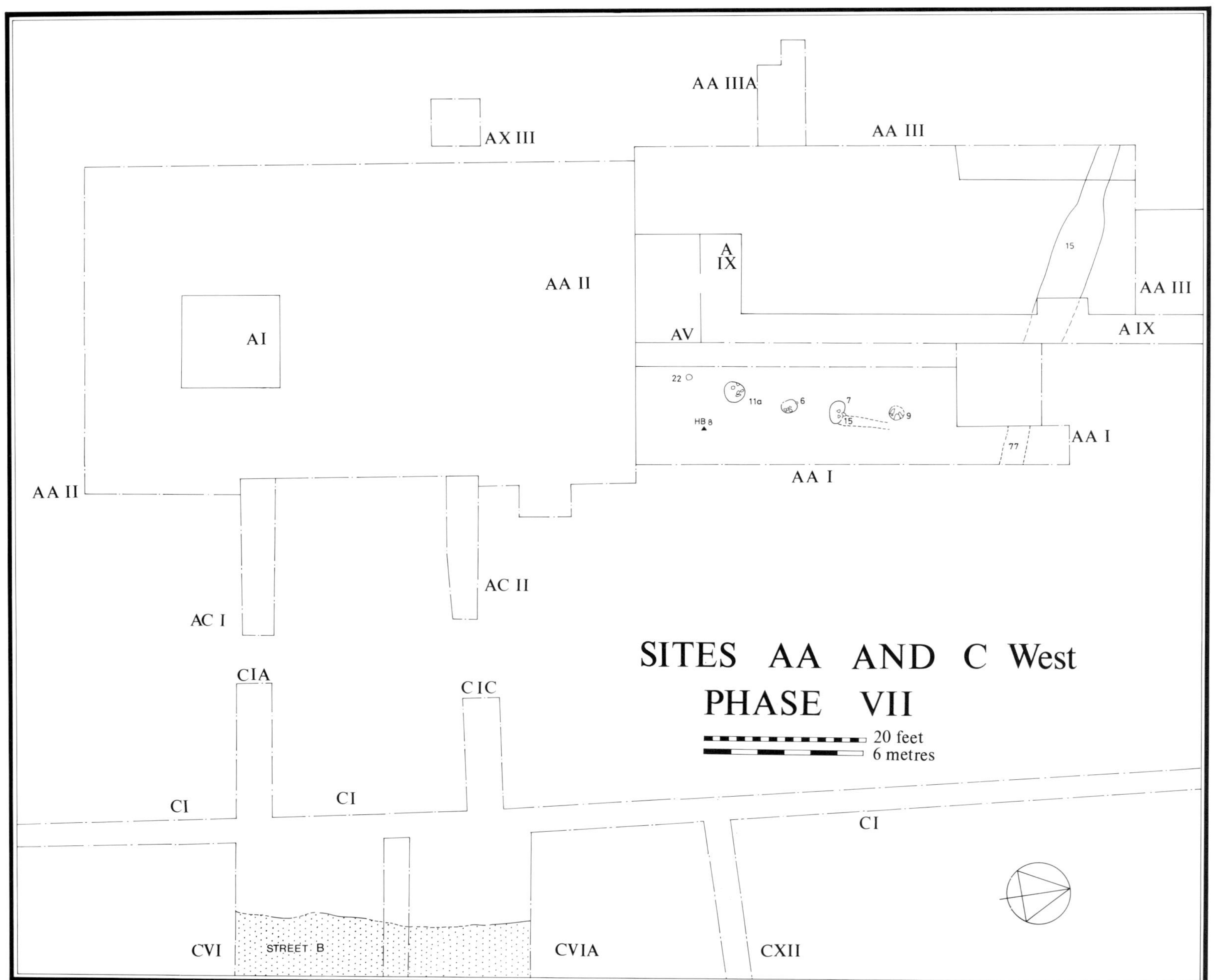

Figure 20 Sites AA and C West, phase VII

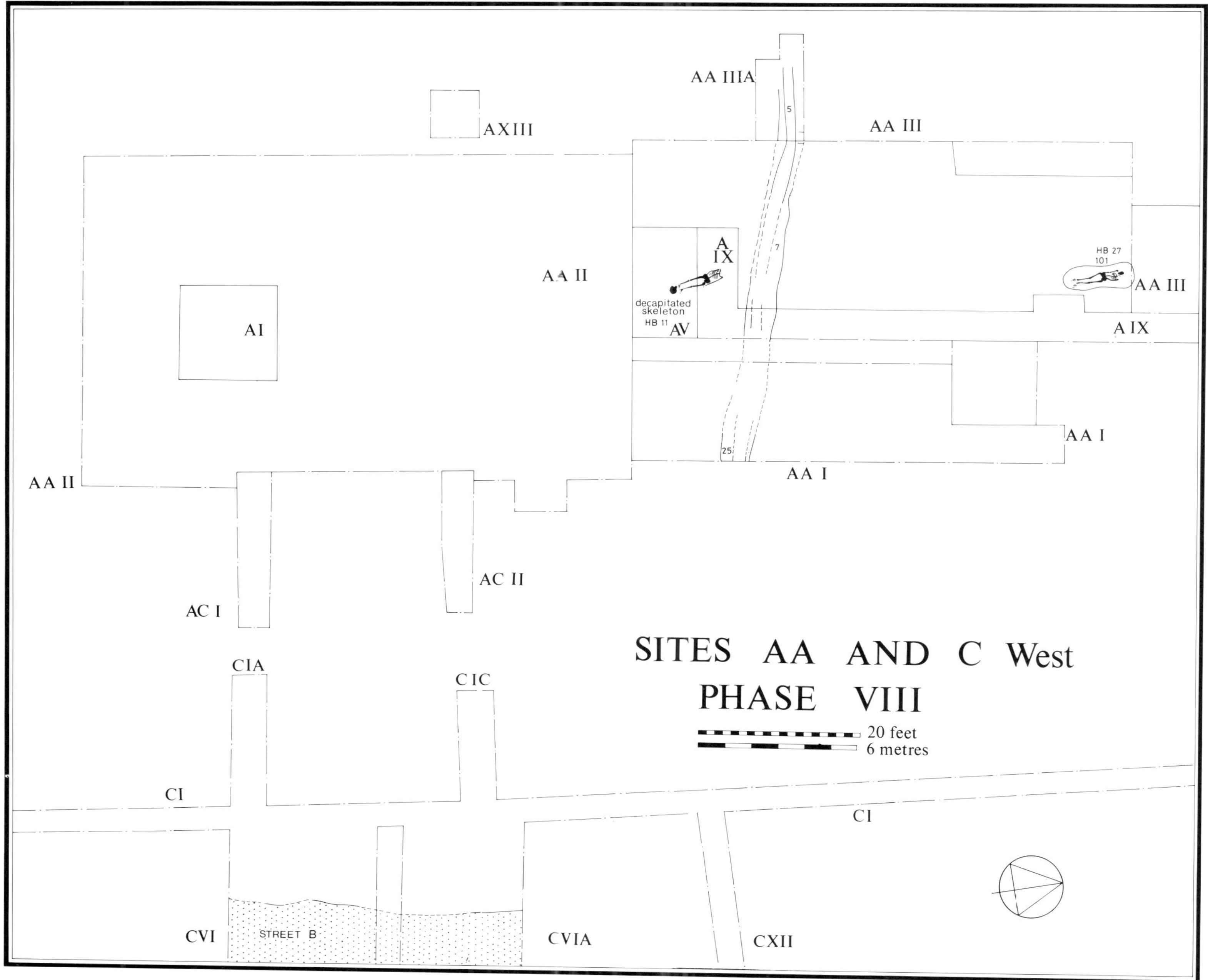

Figure 21 Sites AA and C West, phase VIII

39

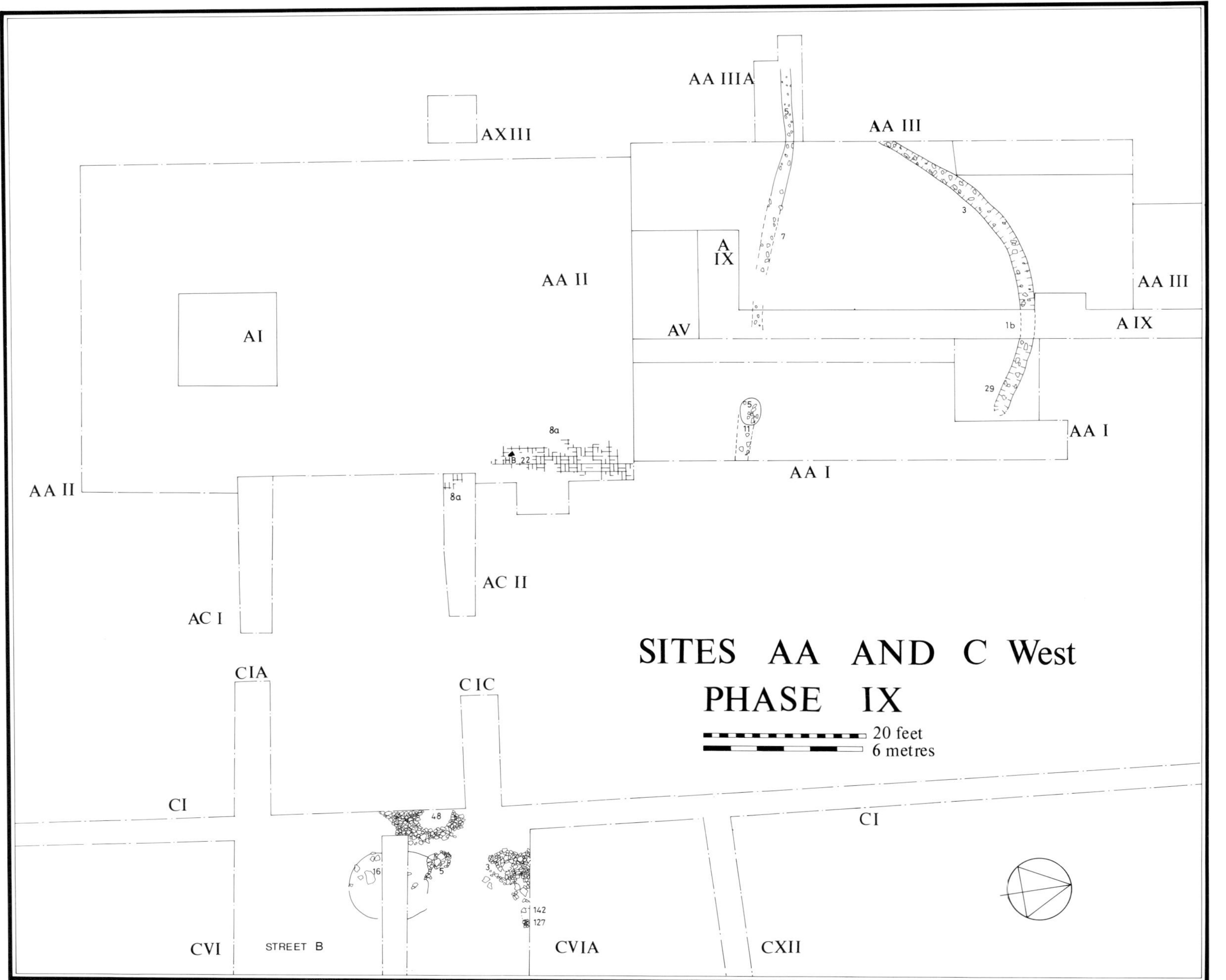

Figure 22 Sites AA and C West, phase IX

40

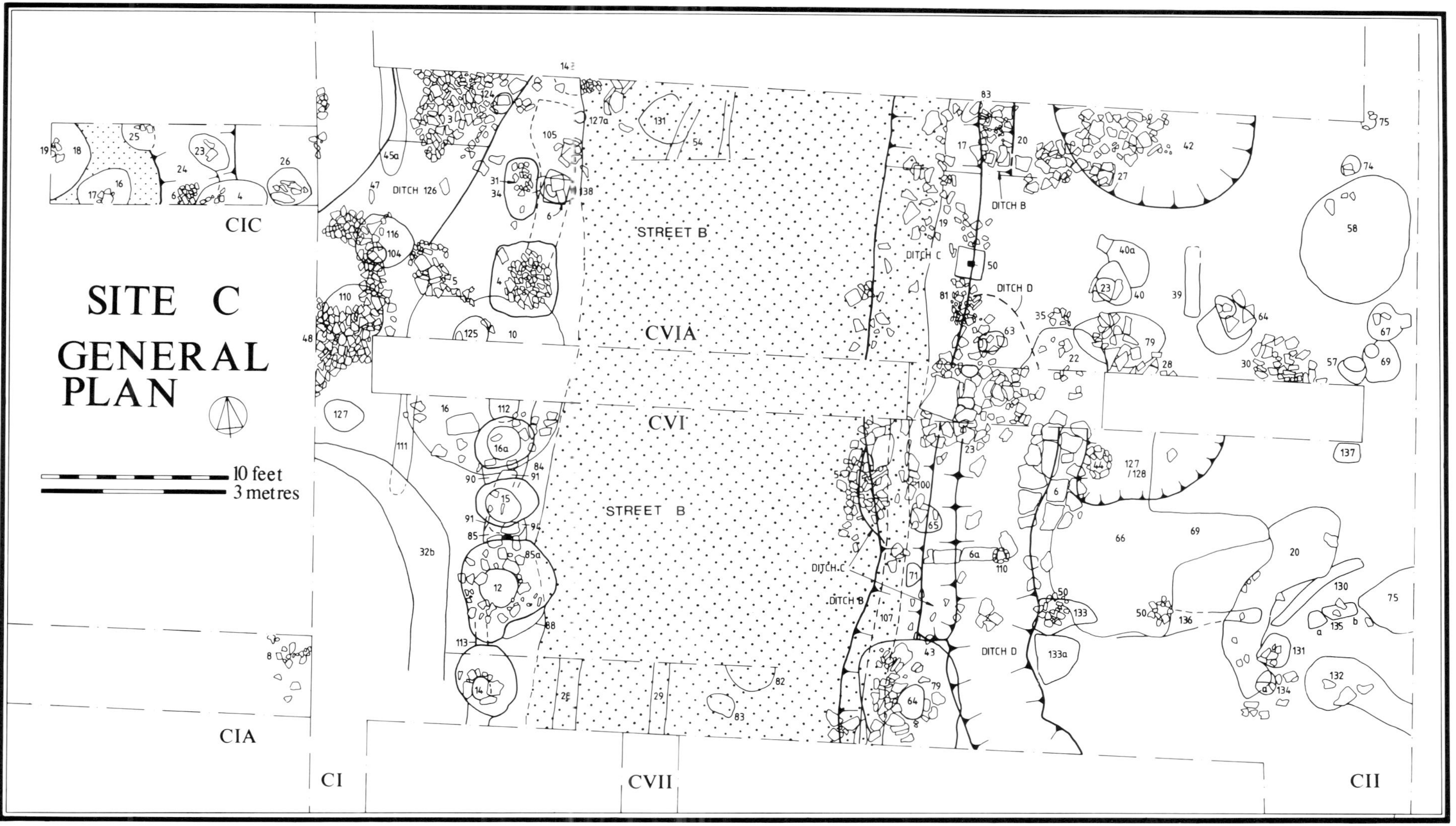

Figure 23 Site C, general plan

41

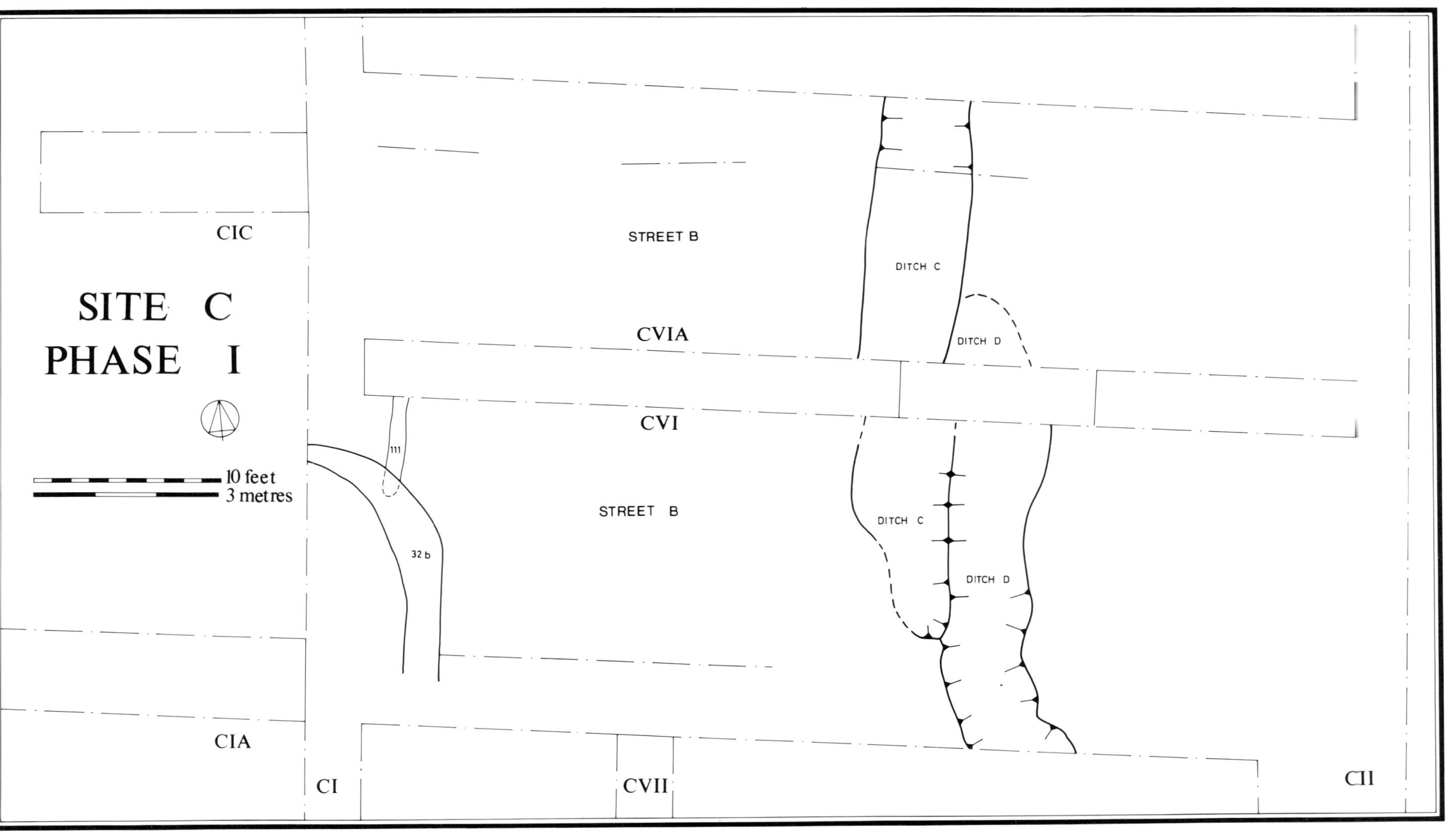

Figure 24 Site C, phase I

42

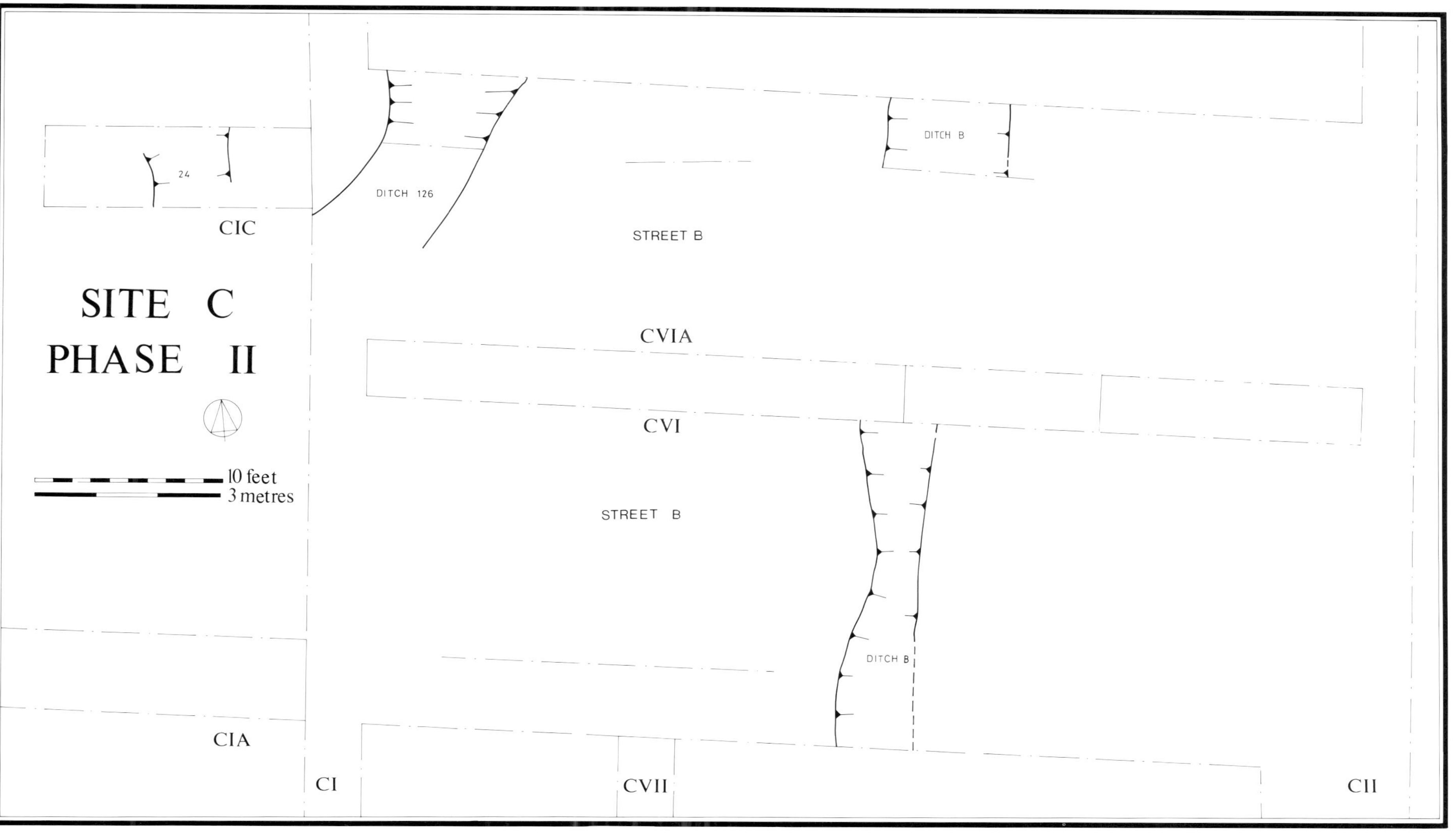

Figure 25 Site C, phase II

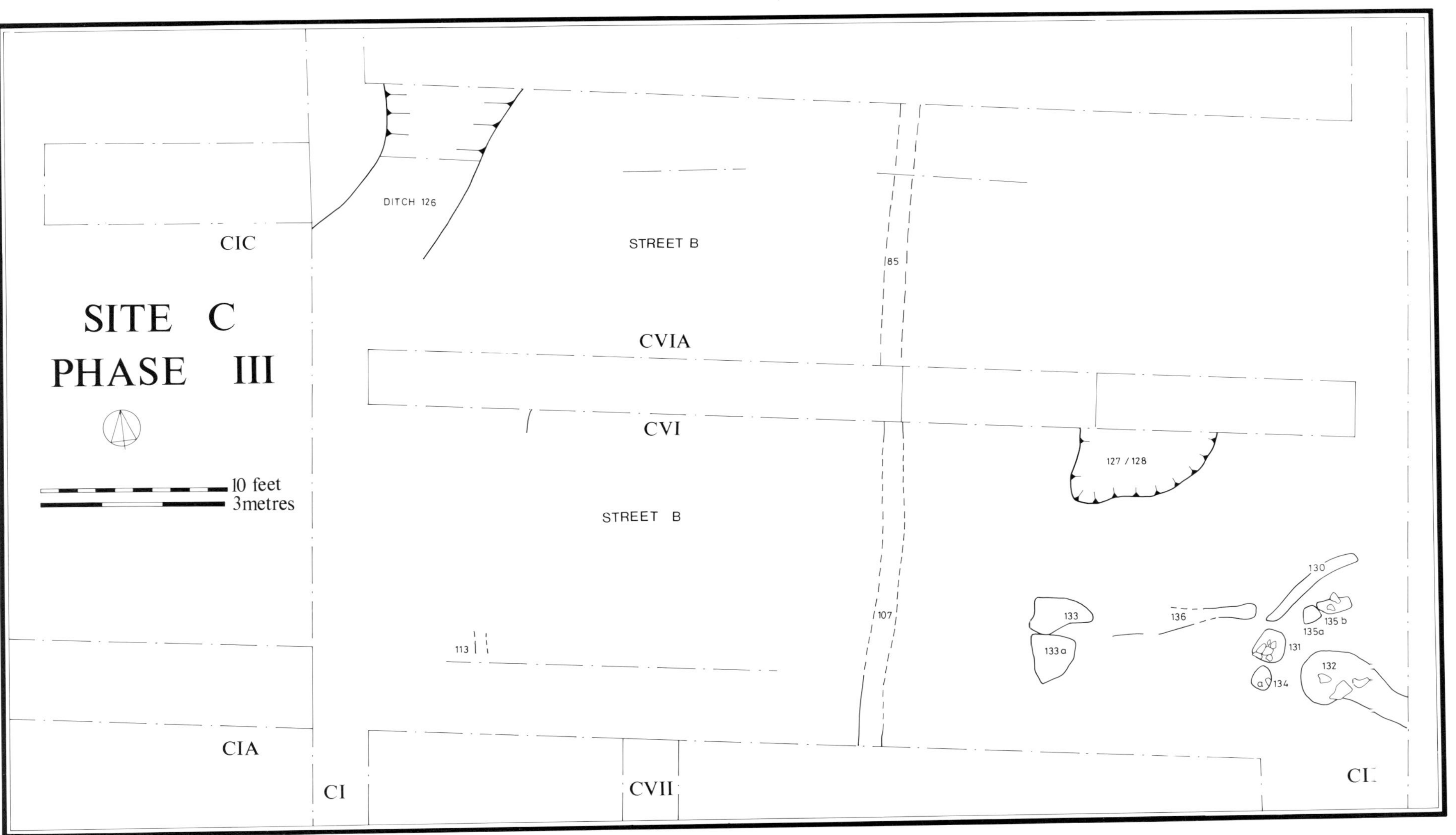

Figure 26 Site C, phase III

44

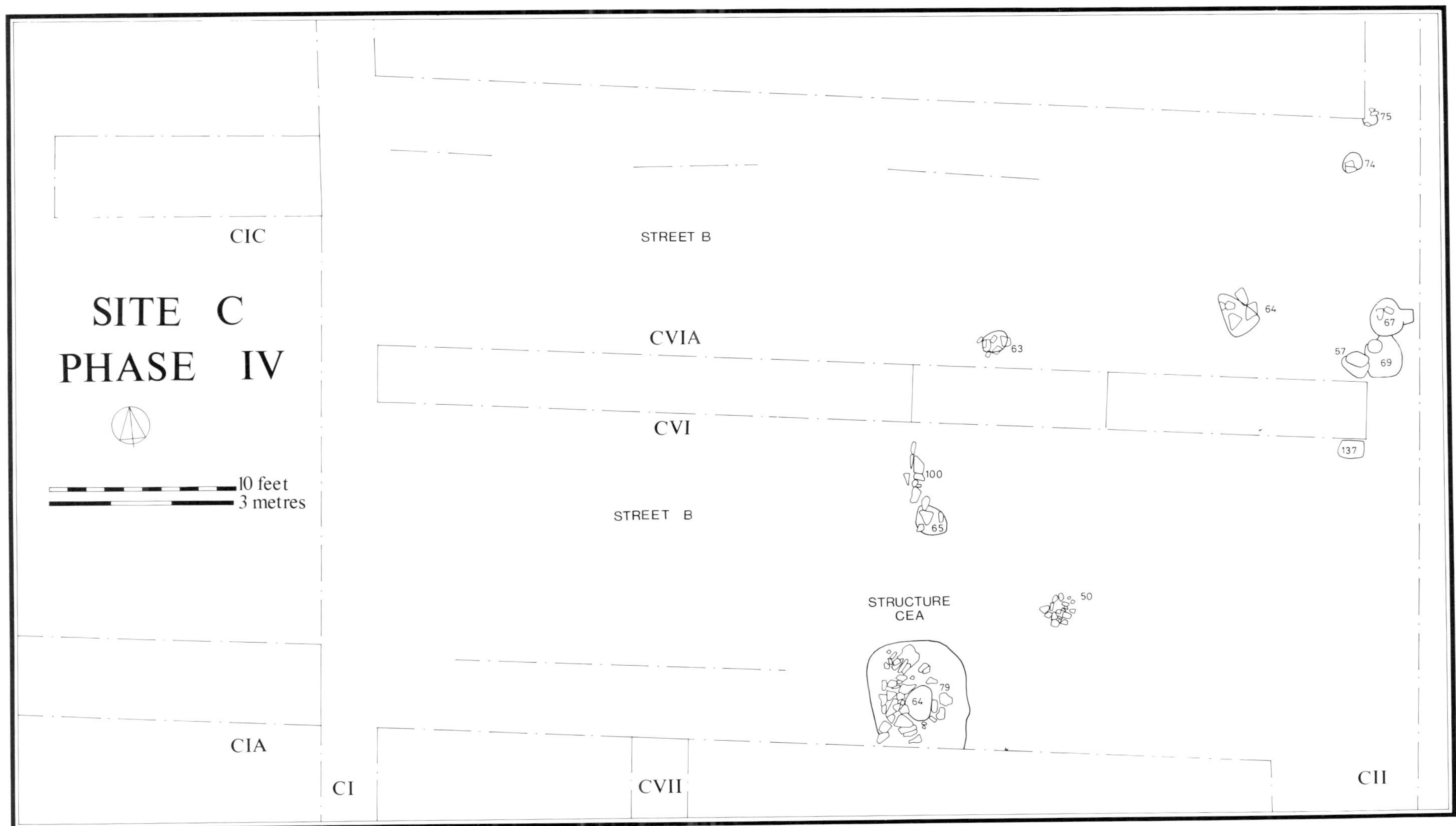

Figure 27 Site C, phase IV

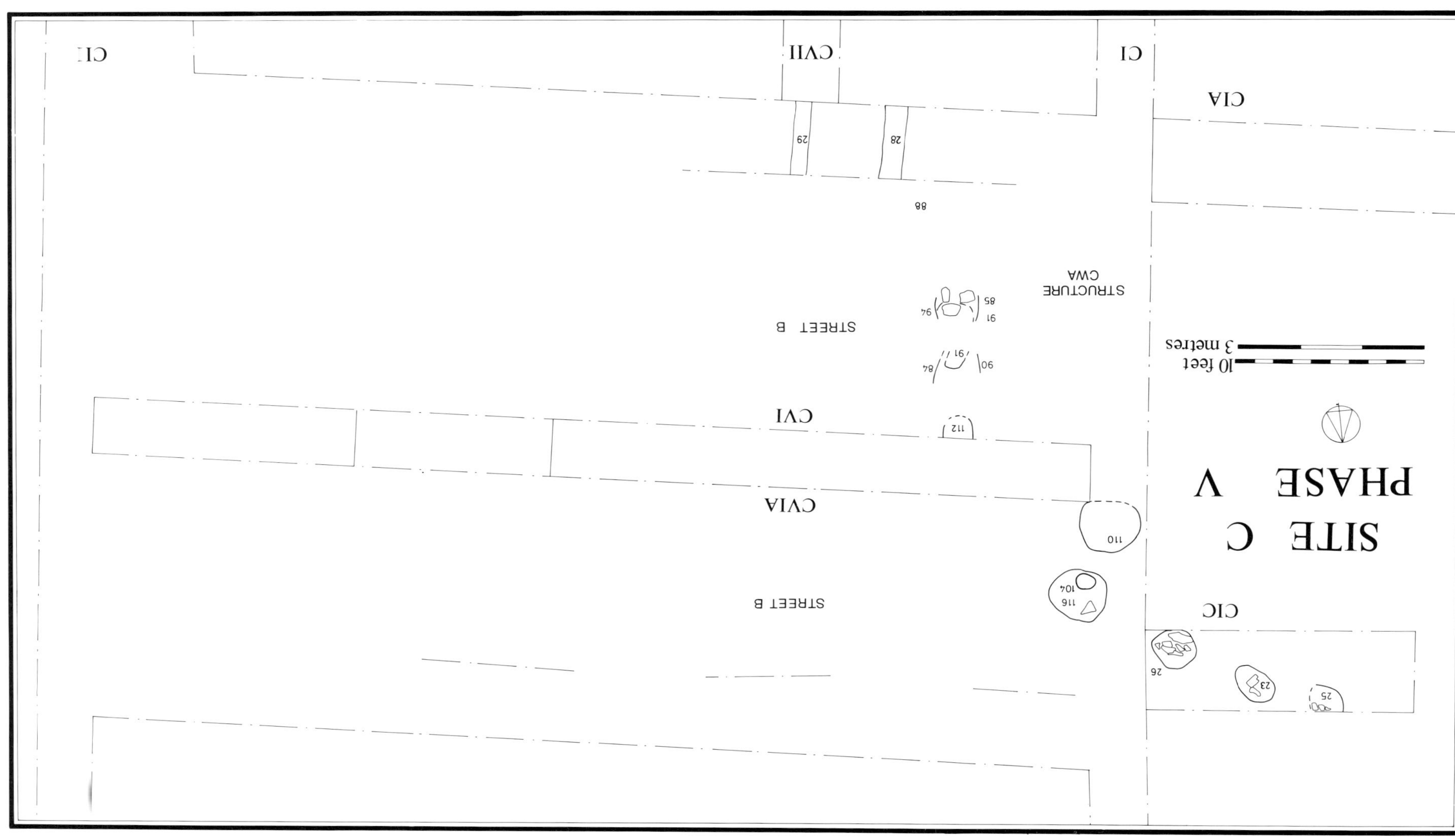

Figure 28 Site C, phase V

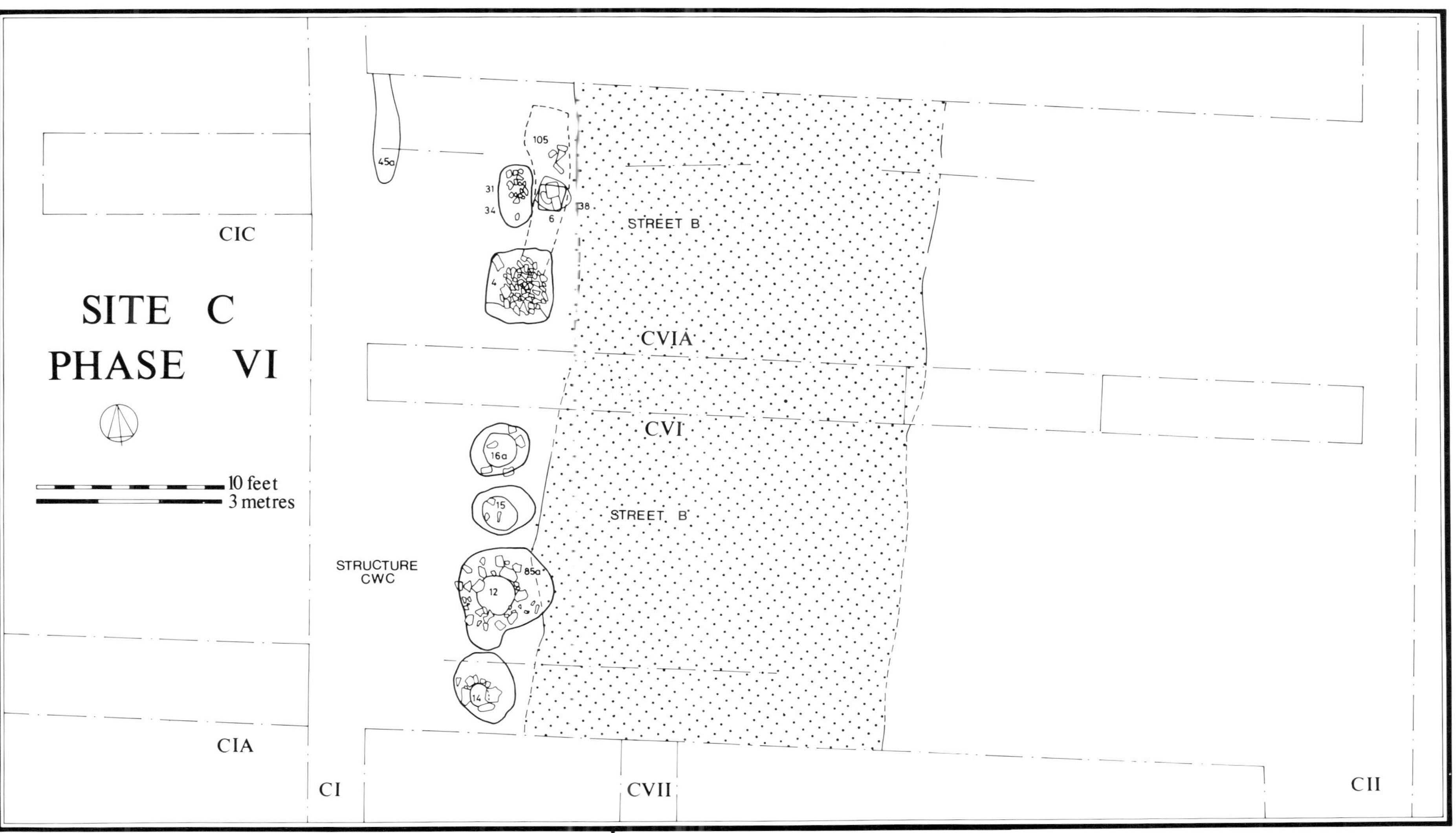

Figure 29   Site C, phase VI

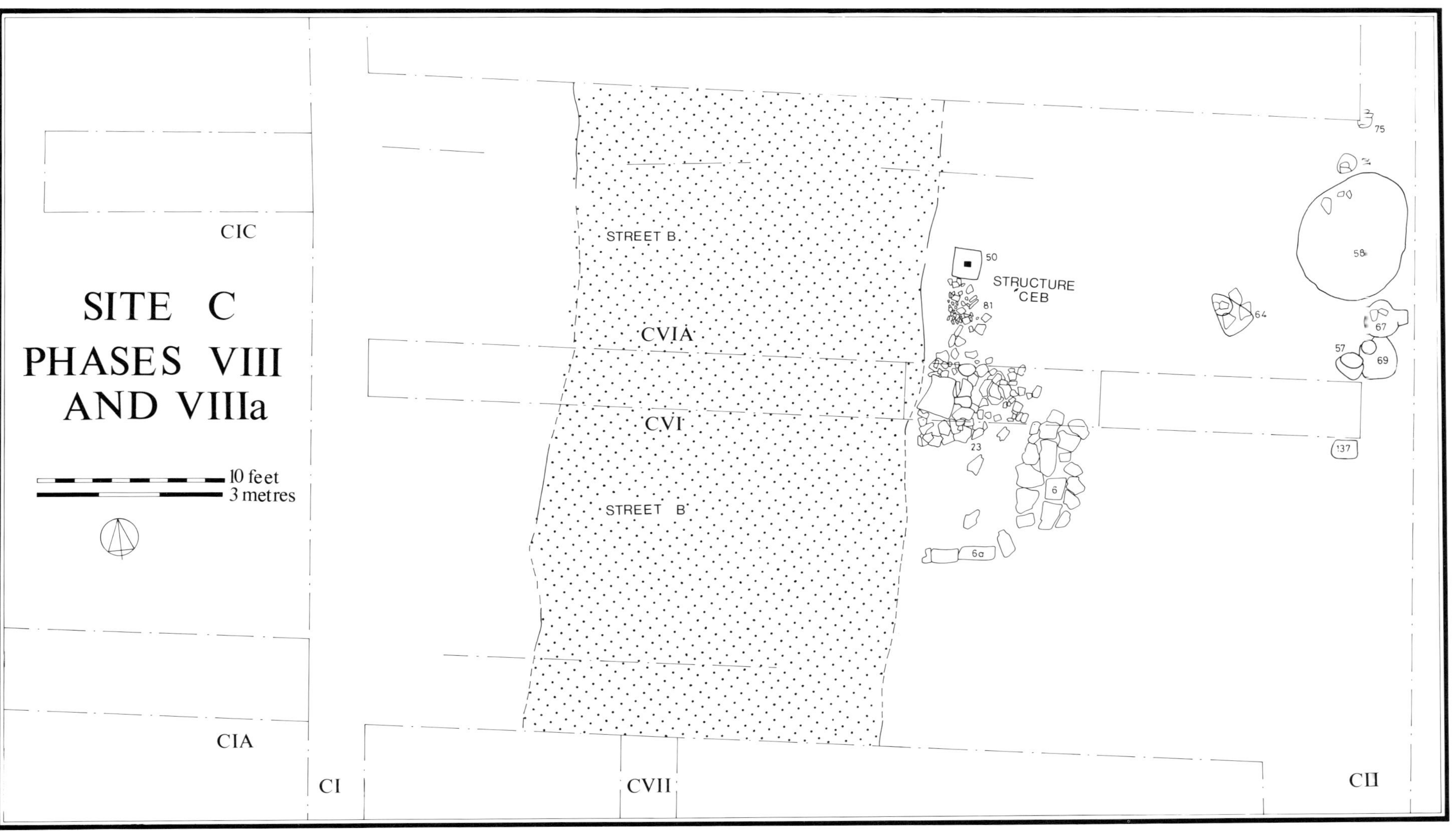

Figure 30 Site C, phases VIII and VIIIa

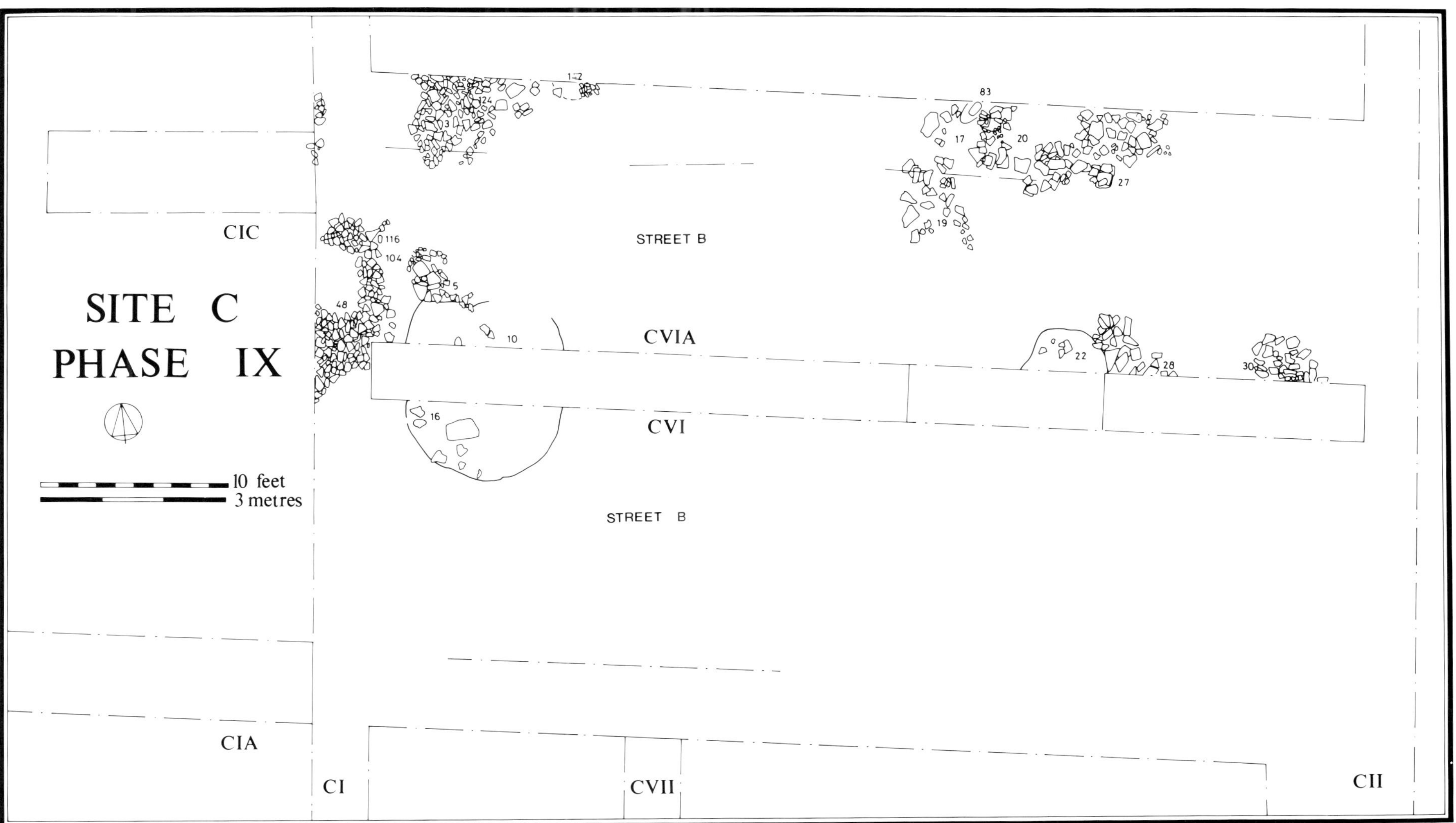

Figure 31 Site C, phase IX

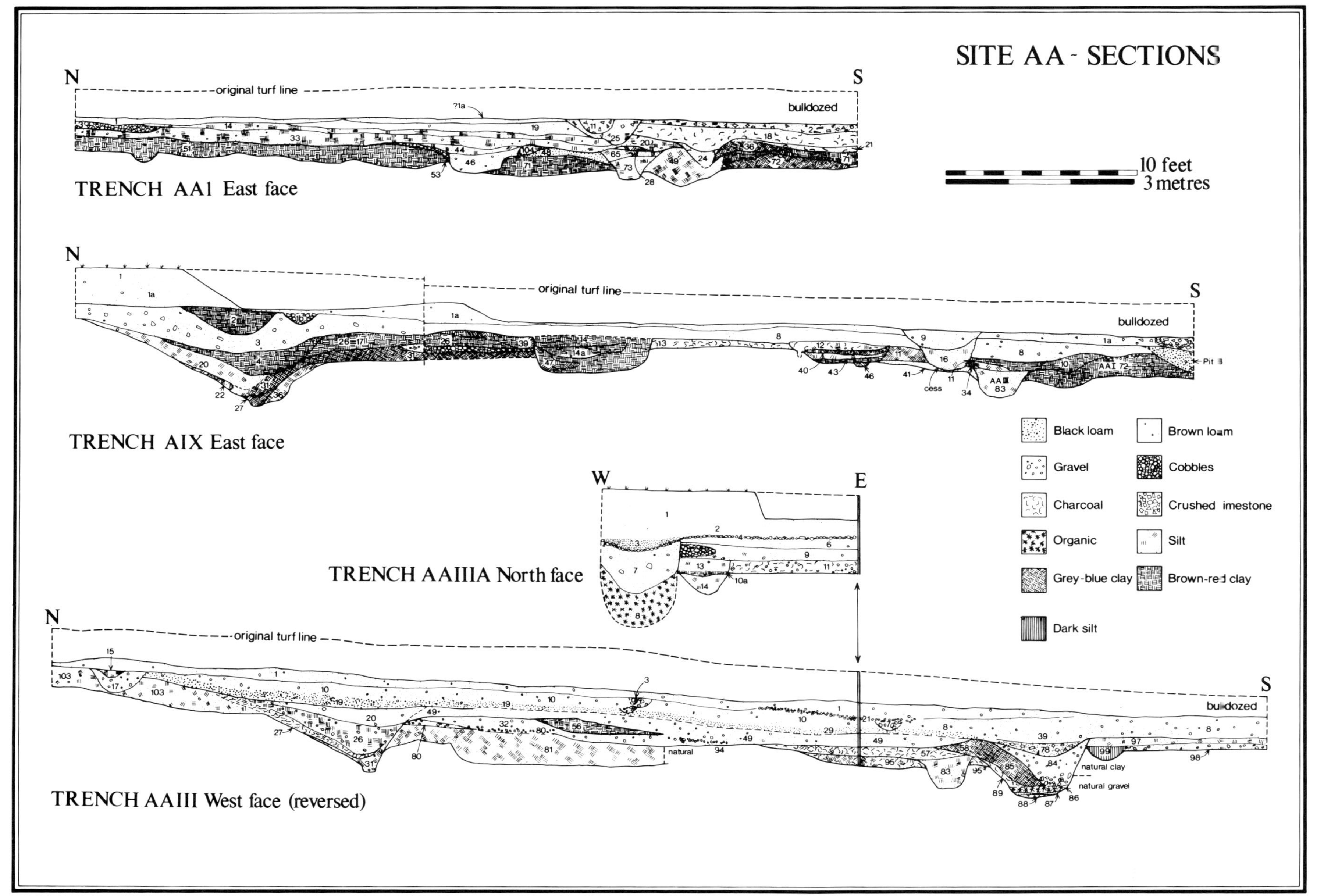

Figure 32 Site AA sections. Trench AA I, east face; trench A IX, east face; trench AA IIIA, north face; trench AA III, west face (reversed) (plan: fig 14)

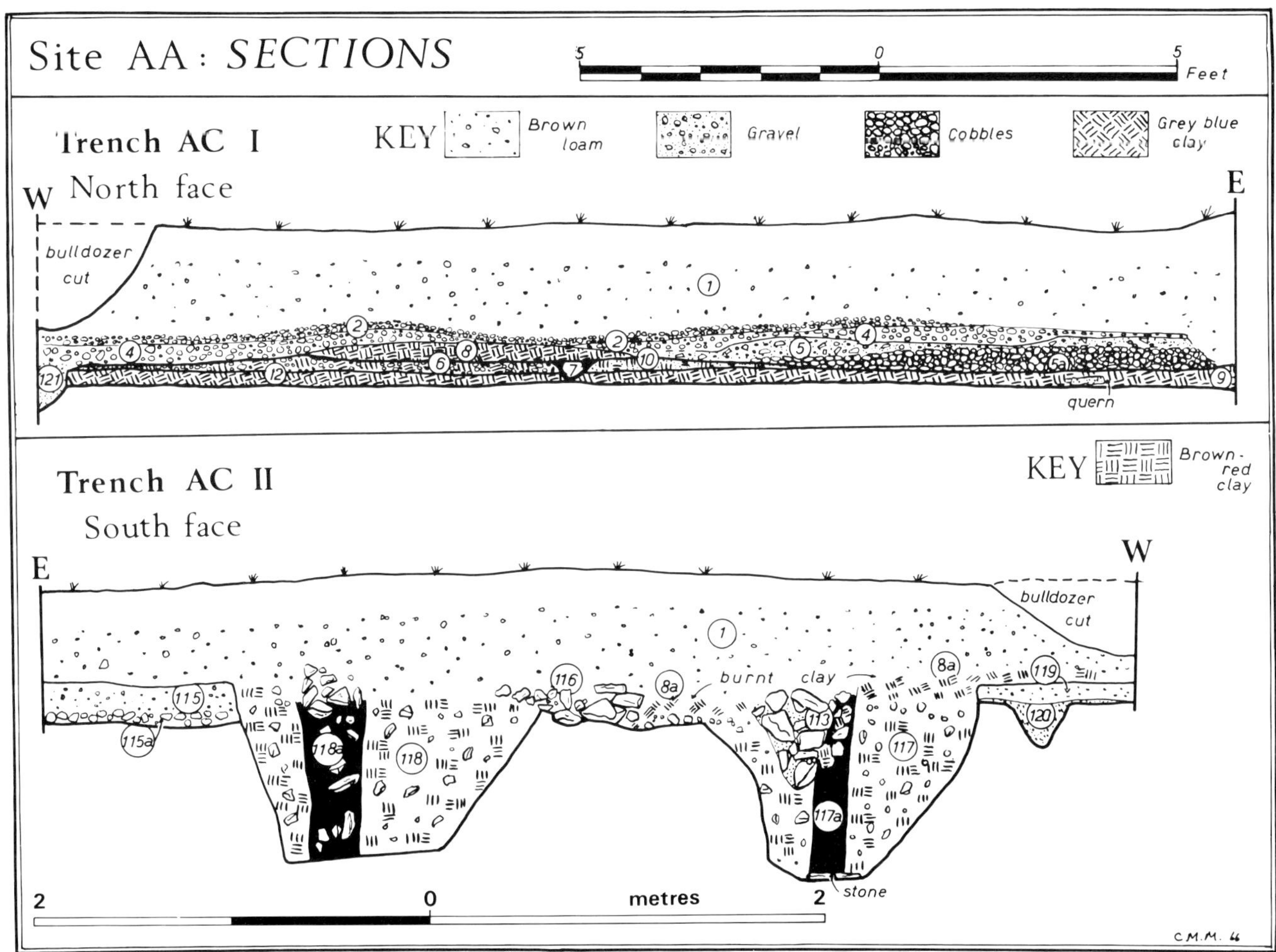

Figure 33   Site AA sections. Trench AC I, north face; trench AC II, south face (plan: fig 14)

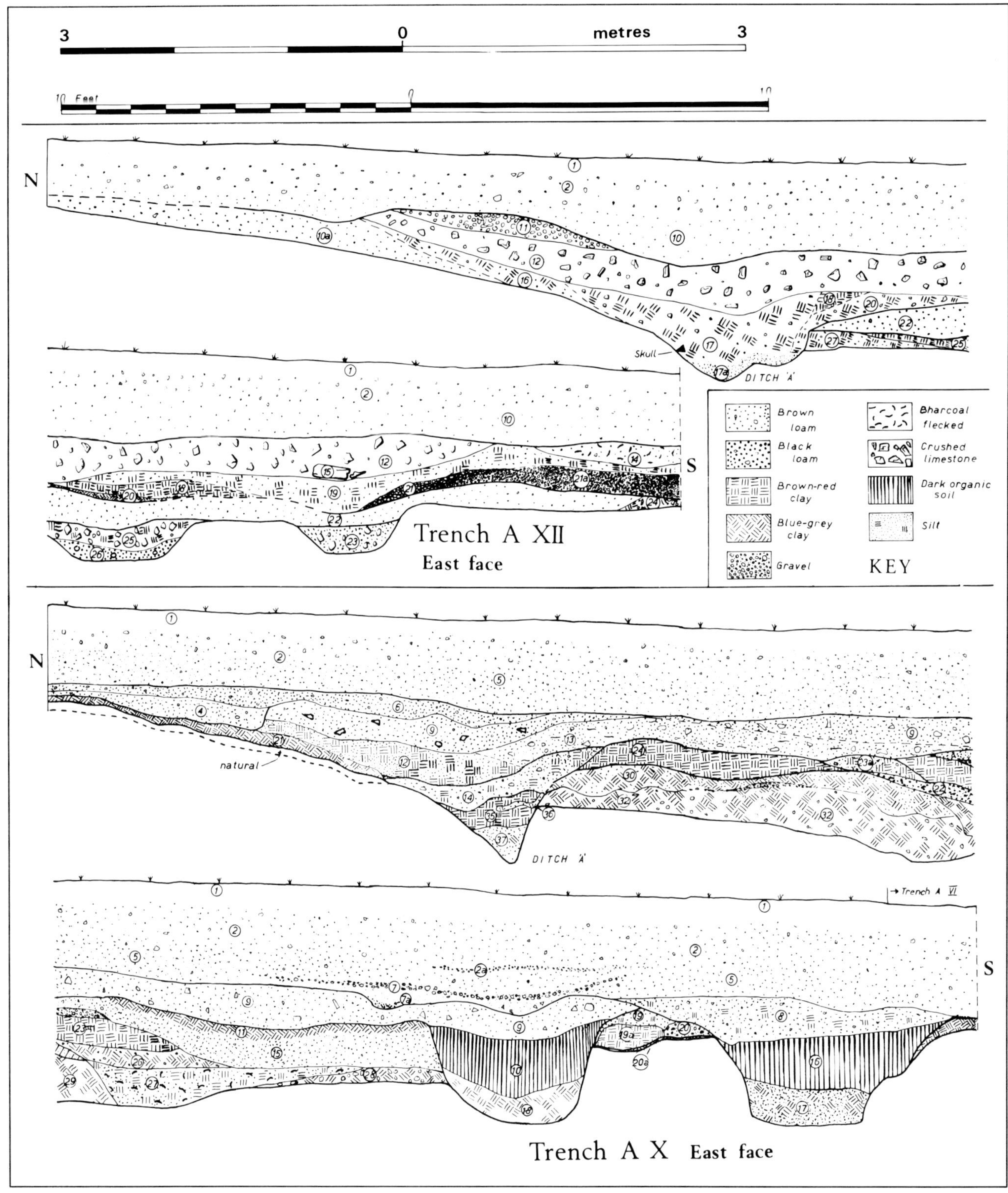

Figure 34   Sections of ditch A and area to south. Trench A XII, east face; trench A X, east face (plan: fig 4)

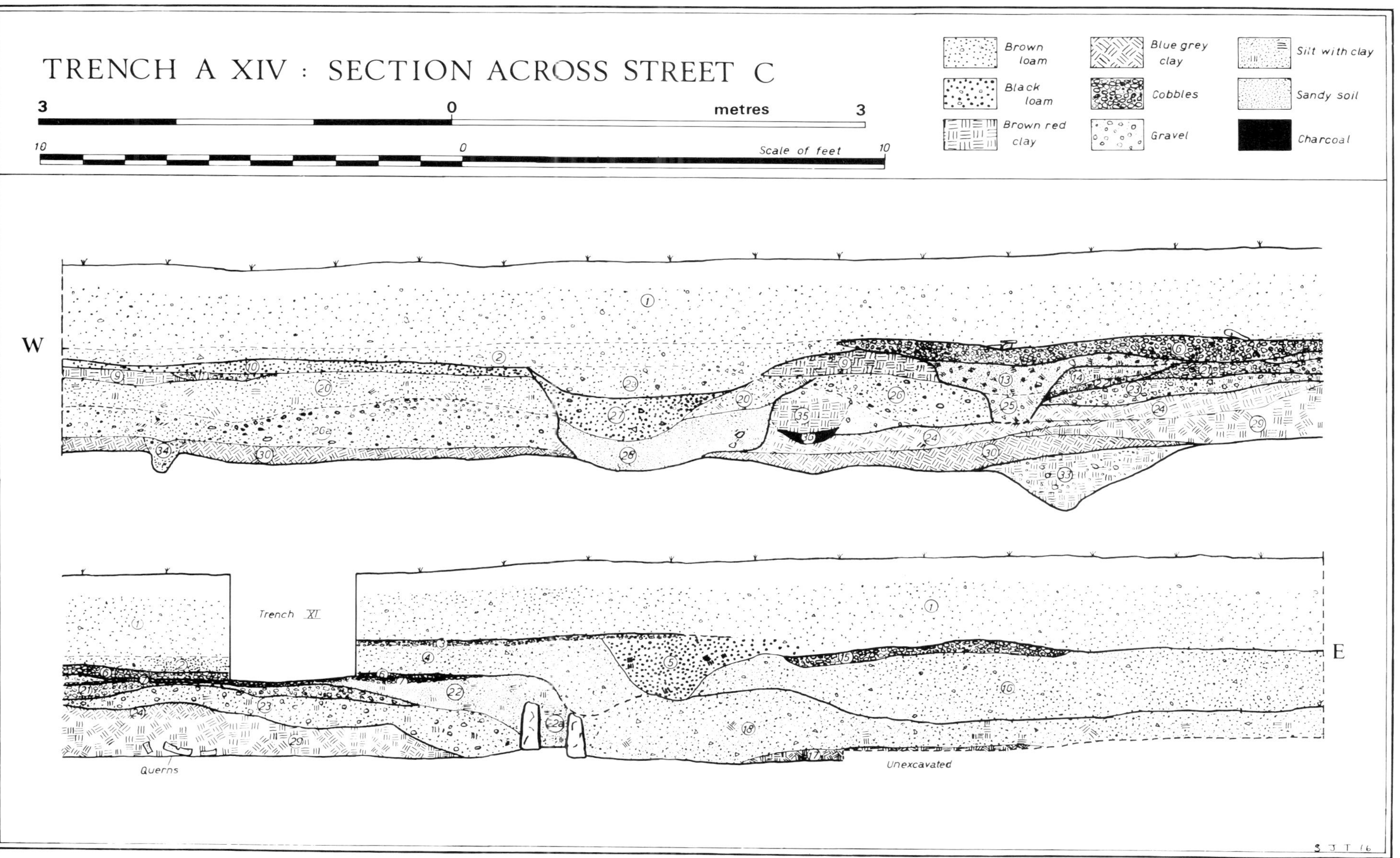

Figure 35 Trench A XIV. Section across street C. North face (plan: fig 4)

53

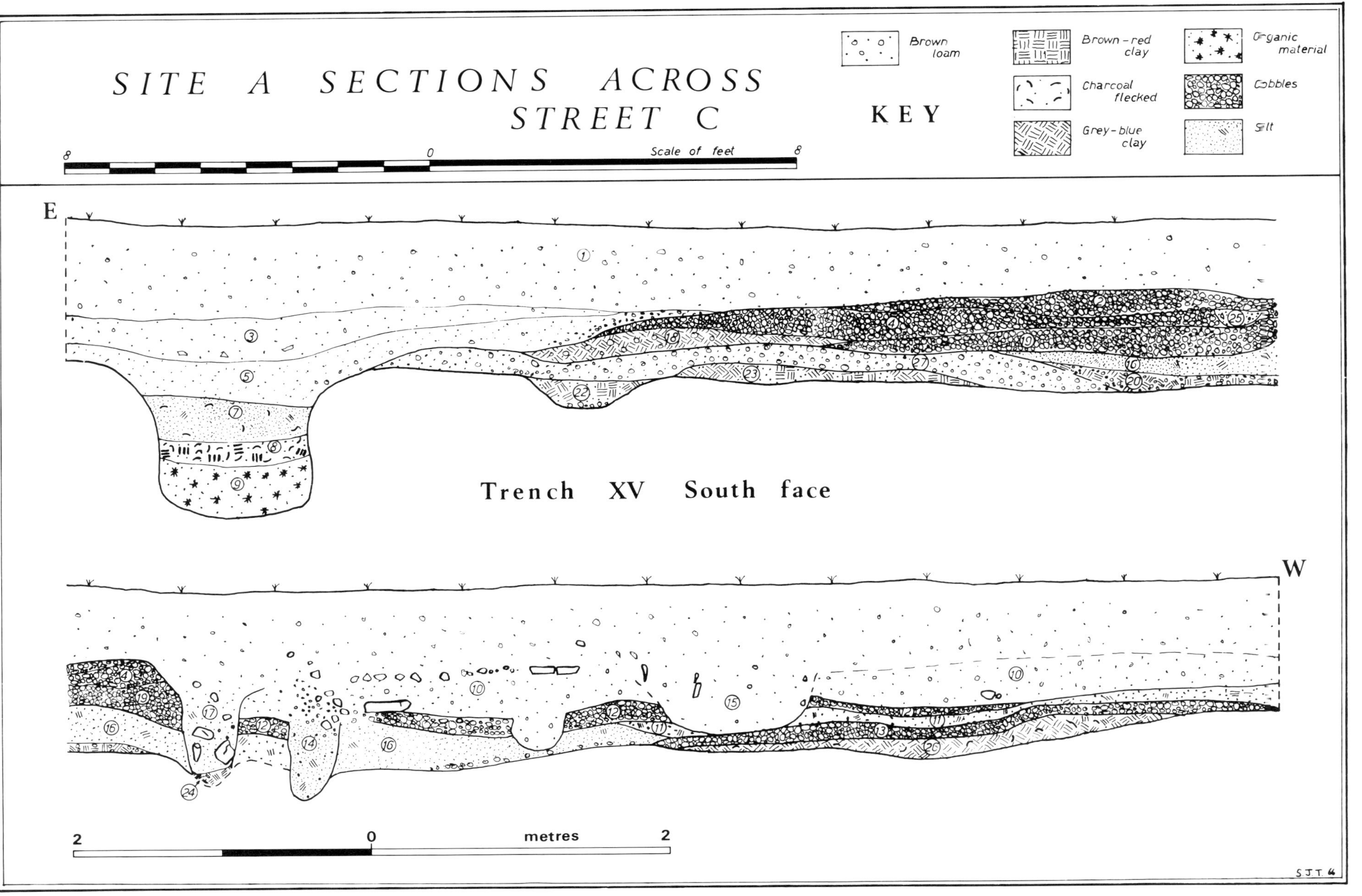

Figure 36 Site A sections across street C. Trench XV, south face (plan: fig 4)

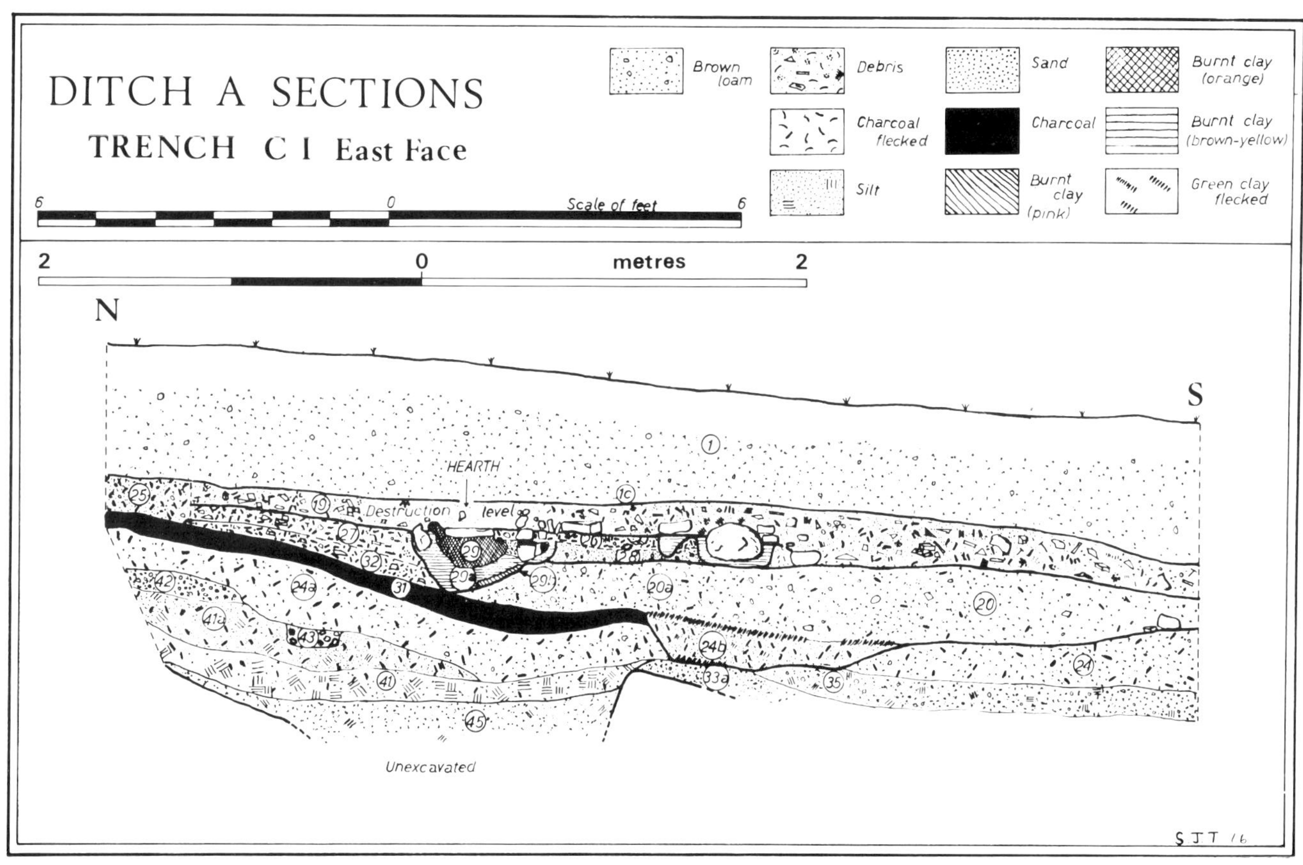

Figure 37   Ditch A sections. Trench C I, east face (plan: fig 16)

55

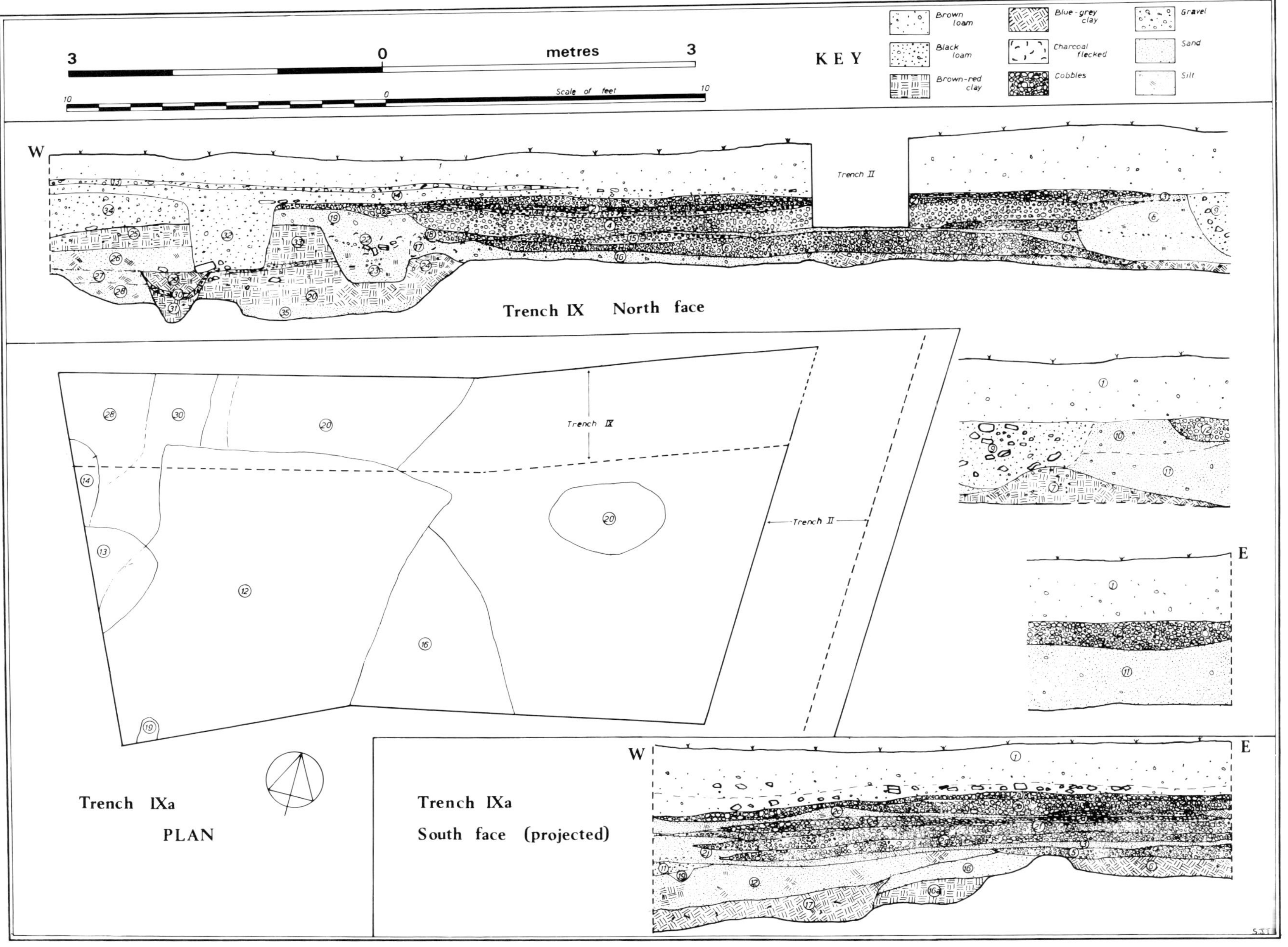

Figure 38   Site C sections. Trench IX, north face; trench IXA, plan; trench IXA, south face (reversed) (see fig 4 for location)

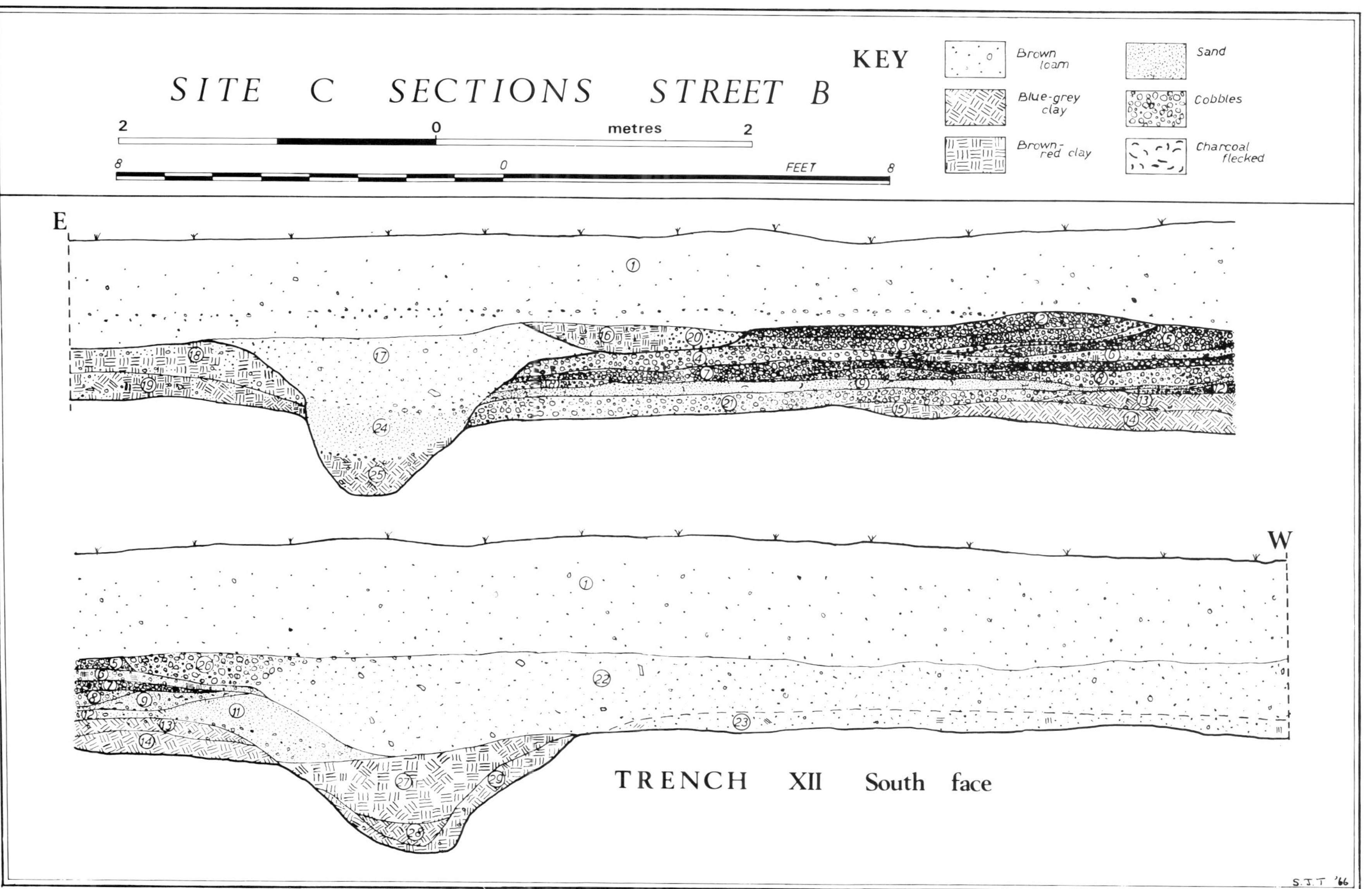

Figure 39 Site C sections, street B. Trench XII, south face (plan: fig 14)

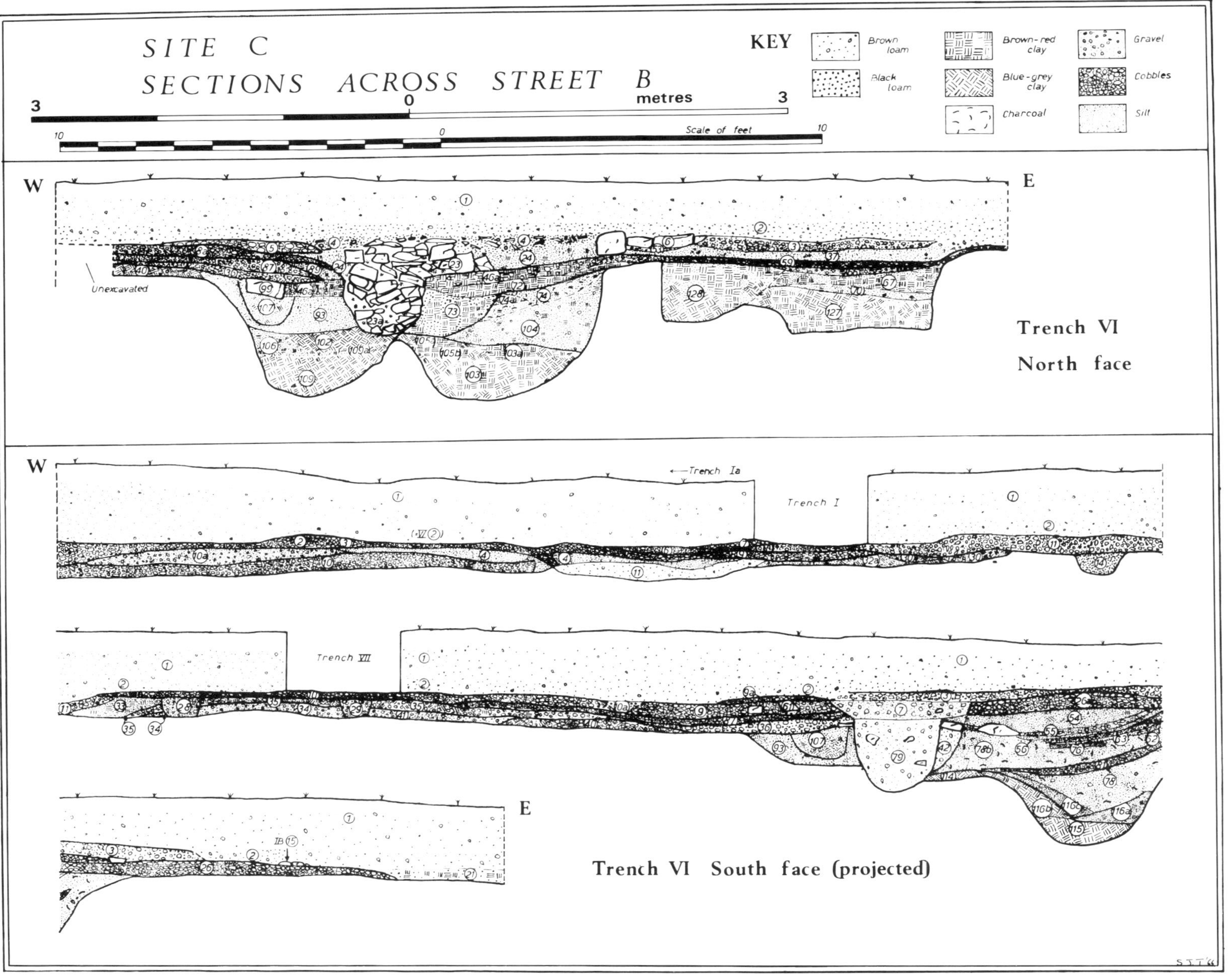

Figure 40 Site C sections across street B. Part of trench VI, north face; trench VI, south face (reversed) (plan: fig 23)

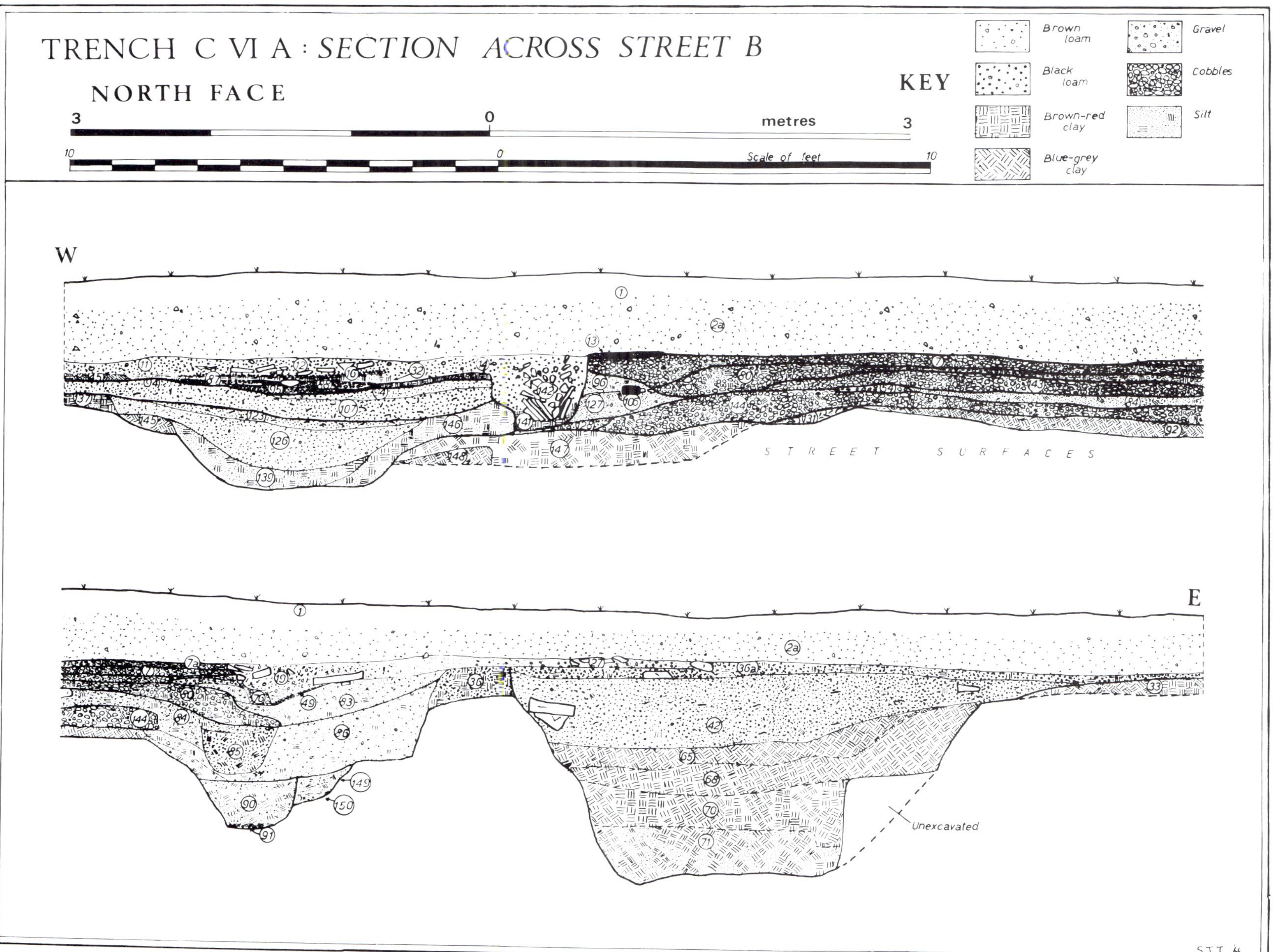

Figure 41 Trench C VIA. Section across street B, north face (plan: fig 23)

Site D

R S Langley

[M1·C10] Site D lay in the northern central part of Birch Abbey at the top of the gravel terrace (fig 3 no **35**, and figs 4, 42, 54). There were two main areas, trench D I covering some 320sq m on the north side, trench D II some 315sq m to the south. A small extension, trench D IV, lay on the north-eastern side.

The area lay immediately to the south of the main Stratford–Droitwich road, street A, and on either side of a minor road, street C, extending south along the western edge of trench D I and the eastern edge of trench D II. Sections across streets A and C can be seen in figs 62 and 61.

Adjacent excavations by Tomlinson (Hughes 1963; Tomlinson 1964; 1965), had revealed substantial stone buildings to either side of the site D area. In contrast, the successive buildings excavated in trench D I were all of timber.

The rear plot, in trench D II, remained an open area for most of the period, initially divided into enclosures and later extensively quarried for gravel.

Phase I (figs 43, 55)

[M1:C10] An unmetalled trackway extended north–south on the line of street C. In trench D II this was clearly defined by pairs of parallel gullies on either side. To the north its course was uncertain, but it might have turned to the east or the west at the south end of trench D I.

The area to the west of the trackway was divided into two ditched enclosures in a system extending south through site H (fig 45). One or more periods of building, structure DA, were represented by timber slots in the centre of trench D I to the rear of the later street C frontage. Two alignments of slots extending north–south for more than 16m were set 2.4m apart at the south end, converging to 1.8m at the north end. These may have been building lines of different periods. Transverse slots — D I 117, 121; 129/193; 197, 198, 174, 179; 175 — extended E for up to 4.8m dividing the area into three or more irregular bays. Postholes set along the western north–south alignment were a further element in the complex and might have been part of a building extending onto the street C frontage, for the most part obscured by a later ditch. At the south end of the complex was a well, which may have been contemporary, or may have been associated with a later building in phase IV (see fig 44). The shaft was cut through gravel and marl to a depth of 3.9m and the upper part was lined with timber.

The features from this phase may have dated from the late 1st to the earlier part of the 2nd century.

Phase Ia

[M1:C14] A secondary feature of the enclosure and trackway system of phase I was a gully extending across the south end of trench D I, realigning the presumed east–west turn of the street C trackway.

Phase II (fig 46)

[M1:C14] The eastern half of trench D I was covered by two successive cobble surfaces. These did not relate to any of the phases of building on the site, but may have been associated with occupation in the area to the east of the excavation. A slot with postholes set in its base extended along the eastern edge of the trench, and may have been part of a building lying to the east. On the north side the cobble surfaces were cut by a well and a pit. The pit, D I 246, contained a large quantity of samian dated AD 125–40 but also late 2nd-century coarse wares. The well (fig 47) was 4.9m deep and the upper part was lined with timber. Most of the pottery was 2nd century. The northernmost of the phase I enclosures was redefined, to the north of its original position, by a narrow, shallow slot with an entrance gap, D I 219, D II 105, the boundary of the enclosure was further defined by a ditch or pits on the eastern side. A large pit in trench D II may have been roofed over for use as a storage pit, D II 29/29A (fig 58). It contained a remarkable collection of samian ware, coarse pottery, and glass ware. The group included 69 samian vessels with the stamps or signatures of 30 Lezoux potters, dating from AD 150 to 160.

Table 3 Site D: phases, dates, and main features

Phase	Features	Date
I	structure DA (slot complex); well; enclosures	1st C to early Antonine
IA	enclosures	
II	cobble surfaces; well; pit; roadside ditches (pits); enclosure	later 2nd C to early 3rd C?
III	roadside ditch	later 2nd C to early 3rd C on
IV	structure DB	later 3rd C?
V	structure DC ('smithy'); smithing hearths; pits	early to mid-4th C
VI	structure DCA, extension to DC; smithing hearths; pits; street C; grave	mid- to late 4th C *tpq* AD 351
VII	street C	mid- to late 4th C
VIII	postholes, structure DD	late 4th C
IX	structure DE and DF; stone pads	late 4th C

Phase III (figs 48, 56)

[M1:D3] In the late 2nd to early 3rd century the line of street C was established by the digging of a ditch on the eastern edge of the road. A number of quarry pits in trench D II can be attributed to phases II and III. There appears to have been no occupation of the site during the middle of the 3rd century.

Phase IV (fig 49)

[M1:D3] Settlement was re-established, perhaps in the later 3rd century. A rectangular structure, DB, measuring 16.5m × 5.8m was erected on the edge of street C in the northern part of the area. The building was represented by postholes set in opposed pairs, defining the side walls. An aisle lay across the south end, projecting at the south-eastern corner. The projection may have housed the well noted above as associated with either phase I or phase IV. A porch may have lain on the western side of the building. The daub walls had been faced with painted plaster.

Phase V (fig 50, plates 3–5)

[M1:D5] In the early to mid-4th century, the phase IV structure was replaced on the same site by a smaller rectangular building, structure DC measuring 6.1m × 4.8m. Postholes were set in five opposed pairs, with double or triple postsettings at each corner. The building housed two possible smithing hearths to the north and south of an internal partition (fig 51). A third hearth lay to the south of the building or was added when the building was extended in phase VI. Waste from the hearths was deposited in a large pit to the south of the building.

Phase VI (figs 52, 57, plates 3, 5)

[M1:D6] The phase V building was extended by 5.5m with the addition of two further pairs of posts at the southern end. The extension, structure DCA, accommodated the third possible smithing hearth. The waste pit at the south end of the building had been backfilled, but further pits lay on the north side and

Plate 4 Site D I, phase V. Iron-working hearth, D I 4, looking east. Scales in 1ft (0.30m) and 1in (25mm) divisions (see also fig 51)

Plate 3 Site D I, phases V and VI. Structures DC and DCA with iron-working hearths, looking south. Scales in 1ft (0.30m) divisions (see also figs 50–2)

Plate 5 Site D I, phases V and VI. Iron-working hearth, D I 3, looking north-west. Scales in 1ft (0.30m) and 1in (25mm) divisions

a water tank, D I 63, lay to the east. A bowl-shaped hearth, D I 130, 1.8m in diameter, lay on the eastern side of the area, covering the phase II pit. Two waste pits lay on its western side. The grave of a woman, aligned east–west, lay close to the western side of the hearth, and was apparently of a similar date. A gravel surface was laid on street C. Quarry pits in trench D II probably relate to the metalling of the road.

Phase VII (fig 57)

[M1:D11] The later phases were of uncertain date, from the mid- to late 4th century onwards. A second road surface was laid over street C. A third surface was also observed in the southern half of the area.

Phase VIII (fig 59)

[M1:D11] At the south end of the area posts were set in five opposed pairs to either side of the road. These appear to have defined a rectangular building, structure DD measuring 4m × 13m, employing the road surface as a floor.

Phase IX (figs 53, 60)

[M1:D12] The disuse of the road was further indicated by a structure, DE, built over it in the northern half of the area. Stone settings forming raised pads lay on an alignment extending north–south, representing the eastern side of a building lying mostly to the west of the excavated area. A line of similar bosses extended east–west in the northern part of trench D II representing a second building, DF, also lying for the most part beyond the excavated area.

Site D phase dates

Site D contained a series of postholes and building foundations with a large group of associated pits, ditches, and cobbled road surfaces.

The bulk of the coarse pottery is represented by local grey wares (38%) and Severn Valley ware (28%). These vessels are utilitarian with an inordinately high proportion of storage jars in comparison to the other sites, with the exception of site G. This may be partly a result of the nature of the site, with large storage vessels being more likely to be discarded in rubbish pits, and ditches. The quantity of rusticated vessels appearing in all phases on the site illustrates the residual nature of much of the material.

In the later phases of the site (phase V onwards), Severn Valley wares would appear to increase in proportion to the local grey wares, becoming the dominant ware. The exception to this is fabric DA which apparently reached its peak during the 2nd to early 3rd century.

Black-Burnished ware accounts for 18% of the pottery from site D, increasing steadily in quantity during the late phases, with bowls and dishes particularly important. Shell-gritted ware, which is generally held to be late Roman in date, appears on site D from phase IV onwards.

The fine wares were produced at a number of centres. The Continent produced the North Gaulish, Gaulish, and Rhenish vessels, whereas British colour-coated wares were produced in Oxfordshire and the Nene Valley, with Mancetter responsible for the white wares.

Phase I: 1st century to early Antonine

Local grey wares predominated during this period, with storage jars and rusticated jars the prevalent types. Black-Burnished and Malvernian wares were also present but not prolific.

This phase contains a good collection of 1st-century to Antonine material. The latest samian came from the enclosure system: Antonine from context D II 68, and *c* AD 145–75 from D I 145. Hadrianic–Antonine vessels (R.95, R.96, R.173, R.184, R.190, R.362, B.14, and B.28) are recorded from twelve contexts.

A pit, D I **107**, contained an Aucissa-Hod Hill brooch (cat no 68) dated to the mid-1st century and a brooch fragment (cat no 26) which may be 1st century. The datable pottery was 1st to 2nd century (R.239), 1st century? (O.32), and early to mid-4th century (B.24). The last sherd is certainly intrusive but the pit could well be 1st century.

A Flavian bronze mirror (cat no 72) was found in a slot, D I **174**, part of structure DA but it also contained 2nd-century pottery (as well as an intrusive sherd). A nearby slot, D I **175**, also part of the structure of DA, contained two Claudian coins (cat nos 8, 17), a further illegible 1st- or 2nd-century coin (cat no 424), a brooch fragment (cat no 27) perhaps dating to the 1st century, and a glass unguent bottle (cat no 21A) of late 1st- to late 2nd-century date. The pottery, however, provides a Hadrianic or later date for the filling of the feature (B.14 and B.28). D I **175** also contained an intrusive medieval sherd.

Part of the enclosure system, D II **89**, was cut by a pit, D II **29A**, which contained a good group of pottery dating to the mid-2nd century. It is therefore likely that the enclosures belonged to the earlier part of the 2nd century or earlier.

A 1st-century to early Antonine span would seem appropriate for this phase.

Phase II: later 2nd century (to early 3rd?)

This phase contains a considerable amount of 1st- to early 2nd-century pottery and a smaller collection of Hadrianic–Antonine material. Antonine samian is present in D I **170**. There is an obtuse lattice decorated dish (R.389) from D I **173** which must date to after *c* AD 200.

The majority of the features cutting the cobbled surface were undatable, with little or no information provided by the pottery. However, the pit D I **246** was well sealed beneath a late 3rd-century oven and the material here included a large quantity of samian dated *c* AD 125–40 and 2nd-century coarse pottery, including a late 2nd-century Black-Burnished BB1 dish with intersecting arc decoration (B.74; see Part 2).

A pit near the western edge of the site, D I **173**, contained a range of pottery, mostly indicating a 2nd-century date, but it is notable that the non-ceramic items are 1st century: a Polden Hill spring brooch (cat no 7), a copper alloy spoon (cat no 117), and two pillar moulded glass bowls (cat nos 2 and 6).

Contexts D I *100* and D I *126* contain a late 3rd-century or later Black-Burnished BB1 flanged bowl and a late 3rd-century jar (B.50 and B.20 respectively) which are presumably intrusive. It would appear that the phase dates from the later 2nd to perhaps the early 3rd century.

Phase III: later 2nd century on

Phase III contained only a small proportion of site D's finds; all the material appears to be residual so the dating relies on the previous phase.

Phase IV: late 3rd century?

Most of the ceramic material from this phase is residual late 1st- to early 2nd-century pottery with some residual Hadrianic–Antonine vessels. Possibly contemporary material is restricted to an early to mid-3rd-century Black-Burnished BB1 flanged bowl (B.44) from D I **69**, a shell-tempered ware everted rimmed jar (R.109) from D I **30**, and an Oxfordshire parchment ware bowl (W.38) dated to after *c* AD 240. The shell-tempered ware is most unlikely to have appeared on the site before the late 3rd century. There was a Crummy type 3 bone pin (cat no 30) which is datable to after AD 200.

This phase is 3rd century as it succeeds phase II, and may be late 3rd century.

Phase V: early to mid-4th century?

This phase contains much residual 2nd-century ceramic material and some 3rd-century. Roughly contemporary material includes a 4th-century Black-Burnished BB1 jar (B.24) and a late 3rd-century jar from D I **71** (B.20), and 3rd- to 4th-century Severn Valley ware (O.136, O.146, and O.152). There were 4th-century glass fragments (GL 191 and 163) from D I **46** and D I **71**.

Perhaps early to mid-4th century given the number of succeeding phases.

Phase VI: mid- to late 4th century?

This contains a great deal of 1st- to 2nd-century pottery. Contemporary material only comes from D I **6**, D I **26**, and D I **36**. D I **6** contains O.156 and two late shell-tempered jars (R.43 and R.107) giving it a later 4th-century date. D I **26** and D I **36** contain sherds of B.27 which may be 4th century. A coin dating to AD 351–3 was recovered from a grave D I **120** but there is no stratigraphic link between this and the structures on the site so it is not very useful for dating the phase.

Phase VII: mid- to late 4th century?

This phase produced only a small quantity of pottery, most of which is residual. There is, however, a late shell-tempered ware jar (R.43) from D I *195*, mid- to late 4th century, probably late 4th century. There is no useful non-ceramic dating material.

Phase VIII: late 4th century

The five postpits cutting the western edge of the road all contained residual 1st- and 2nd-century ceramics, while disturbance of the layers covering the south-west of trench D I and the roadside ditch is illustrated by the mixture of both Flavian and medieval material.

D II *15* produced a late shell-tempered ware jar (R.43), whilst late 3rd to 4th-century Oxfordshire ware comes from D I 2 and D I 2A (C.31 and C.57).

There were three contemporary coins from rubbish deposits: from D I 2 dated to AD 353 on (cat no 322); from D I 2A dated AD 346–8 (cat no 278); from D II *15* also dated AD 346–8 (cat no 364).

This phase is late 4th century.

Phase IX: late 4th century

The residuality and disturbance of the features in phase IX is illustrated by the quantity of rusticated jars it contains. There are two late shell-tempered ware vessels recorded from D II 2 and D II **7** (R.112 and R.43). Presumably the phase is late 4th century.

D II 29/29A

Although the latest material in this pit dated to the late 3rd to 4th century there was also a large and clearly *in situ* group of mid-2nd-century samian and other material.

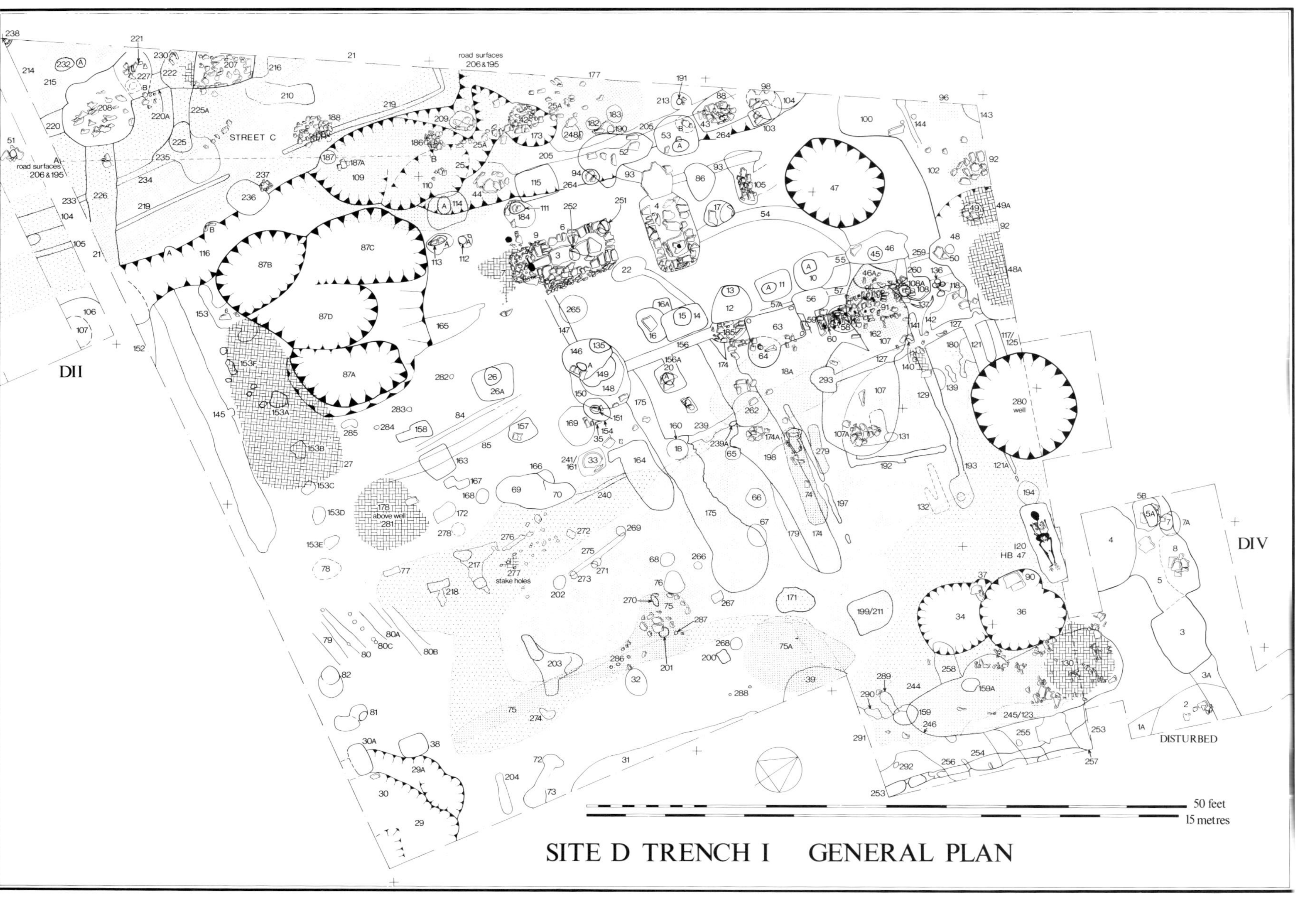

Figure 42   Site D, trench I, general plan

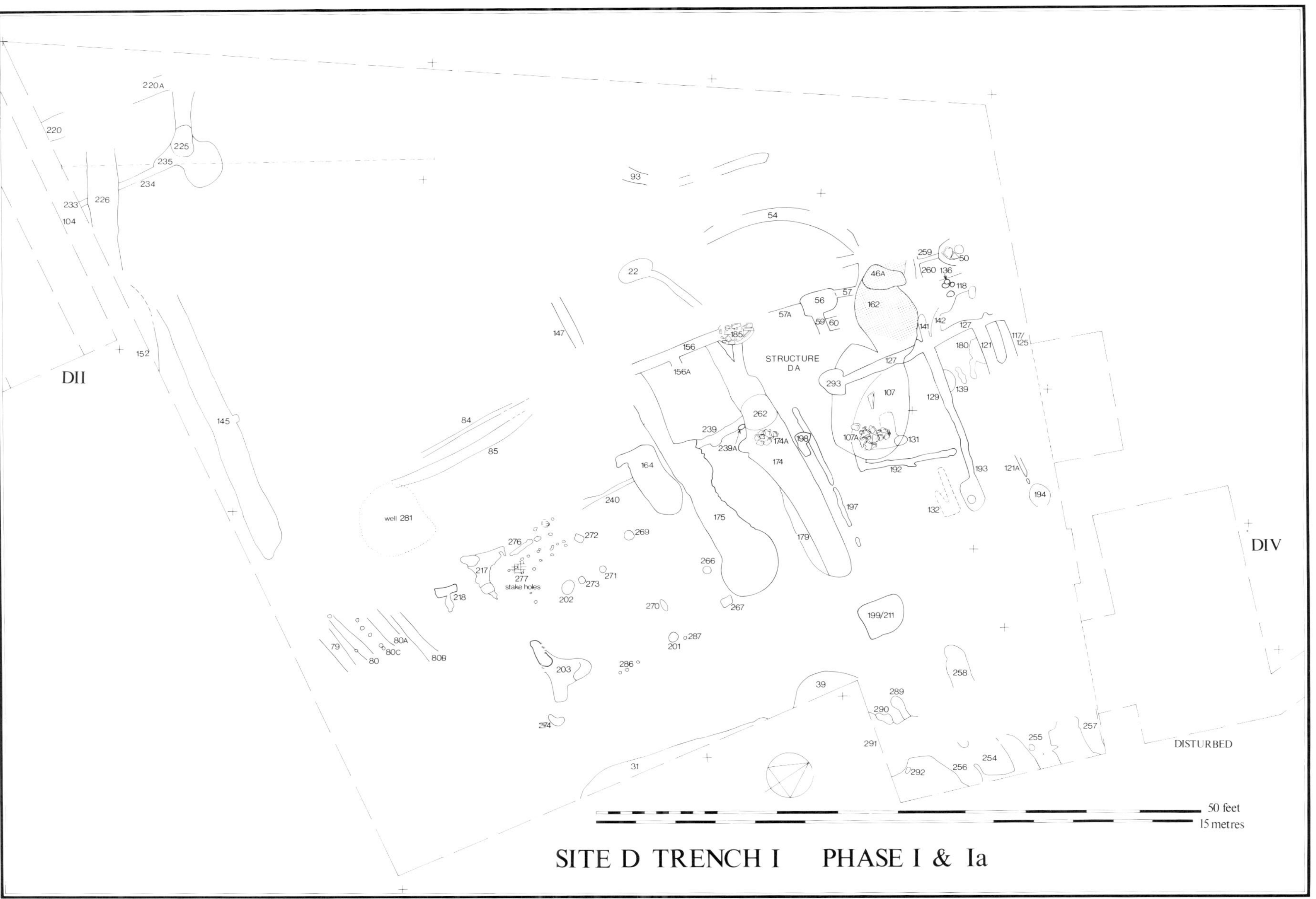

Figure 43   Site D, trench I, phase I and Ia

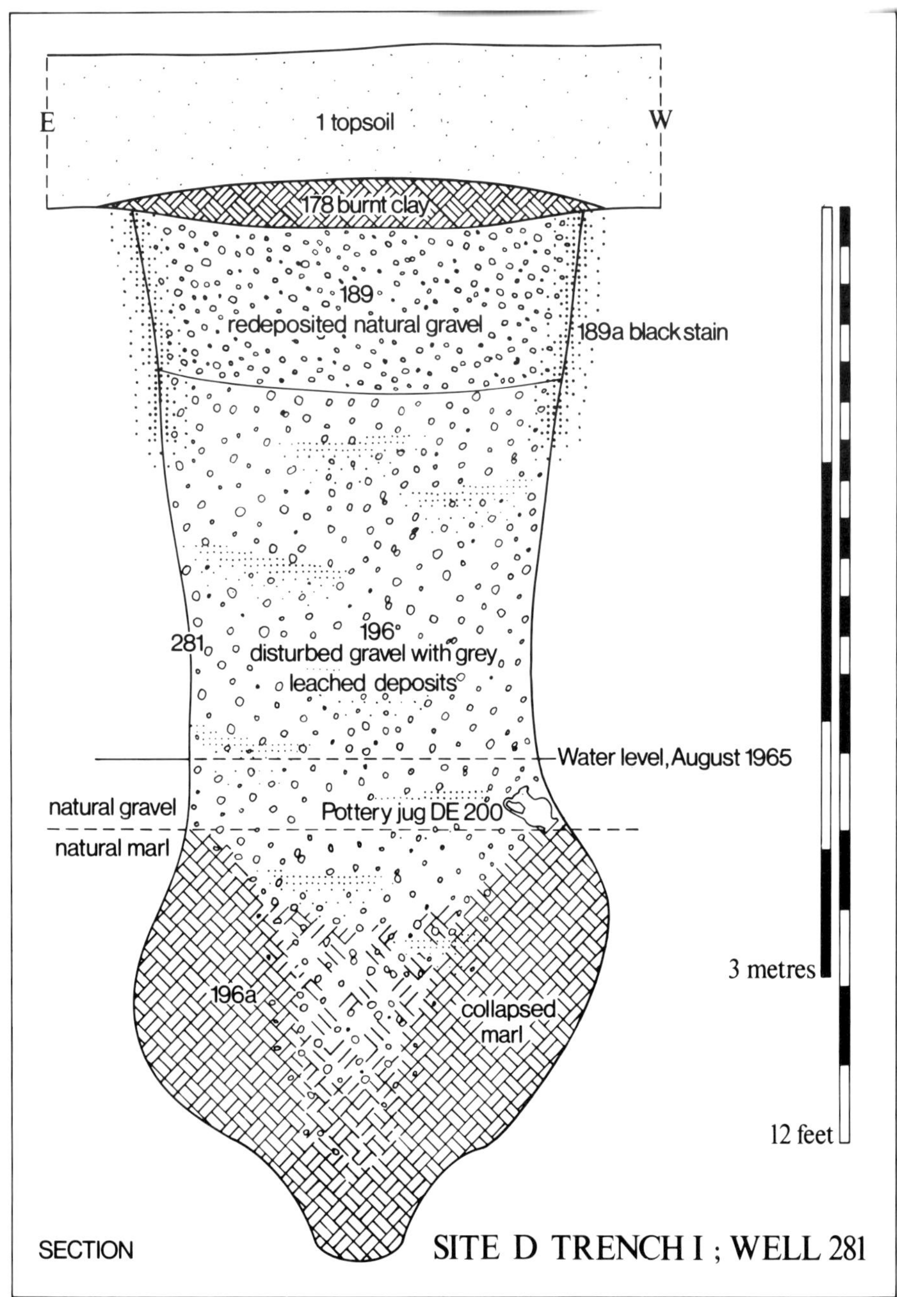

Figure 44   Site D, trench I, well 281 (plan: fig 43)

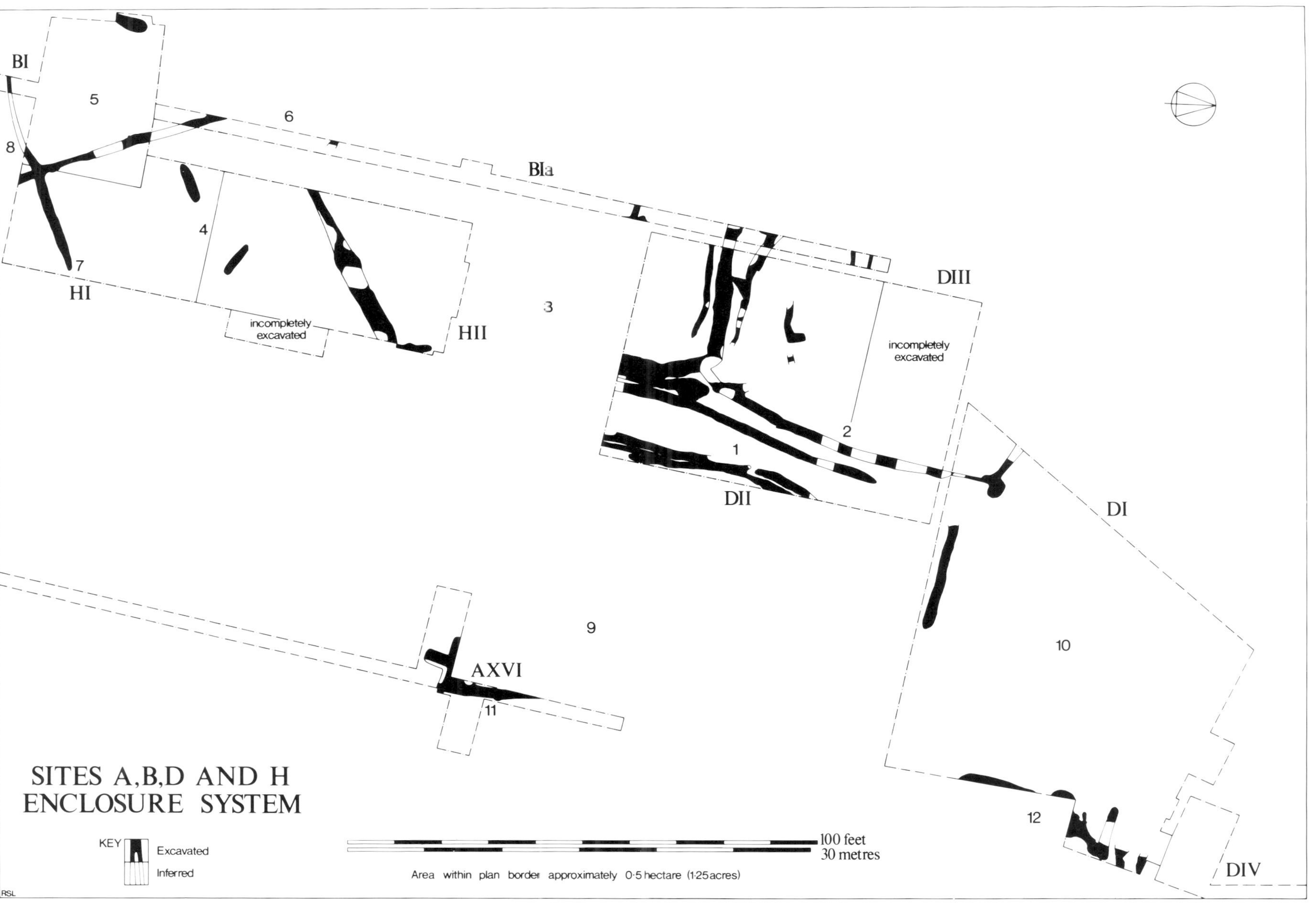

Figure 45 Sites A, B, D, and H enclosure system

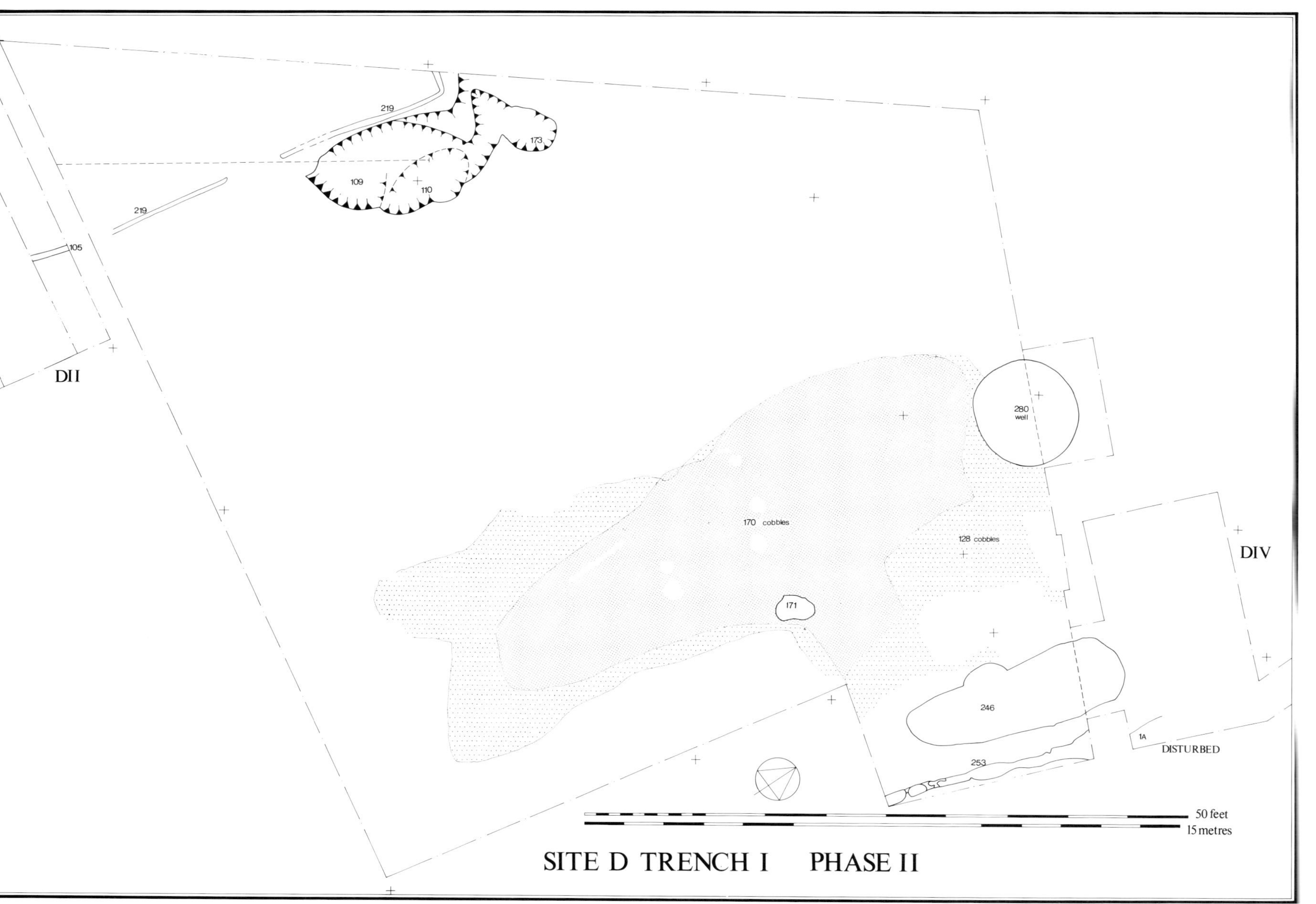

Figure 46   Site D, trench I, phase II

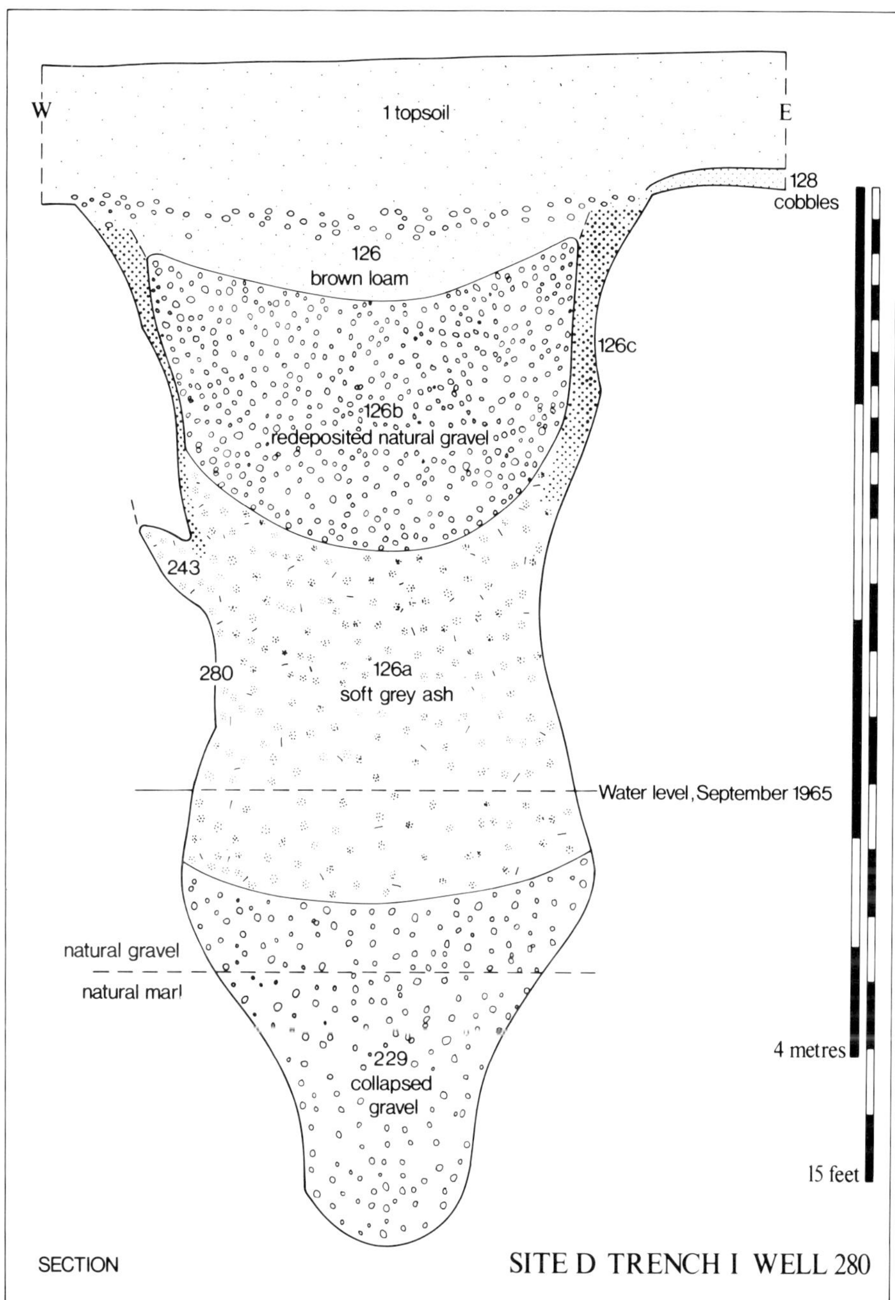

Figure 47   Site D, trench I, well 280 (plan: fig 46)

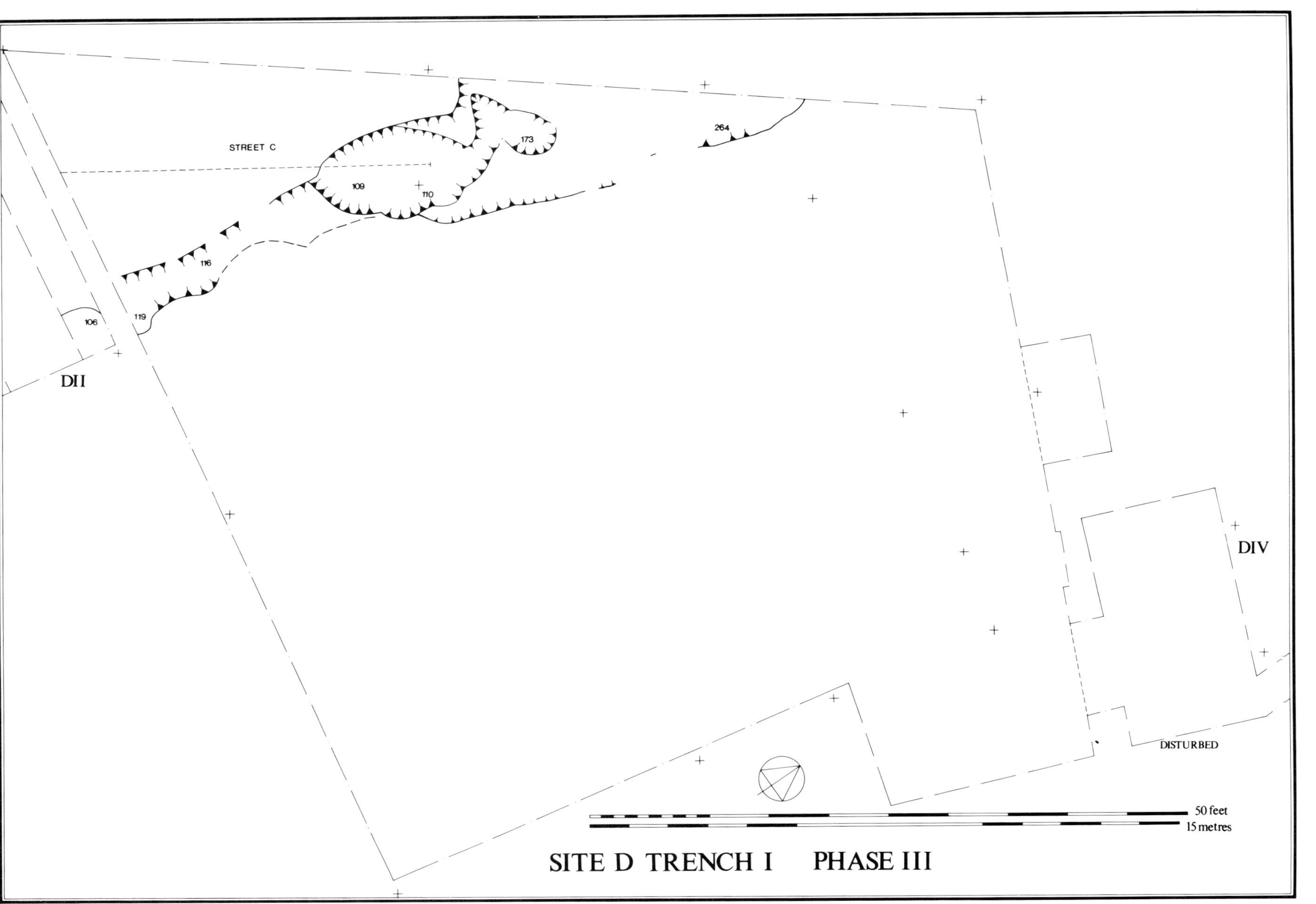

Figure 48 Site D, trench I, phase III

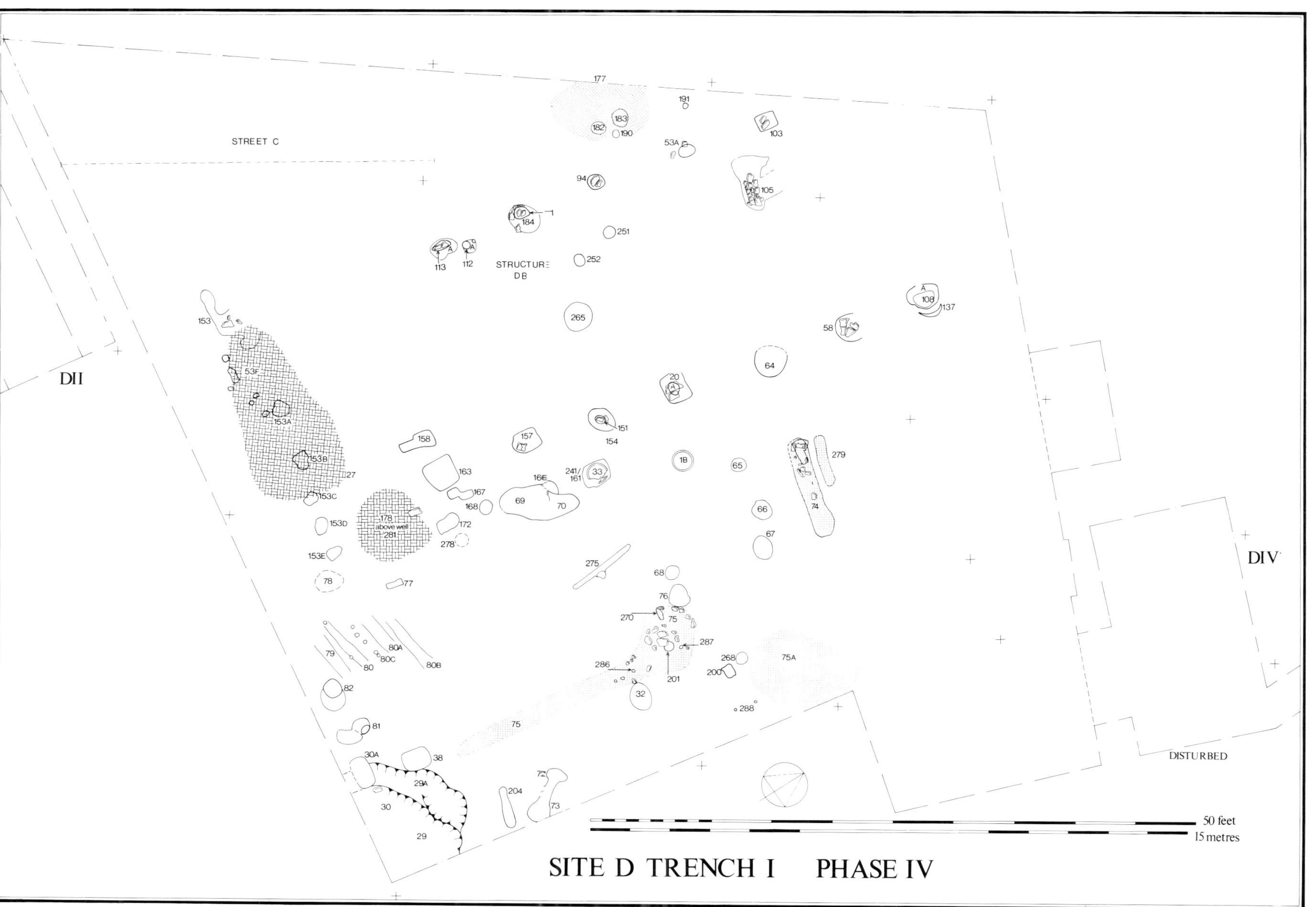

Figure 49   Site D, trench I, phase IV

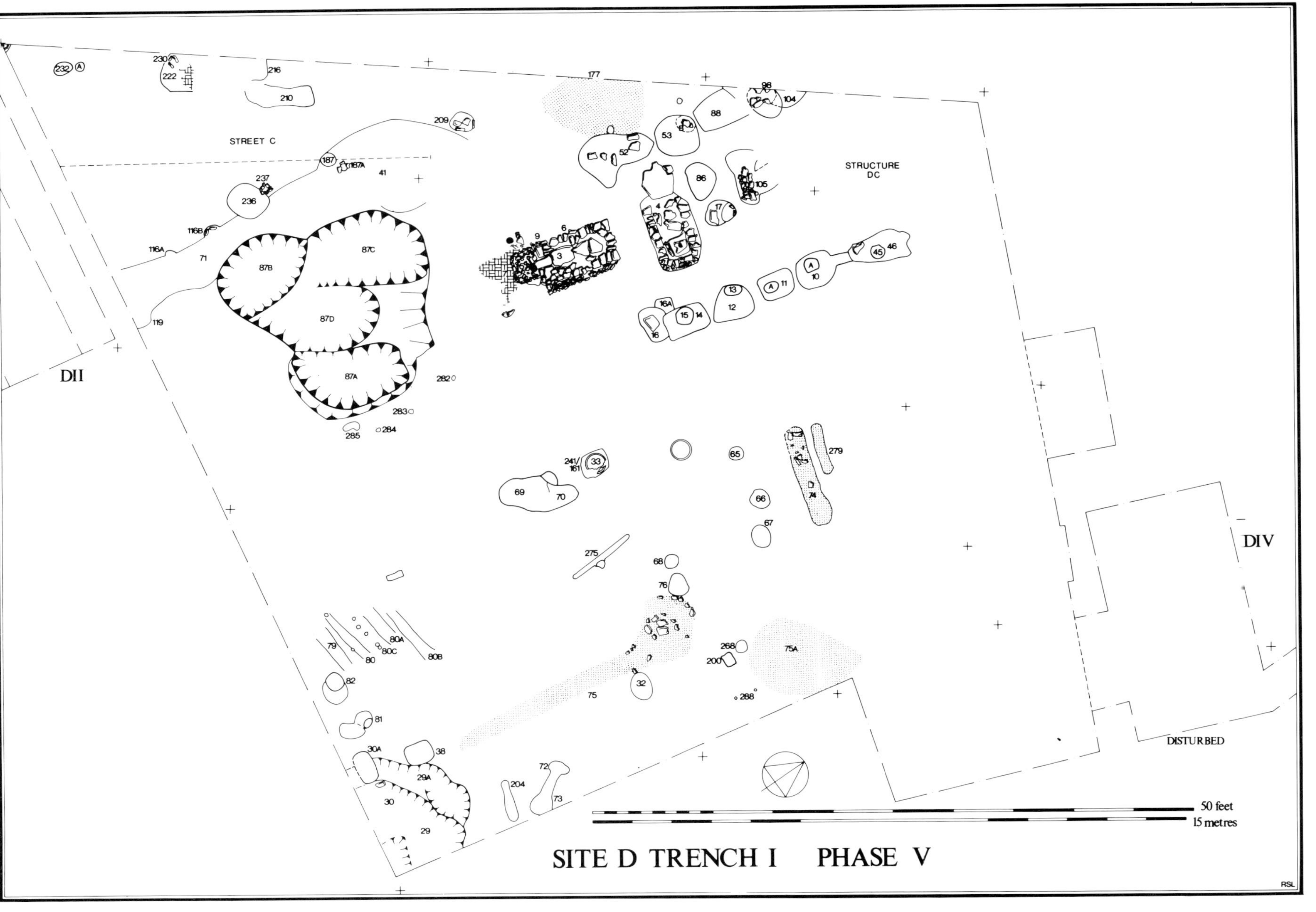

Figure 50   Site D, trench I, phase V

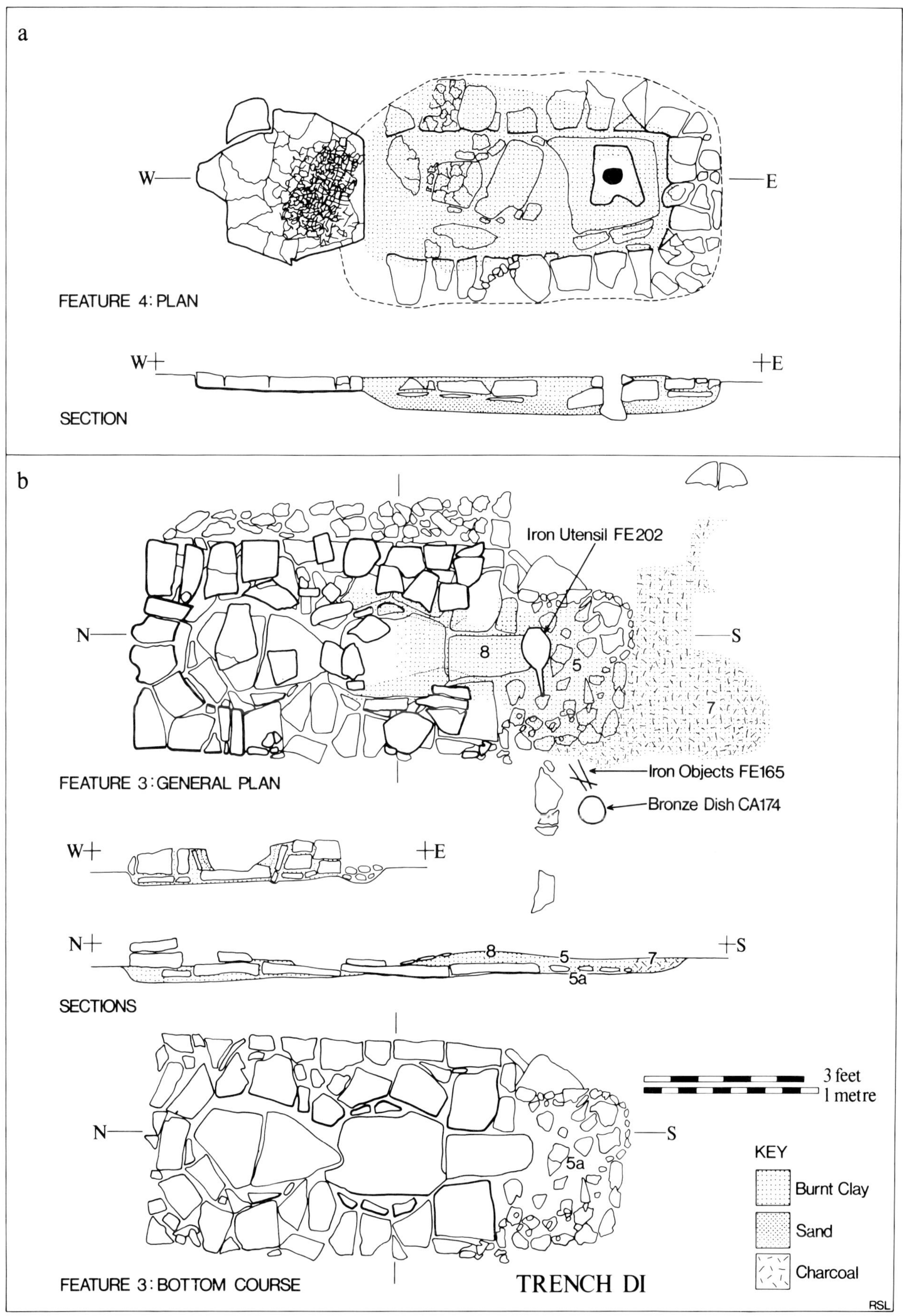

Figure 51 Trench D I, phase V and VI, possible smithing hearths

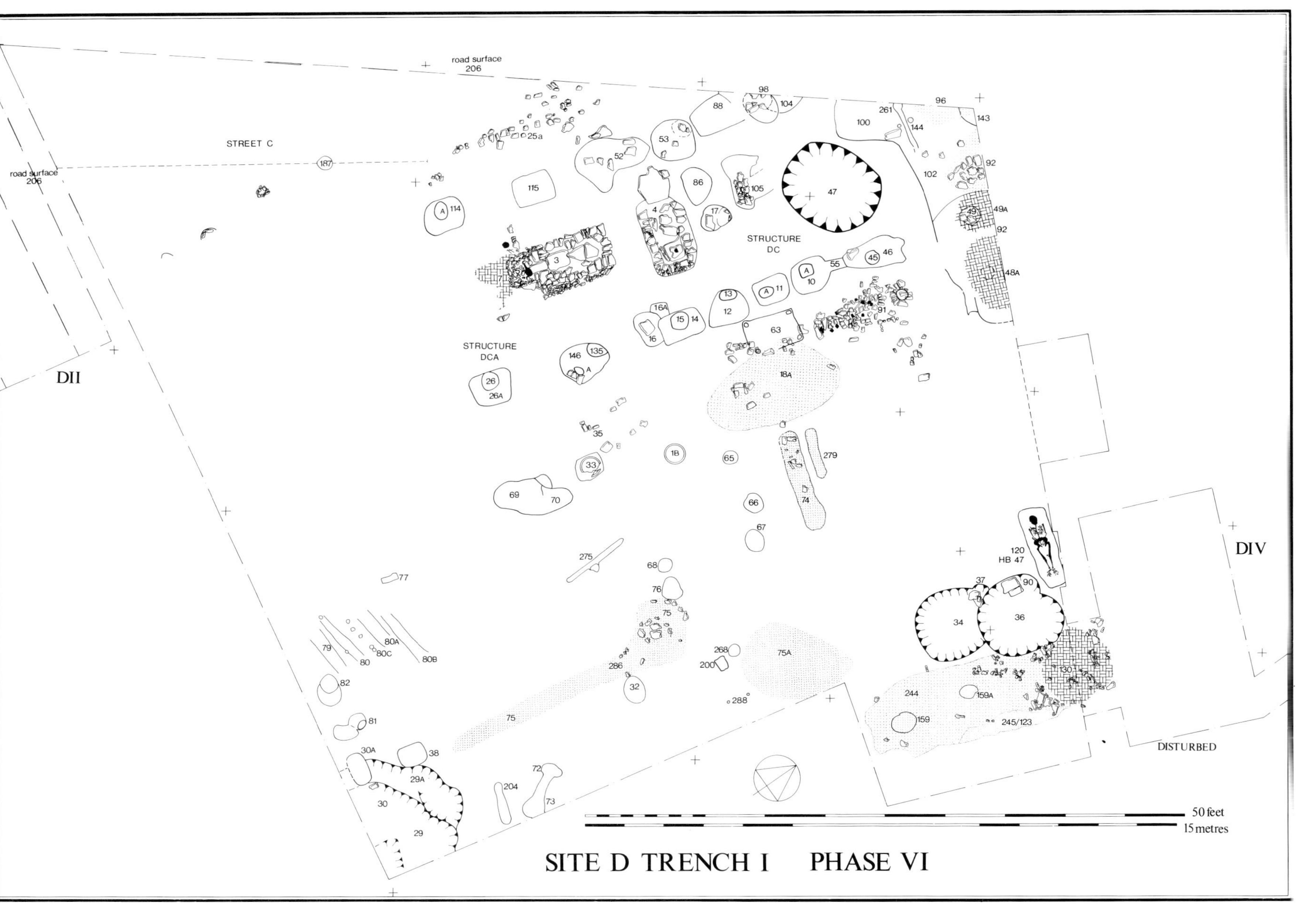

Figure 52   Site D, trench I, phase VI

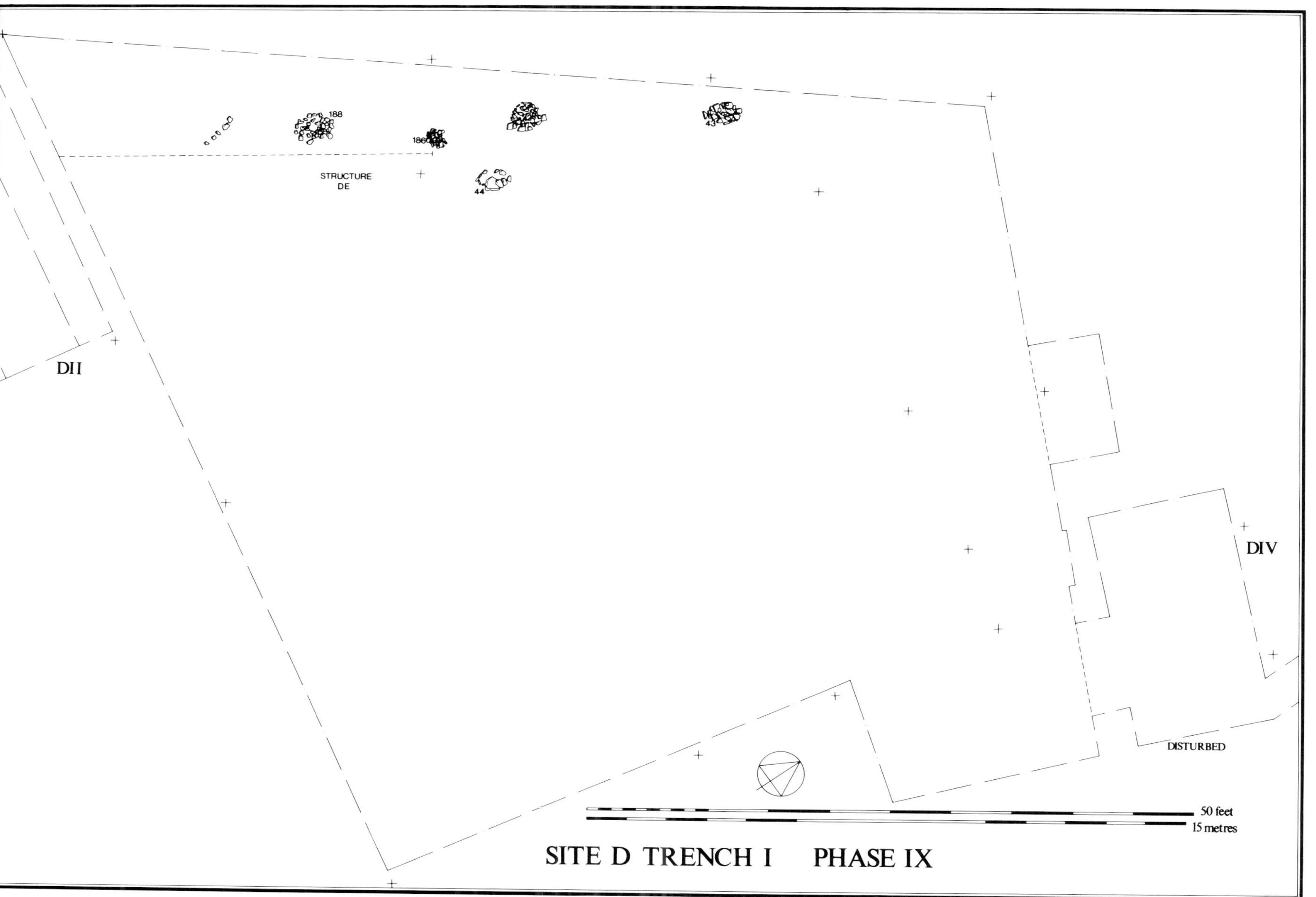

Figure 53   Site D, trench I, phase IX

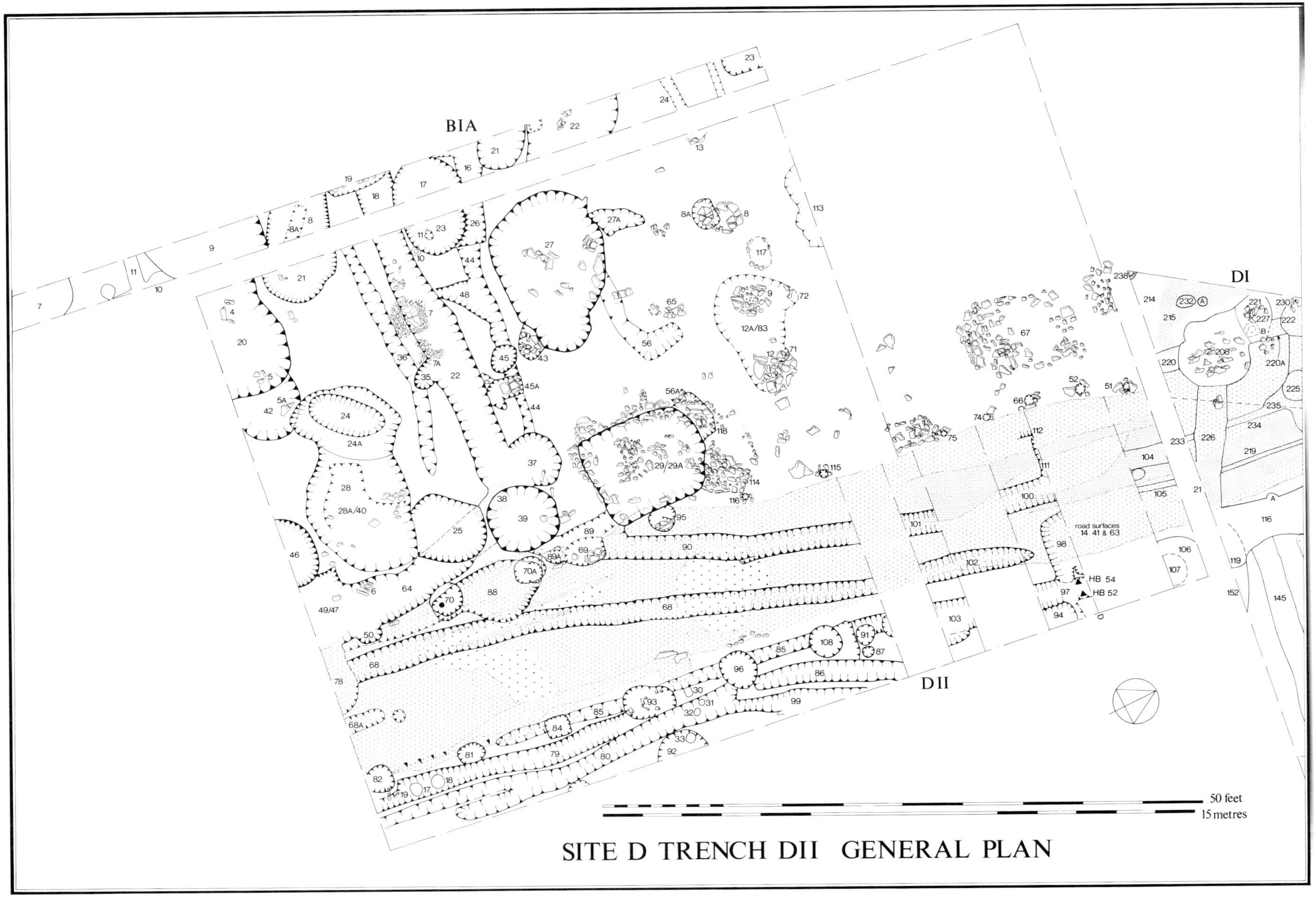

Figure 54 Site D, trench II, general plan

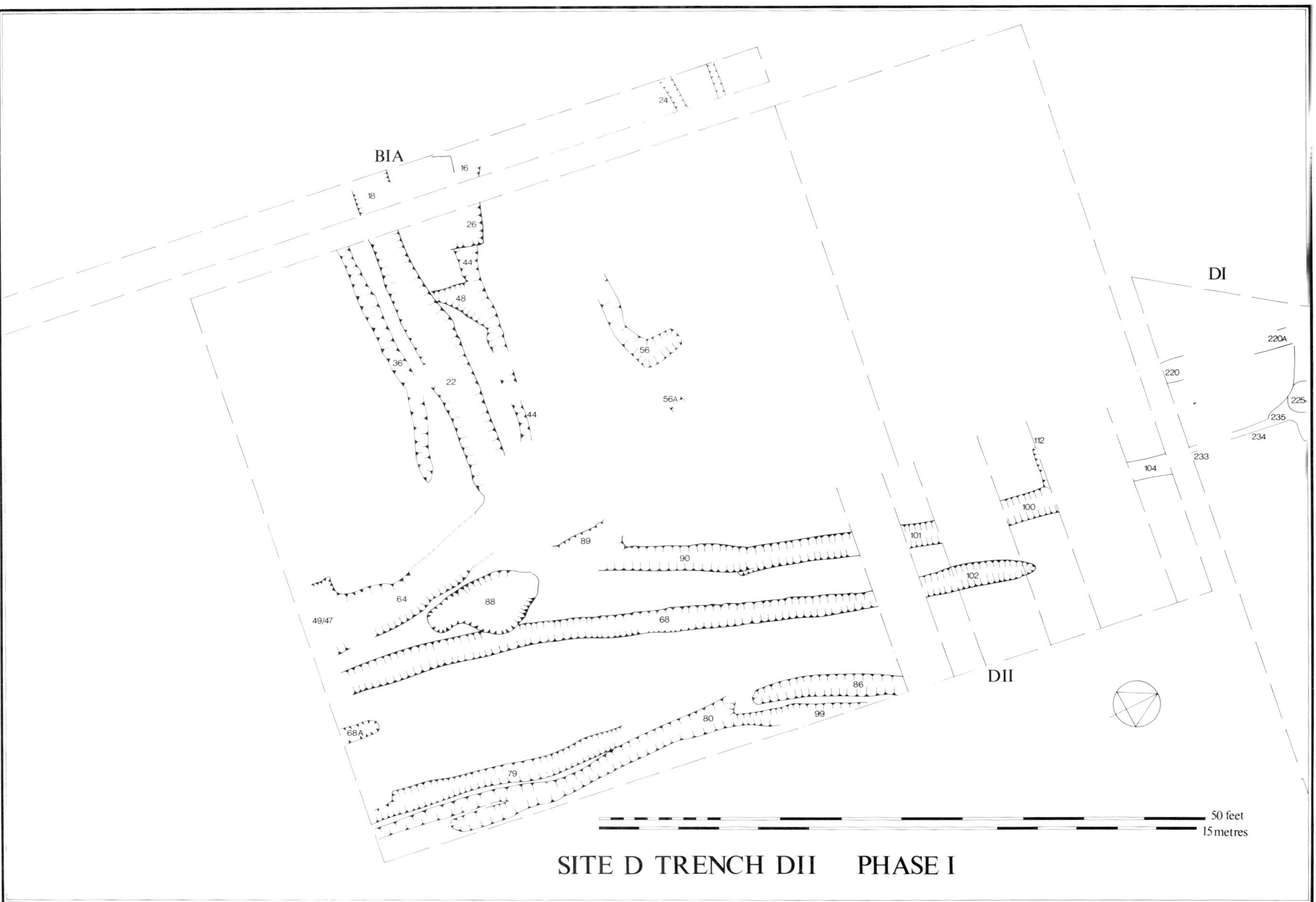

Figure 55 Site D, trench II, phase I

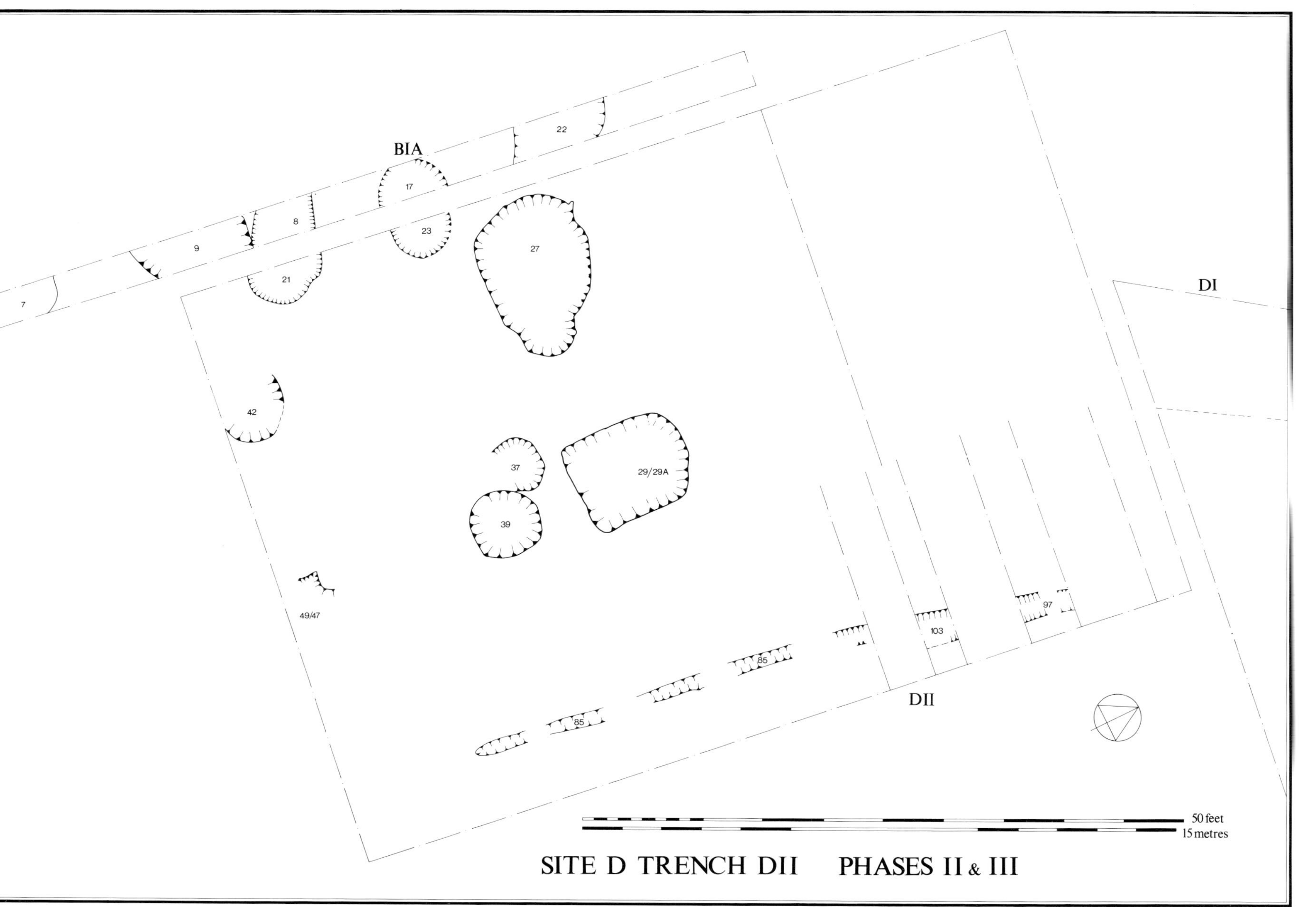

Figure 56   Site D, trench II, phases II and III, with 2nd- to 3rd-century pits

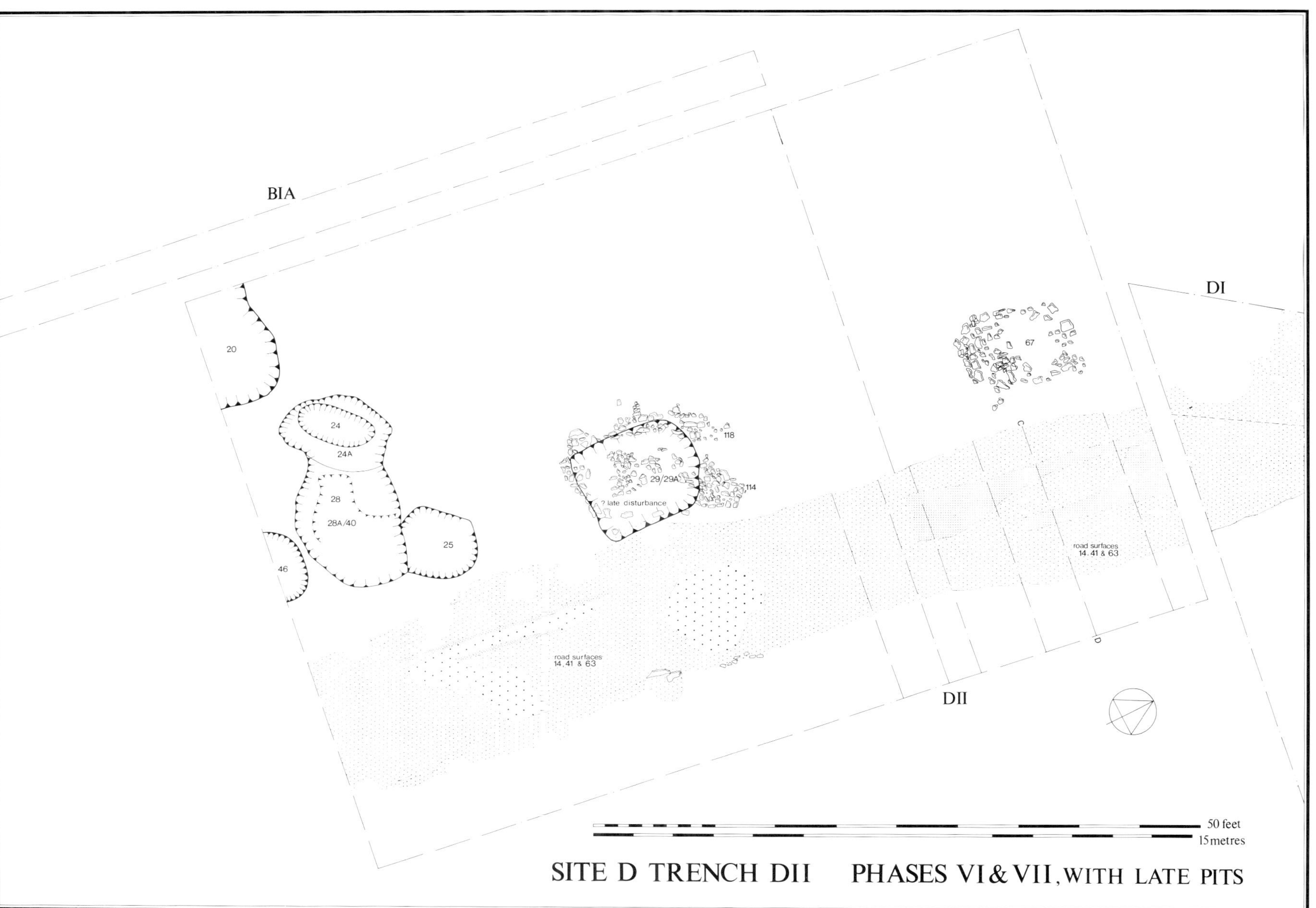

Figure 57   Site D, trench II, phases VI and VII, with late pits

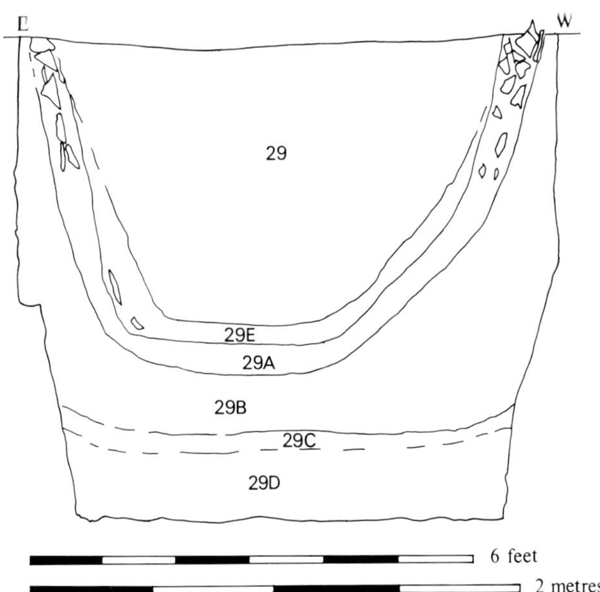

Figure 58 Section of pit D II 29/29A
(plan: figs 56–7)

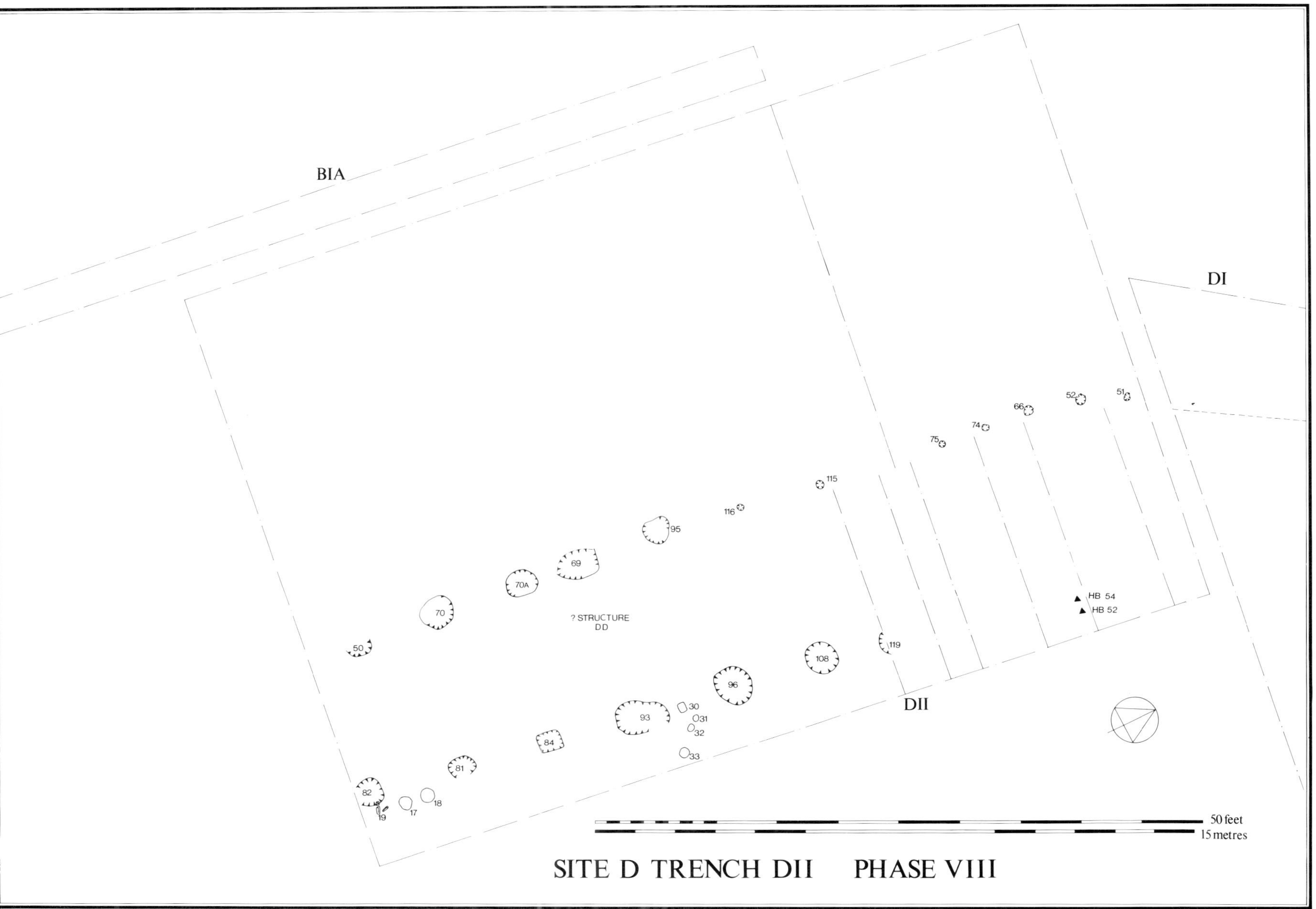

Figure 59   Site D, trench II, phase VIII

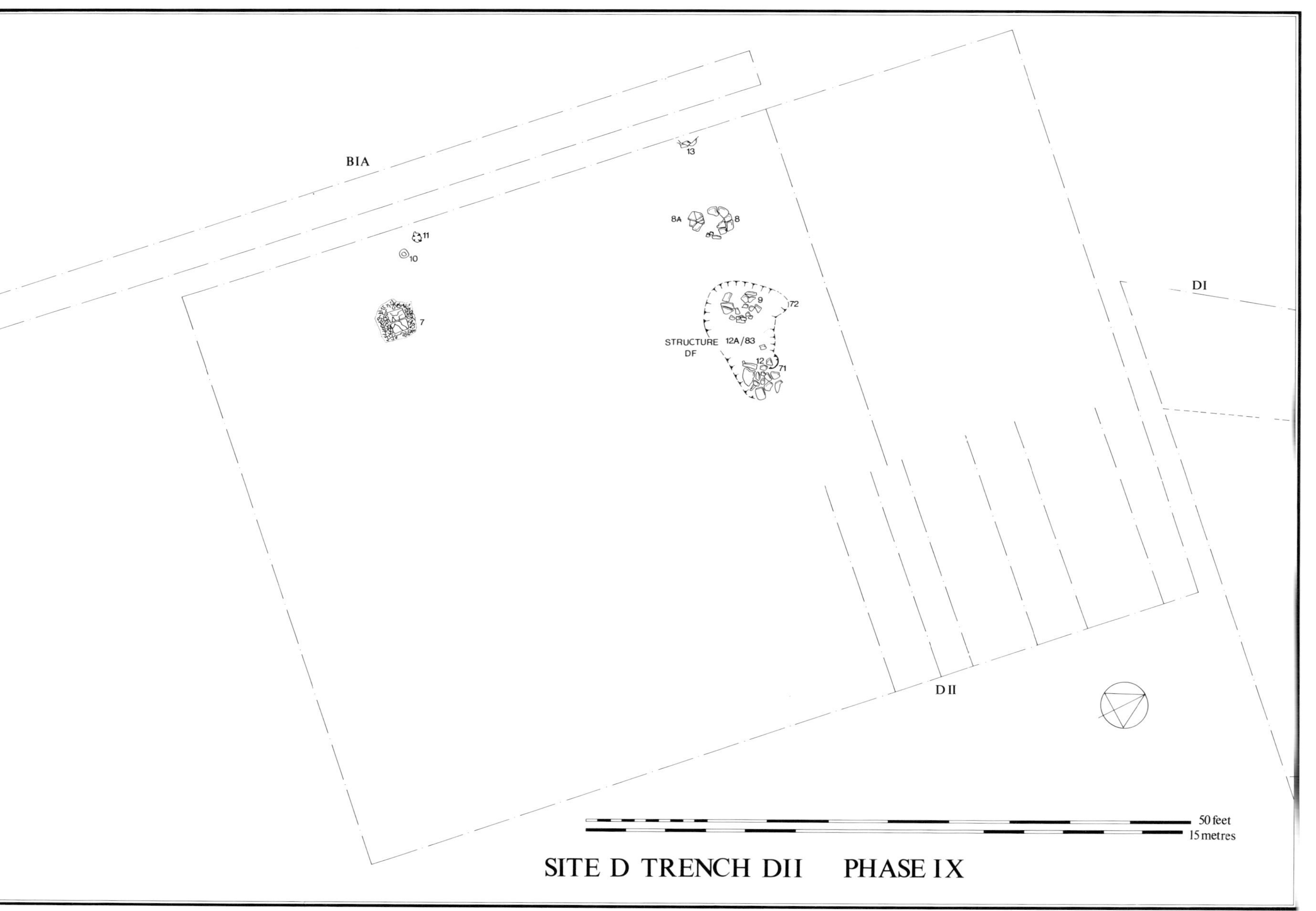

Figure 60 Site D, trench II, phase IX

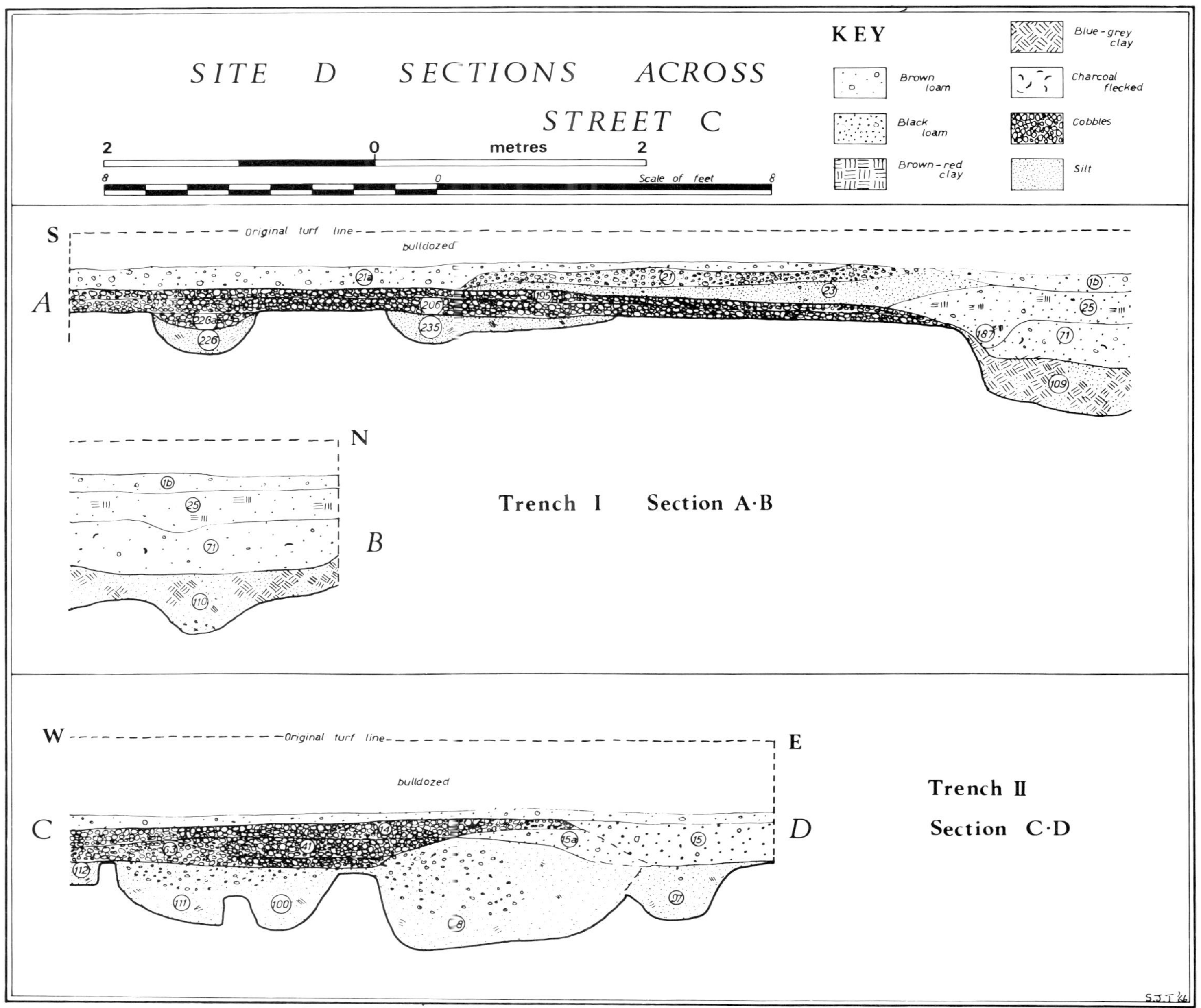

Figure 61 Site D, sections across street C. Trench I, section A–B; trench II, section C–D (plan: figs 42, 54)

83

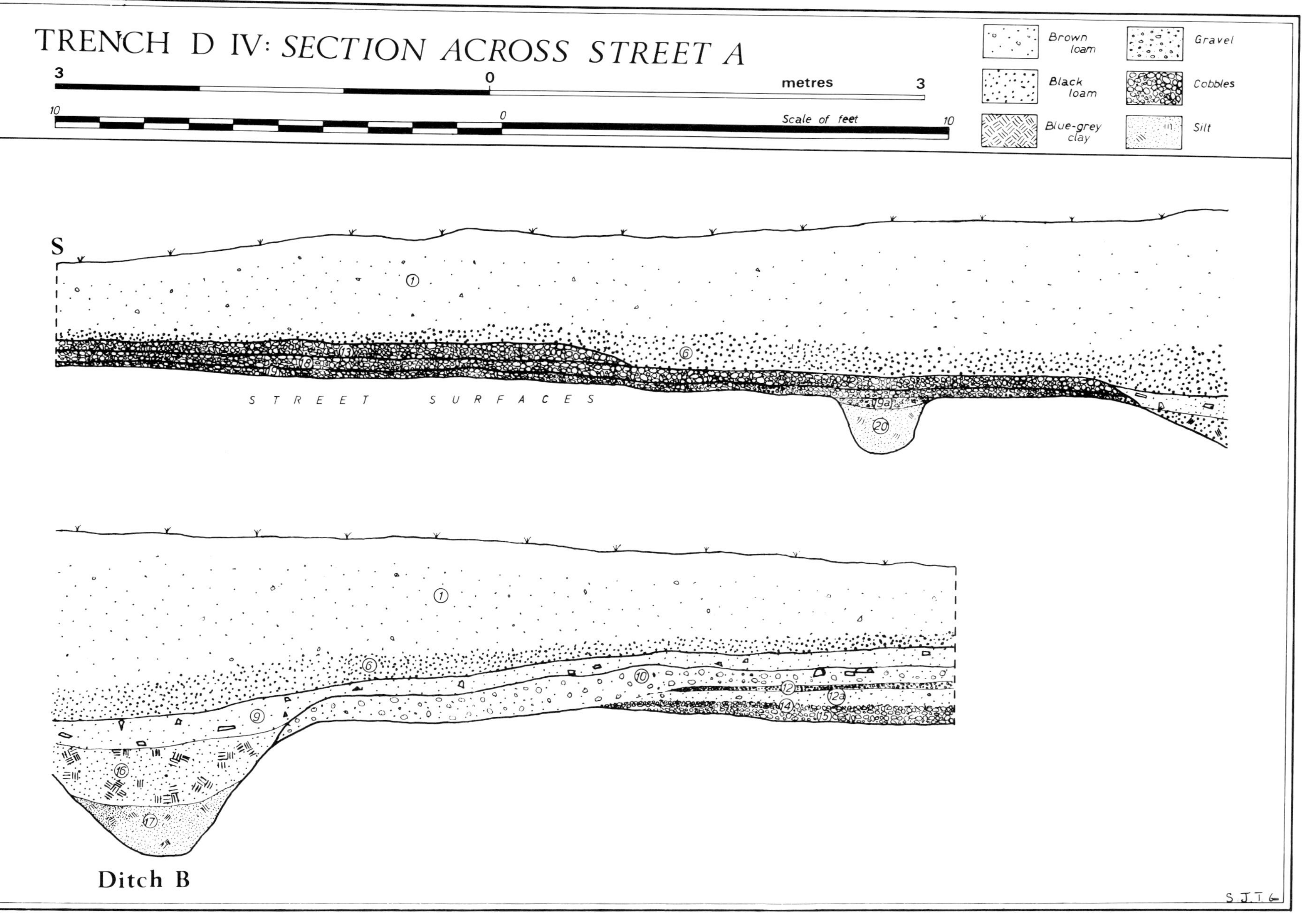

Figure 62 Trench D IV, section across street A, west face (plan: fig 42)

Sites E, F, J, and P
R S Langley with E Allnut

[M1:E3] Sites E, F, J, and P lay in the northernmost part of Birch Abbey, at the top of the gravel terrace (fig 3 nos **36, 37, 40**, and figs 4, 63, 64; plates 6, 7). The sites comprised the largest of the open areas excavated, more than 2000sq m in extent.

The area lay on the northern side of the main Stratford–Droitwich road, street A, and was divided into eastern and western halves by a minor road, street C, extending north–south. At the northern end of the area, street C was diverted to extend east–west through the western half of the area. Occupation was concentrated on the eastern side of street C in the earlier periods, and to the west in later periods but there was also significant early activity on the western side of the road.

The eastern two-thirds of the area were divided into the five trenches of site E (trenches E I–V), with an exploratory trench extending east–west across the centre (trench E VI).

The western third of the area, site F, was initially divided into four trenches (trenches F I–IV), but these were amalgamated at an early stage into a single area (trench F I). Trench F V was separate from the main area, some distance to the west. Site J lay on the northern side of the area (trenches J I–II): on the south-eastern side were a series of trenches excavated by Place's group (trenches P I, P III, P VI) (Place 1964; 1965).

Phase I (fig 65)

[M1:E3] The earliest features, on site F on the western side of street C, were not fully excavated. A slot extending east–west and a slot extending north–south, with associated postholes, might have been the fragmentary remains of a timber building. Two parallel slots extending east–west lay on the western edge of the area. Street C was in use as an unmetalled trackway, defined by two parallel shallow gullies lying on the western edge of the later road.

Phase II (fig 66)

[M1:E3] The east–west slot occurring in phase I was cut away by a ditch 0.40m deep extending south-west to east across the south-western part of the area. Street C was metalled with a pebble surface on a sand bedding. The road appears to have been no more than 5m wide. Postholes and slots lay in two groups on the western edge of the road. In the southern half of the area these were scattered along a line extending south-east to west possibly completing the arc of the ditch to the west. In the northern half of the area the postholes and slots may have defined a small building, some 2m square, of a similar type to those found in several parts of the site in phase V. Phases I and II dated from the 1st century.

Table 4 Sites E, F, J, and P: phases, dates, and main features

Phase	West	East	Date
I	slots; street C trackway		1st C
II	ditch; street C surface; posthole groups		1st C
III	quadrilateral enclosure; street C; cobble surface	ditches; structure EA (round house); pebble surface	Neronian–Trajanic (later on J)
IV	street C	structure EB (round house)	Hadrianic–Antonine
V	street C	structure EC	late 2nd C?
VI	structures FA, FB, EH, EI, EJ (booths)	structures ED, EE, EF, EG? (booths), surfaces	early 3rd C?
VII	structures EK, EL (posthole buildings)		3rd C?
VIII	structures EM, ELA (posthole buildings)		3rd C?
IX	structure FC (slot building)		late 3rd/early 4th C on
X	structure FD (?aisled building)		late 3rd/early 4th C on
XI	structure FE (enclosure wall)		after AD 353
XII	structure FE (enclosure wall); structure FF; street A and ditch		after AD 353
XIII	cobble surface; street A and recut of ditch; structures FG and PA (post alignments on street A)	cobble surface	after AD 353

Plate 6 Site E I, phase VI, structures EH, EI, EJ, with phase III and IV enclosure trenches E I 10, 36, 19, 43, looking north-west. Scale in 1ft (0.30m) divisions (see also figs 67, 68, 70)

Plate 7 Site E, parts of timber buildings at the north end of trench E II, looking south-west. Scale in 1ft (0.30m) divisions

Phase III (fig 67)

[M1:E5] In the Neronian–Trajanic period much of the area to the west of street C was enclosed by two parallel trenches (plate 6). The trenches defined a quadrilateral enclosure in the form of a slightly skewed square, with sides 23m long on the outer circuit and 20.5m long on the inner circuit. Opposed entrances, narrower on the inner circuit than on the outer circuit, bisected the east and west sides. The trenches were 500mm wide and up to 500mm deep, with a U-shaped profile. A line of stakeholes flanked the inner edge of the north-eastern segment of the inner trench and extended west on the north side of the eastern entrance. The enclosure was associated with a cobble surface which covered much of the area to the west of the road. The edge of the cobble surface covered silt lying over the phase II road surface. The road was resurfaced with rammed gravel laid to a width of 3.25m and was bounded by a ditch on the eastern side, E IV 23.

At the northern end of the area this ditch joined a second ditch extending east–west, either blocking the road or diverting it to the west. No metalling was observed on the line of the apparent westward diversion, but it is against this line that the quadrilateral enclosure may have been orientated. It is possible that this east–west ditch is later than the north–south ditch.

A circular building, structure EA, lay on the south-eastern side of the area. The building was defined by a circular slot, 12m in diameter, with an entrance on the eastern side. Stakeholes were set in the slot and larger postholes were widely spaced around the edges of the slot. The circular slot

enclosed floors of clay and sand. A hearth lay at the centre of the building and slots partitioned part of the south-west quadrant. A large number of stakeholes lay in the floor of the western half of the building. A pebble surface extended to the north of the building.

Phase IV (fig 68)

[M1:E9] In the Hadrianic–Antonine period the circular building of phase III was replaced by a concentric, circular structure, EB, which was 13.2m in diameter. Stakeholes lay in the perimeter slot on the western side and larger postholes were spaced along the inside edge of the slot. A posthole was set to either side of the entrance, inside the perimeter slot on the line of the previous building. A gutter or eavesdrip lay on the south-eastern side of the building. The building enclosed a cobble floor, with a hearth at the centre associated with a number of waste pits. Stakeholes were scattered over the western half of the building in a similar position to those associated with the phase III building.

Street C may have been resurfaced at this or a later period. On the eastern side, the road was bounded by two parallel ditches. The road surface extended north across the phase III ditch that had diverted the road to the west. However, at some later date the surface was cut by a ditch similarly diverting the road to the west.

A pebble surface lay on the north side of the circular building. This was associated with a small four-post structure, E IV 52A, 52B, 69, 69B, measuring 2m × 5m. A slot lay between the southern two posts.

A ditch extended south-east from the roadside ditches, cutting the postholes and slot forming the south side of the four-post structure.

Phase V (fig 69)

[M1:E12] In the later Antonine period the site to the north of the former circular buildings was occupied by a rectangular building measuring 18m × 8m, structure EC. This extended parallel to street C and was set back from the road by 4m. The building was defined by slots with stakeholes set at their bases. At the north end was a portico 2.5m deep: the remainder of the building was divided into three rooms with the north-western part of the central room divided off to form a fourth room. At the south end, a 3m square annexe housed a stone hearth. Two small rooms lay to the west of this. A floor of clay and sand was associated with the building. A shallow drain or slot was cut on the edge of the road. It may have replaced the earlier roadside ditches or may have been related to the building.

Phase VI (fig 70)

[M1:E14] In the early 3rd century, a number of small buildings, structures FA, FB, ED–EJ, were erected on both sides of street C. These were all variants on a 2m square plan defined by a slot retaining stakehole settings.

The small square 'booths' lay in four groups: west of street C, a single building, FA, lay near the north-eastern corner of the former quadrilateral enclosure and three or more phases of building, FB, EH, EI, and EJ (plate 6) lay over the enclosure boundary to the south of its eastern entrance; east of street C, two phases of building, ED and EE, stood near the centre of the former rectangular building, and elements of several buildings, structures EF and EG, lay over the south end of the building.

The small buildings could have been merely temporary shelters, corresponding with the apparent abandonment of other parts of Birch Abbey during this period. In the succeeding period the area to the east of street C was permanently abandoned but on the western side larger buildings were erected on the sites of the former 'booths', in what might be seen as a direct line of development from the settlement established with them.

Phase VII (fig 71)

[M1:F3] On the western side of street C in the northern part of the area a rectangular building, structure EK, measuring 12.9m × 7m, was defined by postholes in six opposed pairs. The building lay with the eastern gable end against street C extending east–west between the former 'booth' and the edge of the road.

At the south end of the area, the site of the former 'booths' was occupied by a timber building, structure EL, measuring 10m × 3m and defined by postholes.

Phase VIII (fig 72)

[M1:F4] The building in the northern half of the area was replaced on the same site by a smaller structure, EM, narrower, and one bay shorter at the western end, measuring 9m × 3.5m. The building at the south end of the area was repaired with the replacement of a number of posts, structure ELA. The phases of building on the northern margin of the area might have been contemporary with the structures of phases VII and VIII. Postholes defined a small building over 7m long, 1.5–1.75m wide, which was replaced in a later period by a similar structure, 8.5m × 1.75m, associated with a cobble floor. A third building, 9.5m × 1.75m, may have lain to the east in the later period. The three buildings were aligned along the northern side of the east–west diversion of street C, the building on the eastern side lying across the north–south line.

Phase IX (fig 73)

[M1:F6] Occupation was established on a fresh site on the western side of the area, set back some 10m behind the line of street C. Building was aligned on street A, which crossed the south end of the area, and street C might have been abandoned in this part of the site.

Several periods may be represented by a complex of timber slots, structure FC, extending over much of the western half of the area. The slots delineated buildings, or possibly animal pens, in four bays up to 11m east–west and 4m north–south. There were related slots along the south and west edges of the excavated area and extending south to the edge of street A.

No sequence within the complex could be established but the latest features may have been the two northern bays. This part of the plan was repeated in the structures of the succeeding phases (X–XI).

Phases X–XII (figs 74–7)

[M1:F8] Several of the timber slots of structure FC were replaced by lines of substantial posts. Two corresponding alignments extended east–west defining an area 11m × 8.5m in five or six regular bays. These were divided by a internal parallel alignment of posts set at irregular intervals. The posts in the north and central alignments had been replaced at least once, but the south alignment was of a single period. A line of posts extended north–south across each end. These features were enclosed by a stone wall forming an 18m square equidistant from the north, south, and west alignments but truncating the extremities of the two north–south alignments. Latterly, the south-east corner of this enclosure was divided off by a massive stone wall.

The evidence can support several interpretations of these features, of which two are outlined below. Further discussion can be found in microfiche.

Phase X (figs 74, 75)

[M1:F8] In one interpretation, posthole alignments perpetuating the plan of part of structure FC defined a building some 11m × 8.5m with an aisle 3m wide on the north side, structure FD. Fence lines projected north and south from the west end, and south from the E end of the building. The bay structure of the north wall corresponded closely with the south wall but the intervening aisle posts were set at irregular intervals. The alignment defining the eastern end of the building was not square to the sides, producing an arrangement of five bays on the north side and six on the south. This interpretation stresses the continuity in plan with structure FC and supposes that all the post alignments must have been in immediate succession to the timber slots of the earlier phase.

Alternatively, it can be suggested that the southern east–west alignment did not appear until phase XI. Phase X would then have comprised the two alignments of the north 'aisle' range, defining a narrow building or animal pen some 3m × 11m, between the two north–south fence lines. The lack of continuity with structure FC is a major obstacle to this interpretation.

The north–south fence line at the western end was possibly an independent unit earlier than either of these suggested structures.

Phase XI (fig 76)

[M1:F9] In the first interpretation, the posts forming the north wall and aisle of structure FD were replaced. These repairs may have been contemporary with the erection of a rubble wall 0.6m thick around the building, defining an 18m square enclosure, structure FE. The wall was raised on the most shallow of foundations, in parts only resting on the surface. It lay against the east end of structure FD, and enclosed a passage 5m wide on the other three sides of the building. The wall truncated the fence lines projecting at each end of the building and these may have been removed completely (for location of the fence line see fig 75).

Alternatively, this phase may be interpreted as ranges of buildings 5m wide supported by the enclosure wall, on three sides of a central courtyard. The 'aisle' posts supported a subsidiary structure fronting the north range. This building completely replaced the fence lines or narrow structure suggested above, although it was partly coincident in plan.

Phase XII (figs 77, 78)

[M1:F11] The timber building of phase XI was demolished and the area within the enclosure wall replanned.

Structure FF was a rectangular stone structure built within the south-eastern corner of the enclosure. It occupied the eastern half of the area between the enclosure wall and the former structure FD, or the eastern half of the south range of the possible courtyard structure, and measured 8.4m × 3.6m internally (fig 78). The north and west sides were defined by a substantial stone wall, 0.9m thick, set in a foundation trench 0.4–0.6m deep and butted against the enclosure wall. The shallow foundation of the enclosure wall incorporated in the south and east sides of the structure was not consolidated in any way. A paved yard extended over the area at the centre of the enclosure.

Street A extended from east to west across the south side of the site. The road was more than 7.5m wide and was bounded on its north side by a V-shaped ditch. It appears to have been metalled for the first time when the ditch was dug.

Phase XIII (fig 79)

[M1:F13] There were no certain indications of occupation on either side of street C, but patchy cobble surfaces lay over much of the area. Street A was resurfaced and the ditch on its northern side was recut. Two metres to the north of the ditch and approximately parallel to it, posts were set in two parallel alignments, or may have been arranged in a series of 2.5–3m squares, extending for over 45m to either side of street C (structures FG and PA). On the eastern side of the site, a number of the posts had been replaced on one or more occasions. There was little dating evidence associated with the later phases, except a coin dated to post-AD 353 sealed beneath the enclosure wall of phase XI, and fourteen mid-4th-century coins from phase XIII.

Sites E, F, J, and P phase dates

There was little pottery from these sites. This is probably a result of the almost complete absence of pits from the site, indeed the most substantial quantity of pottery comes from one of the few pits which do exist, F V 14A and F V 14B, with very little material from the habitation area.

Phase I: 1st century

There was no dating evidence for phase I. The dating for this phase is extrapolated from phases II and III.

Phase II: 1st century

A 1st-century nicolo intaglio (cat no 3) was found in the top fill of a curving ditch, F I 126, and an imitation Claudian coin (cat no 15) was found in a layer of clay, E I 55, which covered much of trenches E I and E III.

Phase III: Neronian–Trajanic (site E) and Hadrianic–Antonine (site J)

On site E in phase III the pottery associated with the first round house includes contexts with Neronian samian, E II 71 and E IV 48, and the latest samian is Trajanic–Hadrianic from E VI 9. Most of the coarse pottery is of 1st- to early 2nd-century date, especially Flavian–Trajanic (R.145, E IV **23**; R.137, E VI **9**; R.143, E I **15**, E I **36**, E II **78**, and E III **56**).

A coin (cat no 24) dating to AD 69–79 was found in one of the ditches of the quadrilateral enclosure, E I **19** and another (cat no 22) dated AD 68–9 came from an associated cobble surface, F IV 8. The phase would seem to have a Neronian–Trajanic date range.

A sherd of samian dating to AD 150–80 was found in the enclosure ditch, F I **50B**, but as the ditch continued in use during phase IV this find cannot be used as dating evidence for phase III.

In site J ditch J II **B** contained a 1st-century Dr 18 or 18/31 (SG) and a quantity of 1st- to early 2nd-century pottery. There was also a reasonable number of Hadrianic–Antonine forms (R.173, R.178, R.190, and R.192) from J II 21 and some (R.192 and R.95) from J II 22 and J II 22A respectively, together with a number of 2nd- to 3rd-century Severn Valley wares. A Hadrianic–Antonine date would seem reasonable for the group.

Intrusive medieval material also occurred in J II 22A.

Phase IV: Hadrianic–Antonine

On site E this contained a number of Hadrianic–Antonine pottery forms in Black-Burnished BB1 and grey ware (R.362, B.5, B.36, B.39, and R.377) and a 2nd- to 3rd-century Severn Valley ware bowl (O.348; E IV **36**) together with Antonine samian from E II **41** and E V 24. The non-ceramic items have wide possible date ranges but are consistent with the pottery.

The phase has a good Hadrianic–Antonine date.

Phase V: late 2nd century?

Useful ceramic dating from this phase only occurs on site E: most of it is residual Flavian–Trajanic pottery. E II 31A, E II 34, and E IV 57A contain 2nd- to 3rd-century Severn Valley ware (O.265). E II 34 contains a *mortarium* dated AD 120–60. The non-ceramics are not helpful. Perhaps the phase is late 2nd century.

Phase VI: early 3rd century?

This phase is dated by pottery from site E; there were residual brooches and coins. It contains a large quantity of residual 1st- to 2nd-century pottery and a number of pieces of 2nd- to 3rd-century Severn Valley ware (O.265, E II 19; O.265, E II 19A; O.265, E IV 18; O.274, E II 10) together with a later 2nd- to 3rd-century flagon (O.7, E II 31) and a splaying-mouthed Severn Valley ware tankard (O.267, E II 10). The latter is the typologically latest piece and is probably 3rd century.

The group might, perhaps, be early 3rd century as it succeeds phase V.

Phase VII: 3rd century?

There is very little pottery recorded from this phase on site E and it is all residual.

On site F there is also very little pottery recorded. It does, however, include an intersecting arc-decorated Black-Burnished BB1 dish (B.71, F I **99**) which must date to the late 2nd century or later and a wide-mouthed Severn Valley ware jar of 2nd- to 3rd-century date (O.132, F I **125**). The phase might be dated to the 3rd century as it succeeds phase VI.

Phase VIII: 3rd century?

This contains little ceramic or other material on site E but the finds include two obtuse-lattice-decorated Malvernian ware dishes of 3rd-century or later date (R.388 and R.389, E III **31**). Probably 3rd century.

Phases IX and X: late 3rd to early 4th century on?

No dating evidence; the proposed date is based on the dates of phases VIII and XI.

Phase XI: after AD 353

The date of this phase is based on the discovery of a coin (cat no 334) in the foundation trench of wall 1: the coin is an FTR copy dated to after AD 353.

Phase XII: after AD 353

Site F contains only a little, residual 2nd-century pottery and a coin (cat no 197) dated AD 330–5 from the gravel surface, F I **14**, which overlay the phase XI timber structure. The date for the phase is based on the preceding phase.

Phase XIII: after AD 353

Site E contains a fair amount of residual 2nd- to 3rd-century ceramic material but little which is later. There is an Oxfordshire parchment ware bowl (Young 1977, WC7, *c* AD 240–400+) which is unlikely to have arrived at Alcester before the late 3rd century (W.39, E IV 15), a wide-mouthed Severn Valley ware jar (O.136, E IV 15), and a later 3rd-century Black-Burnished BB1 jar (B.20, E V 4). Nothing from this group need be later than the end of the 3rd century.

However, there were eight coins with mid-4th-century dates ascribed to this phase. The coins were found in cobble surfaces — E I 4 (cat no 277, AD 346–8), E II 5 (cat no 306, AD 346–8), E II 9 (cat no 193, AD 330–1; and cat no 272, AD 337–40), E IV 15 (cat no 195, AD 330–1; and cat no 398, AD 367–75) — and in a hollow, E IV 6 (cat no 341, AD 353+; and cat no 395, AD 364–7).

On site F the phase contains a good number of shell-tempered ware vessels (R.112, R.43, R.435, and R.437, F I 5; R.43, F I **18**; R.107, F IV 14) and later 4th-century Nene Valley types (CW.1, F I 5, F IV 14; CW.12, F I 5, F I 8; CW.13, F IV 14). The datable non-ceramic finds included a late 4th-century copper alloy bracelet (cat no 27) and eight coins (cat nos 180, AD 319; 214, AD 332–3; 217, AD 335; 240, AD 330–1; 282, AD 346–8; 293, AD 346–8; 308, AD 346–8; 315, AD 353–4).

The dating evidence for this phase all points to the late 4th century with a convincing *terminus post quem* of AD 353.

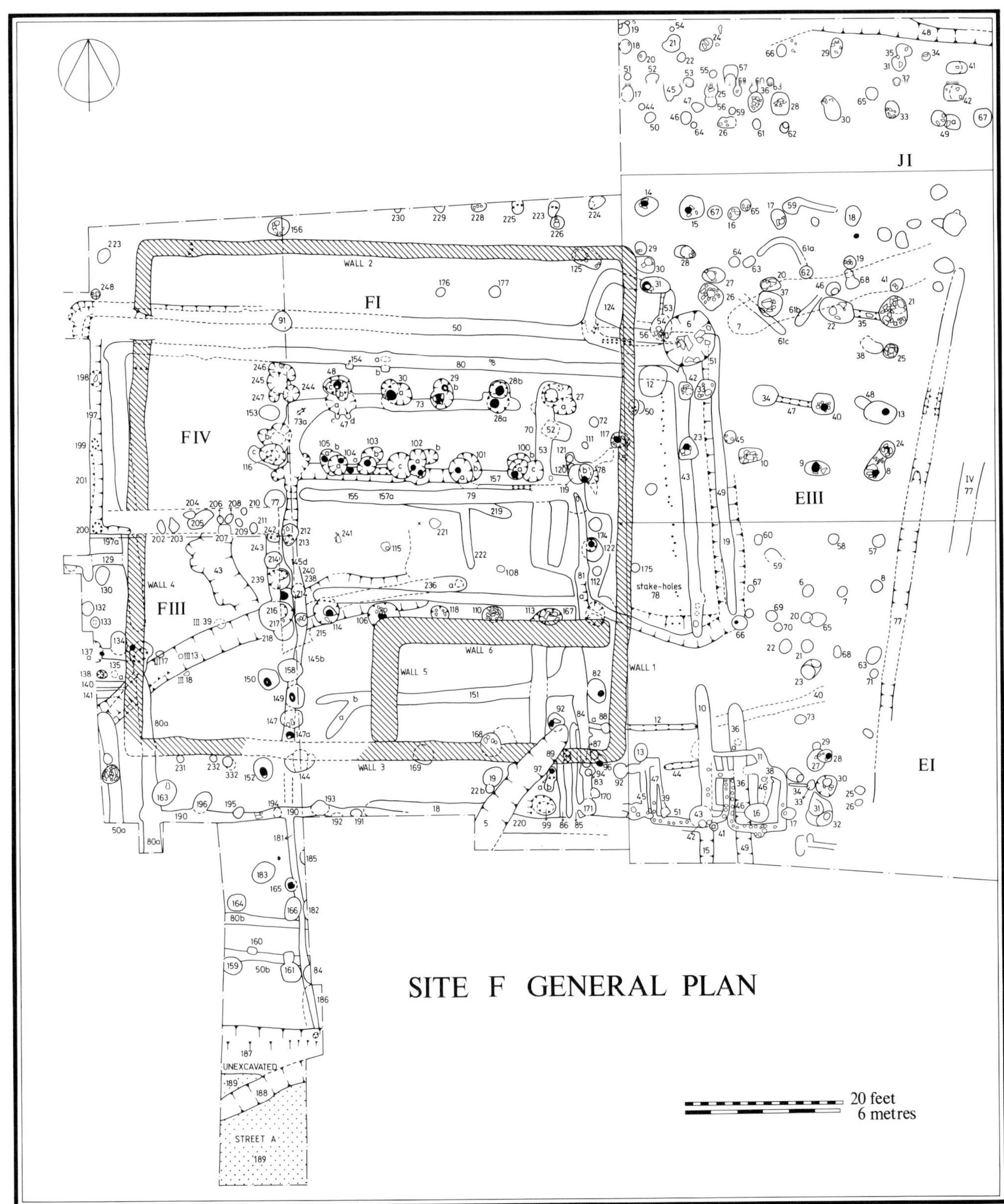

Figure 63   Site F and parts of sites E and J, general plan

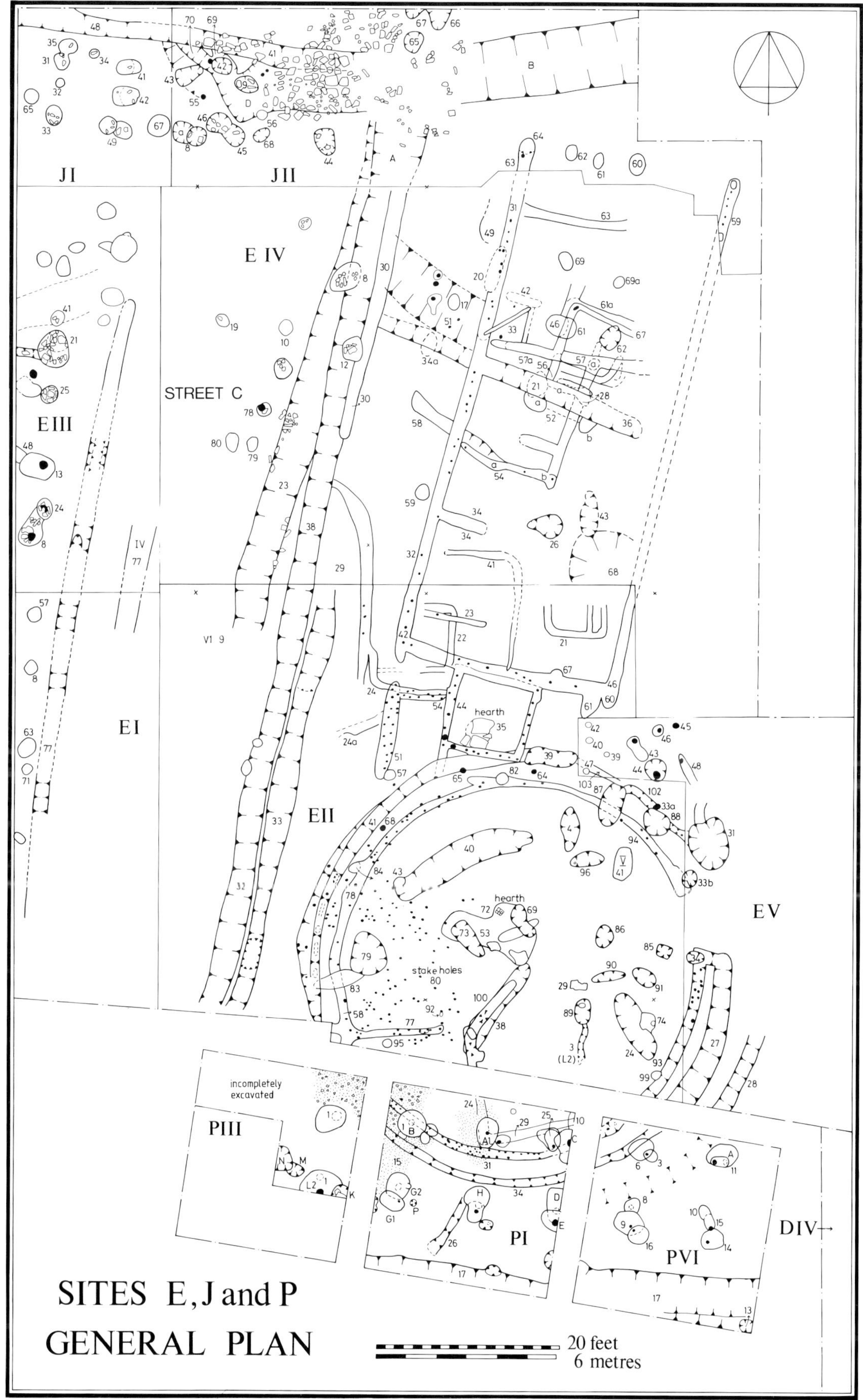

Figure 64   Sites E, J, and P, general plan

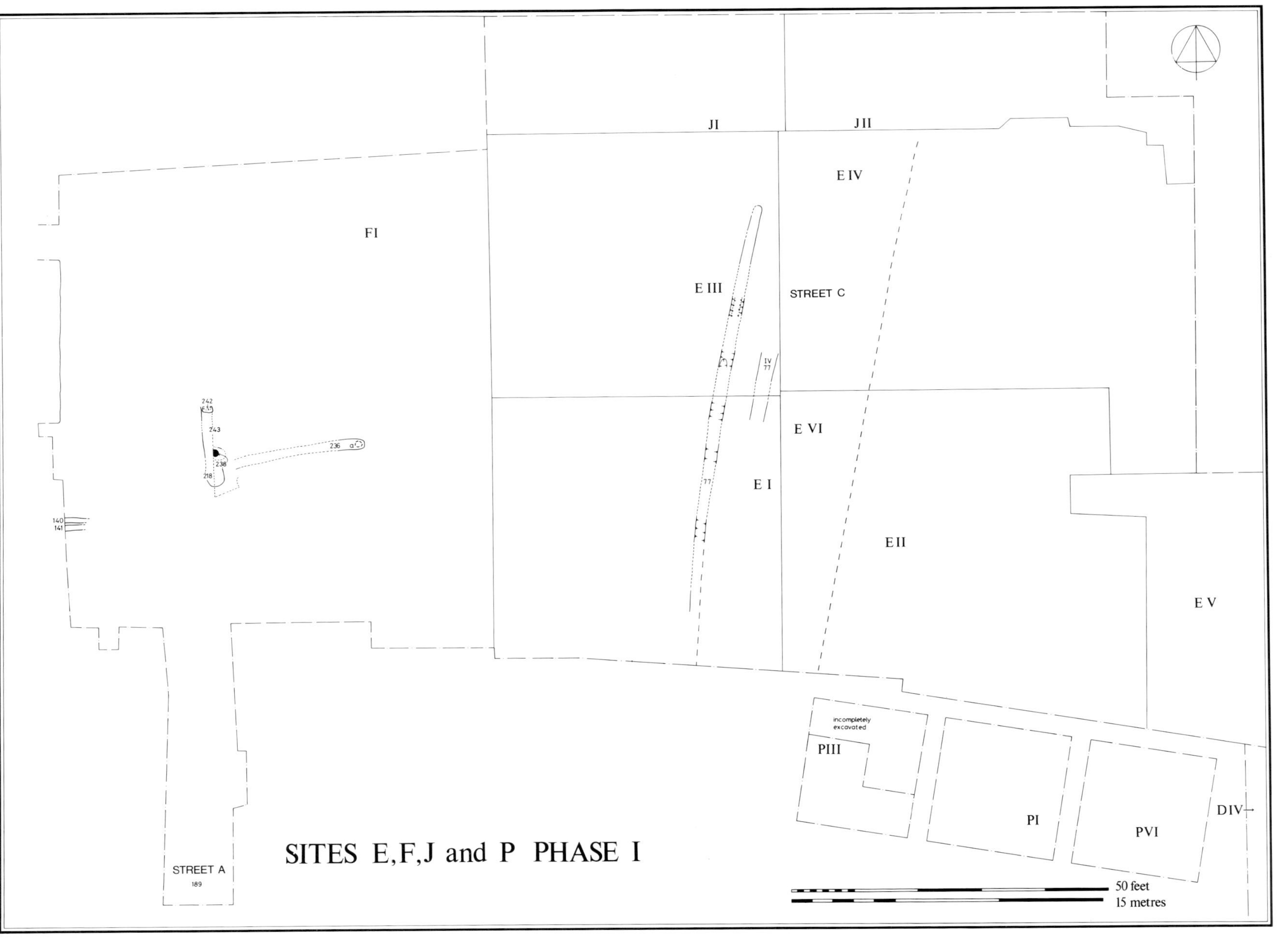

Figure 65   Sites E, F, J, and P, phase I

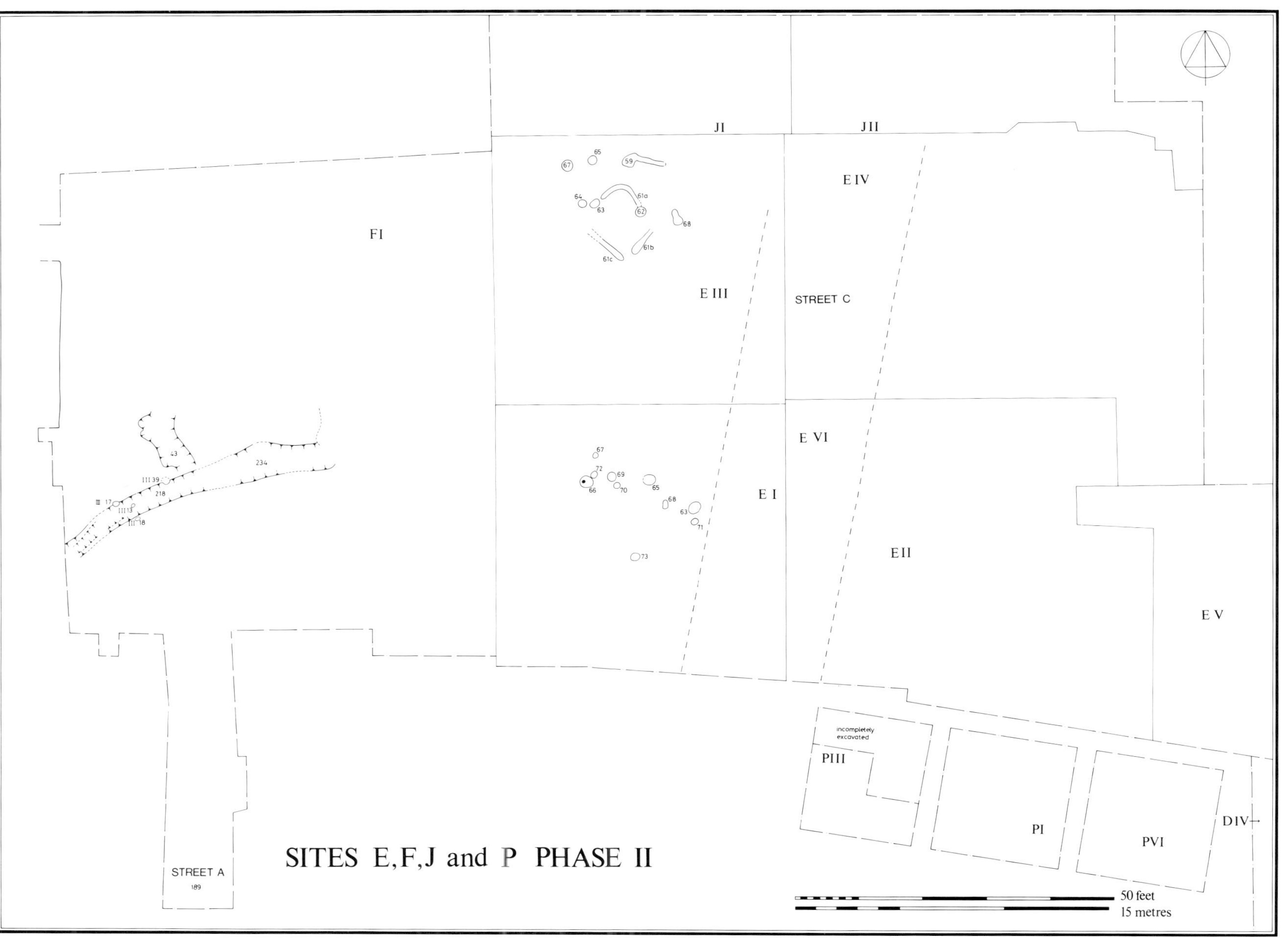

Figure 66 Sites E, F, J, and P, phase II

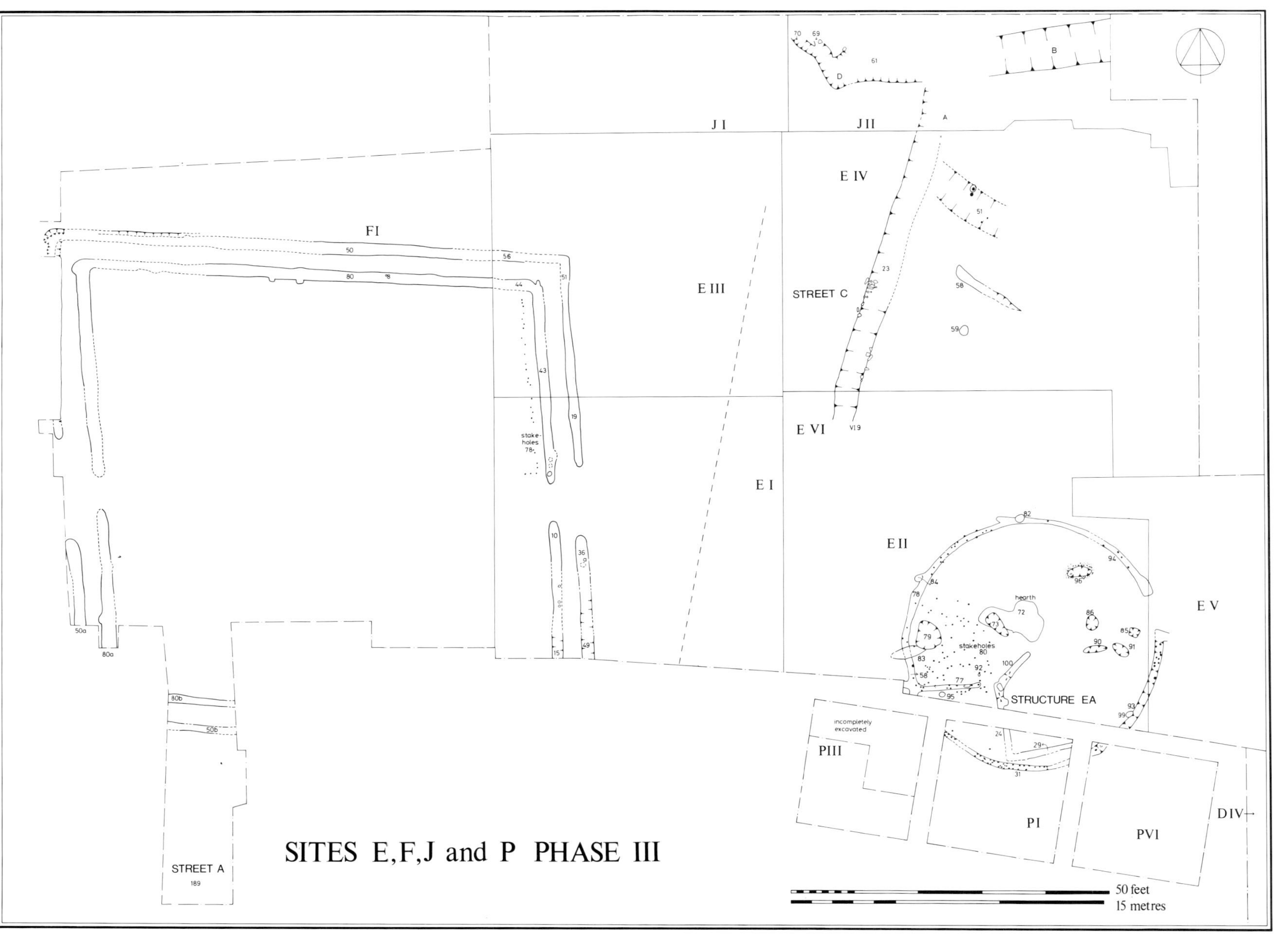

Figure 67 Sites E, F, J, and P, phase III

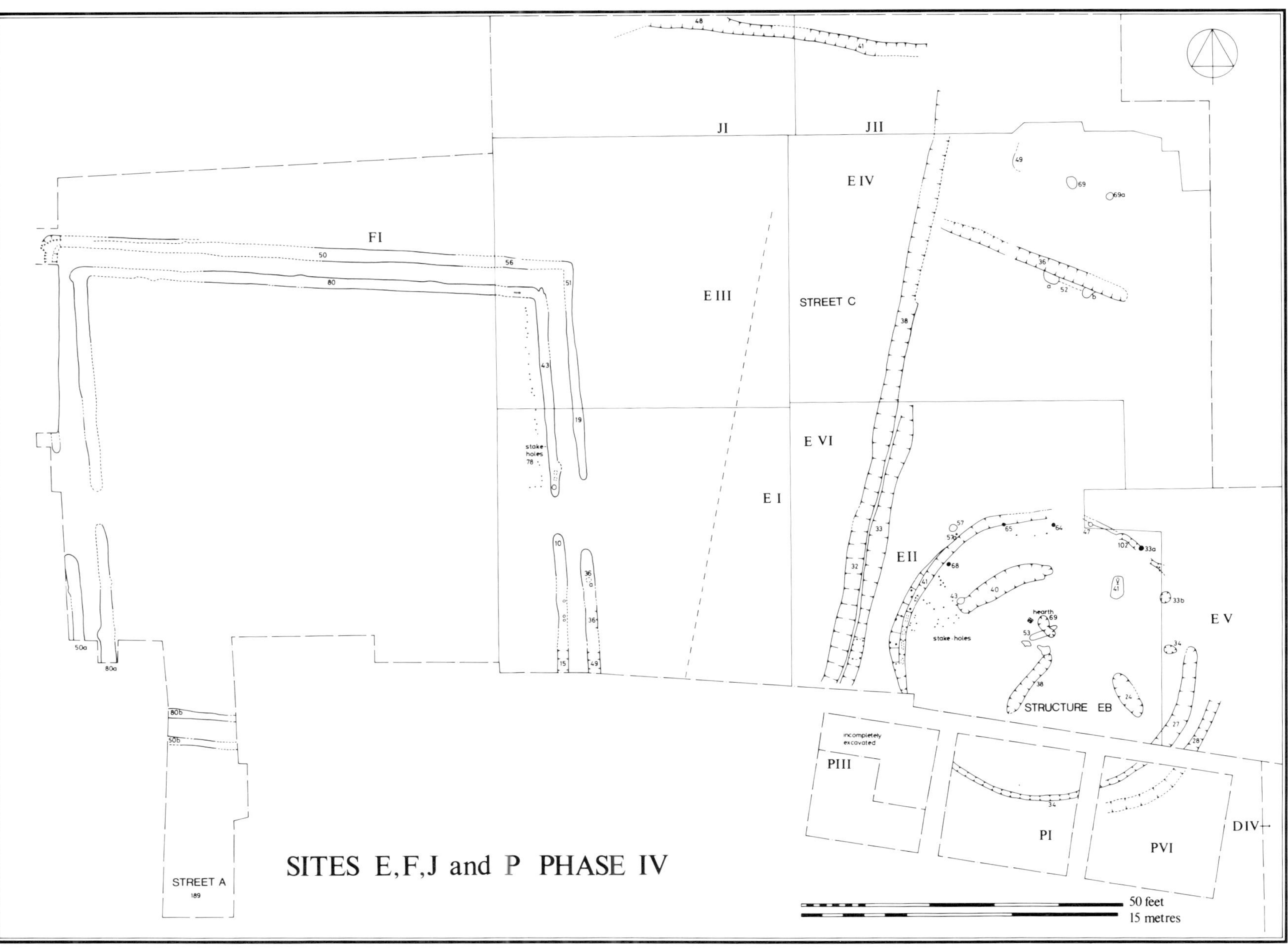

Figure 68 Sites E, F, J, and P, phase IV

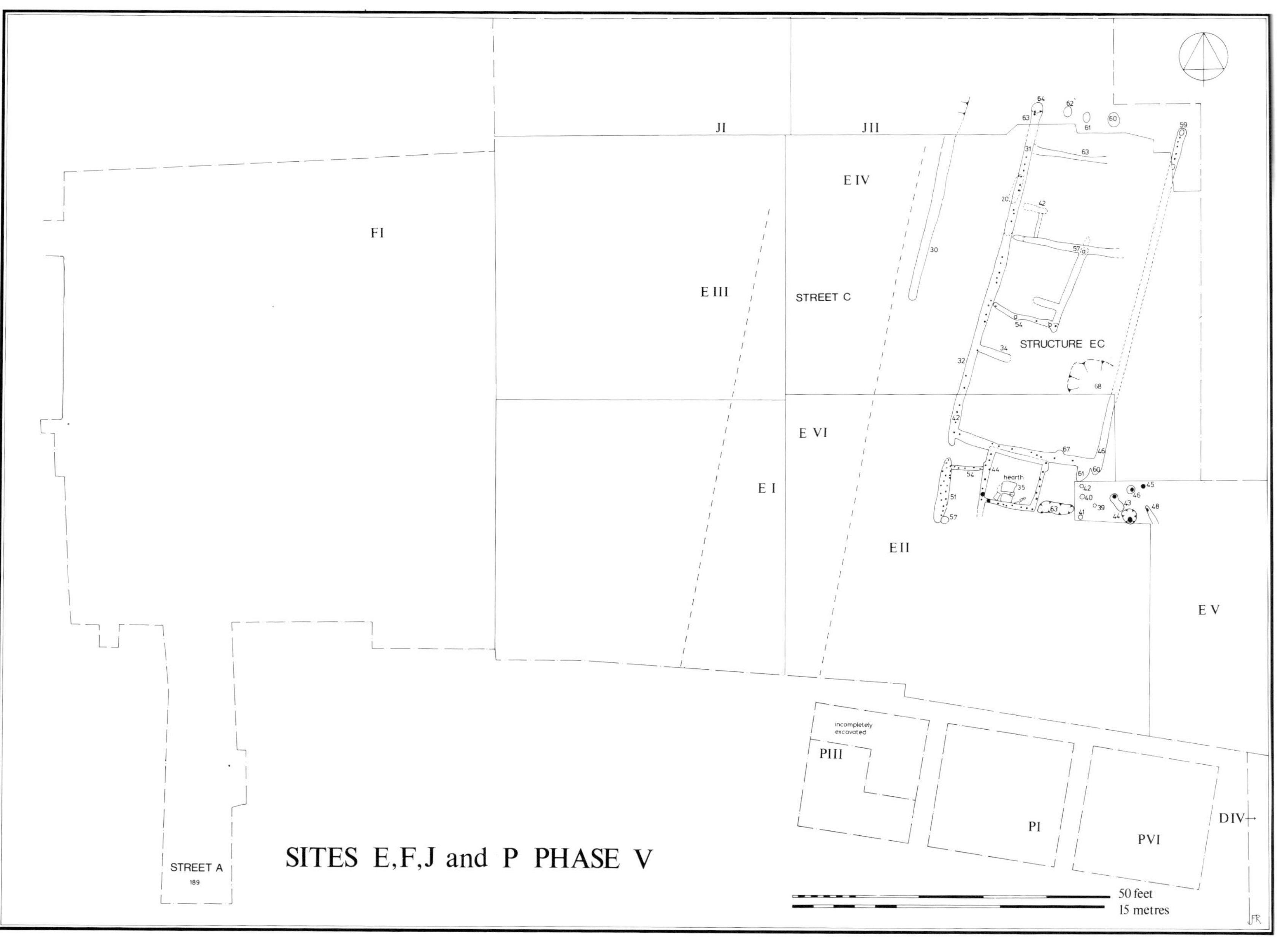

Figure 69 Sites E, F, J, and P, phase V

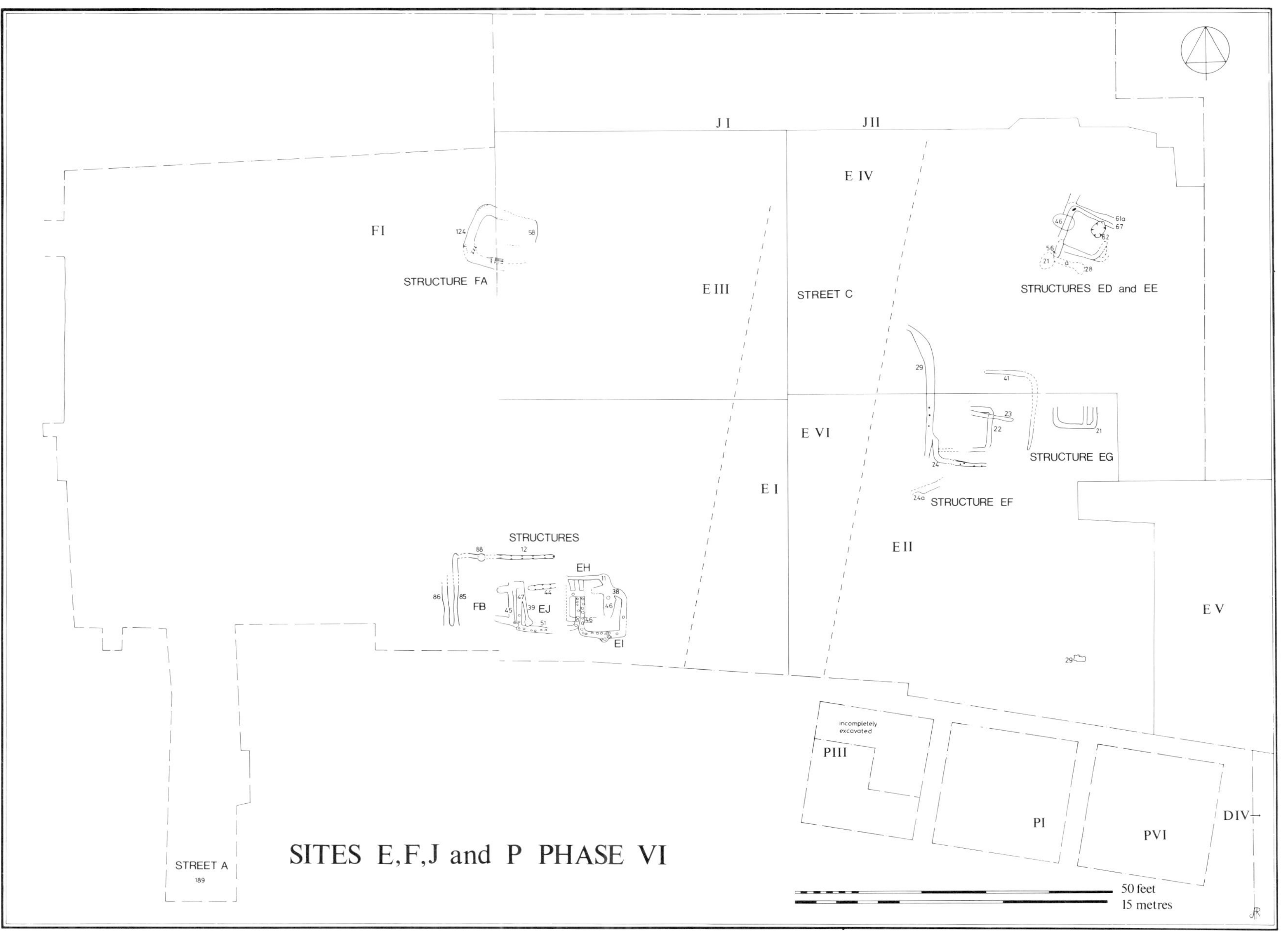

Figure 70 *Sites E, F, J, and P, phase VI*

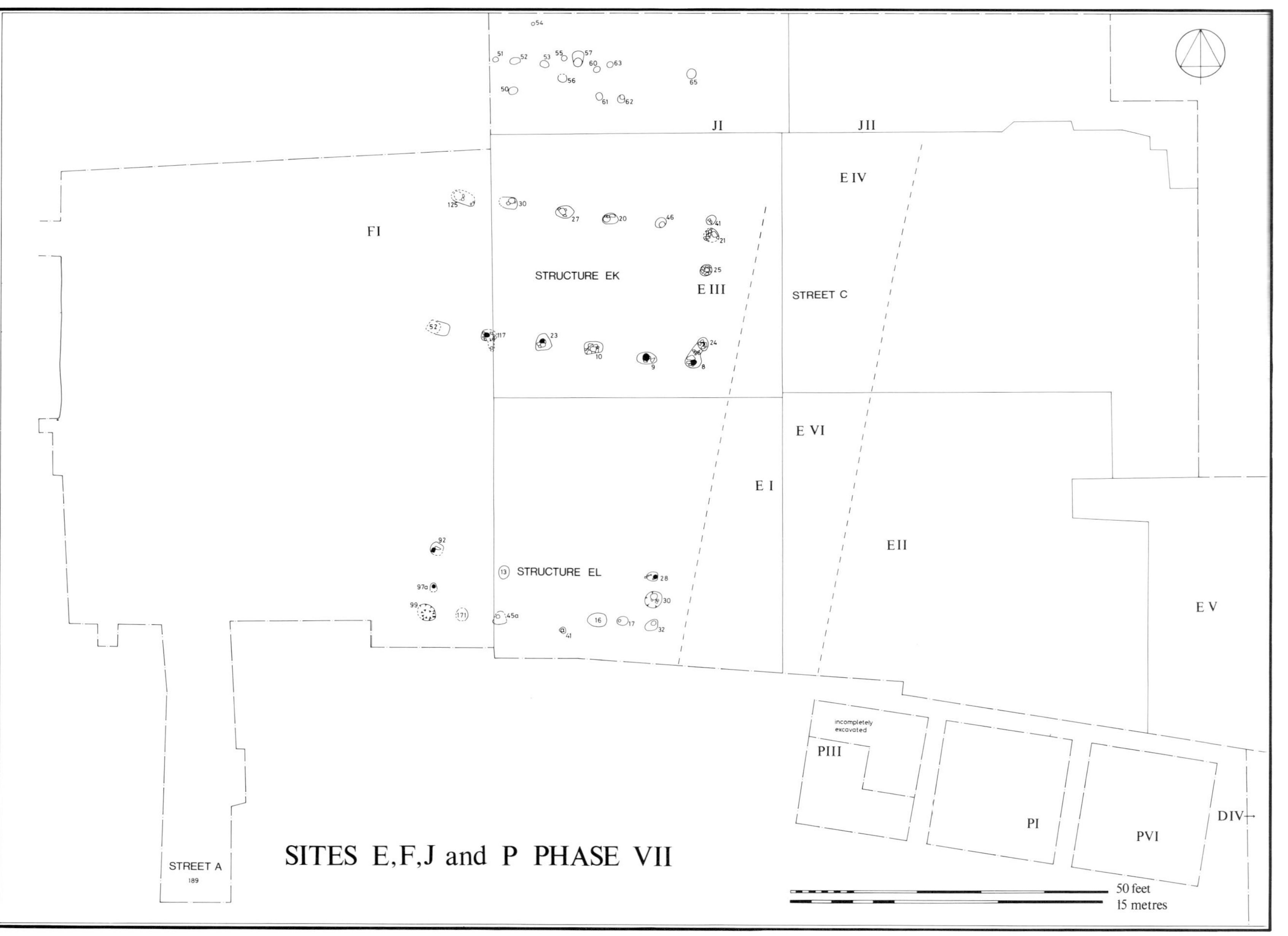

Figure 71 Sites E, F, J, and P, phase VII

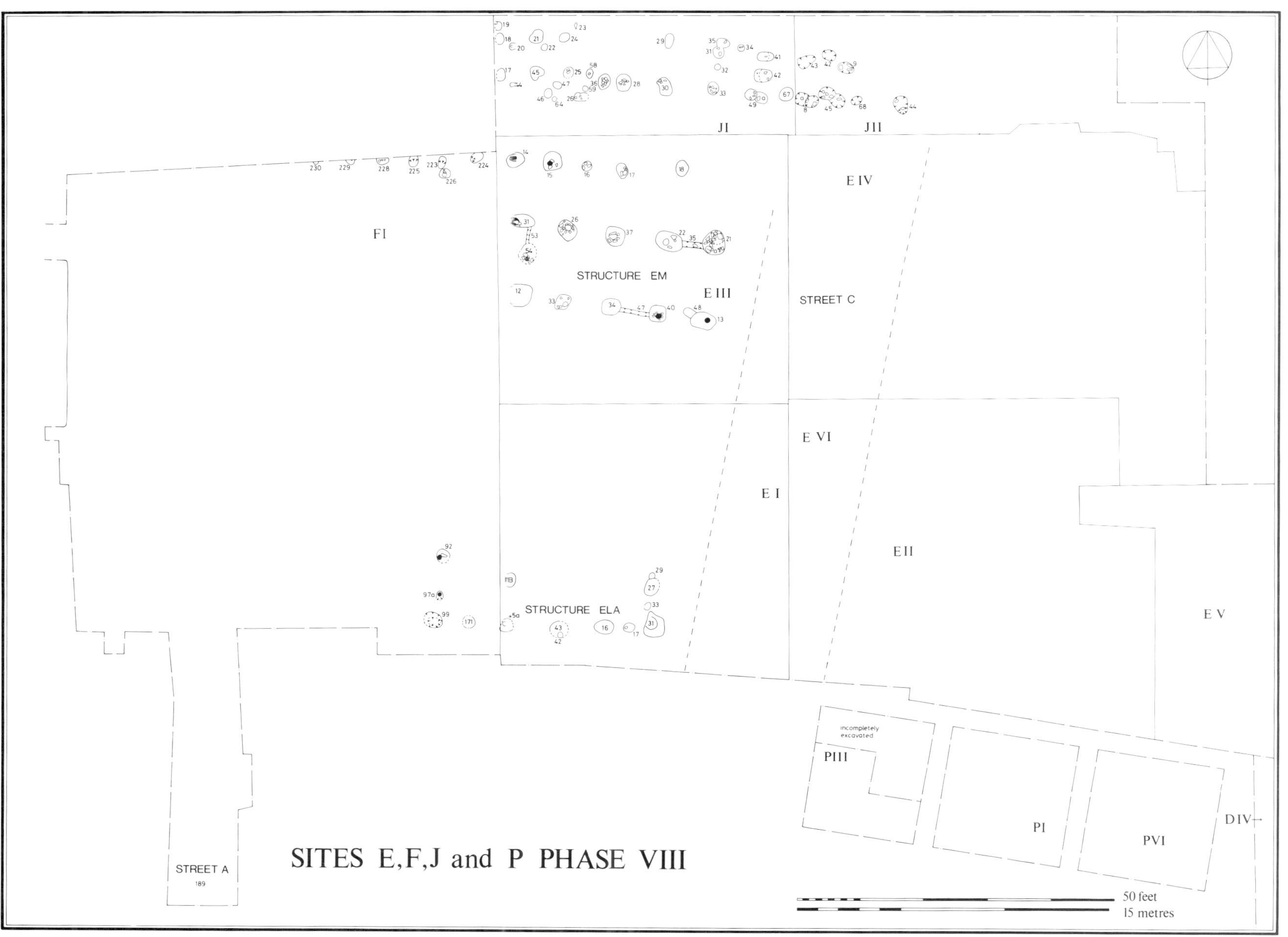

Figure 72   Sites E, F, J, and P, phase VIII

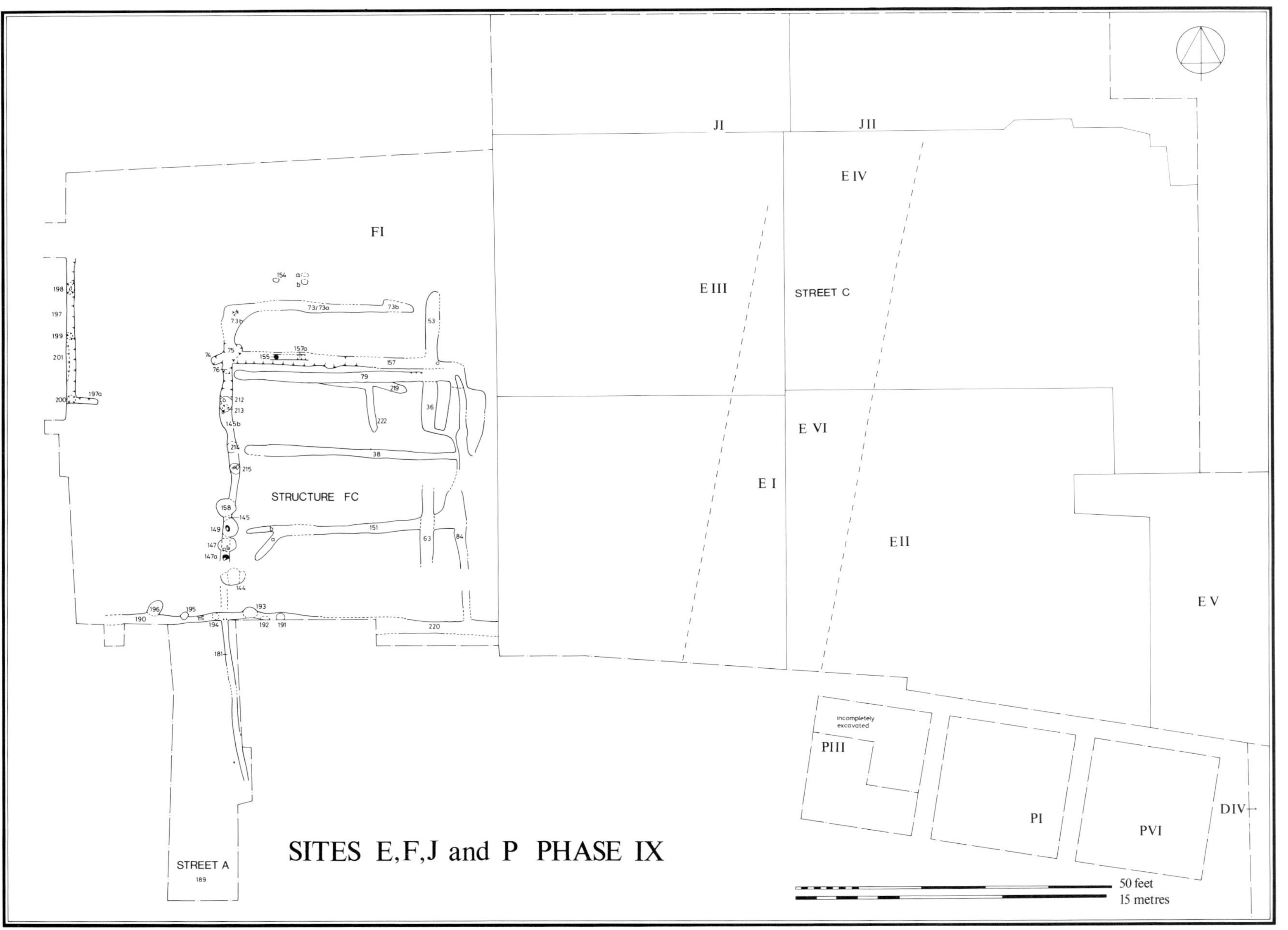

Figure 73 Sites E, F, J, and P, phase IX

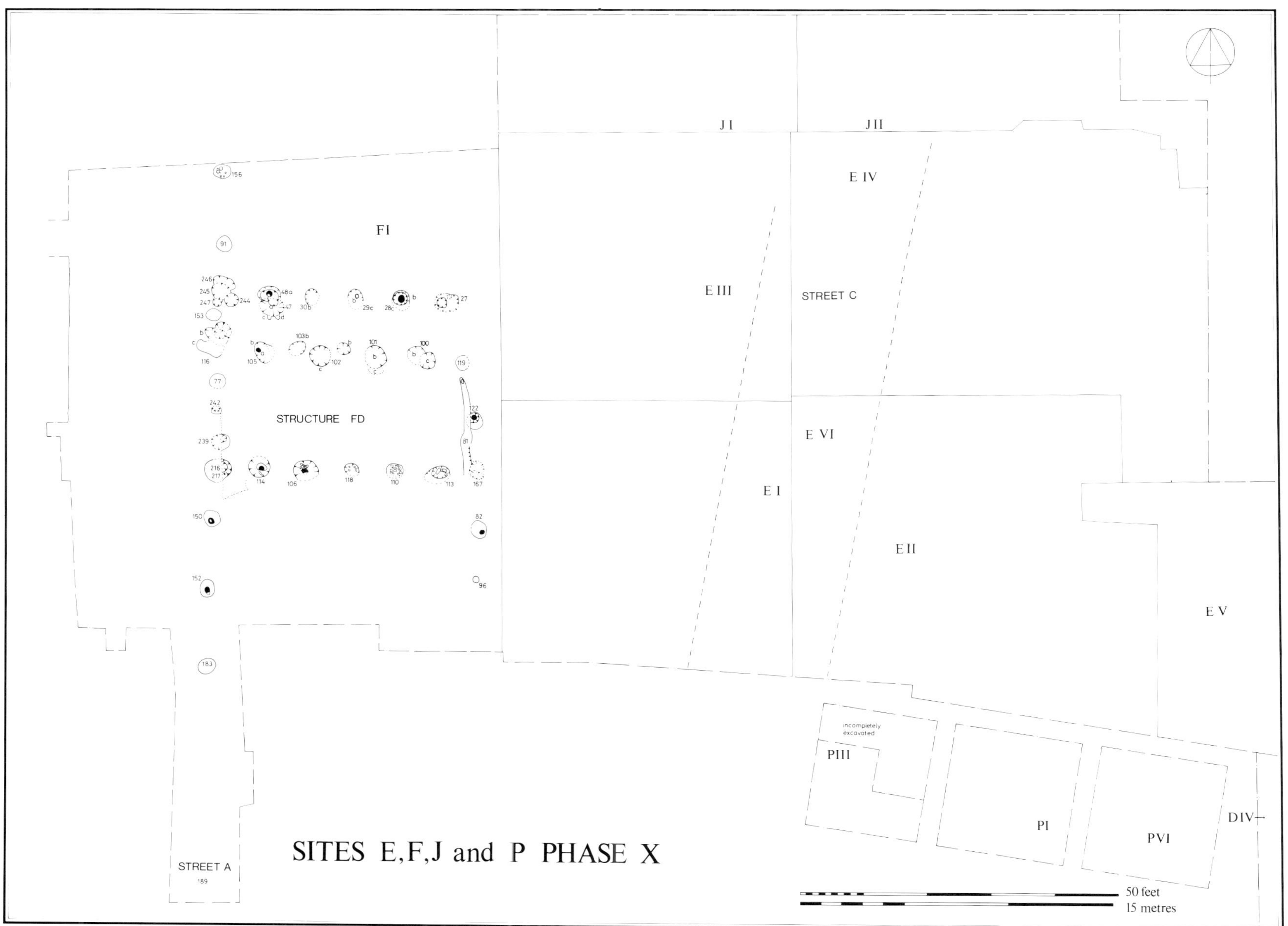

Figure 74 Sites E, F, J, and P, phase X

101

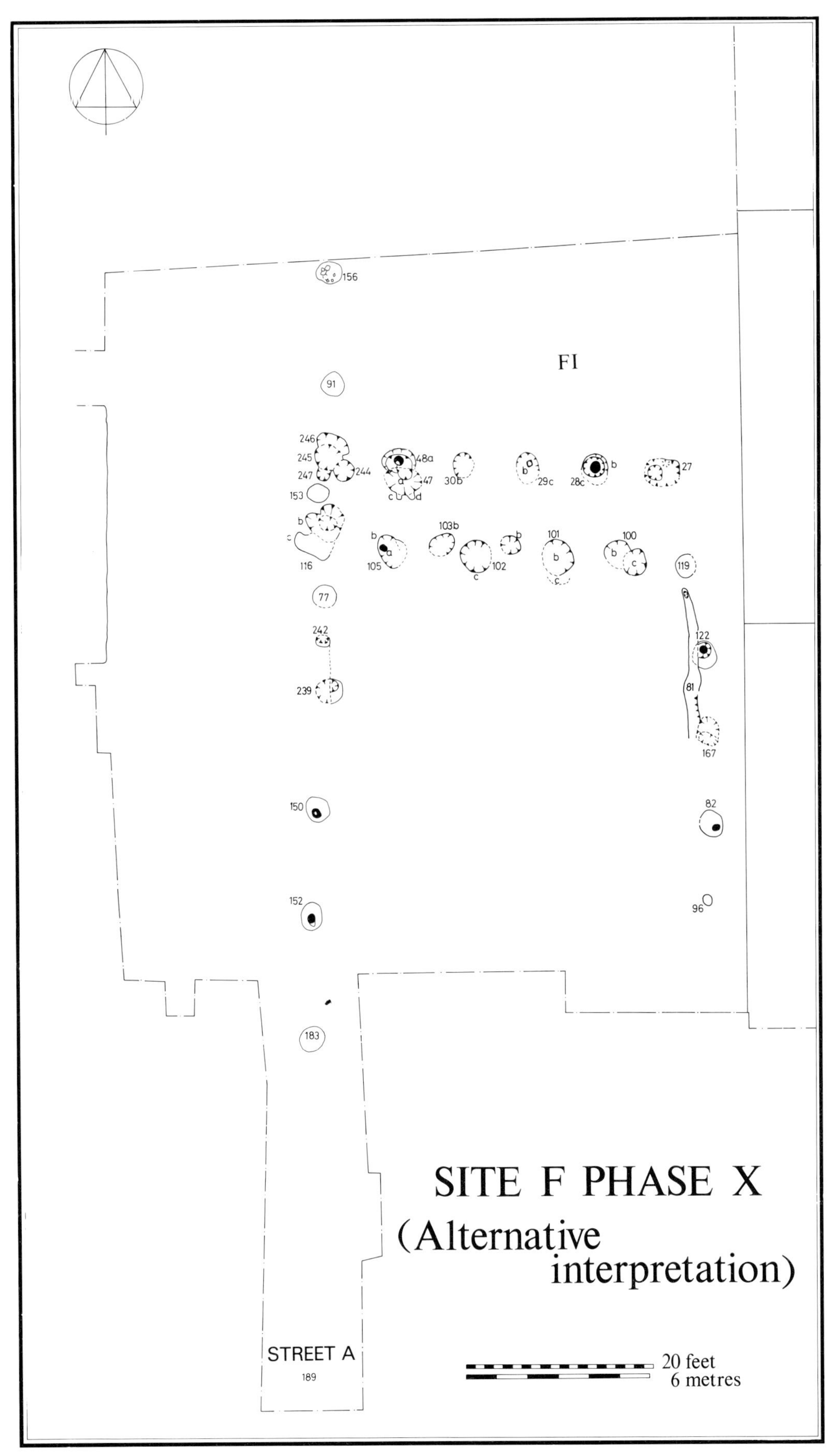

Figure 75 Site F, phase X, alternative interpretation

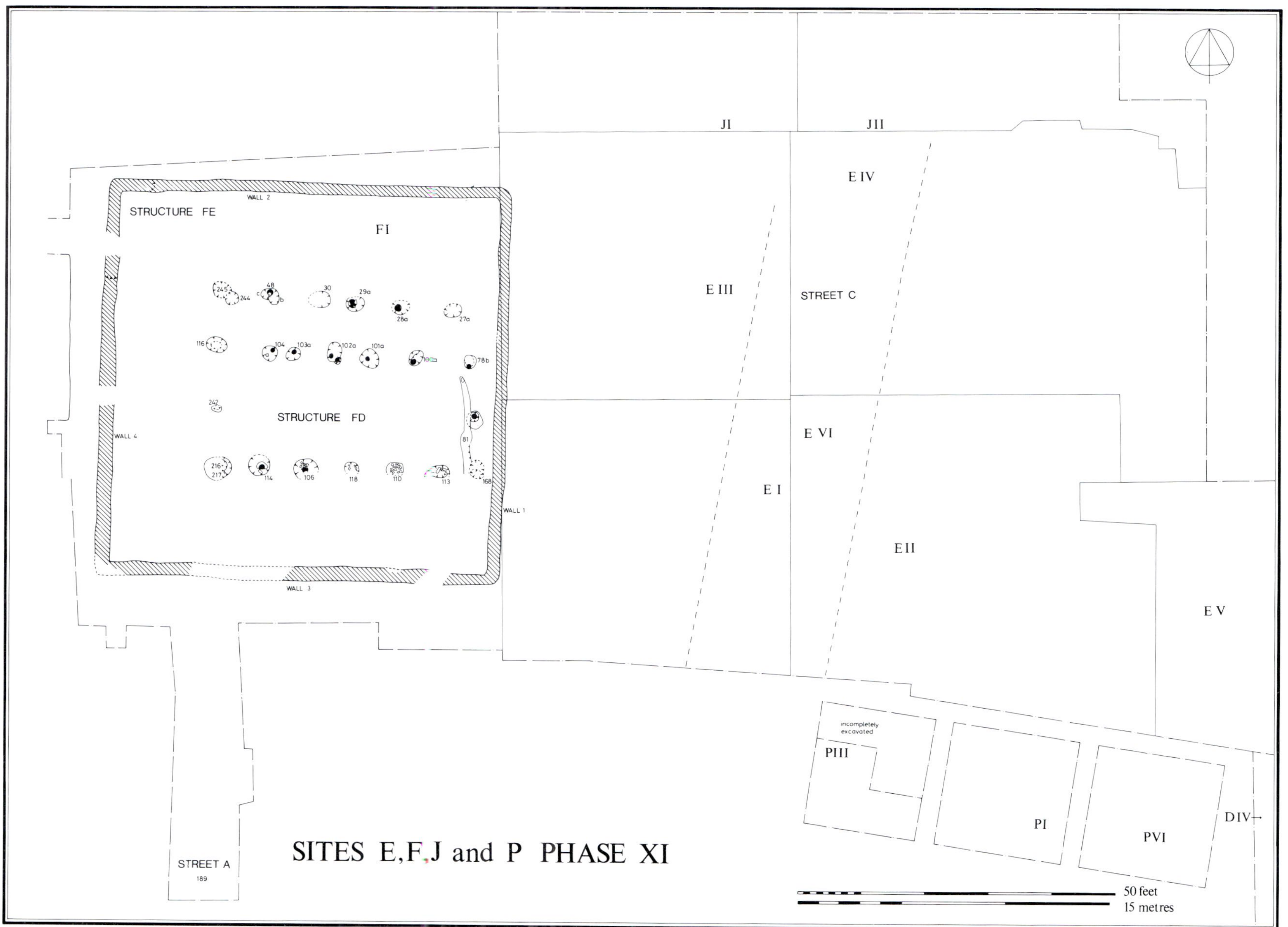

Figure 76 Sites E, F, J, and P, phase XI

Figure 77 Sites E, F, J, and P, phase XII

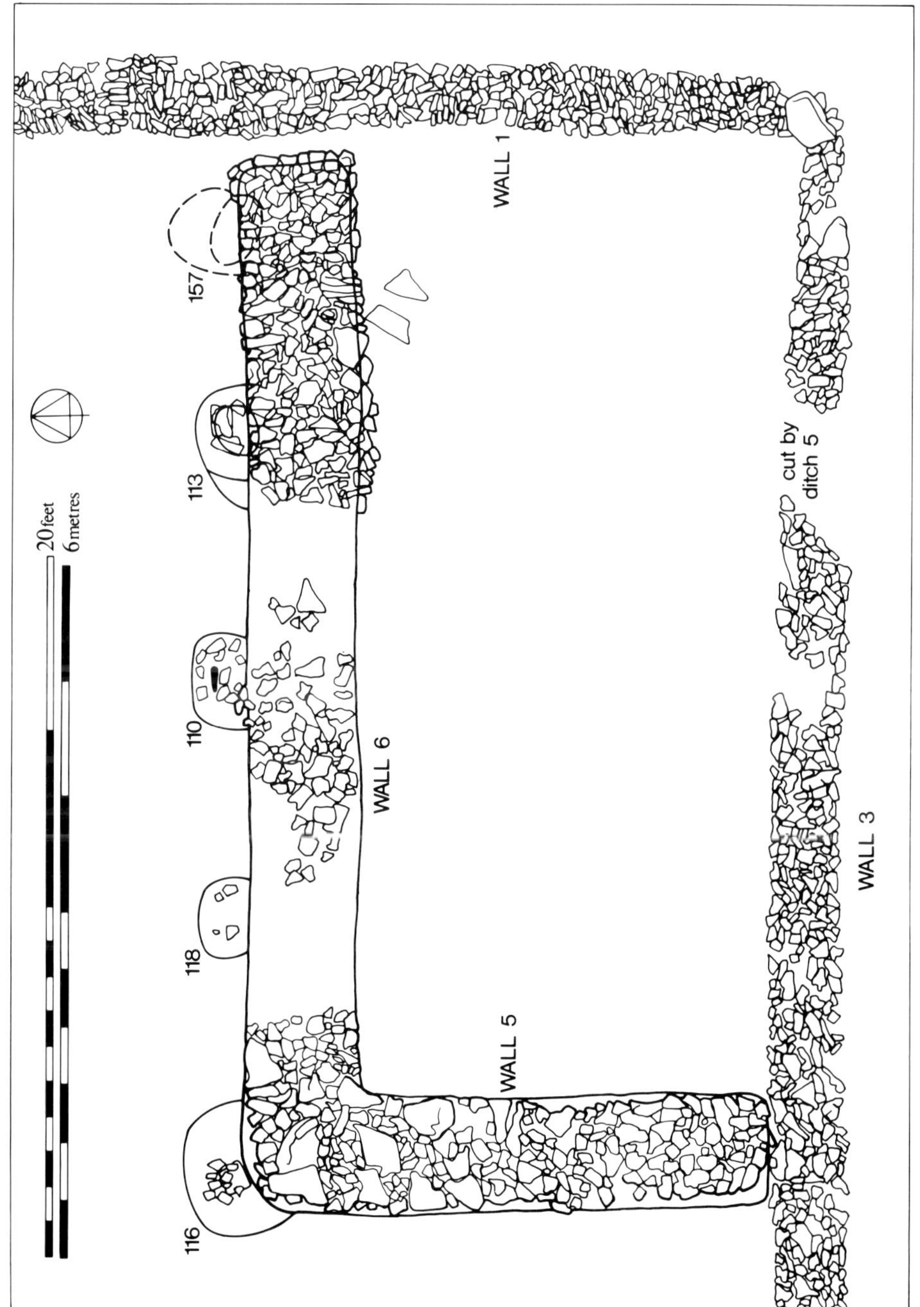

Figure 78 Stone walls on site F (detail), phase XII

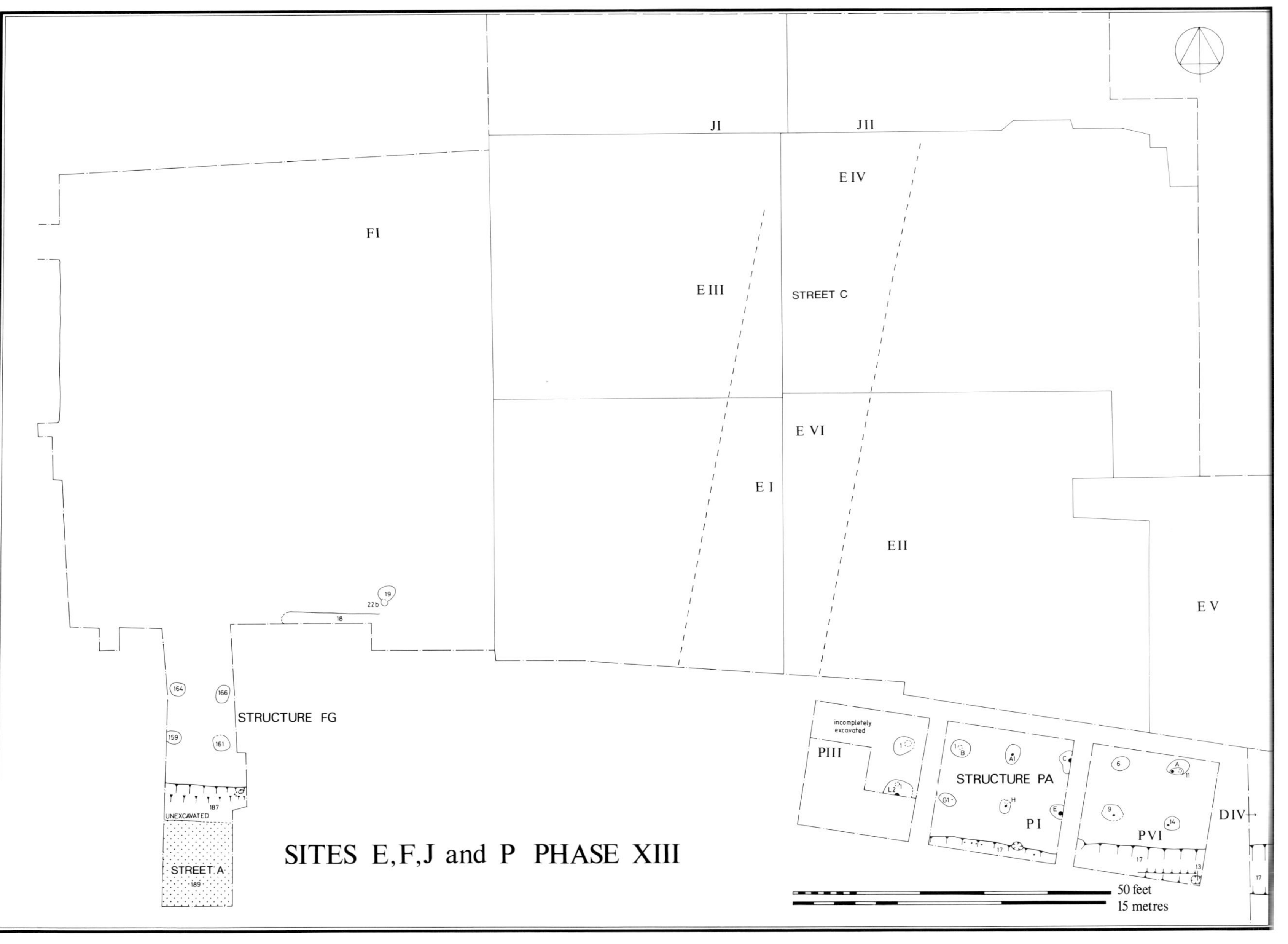

Figure 79 Sites E, F, J, and P, phase XIII

Site H, trench B I extension, and trench B IA

R S Langley

[M1:G3] Site H lay on the edge of the gravel terrace and covered an area of 250sq m; trenches B I and B IA were expanded to take in a further 81sq m contiguous with trench H I (fig 3 nos **33, 39**, and figs 4, 80; sections in fig 85).

The natural gravel had weathered in places to form spreads of sterile sand and pebbles and this was displaced over man-made features in some places.

Phase I (fig 81)

[M1:G3] The earliest features on the site were three gullies and three fragments of gullies belonging to a late 1st- to early 2nd-century enclosure system. This system is discussed in detail under site D (see also fig 45). Two of the gullies had postholes and stakeholes set at the bottom of them.

Phase II (fig 82)

[M1:G4] Several slots are grouped together in this phase on the basis of similarities in form. Their function is obscure, although they may have formed a subsidiary enclosure. However, pits were the main features of the phase. These were mostly dug as quarry pits and filled with rubbish, with some of them cutting the phase I enclosure gullies. The pit complex in the centre of the site was only partly filled in when it was covered with soil and the phase III structure built on top. An Antonine to 3rd-century date is indicated.

Phase III (fig 83)

[M1:G6] Structure HA, a post-built rectangular building, 12m long, was erected on top of the phase II pits. It may also date to late in the 2nd century or to the 3rd century. The east side of the building faced onto street C; the west side probably lay outside the excavated area. The packing stones of the postholes included burnt stone and stone roofing slabs, which also occurred in small groups on the surface. The irregular spacing of the postholes suggests that some of the posts were replaced during the lifetime of the structure. There may have been an entrance on the east side and there is some suggestion of posts set in front of the main wall-line. Inside, the building was floored with cobbles.

Table 5   Site H and trenches B I extension and B IA: phases, dates, and main features

Phase	Features	Date
I	enclosure system	1st C to Hadrianic
II	slots and pits	Antonine to 3rd C
III	building HA, well	Antonine to 3rd C
IV	filling of well	mid- to late 4th C

Two groups of postholes of uncertain date and function lay at the south end of the trench (see general plan, fig 80, B I 47–51, H I 22–5).

A well was excavated in trench B IA (fig 84, plate 8). It was 0.85m in diameter and was lined with stone to its full depth of 3.75m. Finds from the fill of the construction shaft suggest a late 2nd-century to early 3rd-century date for the digging of the well.

Phase IV

[M1:G8] The finds from the bottom of the well dated to the mid- to late 4th century, indicating that it had been repeatedly cleaned during its lifetime (fig 84). The silt at the bottom of the well covered two small, uninscribed stone altars and other finds included the bones of bird, dog, horse, and pig, fragments of wood, walnuts, and glass, an iron object, a piece of tufa, a pierced piece of sandstone, a quernstone, flue tiles, and roof tiles. The assemblage is similar to those from the wells at Bar Hill, Carrawburgh, Wroxeter (Ross 1968) and, in the territory of the Dobunni, Lower Slaughter (Green 1976, 175). It may be regarded as a religious dedication and associated offerings. Deposits blocking the upper part of the well included a human vertebra and a human phalanx.

Sites H, B I extension, and B IA phase dates

Most of the coarse pottery from site H consisted of local grey wares and Severn Valley wares. Black-Burnished ware also appeared in considerable quantities, and there were a dozen or more Malvernian sherds dated to the 2nd century, mostly appearing in phases II and III.

Plate 8   Site B IA, phase III, well B IA 25, looking south-west. Scale in 1in (25mm) divisions (see also figs 83–4)

The table wares present on the site in the form of flagons, jugs, beakers, cups, and samian-derived bowls were mostly produced in fine Severn Valley wares, while the remaining vessel types were utilitarian, with jar forms (particularly storage jars and cooking pots), large tankards, and bowls predominant.

Phase I: 1st century to Hadrianic

On site H there is Flavian–Trajanic samian from H I **28**. There is also a white butt beaker (Part 2, fig 42, no W.25, H I **27**) and a late 1st- to early 2nd-century grey ware jar (R.143, H I **33**). In site B there is a Hadrianic–Antonine Black-Burnished BB1 jar from B I 35 (B.3) and *mortaria* dating to AD 100 on. There are no datable non-ceramic finds.

A 1st-century to Hadrianic date range would seem to cover the phase in both areas.

Phase II: Antonine to 3rd century

In site H there is a good collection of Hadrianic–Antonine material. The latest samian is dated *c* AD 150–80 from context H II 74A. There are Antonine or later Malvernian vessels from contexts H II 49 and 80 (R.89 and R.91) and later 2nd- to 3rd-century Severn Valley ware from contexts H I 7 and 19 and H II 49 and 74A (O.265). There are also 3rd- to 4th-century wide-mouthed Severn Valley ware jars (O.136) from contexts H II 74 and 80 and an everted-rimmed shell-tempered ware jar (R.111) from H II 74. The latter, at least, may be intrusive, or this feature must have continued to be filled until the late 3rd century.

In site B the latest samian recorded is dated *c* AD 150–80, from B I **16**. The coarse ware includes much Hadrianic–Antonine material, a considerable quantity of 2nd- to 3rd-century Severn Valley ware (O.193, O.166, O.274, O.278, O.279, O.282, O.344, O.380, O.287, B I 3; O.265, B I **16**), and a 3rd-century Severn Valley ware flanged bowl (O.345) from B I 3 together with an obtuse-lattice-decorated dish (R.389). Two *mortaria* from B I 3 may date to the early to mid-2nd century. There are also a painted candlestick (W.47, B I 3), a painted Dr 38 copy (O.422, B I 3), and a wide-mouthed Severn Valley ware jar (O.150, B I 3) which could be intrusive but would probably not be out of place in a phase extending from the Antonine period to the mid-3rd century.

The coin (cat no 92) of Claudius II found in the pit B I 3 must be regarded as intrusive, perhaps introduced when B I **2** was cut through the earlier pit.

Overall the phase would seem to have an Antonine to 3rd-century span.

Phase III: Antonine to 3rd century on

None of the fairly small collection from sites H and B of this phase is later than that from phase II. The latest material is three Severn Valley ware tankards (O.274) with 2nd- to early 3rd-century parallels from H II 6A, 68 and **91** and an Oxfordshire *mortarium* from B IV 3.

Phase IV: mid- to late 4th century

The pottery representing this phase all comes from the use of the well on site B. Alongside residual 2nd- to 3rd-century material are a shell-tempered ware jar (R.43) from B IA *13*, an Oxfordshire C77 *c* AD 340–400+ from B IA *15*, and a flanged bowl (R.432) from B IA *15*.

There are also two coins from the well (cat nos 391, AD 351–3; and 397, AD 364–78) suggesting a mid- to late 4th-century date for the phase.

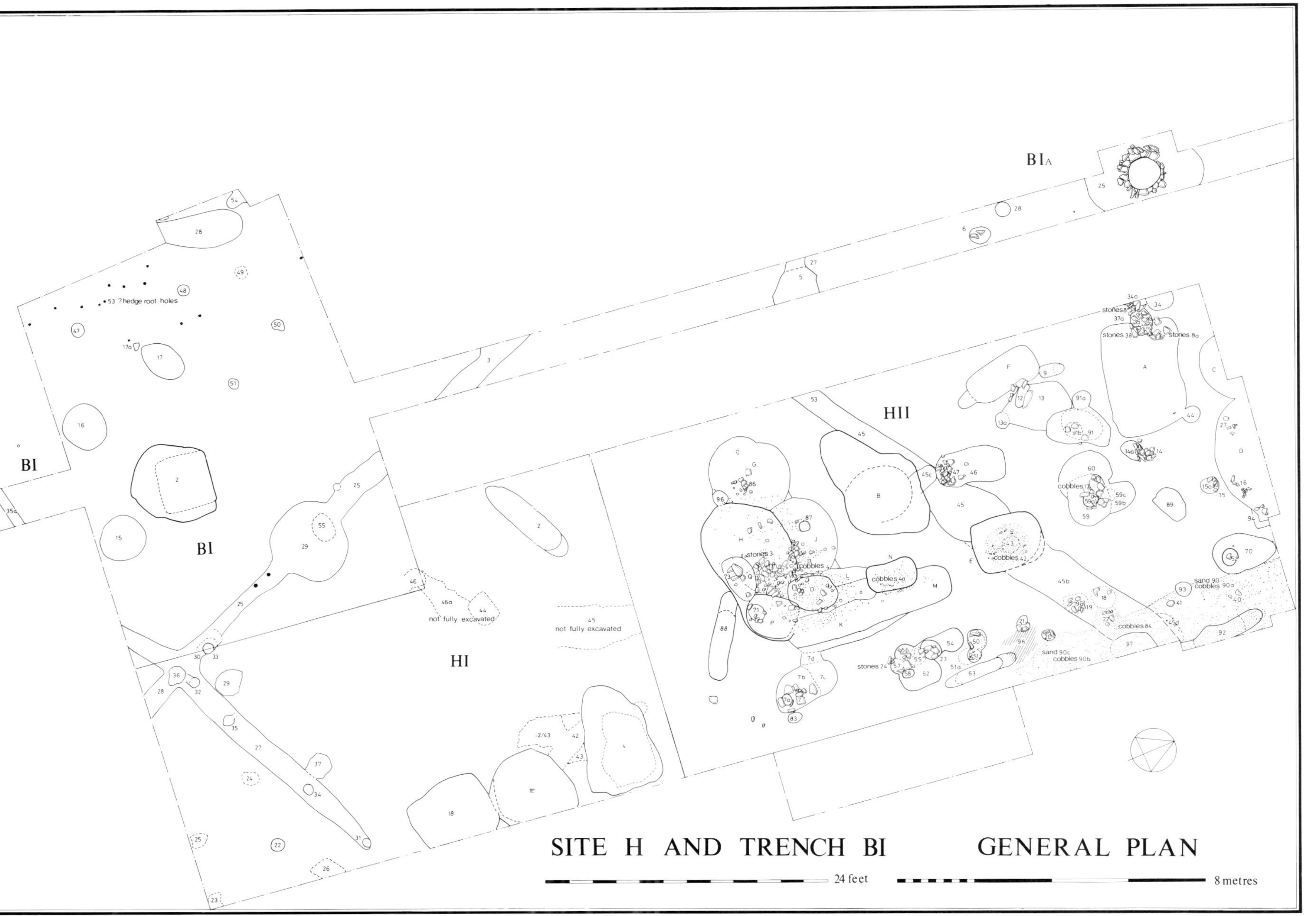

Figure 80 Site H and trench B I, general plan

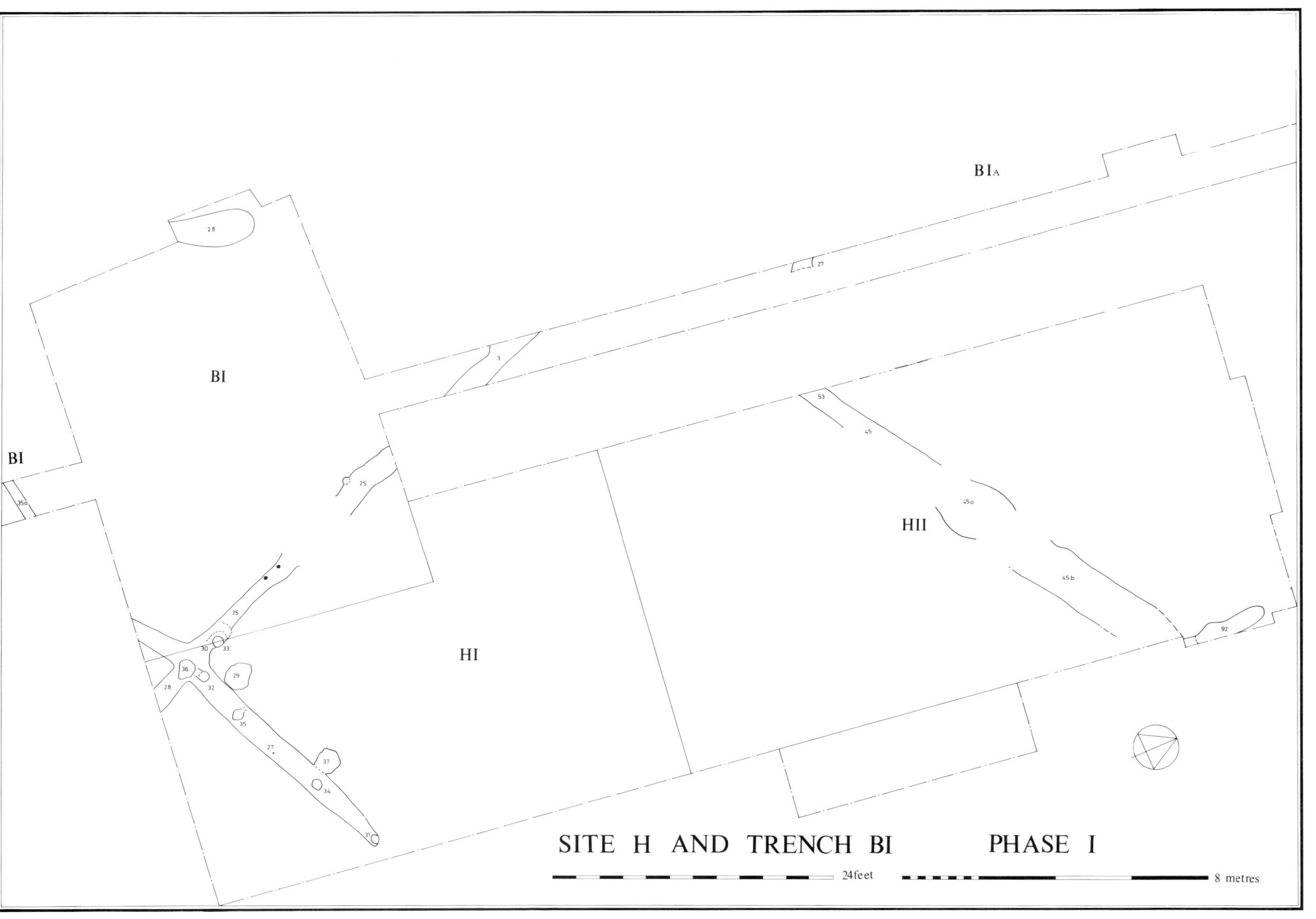

Figure 81 Site H and trench B I, phase I

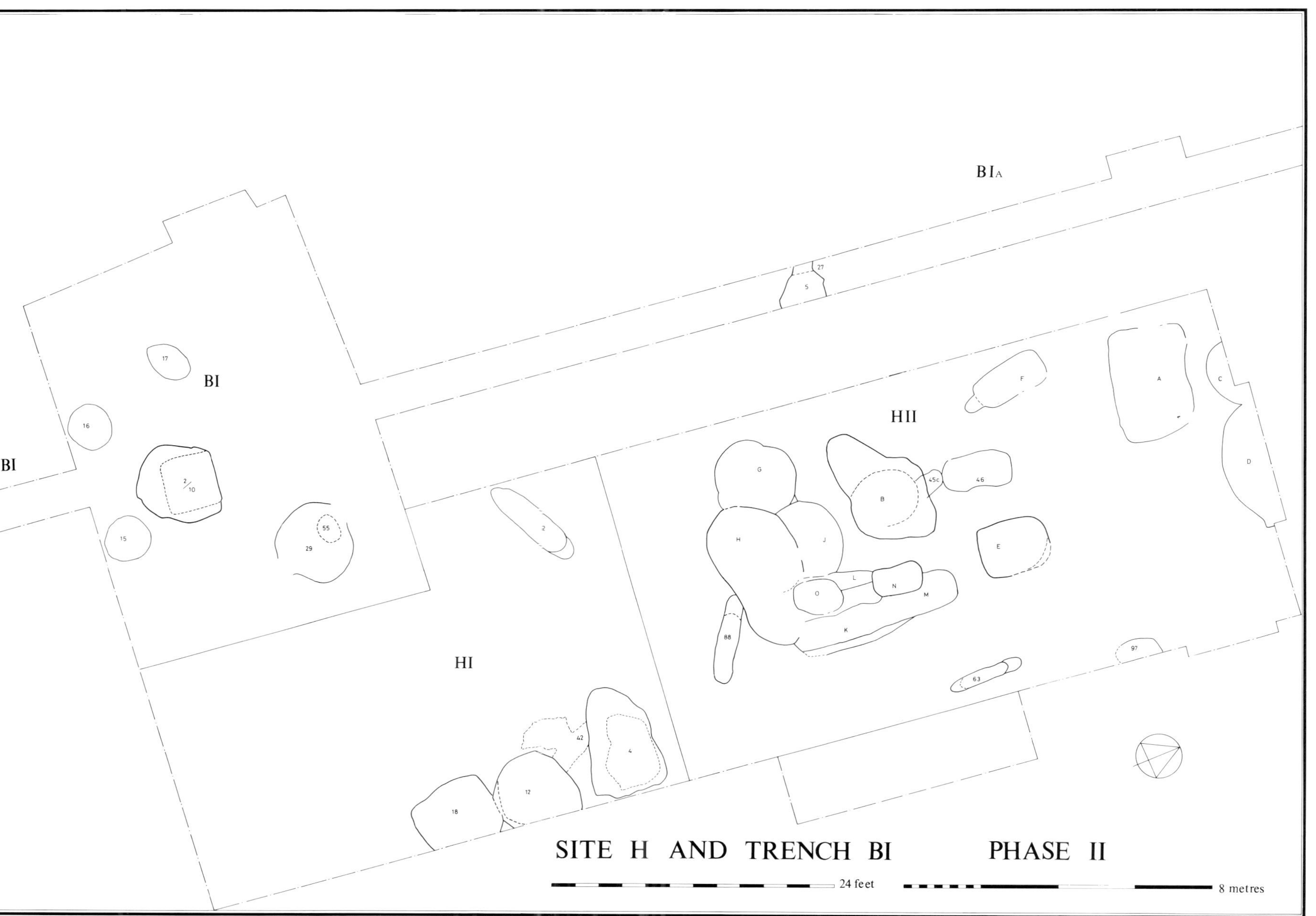

Figure 82   Site H and trench B I, phase II

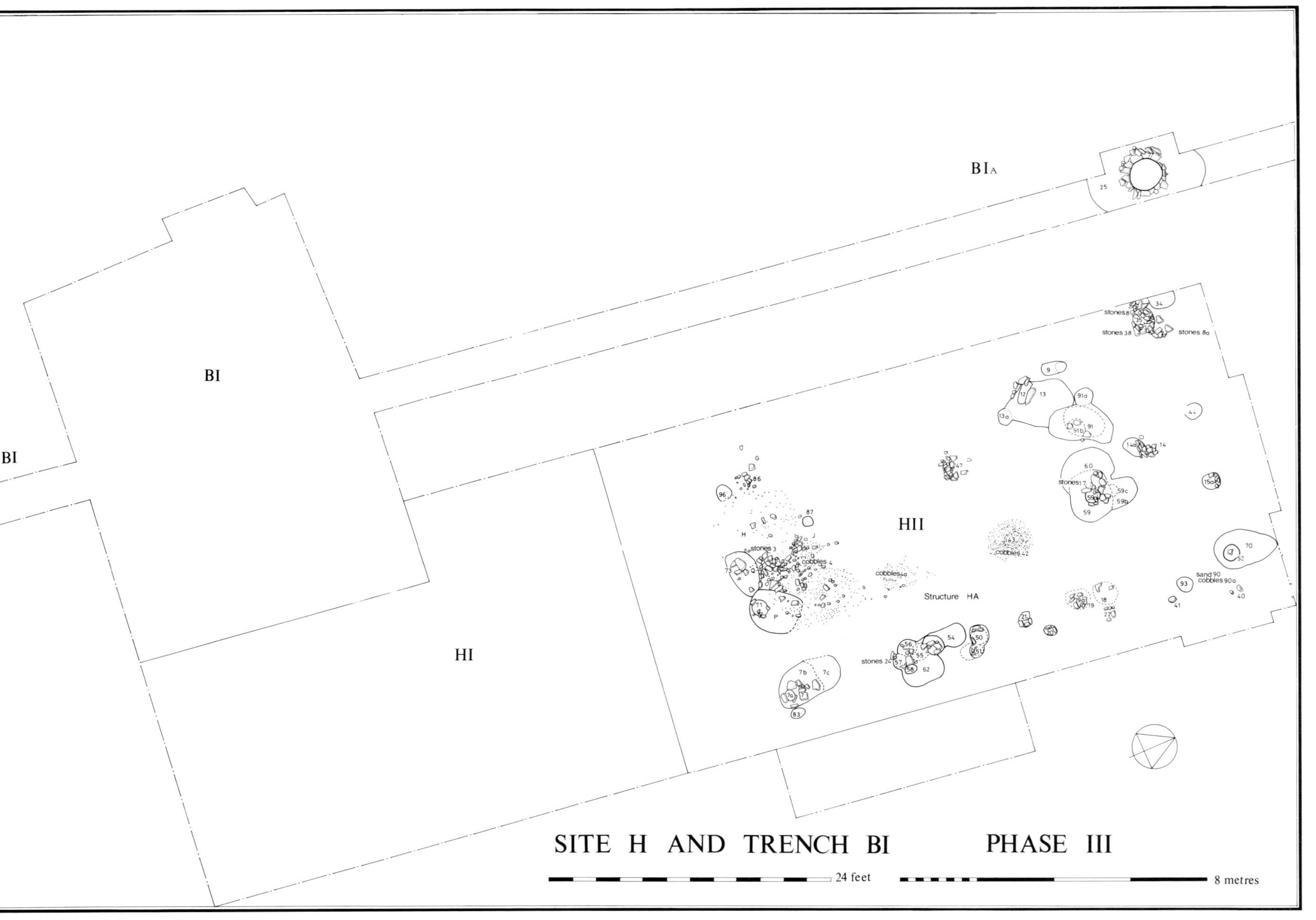

Figure 83   Site H and trench B I, phase III

112

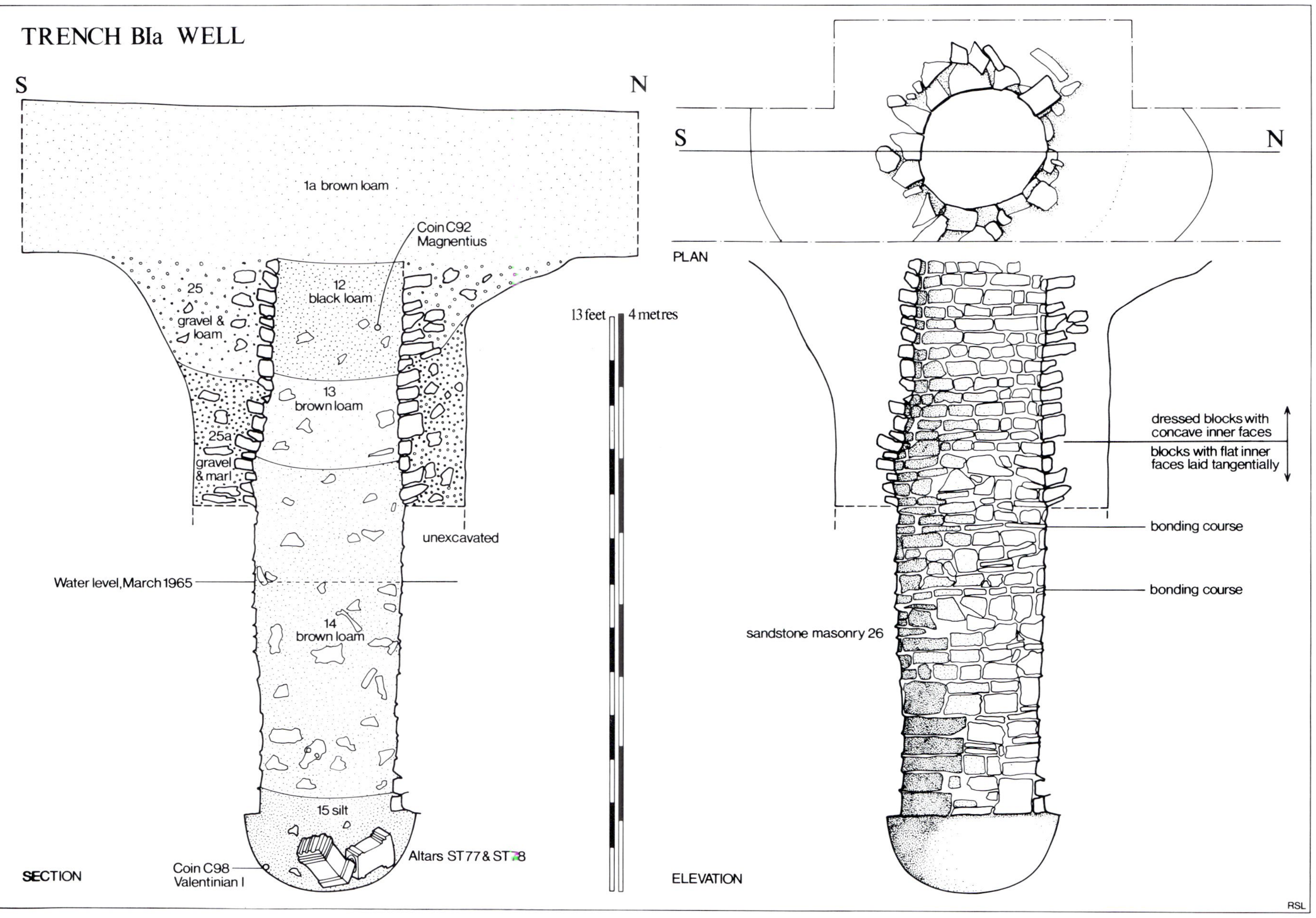

Figure 84 Trench B IA, well (phases III and IV) (plan: fig 83)

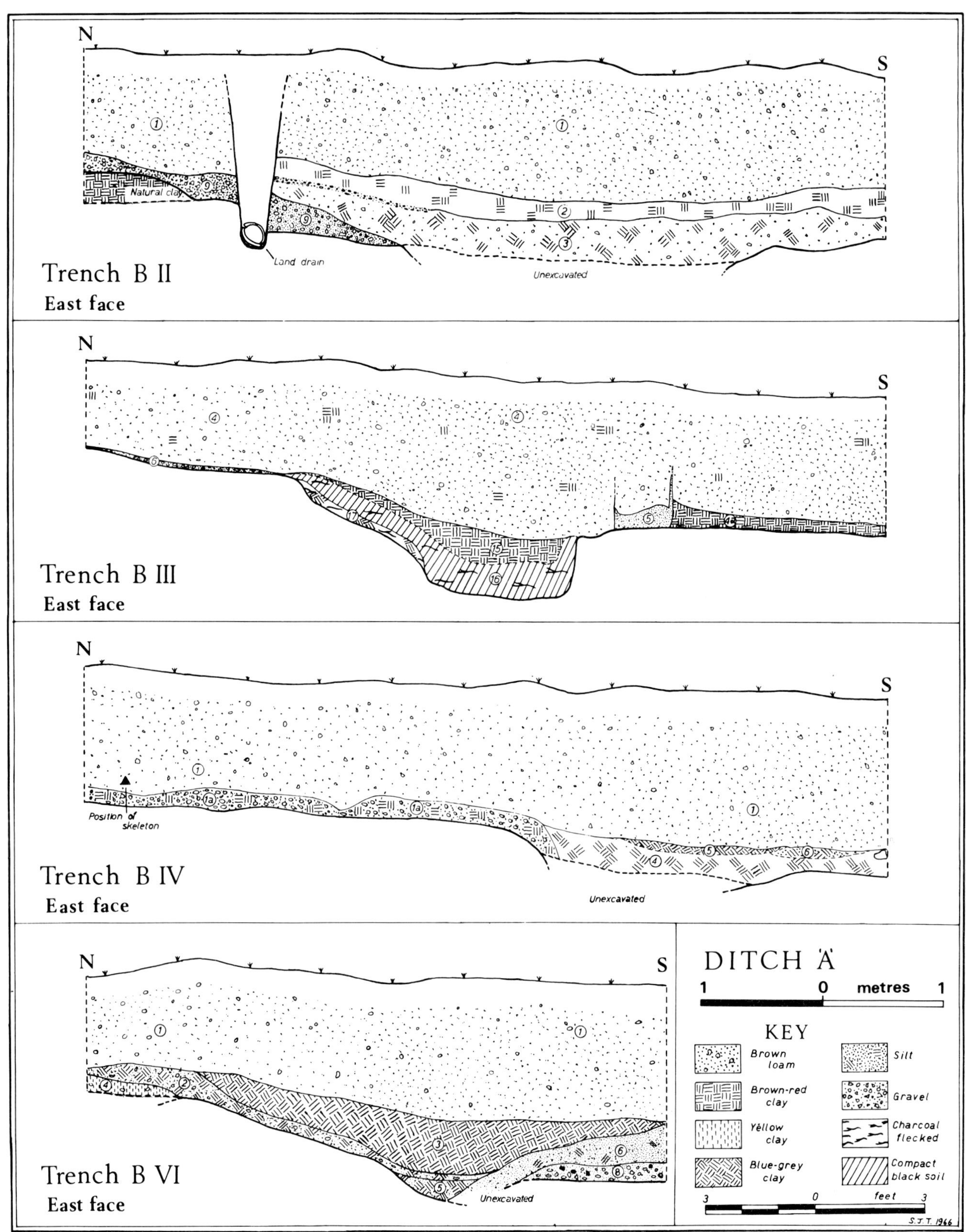

Figure 85 Ditch A sections. Trench B II, east face; trench B III, east face; trench B IV, east face; trench B VI, east face (plan: fig 4)

Site G

E Allnut and Christine Mahany

[M1:G10] Site G was located immediately south of the line of the east–west Roman road, street A, which connected *Salinae* (Droitwich) to the Fosse Way (fig 3 no **38**, and figs 4, 5, 86–8; sections in fig 100). This is marked by the line of the modern lane which runs between Bleachfield Street and Birch Abbey. The large, rich building of villa type excavated by H V Hughes lay to the west.

An area of approximately 600sq m was excavated, divided into five main cuttings separated by baulks, some of which were later removed. A further extension to the north, G IIIA, was started but not investigated thoroughly. Trenches IA and II were not fully excavated.

The interpretation of site G as a whole was difficult as the structures recovered appeared to have no obvious parallels in Roman Britain. The north-west area of the site contained flimsy, timber structures frequently replaced and probably of agricultural function while in the south-east area a series of large, substantially built structures were found. These were at least partially surrounded by a ditch, showing several phases of rebuilding (figs 86–8).

Ten phases of activity were identified starting in the late 2nd to 3rd century and continuing without a break into at least the late 4th century. Phases V–X were all later 4th century and the construction, rebuilding, and destruction of one major building and the associated outbuildings all took place within the last third of the 4th century or later.

Table 6 Site G: phases, dates, and main features

Phase	Features	Date
I	building GA; ditch	late 2nd to mid-3rd C
II	building GA; ditches; fence	mid-3rd C
III	building GA; building GB	mid-3rd to 4th C
IV	building GC; building GD; ditch; slots	early 4th C
V	destruction of GC; minor features	late 4th C
VI	building GE; building GF	late 4th C
VII	building GE; building GG	late 4th C
VIII	building GE; building GH; ?burial	late 4th C
IX	building GE; building GJ	late 4th C
X	destruction; burials	late 4th C

The function of these almost-monumental buildings is problematic. In the absence of any more plausible interpretations, a religious function is not impossible, although negative evidence, ie the absence of cult objects or features, may be significant.

The proximity of the villa-type building in sites T and Tw to the west, with an exterior surface of pebbles similar to the surface seen in G I, suggests a connection between these two buildings. However, the absence of any reliable stratigraphy or dating from sites T and Tw dictates caution in such an interpretation.

Phase I (fig 89)

[M1:G10] The earliest feature on the site was the construction of building GA in the south-east corner, and the digging of the associated ditch to the north-west at least partially surrounding it. In later phases buildings GC and GE were also built on this alignment, and GC was also associated with a ditch. Rubbish pits were dug to the north-east of the building and in trenches I and II. Building GA, represented by a number of slots and postholes, was standing throughout phases I–III (figs 89–91), whilst new structures were erected to the north and west. Although much disturbed by later features, it clearly presaged the more substantial buildings of later phases. It was represented by a partly doubled east–west wall, perhaps of wattle and daub construction. There is some evidence that the walls were treated with plaster. Building GA was demolished with the structures of phase III prior to the building of GC in phase IV.

Phase II (fig 90)

[M1:G12] The features of phase II were located in trenches I and IA, and were contemporary with the continued life of building GA. They comprised a series of boundary ditches, perhaps to be associated with agriculture or stock control, G I 175/181/173, G I 129, G IA 72. A north–south fence bisected trench G I terminating on the north edge of the existing ditch, which had been at least partially filled in, for a further ditch was dug through its lower fill. This ditch had posts along either side and terminated at its junction with the phase I ditch. Other features consisted of postholes, stakeholes, and small pits.

Phase III (fig 91)

[M1:G13] As with phase II, the features of phase III were contemporary with building GA. They comprised a series of slots in G I incompletely delineating a structure GB, with a funnel entrance. Though this may suggest an agricultural function, perhaps for the control of animals, the many sherds of pottery storage jars with graffiti recovered from later phases from this area may rather suggest storage. A hearth was located to the south-west of the building.

Note: an alternative interpretation of phases I–III can be found in the microfiche. This places building

GA in phase II instead of phase I, but the interpretation given here is preferred.

Phase IV (fig 92)

[M2:A2] The destruction layer and associated patches of burning which resulted from the demolition of structures GA and GB were assigned to this phase. The demolition was followed by the features associated with the construction of the large building GC. This building occupied a similar position to its predecessor, GA, and to its successor, GE; like GA, it was at least partially surrounded by a ditch. The building was characterized by a combination of building techniques — multiple posts, some in common pits, and a stone foundation which was later completely removed, presumably for reuse in building GE. It was provided with plastered walls, a hearth, an entrance in the north wall, and an external surface to the west.

There were two elements in the construction: groups of postholes and a foundation trench. Both elements were found together only in the south-west corner and in a small part of the north wall. Otherwise, the building was constructed from posthole groups; here the destruction material in the trench was found over the tops of the holes left by the decaying posts. In construction, therefore, the post-pits were dug first, the posts erected and then the foundation trench dug and filled with stones which were packed around the edges of the posts. Why this unusual construction technique — unparalleled in Roman Britain — should have been adopted cannot be conjectured. The combination of the two elements in the south-west corner may have arisen from a need to strengthen this area. During the destruction of this building the posts were sawn off, and the stumps left to rot in the ground.

The insubstantial nature of the south wall in relation to the others was also very curious. It has been conjectured that the building may have been provided with an open colonnade, but the inclemency of the British winters, and the presence of a hearth and plastered walls, suggest that protection from the elements was a primary consideration and that the wall was filled in. A series of overlapping horizontal planks attached to the posts is a possible construction for this south wall. The planks may have been threaded between the multiple posts in each individual posthole. Otherwise, a timber frame infilled with wattle and daub was presumably built between the posts and on top of the stone foundations in the trenches. Plaster would then have been applied to the daub. However, it should be noted that the paucity of daub recovered makes this interpretation somewhat doubtful.

Wall plaster from this area (see 'Wall plaster', Part 2, p 221) had a predominant theme of yellow ground with stripes and geometrical shapes in red, white, and sometimes pink. Some convex fragments could have come from a window opening or alcove. The building might have been roofed from two conjoining ridges, probably with thatch or shingles. Though tiles were found in small numbers, the south wall appears too insubstantial to have supported such a heavy roof.

North-west of the ditch, in the area G I, were several possible agricultural structures perhaps associated with building GC. Two walls joining at right-angles (GD) define a structure which lay largely beyond the excavated area. They were found associated with drains and postholes cutting a substantial cobble surface.

A number of pits and postholes were also found. There is some evidence that the foundation trenches originally contained the lias blocks which were reused in building GE (phase VI).

Phase V (fig 93)

[M2:A8] The destruction material resulting from the demolition of building GC and its associated outbuildings was found in all areas of the site and also filled the top of the curving phase IV enclosure ditch (fig 92). Areas of burning in G I and G IA were also associated with this destruction. Two ovens with a surrounding clay floor were found in G II. Further minor slots, pits, etc, were found in G I along with the walls of GD (phase IV) which were still standing. This indicates a lack of renewed building activity in phase V.

Phase VI (fig 94)

[M2:A9] Short-lived features between the destruction of GC and the construction of GE were found in trenches G II and G III. A series of postholes delineating a square structure, GF, were found in area G II, G II 17, 11, 10, 16, 24, 19, 20, 21, 15. This structure was possibly contemporary with the construction of building GE or may have been a temporary hut antedating GE's construction. Doubtful stratigraphy in this area made the phasing of these features difficult, and they are therefore included under phase VI.

Building GE was a sturdy and substantial structure, and represented the third and last phase of the building initiated in phase I (GA) and continued in a different form in phase IV (GC). The phase VI building continued the tradition of peculiar plan and construction method noted in the earlier phases. Five large lias-packed postholes linked by a shallow trench formed the west wall. The east wall also had pits and a trench, but here the lias blocks were deposited in a haphazard way, without the careful packing of the west wall (plate 9). Patches of lias blocks irregularly filled a shallow trench in the north wall. The south end of the building was less well defined but was suggested by scattered blocks of lias perhaps representing a disturbed foundation at ground level. There was evidence, in a wall trench, of the south-west corner of the building repeating the dog-leg pattern seen in GC. The very uneven surface of the lias groups in the north and east walls makes it difficult to suggest what kind of structure they could have supported. Some kind of levelling off at a higher level must be assumed. Various possible interpretations are discussed in the microfiche. A

Plate 9   Site G IV, phases VI–IX, east wall of
structure GE, G IV 15, looking south-west. Scale
in 1ft (0.30m) divisions (see also figs 94, 95,
97, 98)

Plate 10   Site G IV, phases VI–IX. Milestone in
north wall of structure GE, G IV 10, looking south.
Scale in 1in (25mm) divisions (see also figs 94, 95,
97, 98)

possible internal hearth was found just east of the
west wall.

Over much of the rest of the site a cobble layer was
laid down, and a series of pits was dug south of the
building.

A notable find was a milestone of Constantine (ST
174) incorporated into the lias foundation of the
north wall (plate 10).

Phases VII–IX

[M2:B4] These phases are concerned with structures
surrounding building GE described under phase VI.
Their relationship with this building is stratigraphically tenuous, but they are thought to have been used
during its life. It is thought that structure GF was by
now demolished.

It is considered that the buildings GG, GH, and GJ
were very closely related (figs 95, 97, 98). A north–
south alignment was found in all three phases,
probably representing the west wall; a posthole
construction was followed by a timber slot construction, and this was followed by a further posthole
structure. The features of GG and GJ, the first and
third structures, were aligned almost directly above
each other, but the intervening slot structure was
found some 4m to the south-west. The provision of a
water tank (fig 96) might seem to reinforce the
suggestion that this area had a primarily agricultural function associated with livestock.

A grave (HB 66) shown on the plan of phase VIII
(fig 97) may be of any date in the later life of building

GE, or may date to the period of its disuse. This is
perhaps more likely in view of the nearby presence
of a further inhumation (HB 65) assigned to phase X.
It contained the bones of an adult male, pottery, and
a fragment of glass.

Phase VII (fig 95)

[M2:B5] The major activity in this phase was the
erection of an insubstantial agricultural building,
GG, in area GI–GG, contemporary with and probably
serving GE. The walls of GD (phase IV) were
probably robbed at this stage.

Structure GG was a long narrow barn-like building
with a wattle and daub infill between the posts, G I
125, 51, 75, 26, 98, 71 (see fig 88), 86, 79 (see fig 88),
102, 146 (see fig 88), indicated by the presence of
burnt clay. The north wall was probably situated
beyond the excavated area, and the south wall
somewhere in the region of the baulk. The eastern
part of the building was provided with a red clay
floor, and there was slight evidence for a central ridge
support.

In area G IA a tank was found, sunk into the
ground, for water retention (fig 96). It was of
post-and-plank construction on a clay lining, with a
floor of limestone slabs. It could have been replen-
ished from the eavesdrip of building GE. It may have
been constructed during the lifetime of structure GG
or during either of its rebuild phases, GH and GJ.
North of the tank some miscellaneous postholes were
found.

Phase VIII (fig 97)

[M2:B9] This phase marks the rebuilding of structure GG on a similar alignment but somewhat to the west. The new building, GH, was represented by horizontal timber slots in the ground, and was provided with a cobble floor, which was divided by further slots into possible livestock pens. The walls of the building were of wattle and daub. Evidence of a possible fenced enclosure to the west in area G IA suggests a continued agricultural use, as perhaps do the traces of wattle and daub associated with the tank. This, too, may have been fenced off, to protect animals falling into it.

The human interment found south of building GE has been discussed above (phases VII–IX).

Phase IX (fig 98)

[M2:B11] In this phase building GH was replaced by a further posthole structure GJ, represented by a clear alignment of postholes extending in a northerly direction from the north-west corner of the still-surviving tank. Since this so closely mirrored the alignment and nature of the building described under phase VII (GG, fig 95), it is very probable that this structure too had an east wall. However, structure GH was insufficiently clearly stratified in the area where the east wall might have been expected for it to be entirely clear whether some of the postholes of GG should properly be assigned to this period. The presence of oolitic limestone and lias limestone in and to the west of the structure may suggest destruction material from stone footings, but nowhere could these be defined.

Phase X (fig 99)

[M2:B13] This phase marks the last stage of activity on the site. A thick widespread demolition layer was found, originating from the destruction of building GE and structure GJ. It filled the tank, suggesting that up to this time the tank had remained open. Some of the destruction material, which included pierced limestone roofing tiles and possible hypocaust tiles, may well have been derived from the villa-like building excavated by Hughes to the west of the site (see fig 12).

The area was then used for burial. Four graves were found containing three infant and two adult burials. The adult male had been buried wearing nailed sandals. This grave also contained a colour-coated beaker. Another grave contained the bodies of an adult female and infant, perhaps mother and child. For further discussion, see microfiche and 'Birch Abbey burials' below (p 144).

The topsoil above site G contained unstratified material including coins with a latest date of Valentinian I (367–75).

Site G phase dates

Site G contained several lightly built structures in the north-west of the site, possibly with an agricultural function. In the south-east there was a succession of substantially built structures at least partially surrounded by a ditch.

The pottery was mostly residual with equal proportions of local grey, Severn Valley, and Black-Burnished wares. The fine wares from the site were scarce, with a handful of white wares appearing in phase IV onwards. The remaining table wares were mainly the products of the late British fine ware industries, including Oxfordshire, Nene Valley, South-Western brown slip, and local colour-coated vessels. There were a couple of Rhenish beakers appearing in phases IV and V which were presumably residual. The local grey wares and Severn Valley potters were producing the utilitarian vessels in demand by the community, with jars and bowls predominating.

Site G is interesting in that it contains a very high proportion of storage jars in comparison with the other sites at Birch Abbey, suggesting that the structures were providing some form of storage facility.

The remaining third of the vessels were Black-Burnished wares. These appear in fluctuating quantities, but with a notable increase during the 4th century. This illustrates the strength of the Black-Burnished industry until the end of the Roman occupation at Alcester and also reflects the decline in the amount of local wares being produced in the later period.

Phase I: late 2nd/3rd century

The earliest activity on site G was the construction of building GA and the digging of the associated ditch and rubbish pits.

The vessels appearing in this phase were all utilitarian vessels with Black-Burnished ware the only fabric not produced locally. The vessel forms were predominantly containers, for example storage jars.

This phase includes two contexts with pre-Flavian samian (G IA **85**, G IV **38**), one of which also contains late 2nd- to 3rd-century samian (G IV **38**). The coarse pottery, alongside 1st-century material, includes Hadrianic–Antonine vessels from G IV **38** and 58 and G II 14 (R.94, R.173, R.205, B.5, B.39, and B.60) and an Antonine vessel (R.99) from G IV **38**.

The only datable non-ceramic was a 3rd-century Henig type IX copper alloy ring (cat no 5). This was found in a pit, G IV **41**. The stratigraphic position of this pit is uncertain and the recovery of the ring suggests it could be placed in phase II.

There was a significant concentration of 1st-century coins and brooches on site G, although not from contexts attributed to phase I. Four (cat nos 1, 40, 44, and 45) of the nine iron brooches from the excavations were found there and three (cat nos 1, 3, and 5) of the five Dobunnic coins.

This seems to indicate a late 2nd/3rd-century range for the phase. Intrusive medieval sherds were discovered in pit G IV 46.

Phase II: mid-3rd century

The features from this phase were contemporary with building GA and were represented by a series of boundaries with the digging of a new ditch. The latest recorded material is Hadrianic–Antonine (R.96 and R.205) from G I **173** and G I **150**. There was no useful non-ceramic dating evidence. Presumably the phase is mid-3rd century or later. In slot G I *175*/175A there was an intrusive medieval sherd.

Phase III: 3rd/4th century

The features in phase III represented a series of slots delineating a structure, GB, contemporary with building GA. The pottery was again scarce, and included one intrusive sherd in feature G I 178 dating to the medieval period. The coarse grey utilitarian vessels predominated with one Black-Burnished and one Malvernian example. The latest vessel is a 2nd- to 3rd-century reduced Severn Valley ware form (R.44) from G V **46**. There was no non-ceramic dating evidence. Intrusive medieval sherds were found in the charcoal layer G I 178.

Phase IV: early to mid-4th century

The foundation trench G IV **24** for building GC provided material dating to the later 3rd or early 4th century (B.20, later 3rd century and CW.13, 4th century). There were also three Black-Burnished BB1 bowls dated to the late 3rd to mid-4th centuries from the phase (B.50, G I **105** and G IV **24**; B.54, G I *105*). The majority of the vessel forms were storage jars and jars, with four sherds of *amphorae*, suggesting that building GC and its related structures had some storage function.

The non-ceramics included two 4th-century glass fragments (cat nos GL 190, 193) and two coins. One of the coins (cat no 207), which was dated to AD 330–1, came from the eastern wall trench of structure GC, G V **26**. The other (cat no 344), dated to AD 353 on, came from the wall of structure GD, G I *2*. A further significant factor is the inclusion of a Constantinian milestone (dated after AD 337) in the foundations of structure GE in phase VI. The similarity of the plans of GC and GE indicates that they were not far separated in time.

The phase is early to mid-4th century.

Phase V: later 4th century

This phase contained the destruction material from the demolition of building GC. The pottery contained some late Roman wares, for example British colour-coated vessels produced in the Oxfordshire kilns (C.49, dated *c* AD 300–400), but is in the main residual, with some intrusive medieval sherds, suggesting that the material from this phase was disturbed. Amongst a mass of 1st- and 2nd-century material there is a late 3rd to 4th-century Severn Valley ware jar (O.136) from G IV *12* and another of 4th-century date (O.281) from G V *7*.

There were ten coins from phase V contexts:

Cat no	Date	Context no	Context description
99	270	G IV *12*	destruction of GC
119	273+	G IV *12*	destruction of GC
227	341–6	G II **6**	oven
269	337–40	G IV 2	destruction of GC
312	353–4	G IV *12*	destruction of GC
379	335–41	G IV *12*	destruction of GC
412	367–75	G I *106A*	destruction fill in ditch
421	388–402	G IV *12*	destruction of GC
438	4th C	G IV *12*	destruction of GC
439	4th C	G IA *60*	?destruction of GC

Although the latest dated coin is AD 388–402 it would be unwise to take this as a *terminus post quem* for the destruction of GC since destruction deposits in general are not well sealed and can be contaminated. However, the coin and pottery assemblages together provide a reliably later 4th-century date for the phase.

Three sherds of intrusive medieval and post-medieval pottery were found in G IV *12*, G I **97**, and G I **92**.

Phase VI: late 4th century

This phase saw the excavation of a series of short-lived pits followed by the construction of building GE. Black-Burnished ware was the predominant fabric type, although local grey and Severn Valley wares appeared in considerable quantities. Most of the material appears to have been residual, with the numismatic evidence providing a late 4th-century date. The latest pottery, apart from some early to mid-4th-century Black-Burnished BB1, is 4th-century Severn Valley ware tankards (O.281) from G V **107** and G V **100**, shell-tempered ware vessels (R.43 and R.437) from contexts G IV **23** and G IV **33**, an Oxfordshire beaker (C.38) from G V **6** and a South-Western brown slipped ware sherd (C.36) from G IA *17*.

The non-ceramic dating evidence is provided by a milestone and three coins. The milestone (cat no 1) must originally have been erected elsewhere during the reign of Constantine I and is unlikely to have been moved until well after the end of his reign in AD 337. It was then reused as part of the foundations of structure GE. The coins (cat nos 302, 352, 384) have dates of AD 337–40, 353+, and 350–1 respectively. Of these no 302 was the most useful, coming from the wall trench of structure GE, G IA **25**.

This phase is securely dated as late 4th century.

Phase VII: late 4th century

There was very little pottery found in association with the features from this phase, which saw the construction of an insubstantial building, GG, and the digging of a tank. All of it was residual. The non-ceramic evidence was equally unhelpful and the dating relies on the date of phase VI.

Phase VIII: late 4th century

This phase saw the rebuilding of the phase VII structure as structure GH. All of the pottery was residual and of 1st- and 2nd-century date. The single coin (cat no 408) from cobble layers in building GH, G I *12*, was dated as AD 367–75, confirming the late 4th-century date for the phase derived from the date of previous phases.

Phase IX: late 4th century

This saw the second rebuilding of the phase VII structure, with a post construction GJ. The pottery, amongst much residual material, included a shell-tempered ware bowl (R.112) from G I **7** and Oxfordshire beakers of Young's (1977) types C16 and C31 (C.10 and C.39) from G I **24**.

Further confirmatory dating evidence was provided by two mid-4th-century coins (cat nos 234 and 374) from a cobble surface, G IA *2*, although this was not strongly linked with structure GJ. Again, the date relies largely on the date of phase VI.

Phase X: late 4th century

Phase X saw the last stage of activity on the site when it was predominantly a demolition area. The only non-residual vessels recorded from this phase are an Oxfordshire beaker (C.3) from G III 2 and a late shell-tempered ware jar from G IA 21. There was one mid-4th-century coin (cat no 375). The date is extrapolated from phase VI.

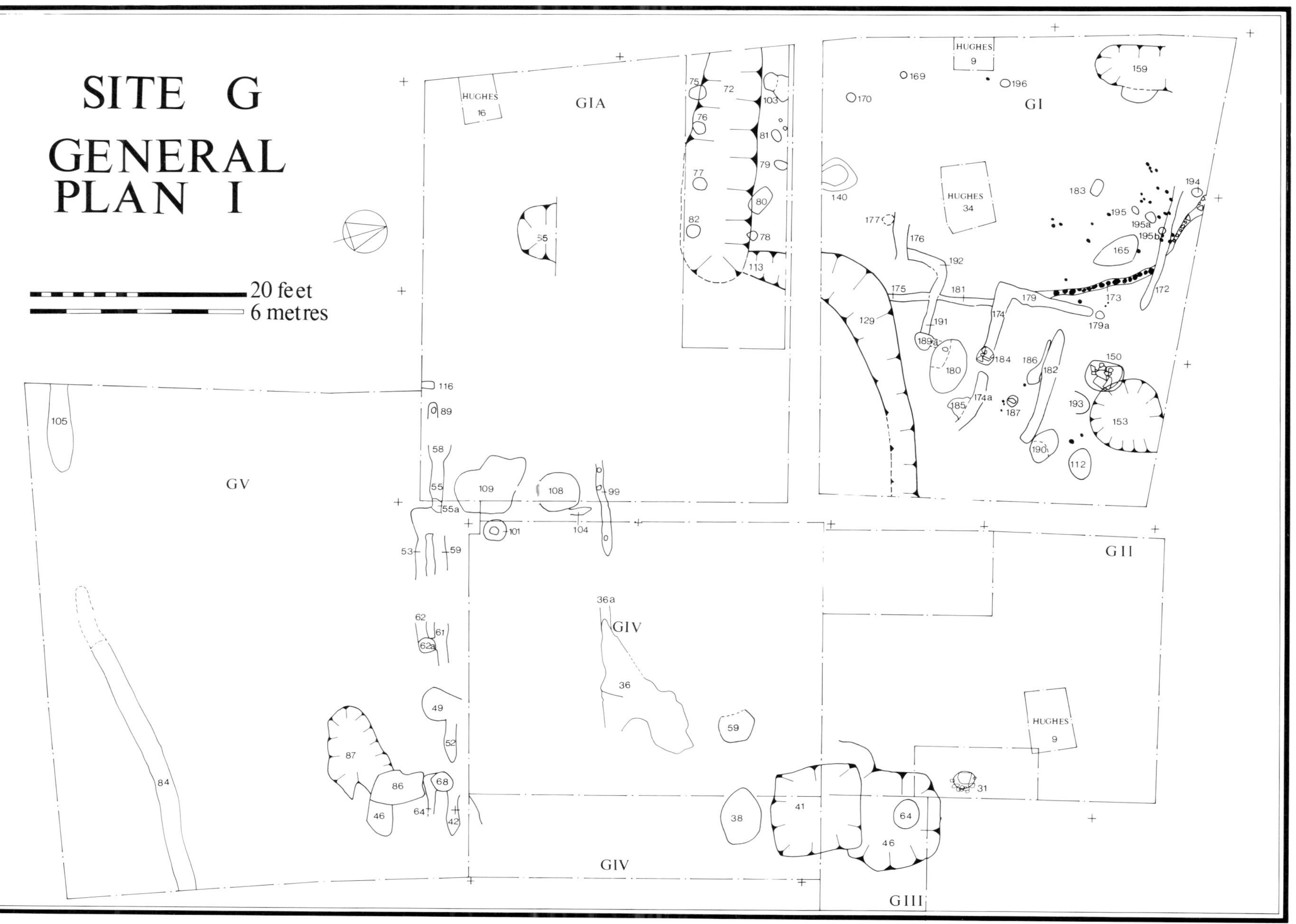

Figure 86 Site G, general plan I

121

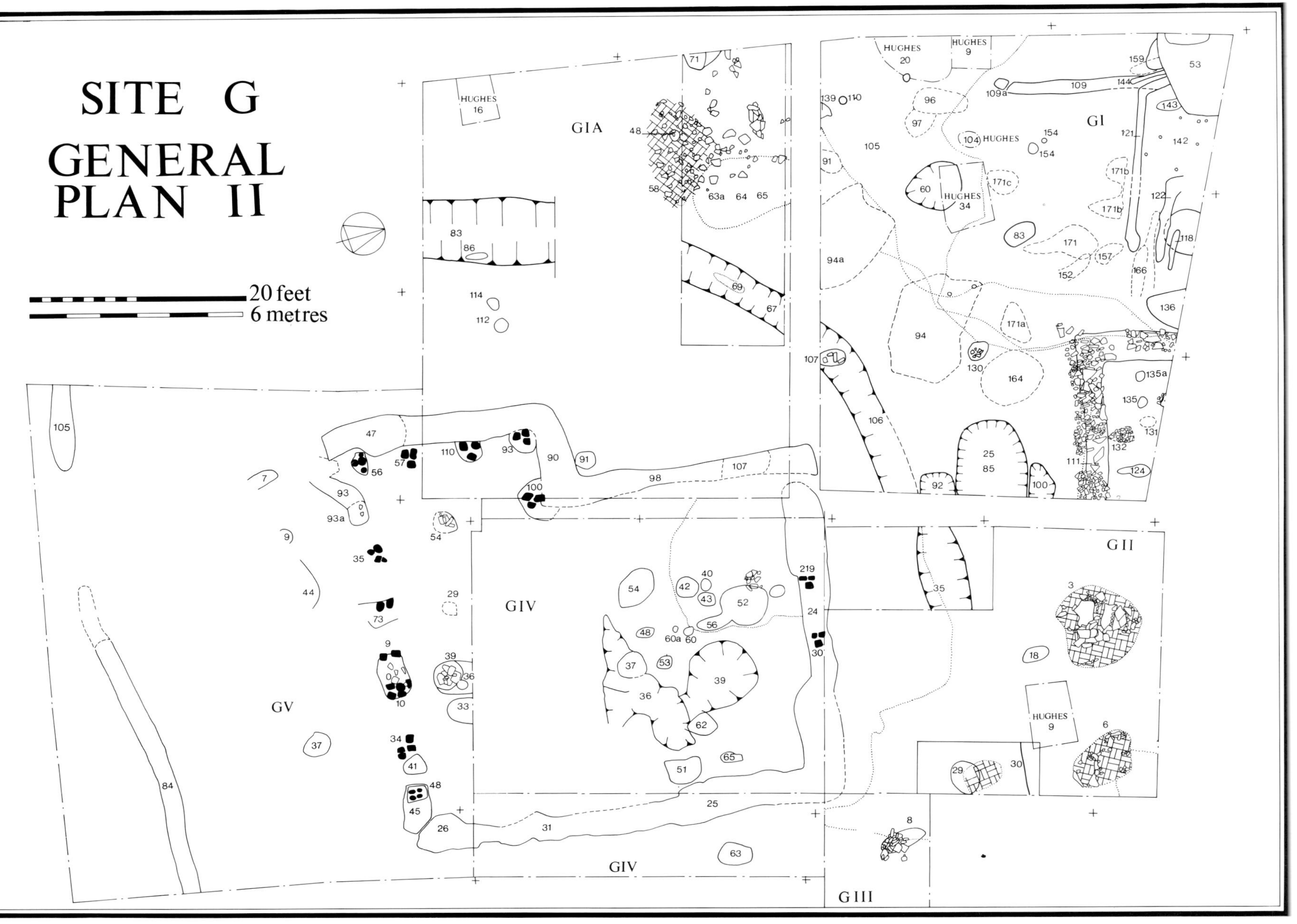

Figure 87 Site G, general plan II

122

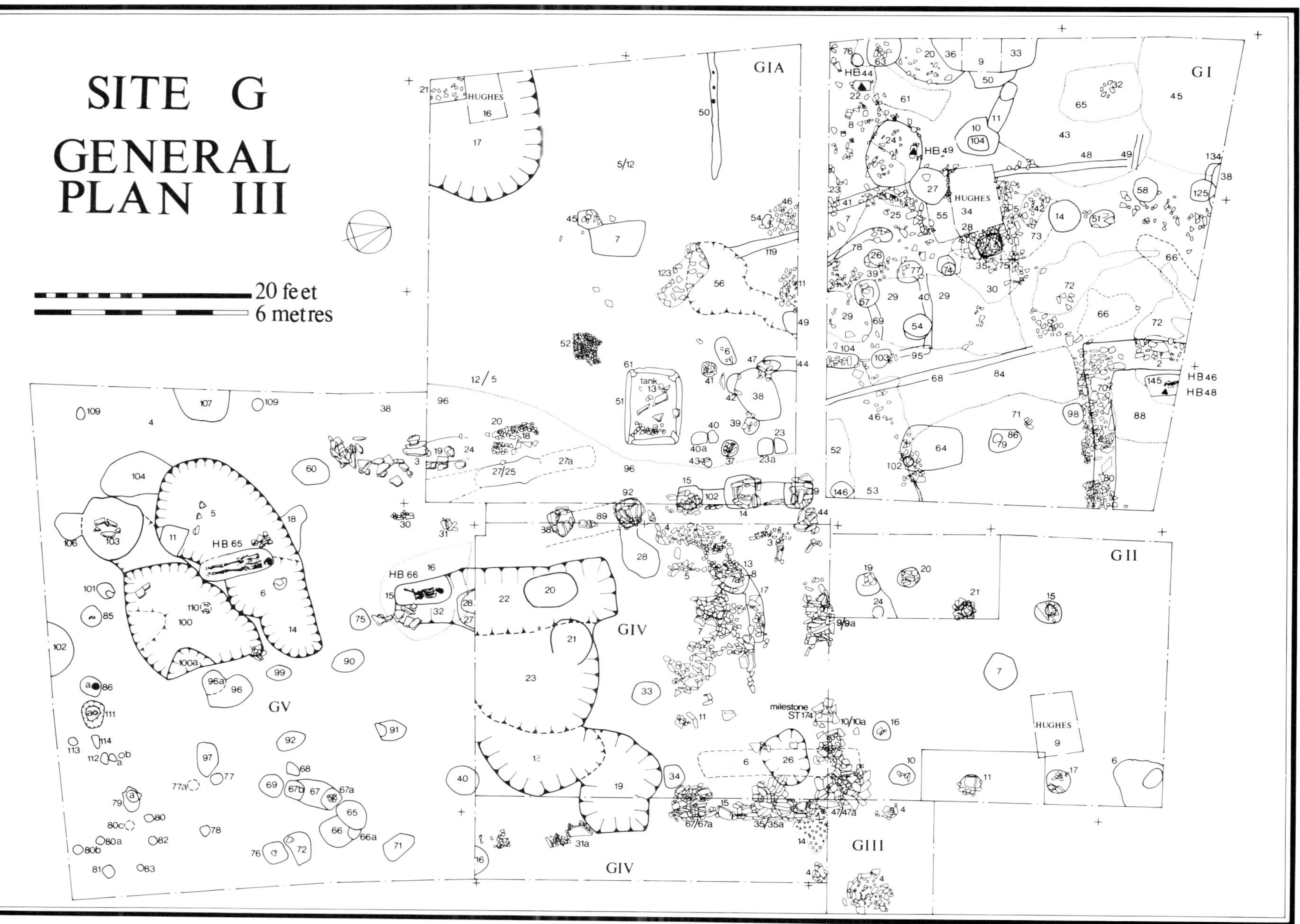

Figure 88 Site G, general plan III

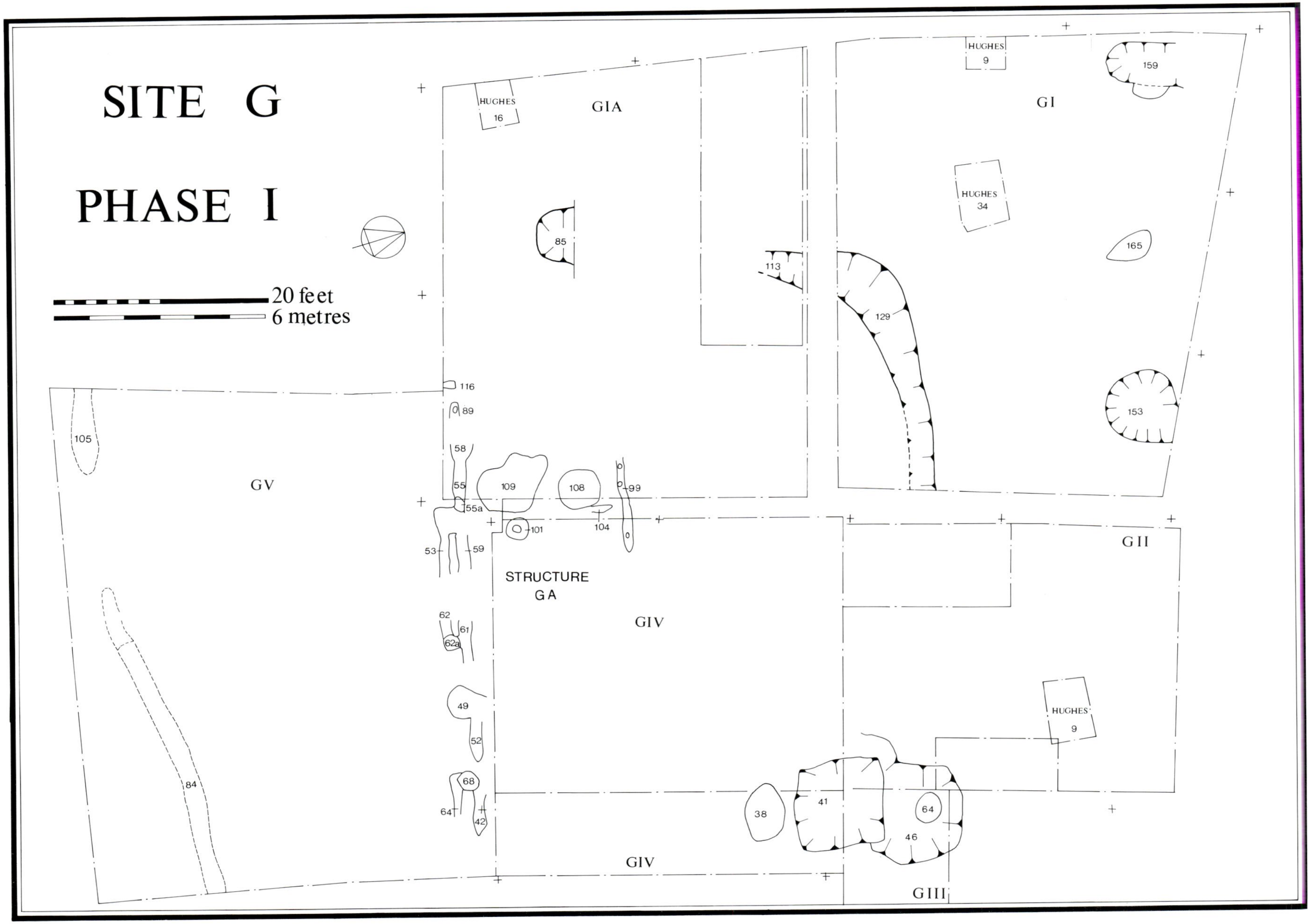

Figure 89 Site G, phase I

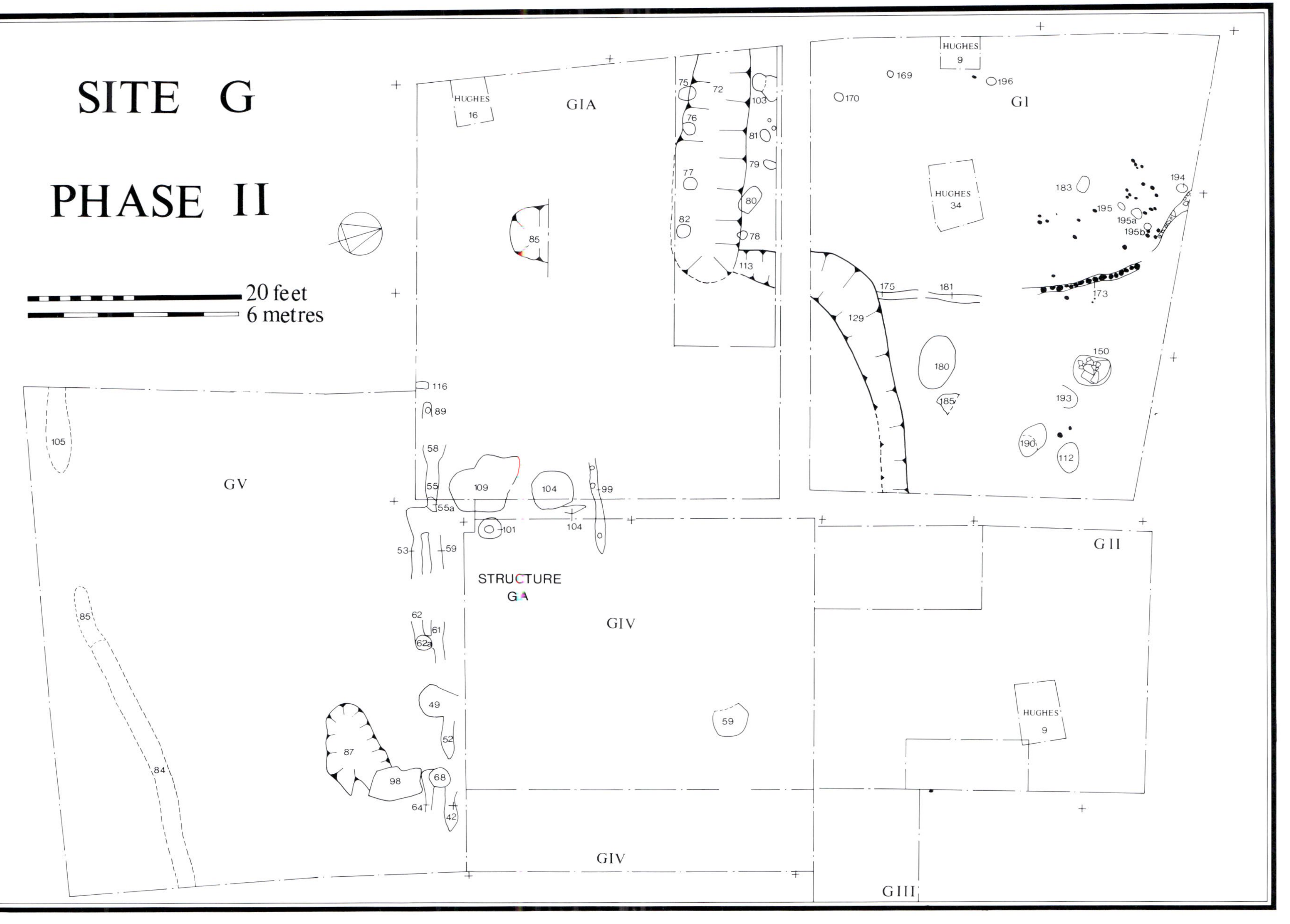

Figure 90 Site G, phase II

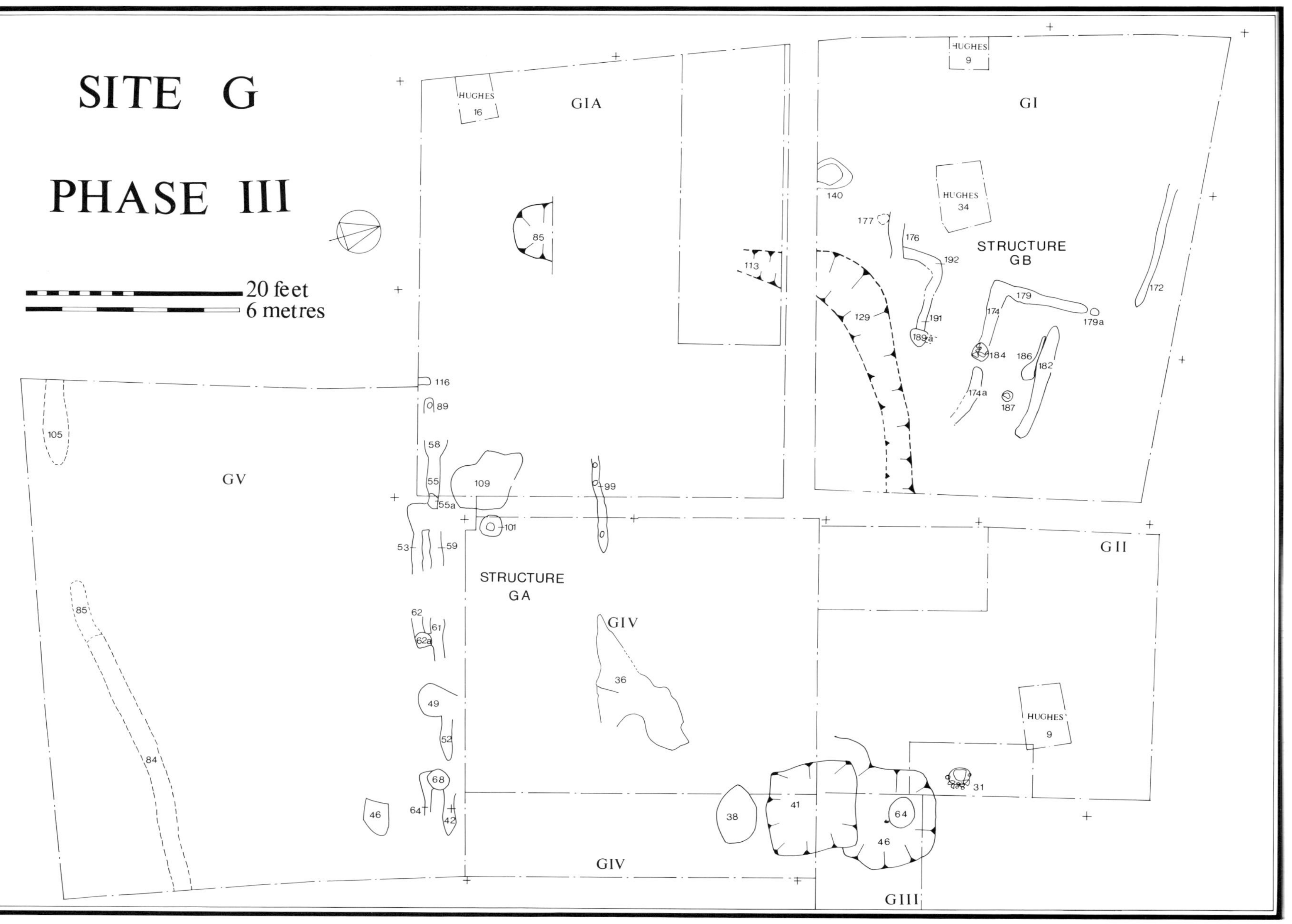

Figure 91 Site G, phase III

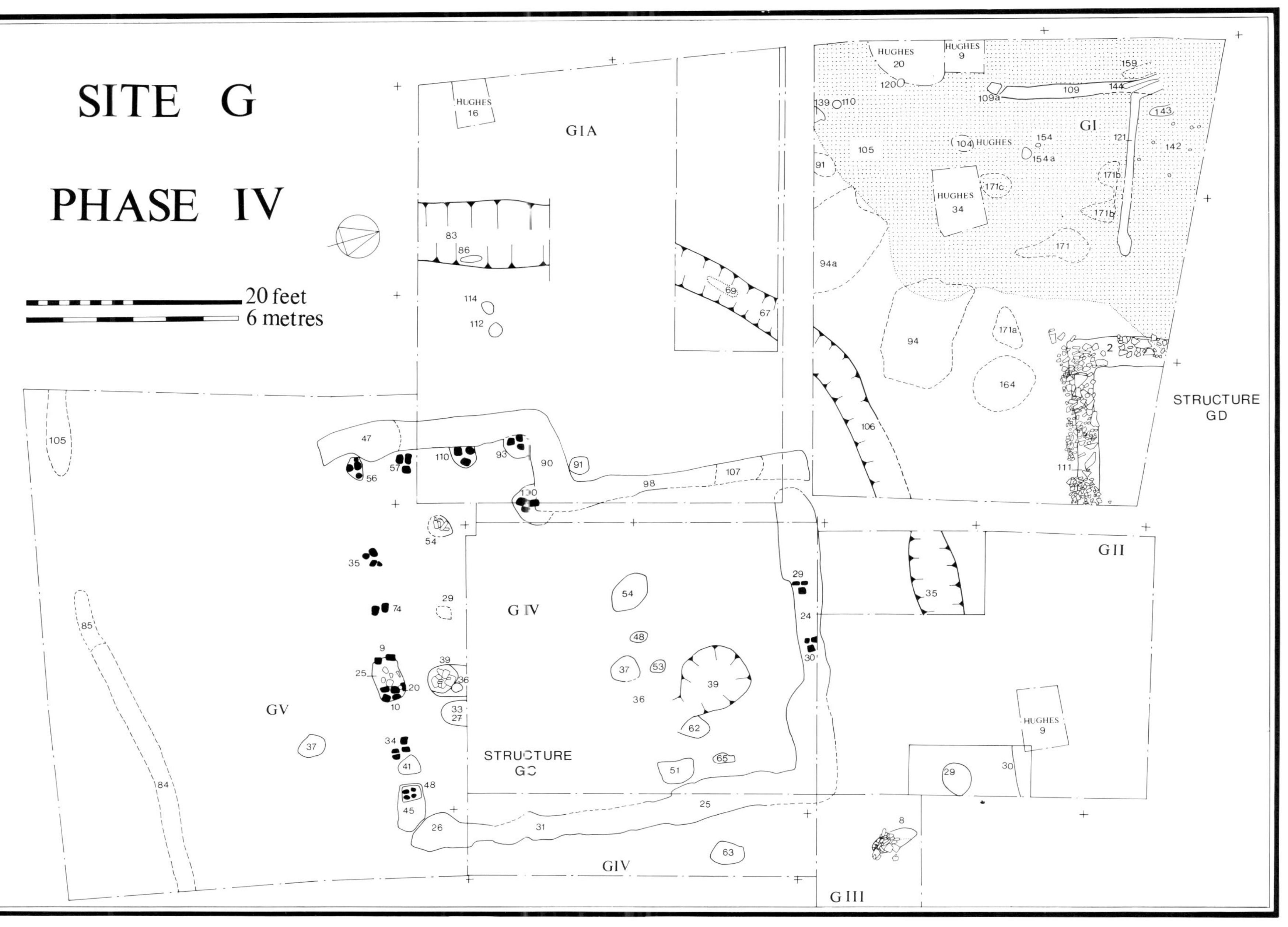

Figure 92   Site G, phase IV

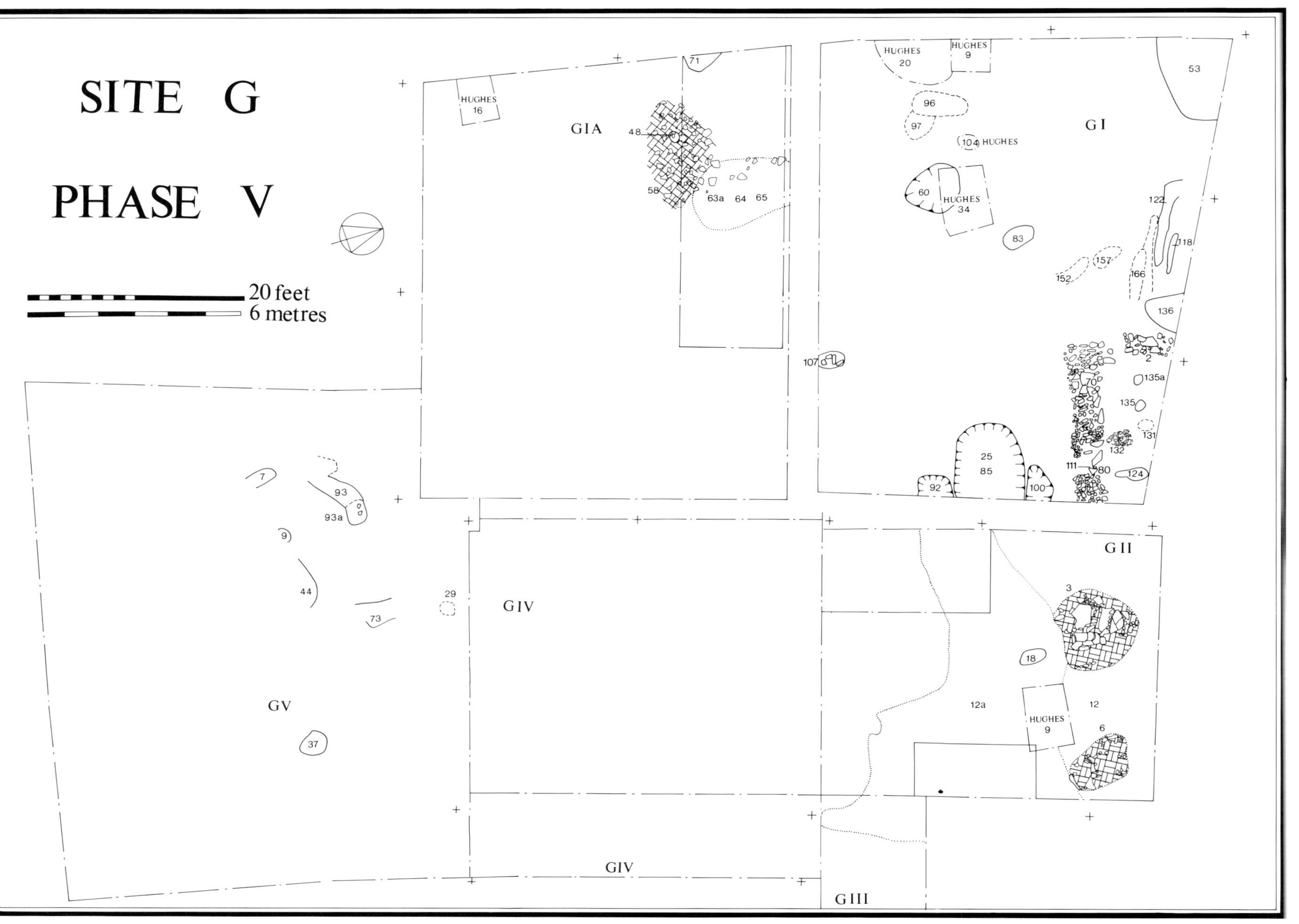

Figure 93   Site G, phase V

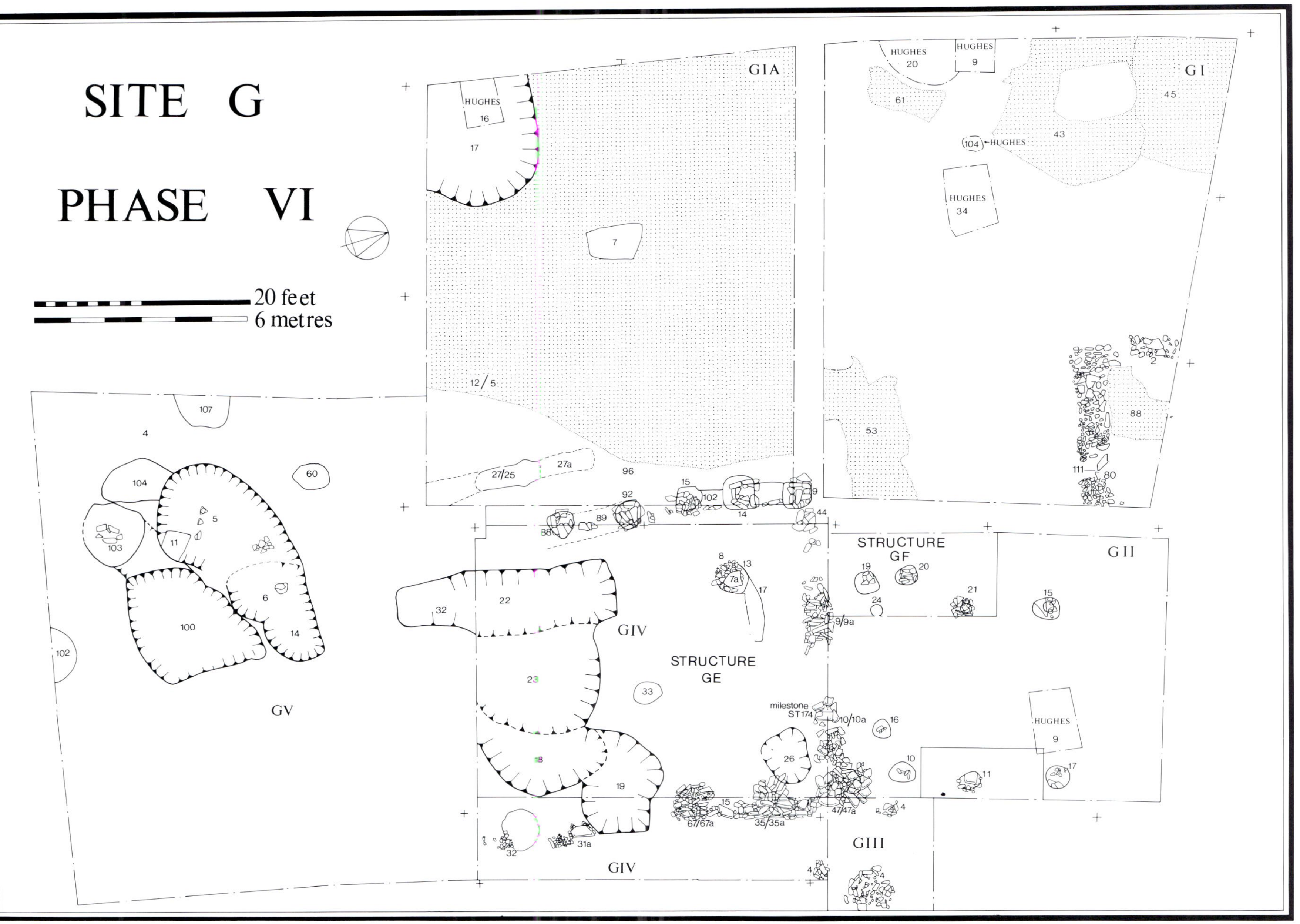

Figure 94 Site G, phase VI

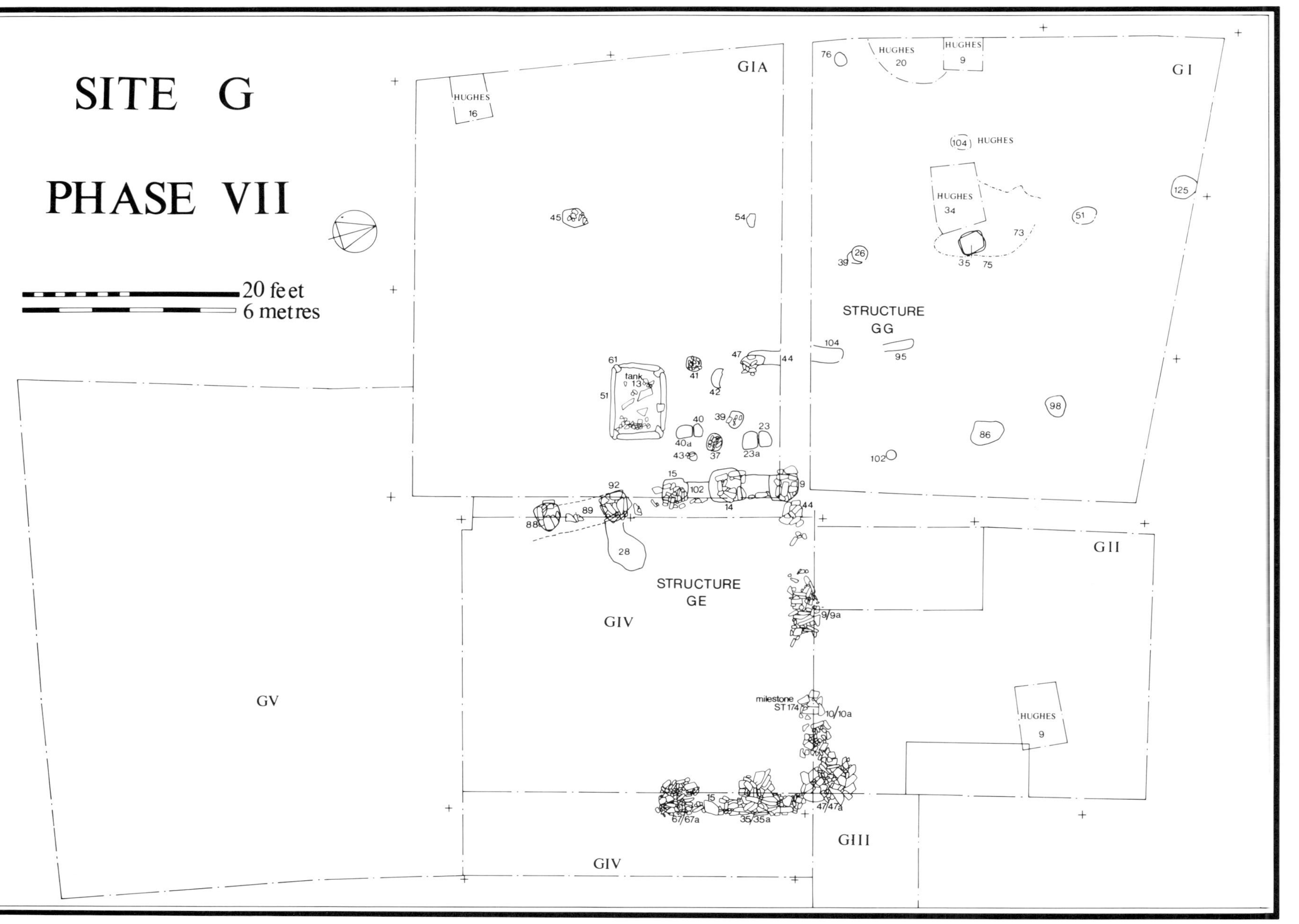

Figure 95   Site G, phase VII

130

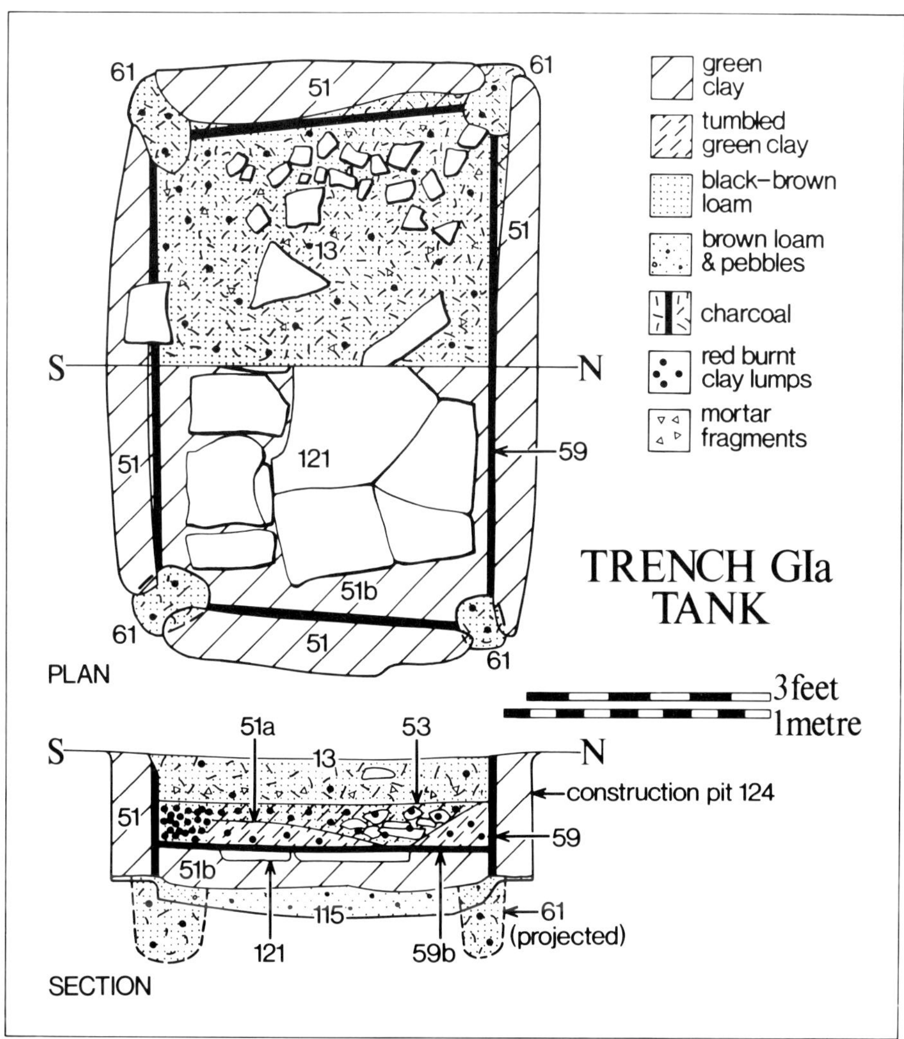

Figure 96   Trench G IA, phases VII–IX, tank

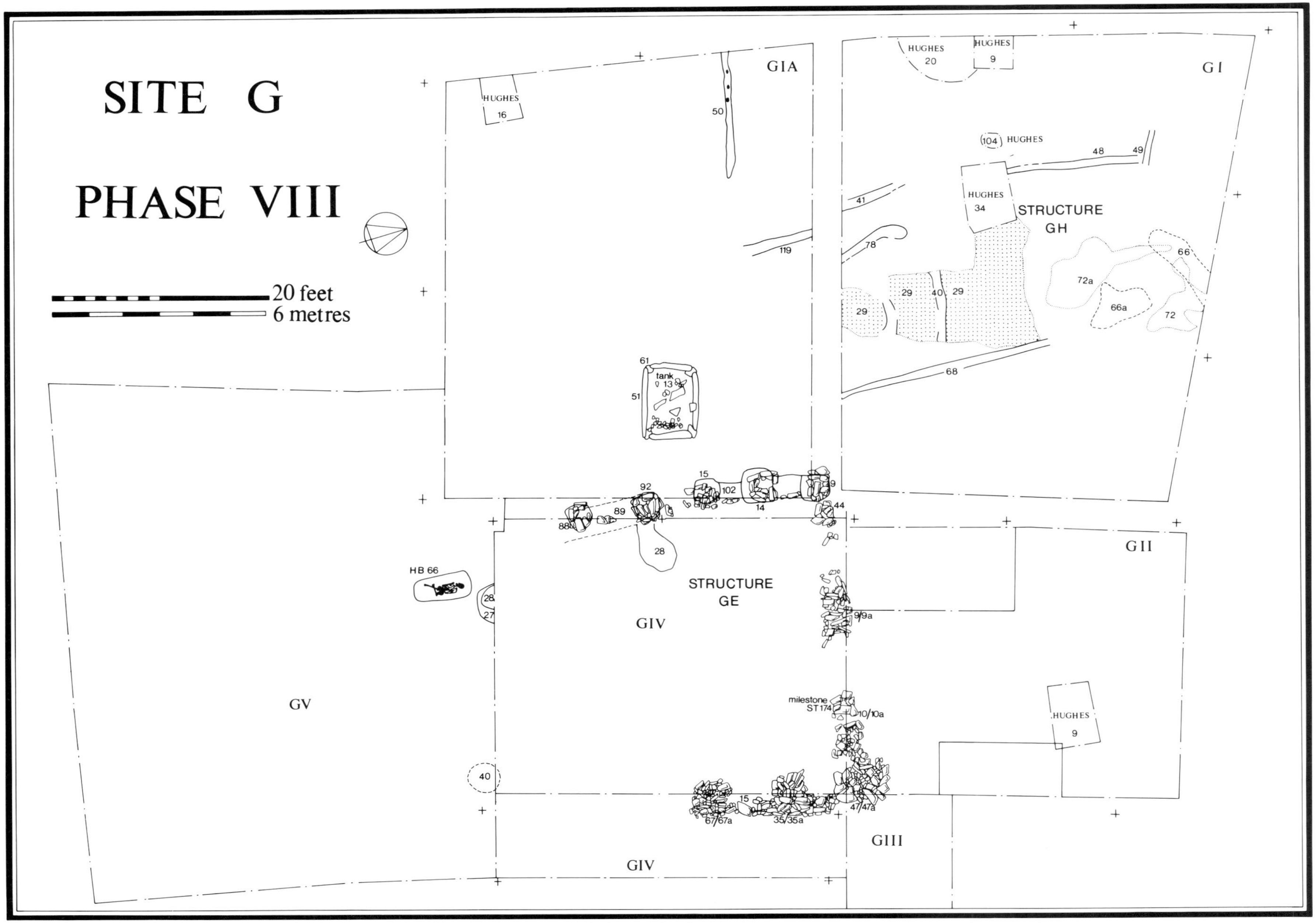

Figure 97 Site G, phase VIII

132

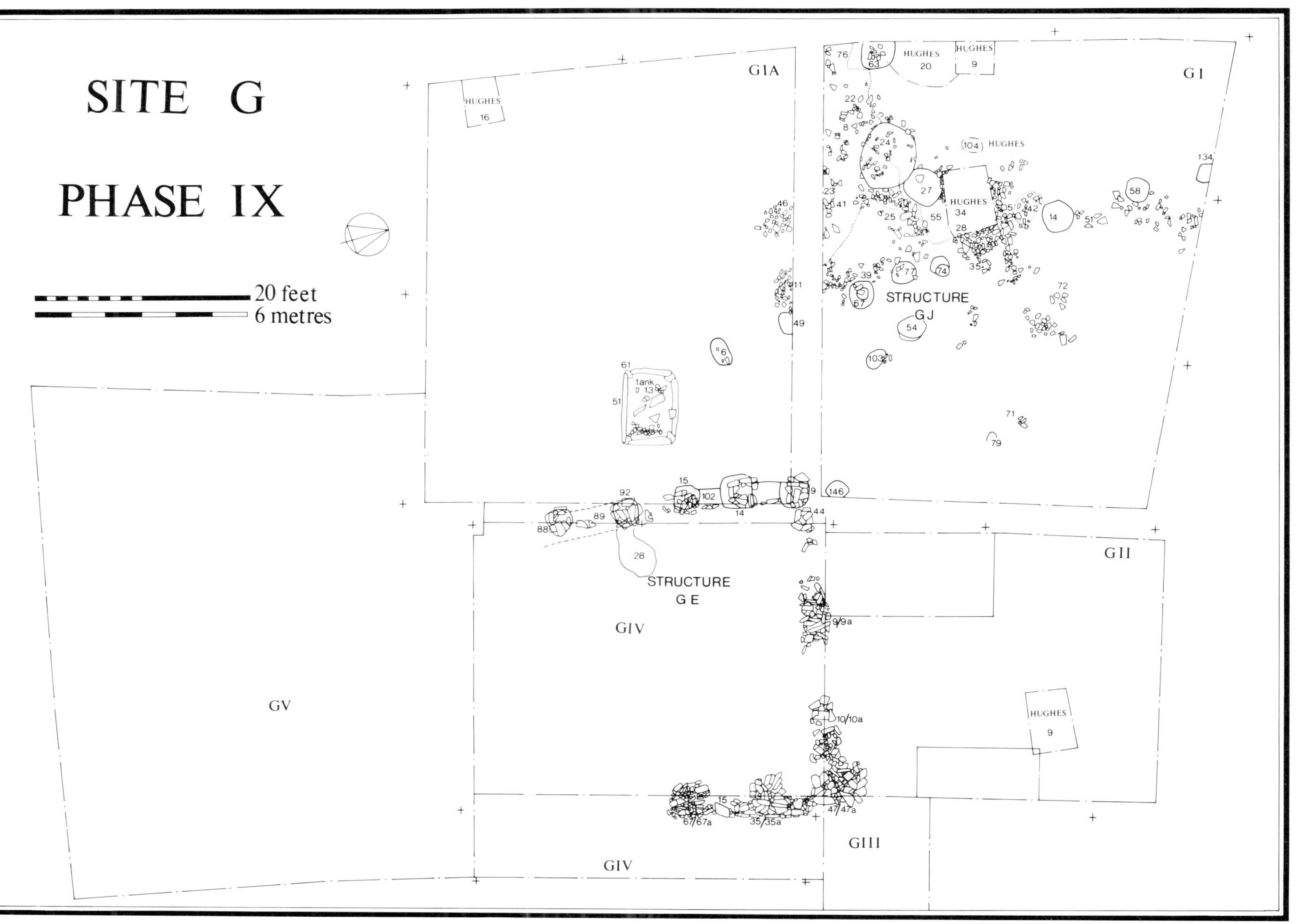

Figure 98 Site G, phase IX

133

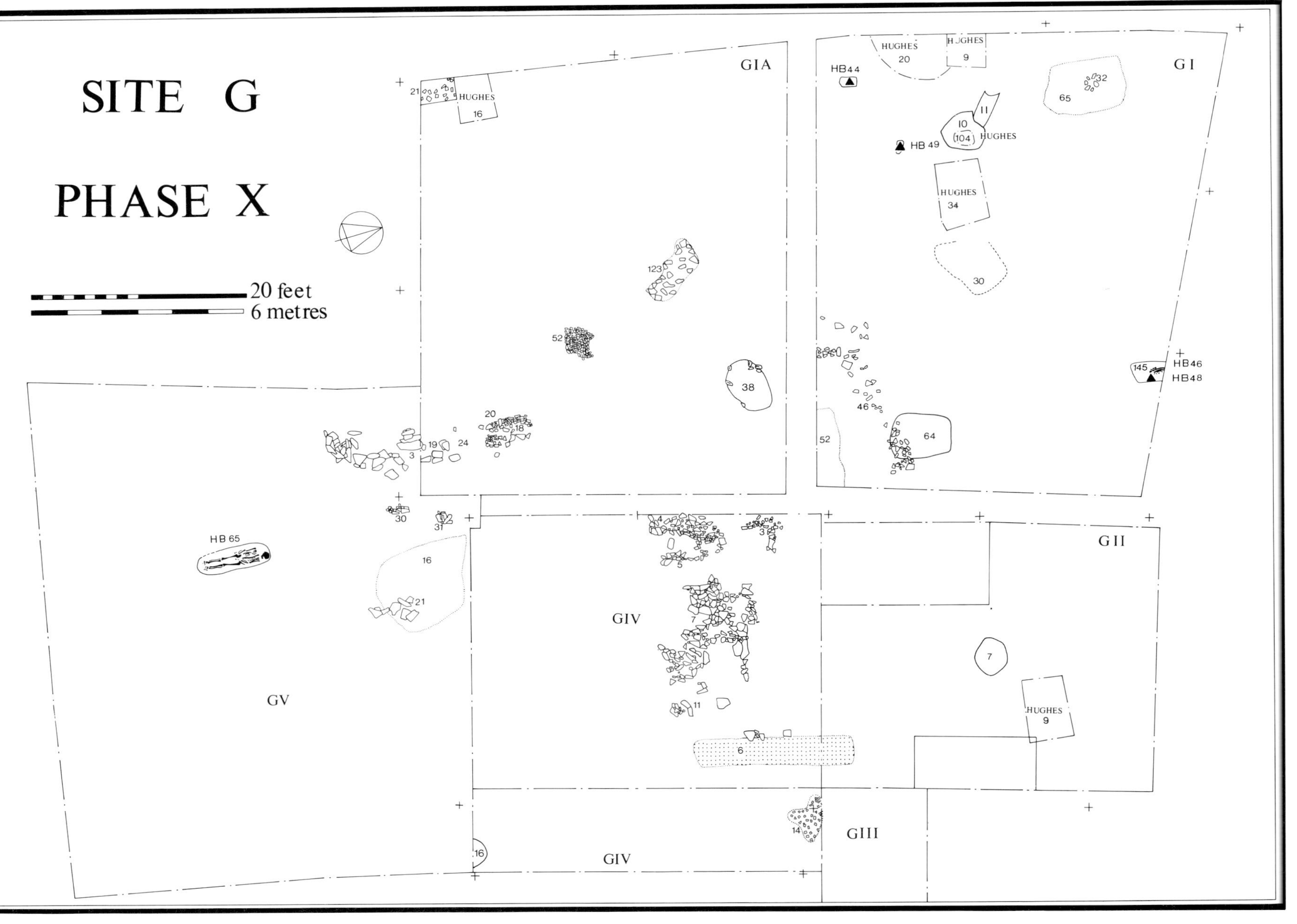

Figure 99 Site G, phase X

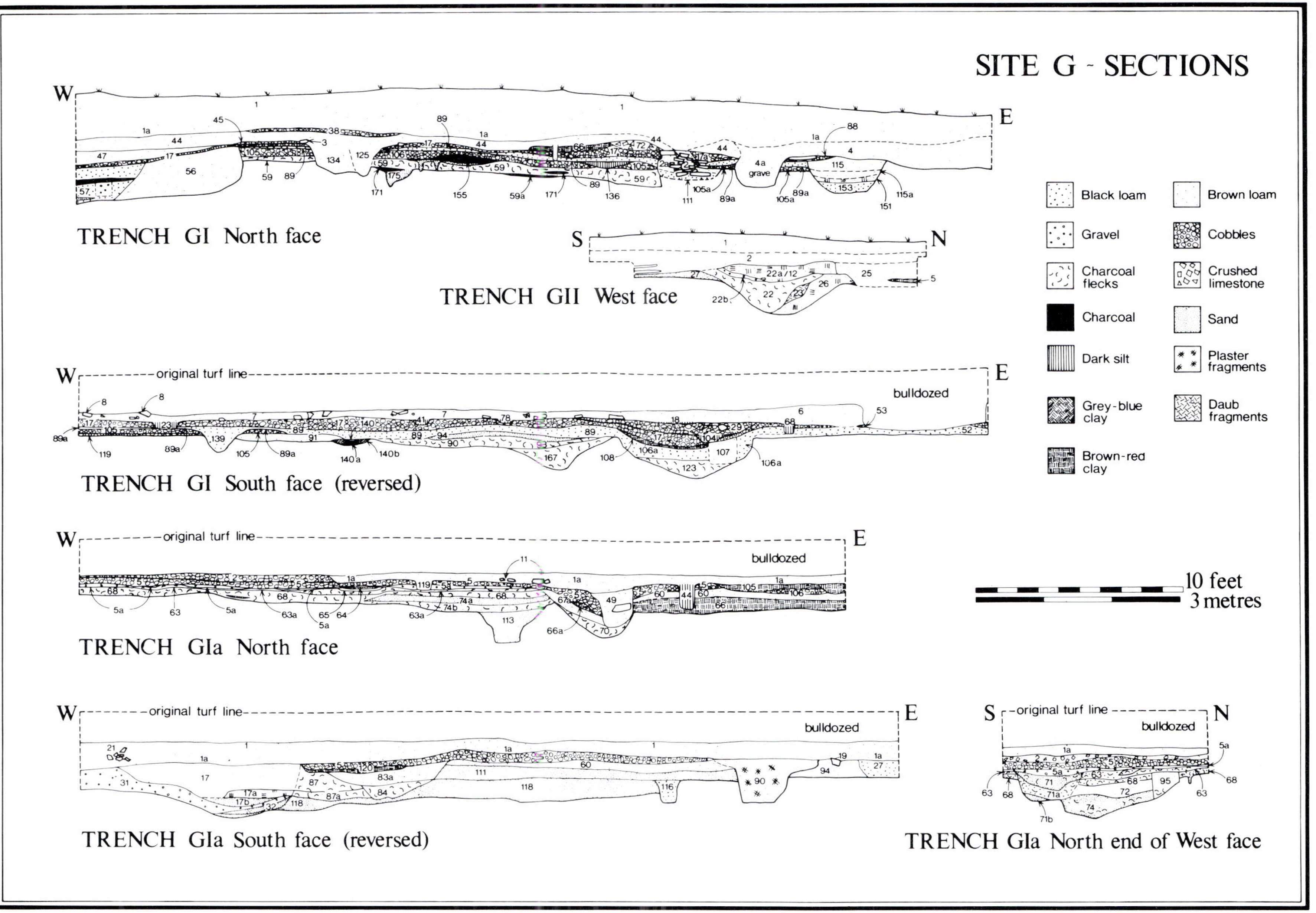

Figure 100   Site G sections. Trench G I, north face; trench G I, south face (reversed); trench G IA, north face; trench G IA, south face (reversed); trench G IA, north end of west face (plan: fig 89)

Site K

R S Langley

[M2:C3] No evidence for the Roman defences was found in these trenches and much of the area would appear to have been marshland in the Roman period (fig 2, fig 3, no **41**, fig 101). However, later excavations on the Gateway supermarket site and in Bull's Head Yard indicate that the defences almost certainly passed through this site (Cracknell forthcoming). The traces must have been removed by the watercourse which extended through the area from north-east to south-west in the medieval period.

Trenches K I, K II, and K III contained two beds of peat, the lower one up to 0.4m thick. The upper part of the deposit produced two Roman sherds and a tile and may be compared with the peat found at Bull's Head Yard (Booth 1980, 20), with a radiocarbon date of 1760±80 bp.

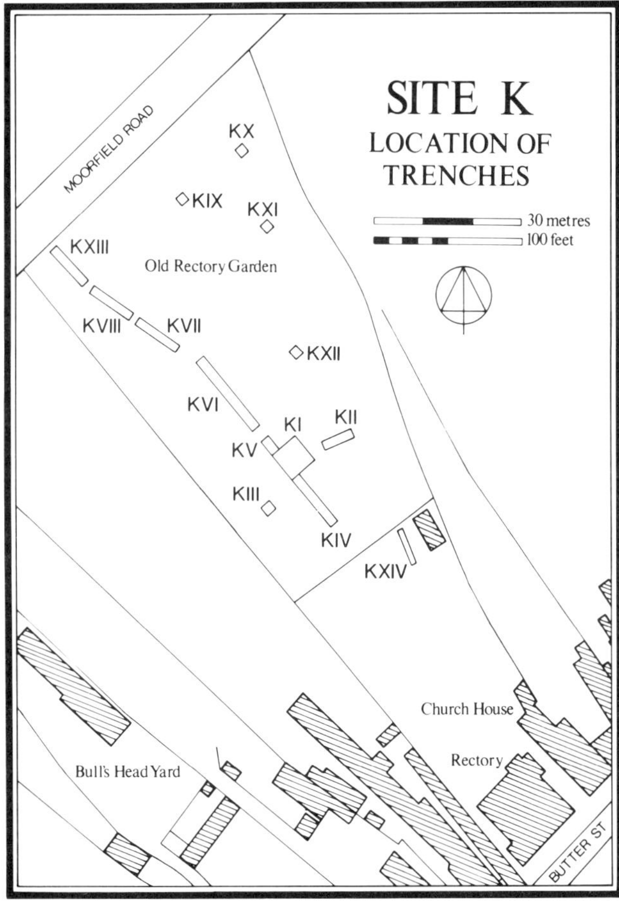

Figure 101   Site K, location of trenches

Site L

R S Langley

[M2:C5] An area of 0.44ha was explored by machine trenches in advance of construction of a chemical works on the site (fig 2, fig 3, no **42**, figs 102–4).

Trenches L XI and L VIII

Phase I

[M2:C6] A ditch containing late 1st- to early 2nd-century pottery extended east–west in trench L VIII, L VIII 26, but did not appear in trench L XI.

Phase II

[M2:C6] In trench L VIII a series of floor layers — one of mortar — and occupation deposits survived between two robbed-out walls, one in the middle, L VIII 27, one at the northern end of the trench, L VIII 2. In trench L XI there were two stone walls at right-angles to each other, L XI 17, 20, with a mortar floor between them. Both this and the phase III structure were aligned on street A.

Phase III

[M2:C7] The second structure was seen at the south end of trench L VIII. Although this building was partly constructed of timber it contained a hypocaust, possibly related to the building excavated by Hughes (1958, 15–16). *Tesserae* found in the topsoil and in the phase IV robbing may be attributable to the hypocaust floor. The area to the north of the building was twice resurfaced whilst it was still standing.

The phase II structure was partly rebuilt at this time. Five successive floors of mortar, *opus signinum*, and clay with interleaving burnt layers were associated with this new structure. One of the floors contained a coin (cat no 377) dating to AD 335–41.

Phase IV

[M2:C9] Both buildings were robbed out at this time. The fill of the hollow, L VIII 49, where the hypocaust had been, included a coin (cat no 220) dating to AD 332–3.

Trenches L III, L IV, and L IX

[M2:C9] In phase I a series of beam slots supported a timber structure of uncertain size which perhaps extended into trench L I (fig 103). In phase II the slots were cut by a ditch, L III 14, after which time the site was abandoned.

Reoccupation of the site in the 3rd century or later was indicated by a cobble surface, a robbed-out wall, and a possible hearth in phase III. A robber trench and post-Roman features were assigned to phase IV.

Trenches L I and L XIII

[M2:C10] The only structural feature in phase I was a timber slot, L I 17, which may have been related to the features in trenches L III, L IV, and L IX.

In phase II a large ditch with a slot at the bottom cut through the trenches on a north-east to south-west alignment. The secondary fills of the ditch contained Antonine samian. The upcast was deposited on the north-west side.

In phase III the ditch filled in and a flat-bottomed gully, L I 20, and a posthole, L I 15, were dug. The remaining features were probably post-medieval.

Trenches L II and L X

[M2:C12] The main feature of these trenches was a wall apparently parallel to the ditch seen in trenches L I and L XIII. The wall was associated with a flag floor and a cobble surface.

Trench L XII

[M2:C12] The eastern half of the trench cut across a broad, flat-bottomed ditch which may have been the same as that seen in trenches L I and L XIII although it was broader and on a slightly different alignment. The features in the western half of the trench might be supposed to be post-medieval.

Trenches L V, L VI, and L VII

[M2:C13] These trenches revealed little but post-medieval quarry pits. At the northern end there was a flat-bottomed, curving gully.

Site L phase dates

Trenches L XI and L VIII

Trench VIII contained a late 1st to early 2nd-century vessel type in phase I (L VIII *26*).

Phase II contained 1st-century samian.

Phase III contained a coin (cat no 377) dating to AD 335–41 from a mortar floor, L XI *13*.

Phase IV contained an Oxfordshire vessel (C.56) dated *c* AD 270–400+ from L VII 49. There was also a coin (cat no 220) of AD 332–3 from a layer postdating the destruction of the hypocaust, L VIII *49*.

Thus, this part of site L was occupied from perhaps the late 1st century to the mid-4th century.

Trenches L III, L IV, and L IX

The main pottery fabric found within these trenches is Black-Burnished ware with equal proportions of Severn Valley and local grey wares. Utilitarian jars and bowls are the main vessel types, with Black-Burnished bowls particularly predominant. There is no useful non-ceramic dating material.

Phase I: date uncertain

In this phase no samian is recorded and there are two Hadrianic–Antonine vessels (B.5 and R.205) from L III *1* and **8**. However, there are also 4th-century pieces (B.56 and O.281) from L III *1* and **16**.

Phase II: 3rd century

In phase II, L III *11* and **14** contain samian of *c* AD 170–200 and Antonine date respectively, whilst the coarse pottery includes a Hadrianic–Antonine jar from L III **14** and a late 3rd-century jar (B.20) from L III *11*. The phase is presumably 3rd century.

Phase III: 3rd century on

In this phase all of the material from L III is residual, but there is a 2nd to 4th-century Severn Valley ware piece (O.367) from L IX 3.

Phase IV: late Roman and modern

There is no clear dating evidence for the robber trench and hollow assigned to phase IV. The horse burial is modern.

Trenches L I and L XIII

Trench L I contained mostly Black-Burnished and Severn Valley ware, with utilitarian jars and bowls the predominant forms while site L XIII contained Black-Burnished ware in the majority, with equal proportions of Severn Valley ware and local grey wares.

Phase I: Antonine

There is Antonine samian from L I *14* and an Antonine jar (R.88) from L XIII *4*. An Antonine date would seem appropriate.

Phase II: late 2nd century on

In this phase there is a Hadrianic–Antonine jar (B.3) and Antonine samian from L I **16** and an Antonine vessel (R.211) from L XIII **8**. Probably late 2nd century or later.

Phase III: late Roman / post-medieval

All the material from trench L I is residual but there is a later 3rd-century jar (B.20) from L XIII **9**.

Trench L XII

This contained essentially local grey and Malvernian wares with a handful of Black-Burnished and Severn Valley wares. Utilitarian jars predominated, particularly late 1st- to early 2nd-century rusticated jars, many of which were residual.

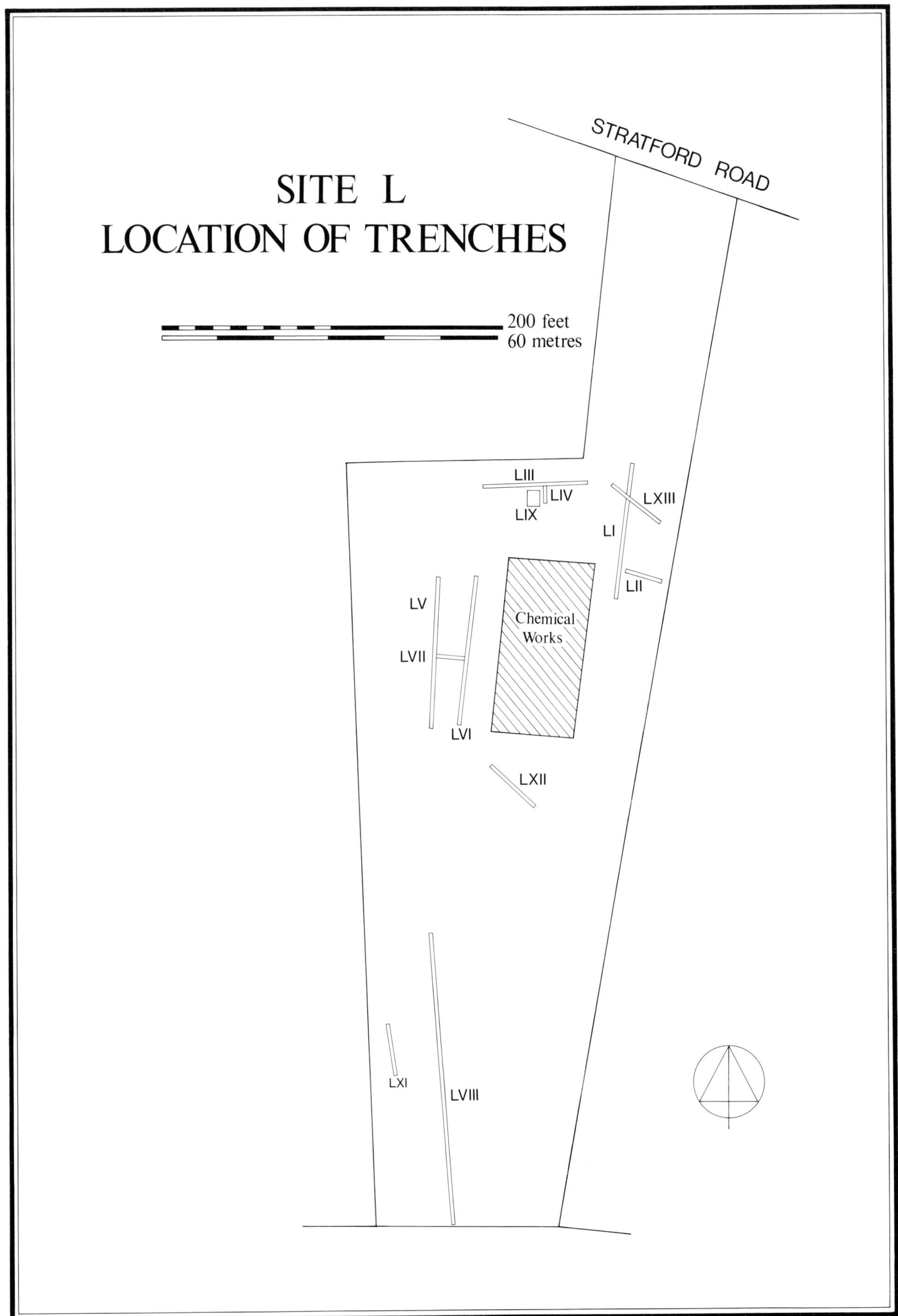

Figure 102   Site L, location of trenches

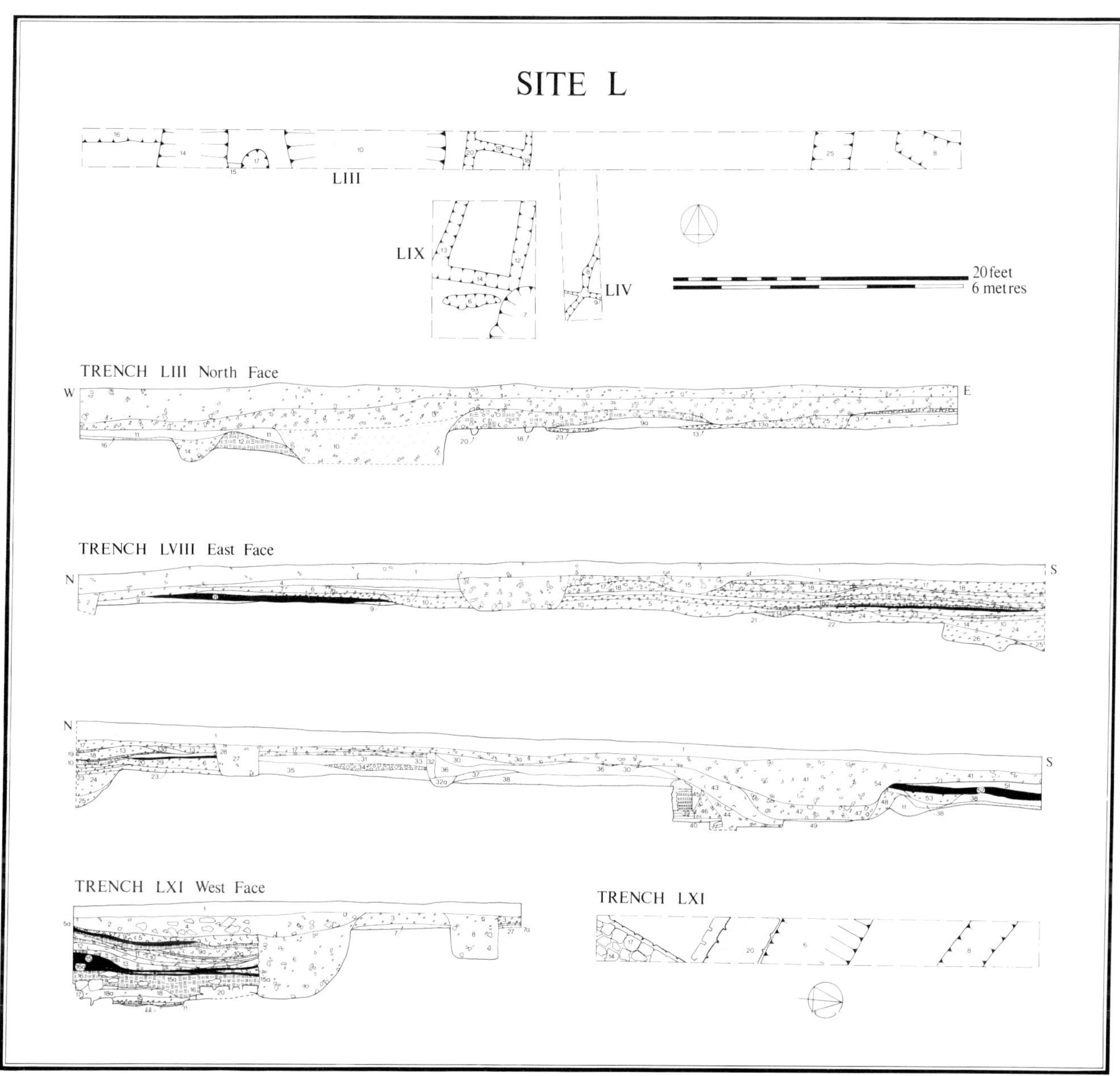

Figure 103   Site L, plan of trenches L III, L IV, L IX, L XI. Sections of trench L III, north face; trench L VIII, east face; trench L XI, west face

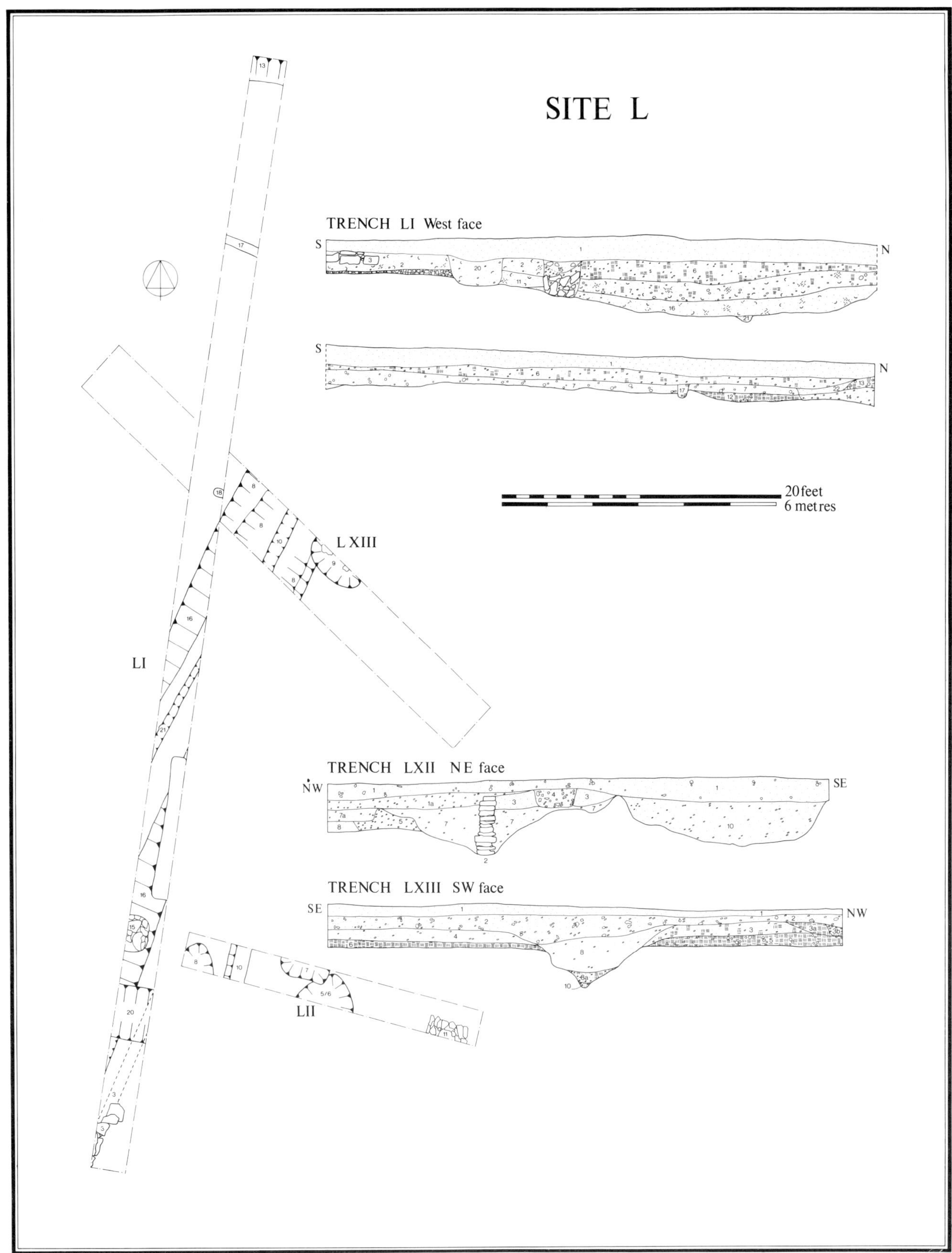

Figure 104   Site L, plan of trenches L I, L II, and L XIII. Sections of trench L I, west face; trench L XII, north-east face; trench L XIII, south-west face

Site M

R S Langley

[M2:C14] Three machine trenches were dug through the town defences on a site on the north-eastern side of the town (fig 3, no 43, figs 105, 106). Recording was mainly undertaken in trenches M I and M III with M II only cleared towards the river end (fig 106).

Phase I

[M2:C14] Several postholes and slots at the south end of trench M I predated the phase III rampart. The varying alignments indicated that several distinct periods were represented. In trench M III five periods were distinguished. The postholes and pits of periods i and ii were superseded by a brown loam, a cobble surface, and hard-packed clay in period iii. This loam was raised in a bank some 0.75m above the general level at its highest point, just behind the later wall trench and this might be an early defensive bank, M III 19. Similar banks have been found on the Gateway supermarket site and at Gas House Lane (Cracknell forthcoming). A layer of clay assigned to period ii and some postholes might also be considered in this context. These layers were cut by a hearth, pits, and other structural features. Periods iv and v consisted of cobble and possible stone surfaces and more postholes.

The pre-rampart occupation dated from the Antonine period or later. A 2nd-century fibula (cat no 76) was found in a period ii context and the period iii pits and slot contained Antonine samian. The presence of obtuse-lattice-decorated Black-Burnished ware may indicate that the phase runs into the 3rd century.

Plate 11   Site M, phase III postholes of the timber pile foundation for the late 4th-century town wall. Scales in 1ft (0.30m) divisions (see also fig 106)

Phase II

[M2:D2] Black loam sealed the pre-rampart occupation in M I and M III, M I 21, M III 6B/14/45.

Phase III

[M2:D2] The defensive wall, which was built in phase III, had been completely robbed out, so the description here only concerns the remains of the foundations.

In trench M III the wall and the construction trench had both been 3.5m wide but in trench M I the construction trench was 5.5m wide with the space behind the wall filled with loam. The bottom of the construction trench had been filled with sand and gravel covered by clay, and timber piles 120–50mm in diameter had been driven into the natural gravel (plate 11). In trench M I the rampart overlay the construction deposits indicating that it was contemporary with the wall. The rampart consisted of at least four distinct tips of clay with an overall eroded width of 11m if a possible refurbishment is included. Smaller layers seem to have been deposited against the front edge of the wall but there was no evidence for a ditch. No datable material was recovered from the rampart or construction trench.

Phase IV

[M2:D4] A series of crushed stone and tile surfaces and cobble surfaces overlay the tail of the rampart and there was a plaster floor and a possible foundation trench in trench M III. In front of the wall in trench M I there were several unstratified features, largely pits and postholes.

The robber trench was filled with limestone rubble and red sandy clay.

Site M phase dates

Phase I: late 2nd to early 3rd century

There is a ?2nd-century Black-Burnished BB1 dish (B.67) from M III **16** and a small reduced rimsherd, possibly from a 1st-century carinated beaker from M I **22**. The remaining coarse pottery from this phase is rather later, with contexts M III *19*, M III **20**, and M III **24** all containing obtuse-lattice-decorated Black-Burnished ware (BB1) jar bodysherds (3rd–4th century) and M III **20** having a 3rd-century Black-Burnished ware (BB1) jar rim fragment. Unless the material from all three of these contexts is intrusive the phase would appear to extend at least into the early 3rd century (Bidwell 1985) suggesting a date of around AD 220 for the appearance of the obtuse lattice (cf Evans forthcoming). Two *mortaria* found in M III **17** date to AD 180–240.

The coarse ware is accompanied by mid- to late Antonine samian from contexts M III 15, **17**, and *23*, together with other Antonine material suggesting a late 2nd-century date. These three features, a posthole, a pit, and a beam slot respectively are all sealed by M III *6B/14*, a phase II black occupation layer beneath the defensive bank associated with the town wall, M III 13.

Two stratigraphically primary features in the site M sequence, pits M III **27** and *28*, both contain rim sherds of middle Iron Age pottery. There was another sherd from M III **30** and a possibly Iron Age sherd from M I **23**.

A patch of clay, M III *32*, contained a plate brooch (cat no 76) perhaps dating to the 2nd century.

Phase II: late 2nd to early 3rd century on?

Phase II contains only five recorded coarse pottery vessel types, one of which (O.143) has a late 3rd- to 4th-century date range. The others are Hadrianic–Antonine? (B.67 (two examples), B.11, and R.93) and late 2nd to late 3rd century (O.349). The samian was largely Antonine. The date is based on the dates of phases I and III.

Phase III: mid-4th century

Phase III has only one recorded coarse vessel type, which must be residual.

The date for the town defences is derived from the opposite side of the circuit, at the Gateway supermarket (Cracknell forthcoming) and the adjacent Coulters Garage sites (Booth 1985). On the supermarket site, three later 3rd-century coins were found in the rampart which backed the town wall but the most significant dating evidence comes from a large stone building which was demolished to make way for the wall. The construction of this building, at Coulters Garage, has been dated by Booth (1985) as *c* AD 300. A coin of Valentinian I dated AD 364–7 was found in a context associated with its destruction, thus providing a probable *terminus post quem* for the building of the town wall.

Phase IV: Roman / post-Roman

Phase IV has five recorded vessel occurrences, all residual types.

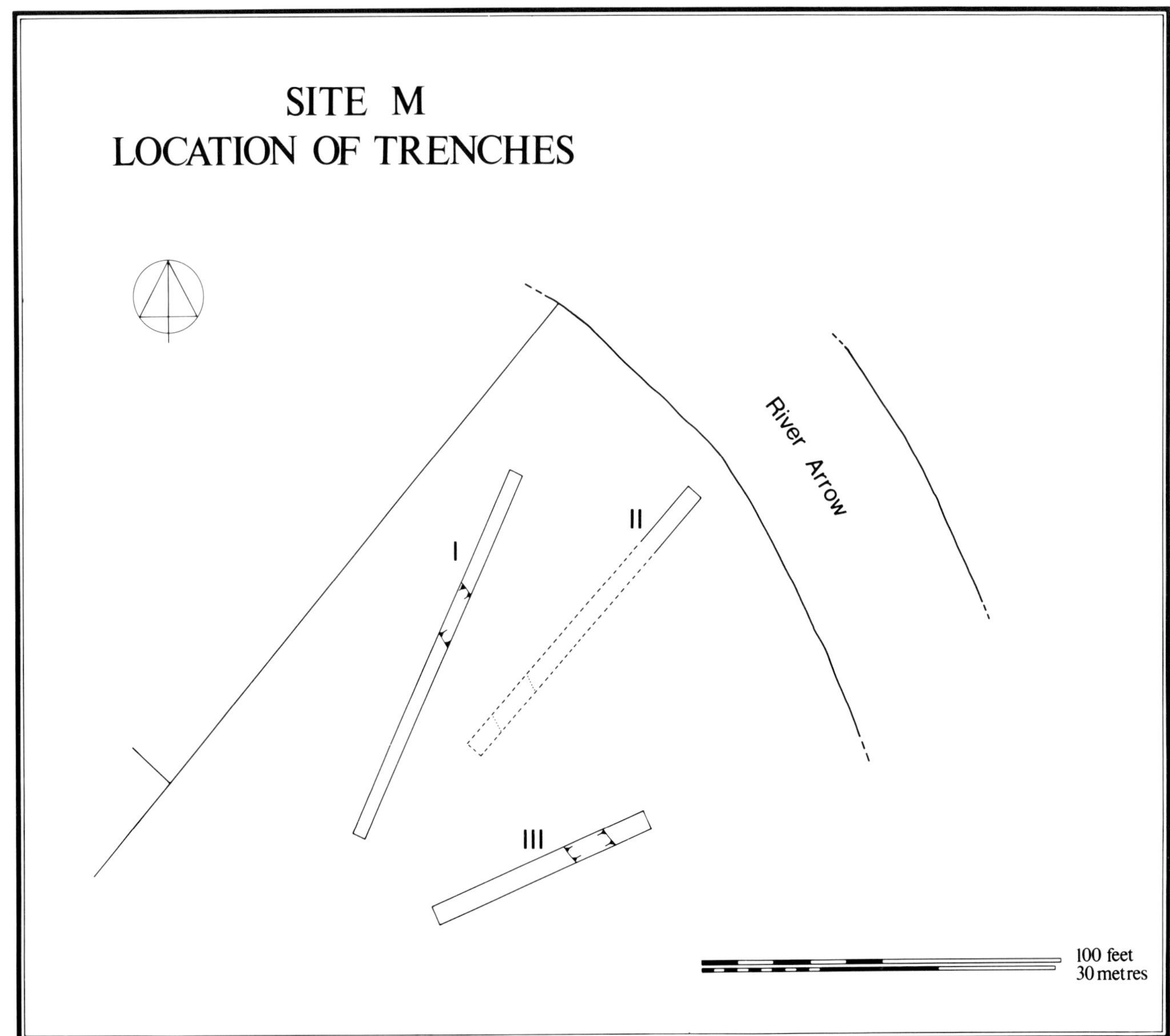

Figure 105   Site M, location of trenches

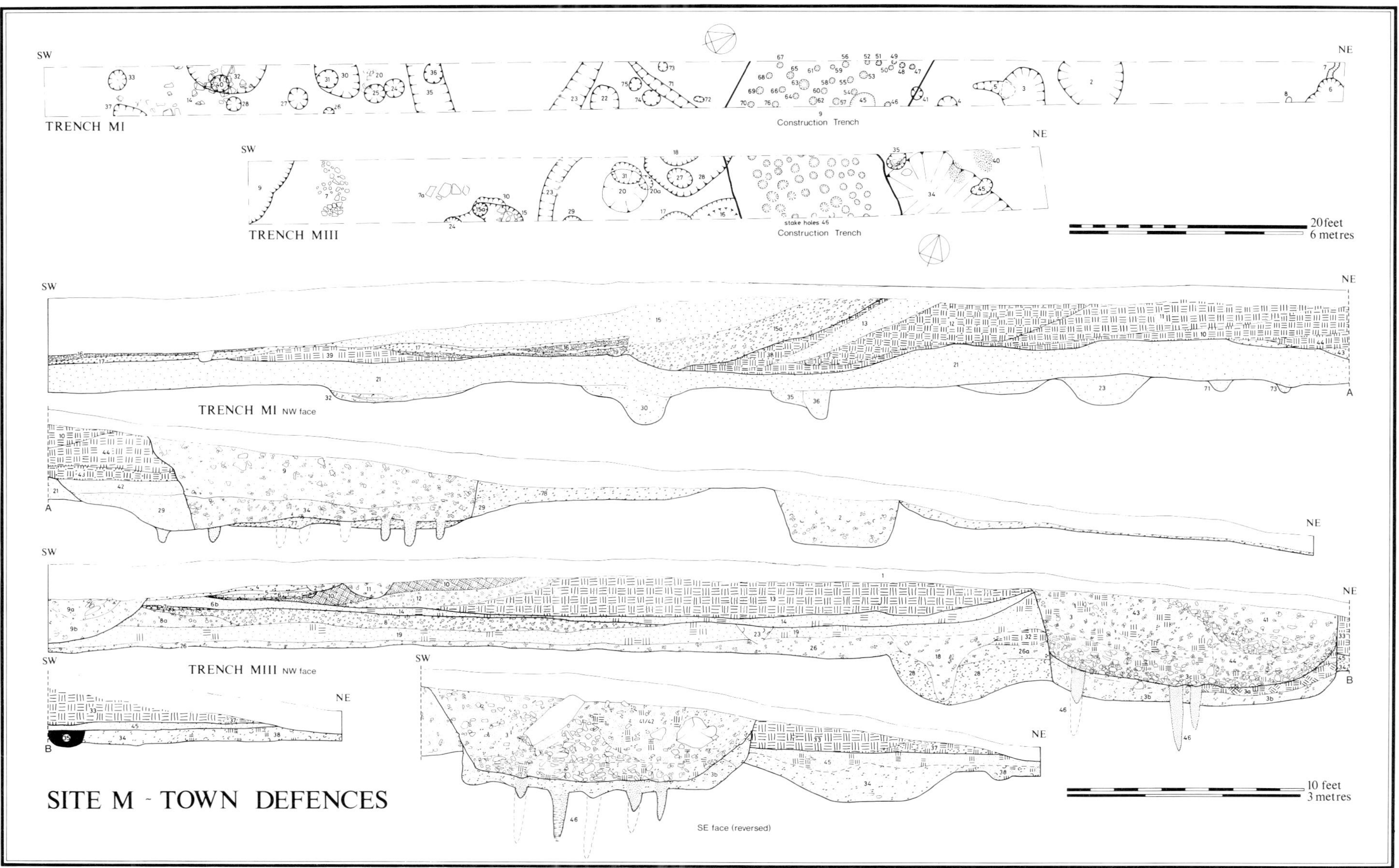

Figure 106 Site M, plan of trenches M I and M III. Sections of trench M I, north-west face; trench M III, north-west face; south-east face (reversed)

Birch Abbey burials *R S Langley*

Thirty-one adult inhumations, 24 non-adult inhumations, and one cremation were found in the excavations (figs 107, 108, table M2 in microfiche). The human bone report (with identifications by C B Denston, in Part 2, p 215–16 and M4:E3–M4:G11) gives details of the pathology; this section deals solely with the methods of interment and cremation.

Of these 27 adult inhumations were identified in context. The discrepancy arises because in one group of four skeletons, some of the bones were disturbed and mixed by the mechanical excavator (HB 4, HB 6A, HB 16). These were bagged and numbered separately from the bones of the same individuals found *in situ* (HB 5, HB 6, HB 7). Two teeth (HB 25) were most probably associated with one of the skeletons from this group (HB 13).

Eight groups of bone each comprised only a single fragment: one fragmentary cranium (HB 3), four cranial fragments (HB 9, HB 42, HB 45, HB 51), one broken and weathered mandible (HB 50), one vertebra (HB 34), and one phalanx (HB 29). (These and the site L skeleton are not plotted on fig 107.) HB 3 and HB 9 possibly resulted from the incomplete recovery of skeletons intersected by machine trenches. The remainder appear to have been redeposited fragments completely dissociated from their original graves. Continuous use of the area for burial over a number of generations might have resulted in the disturbance of earlier graves, and indeed a number of the inhumations found *in situ* had been intercut. Bones disturbed in this way most commonly would have been shovelled back into the fill of the later grave, but could have lain on the surface or have been removed by dogs or other animals. HB 29 and HB 34 were in close association and might represent a single individual. They came from the upper fill of a well which had two altars at its bottom (see trench B IA, phase IV), and could be parts of a dedicatory offering. However, the fragments are small and disparate, and it is most probable that the bones were incidental inclusions in the soil filling the shaft.

Excluding these fragmentary remains, the *in situ* inhumations represented 20 adults: 15 males and four females from the Birch Abbey area, plus one female from site L, east of Bleachfield Street. The immature remains represented 24 individuals. There was a single cremation burial, an adult male.

Earlier records indicate that a cemetery extended over a wide area from Grunthill (Gwinnett 1954, 6) and Folley Field (Davis unpublished notes; Gwinnett 1954, 6–7) west of Ryknild Street to the Spittle Brook on the west side of Birch Abbey. Smaller cemeteries have been found at other locations (fig 2).

Four separate areas of burials can be identified from Davis' notes. Not all, however, were certainly of Roman date. They were, from east to west:

(i) A possible group of four burials found in 1925 beside the old Alcester–Stratford road in an uncertain location perhaps fairly close to the river Arrow north-west of Oversley Bridge (**9** on fig 3).

(ii) A group of three adults and one child in burials apparently aligned north–south, located in the north bank of the river Arrow at the point where this river, having run east–west through the flood plain, turns sharply southwards. This site can be precisely located (**82** on fig 3). It was known to Hughes (1959, 31–2) and was repeatedly visited by Booth between 1975 and 1982. There can be no doubt that a significant Roman cemetery existed at this point and its continual and continuing erosion remains a matter of concern.

(iii) Two crouched inhumations and a group of skulls and other bones were found at various times between 1923 and 1929 in the beds of the old sewage works to the west of Bleachfield Street on the south side of the town (**6** on fig 3). The site cannot be more closely defined. None of these burials was associated with dating material and it seems quite likely from the account of the circumstances of the discovery that they were of pre-Roman date.

(iv) In 1925 Davis excavated 15 inhumations aligned east–west and a cremation in Folley Field and Orchard just west of the former railway line on the west side of the town (**7** on fig 3). Three of the inhumations were contained in crude stone cists and one was associated with a coin of Constans. The burials lay some 180m north of the probable find-spot of a stone coffin discovered in 1866 at the time of the construction of the Evesham Street railway bridge. These finds, together with the later exposure of 'over a hundred burials' in an adjacent area to the east (Hughes 1962), suggest the presence of a major late Roman cemetery, perhaps with earlier antecedents.

On the Birch Abbey site no grave occurred north of street A, although one redeposited bone was found on site E (HB 50). This road may have defined the limits of the burials, although the burial from site L, two burials in a well at Needle Industries (Hughes 1959, 27), and an unusual grave on the Lloyd's Bank site (Evans & Booth 1975, 50) lay some distance to the north and east of these boundaries.

Sixteen graves lay along or immediately north of the line of ditch A, and there were no adult burials to the south; all were later than the backfilling of the ditch but appear to have respected a boundary on the same line. Four graves lay close to street A, but none were recorded over much of the central area of the site. This distribution in part reflects the wider extent of the trial trench sampling in the southern part of the site, and the density of burial may have been fairly constant over the whole of the area. Certainly, in the open area trenches the burials appear to have been very dispersed.

There was a preponderance of males in the group, ranging from one and a half times the number of females in the 31 groups of adult bones identified in the specialist report (the maximum number of inhumations), to three times the number of females in the 20 *in situ* adult graves (the minimum number of inhumations). A weighting of the sexes is apparent also in the distribution of the graves. Males and females were in equal numbers in the northern part of the site, but males were eight times more frequent than females in the area to the south.

Infant burials lay in a different distribution from the adults. Eight occurred in the central area where no adults were recorded, and five (HB 39, HB 40, HB 52, HB 54, HB 37) lay along the edges of street C. No infants were recorded in the south-western area where the adults were mostly concentrated although a child of 9–12 years (HB 12) and another of 13–14 years (HB 41) were found in this area. Six infants (HB 2, HB 21, HB 22, HB 24, HB 26, HB 28) were associated with a building to the south of ditch A, perhaps inserted under the joisted floor (see site AA South, phase III), and three more occurred in associated pits (HB 6, HB 8, HB 19).

Most of the burials were discovered in the course of mechanical trial trenching and recorded under salvage conditions. Grave cuts were not observed in most cases. HB 27 and HB 47 were laid in broad rectangular graves, while HB 65 was in an oval cut scarcely larger than the body; all three graves were shallow. There was no evidence of any grave markers.

Coffin nails and wood were present in five of the inhumations (HB 11, HB 27, HB 38, HB 43, HB 47). In the fill of the grave of HB 47 the horizontal nails securing the lid of the coffin lay 280mm above those which had secured the base. In one grave a coffin or plank lining may have been marked by a soil stain with no traces of nails (HB 17). HB 65 did not appear to have been coffined, but had a curious arrangement of two nails lying one either side of the jaw; a group of nails by the left foot may have been from a small wooden box.

The bodies were usually buried in an extended position with the head to the north. Two males (HB 14a, HB 20) had their heads to the east, HB 20 lying in a flexed position on his right side. A third male (HB 38) had been greatly disturbed, but the legs lay within a closely fitted coffin, defined by horizontal nails, which would suggest an extended burial aligned with the head to the east. HB 66 was aligned with the head to the north but lay in a flexed position. One female (HB 47) was aligned with her head to the west.

An infant (HB 48) was buried at the feet of one female (HB 46). A second female (HB 43) was buried with a child of 13 or 14 years lying above her (HB 41). It is uncertain whether the burials were simultaneous, or if the child had been placed in the grave later; the two may have been intercut at right-angles. Two infants (HB 52, HB 54) were laid side by side in a double grave.

HB 11 was extended on his left side, aligned to the north; the head had been severed at the shoulders and laid beyond the feet, which were associated with boot-nails.

One female (HB 13) had been buried in a prone position. A slab set upright by the left shoulder may have been the remains of a stone cist over the head, of the type recorded by Davis at Folley Field (Davis unpublished notes; Gwinnett 1954, 7). The skull had been removed by a disturbance at the north end of the grave before three males (HB 5, HB 6, HB 7) were buried at a higher level. These were associated with cranial fragments (HB 16) which may have derived from HB 13. The three later burials had been disturbed by the mechanical excavator and were considerably mixed; they might have shared a common grave.

Decapitated and prone burials are common occurrences in Roman cemeteries. Usually it is uncertain whether decapitation was the cause of death or was inflicted *post mortem*. The reason for these practices is unknown, but the intention may have been to deprive and punish the spirit, or to confuse a ghost and prevent it from walking. Most such burials are not remarkable in other respects (Harman, Molleson & Price 1981). HB 11 may have been distinguished in life by the deformity of his left leg.

Objects were associated with seven of the burials (HB 5, HB 11, HB 13, HB 14, HB 20, HB 65, HB 66) and are summarized in table M2. Personal ornaments and equipment were not usually placed with the bodies. The lack of pins and brooches suggests that normally the dead were buried loosely wrapped, or without any clothing. A bone pin associated with the decapitated male burial (HB 11) might have secured a cloak or shroud. The prone female burial (HB 13) included a bronze pin. A stone spindle whorl was found with a male burial (HB 20). Three males (HB 11, HB 27, HB 65) were buried wearing their boots, the hob nails remaining around the bones of the feet. A colour-coated beaker was laid to the left of the feet of HB 65; a group of nails close by might represent a small wooden box, as noted above. The single cremation burial (BB 5) was contained in a pot.

Animal bones were not commonly associated with the burials, but HB 67, the female grave from site L, Stratford Road, included bones of a horse. The cremation (BB 5) included bird bone and bones of a sheep or goat. An adjacent pit contained the bones of a bird in a pot. One infant (HB 49) lay on the scapula of an ox, which may have been used as a shovel to dig the grave (Birss 1985).

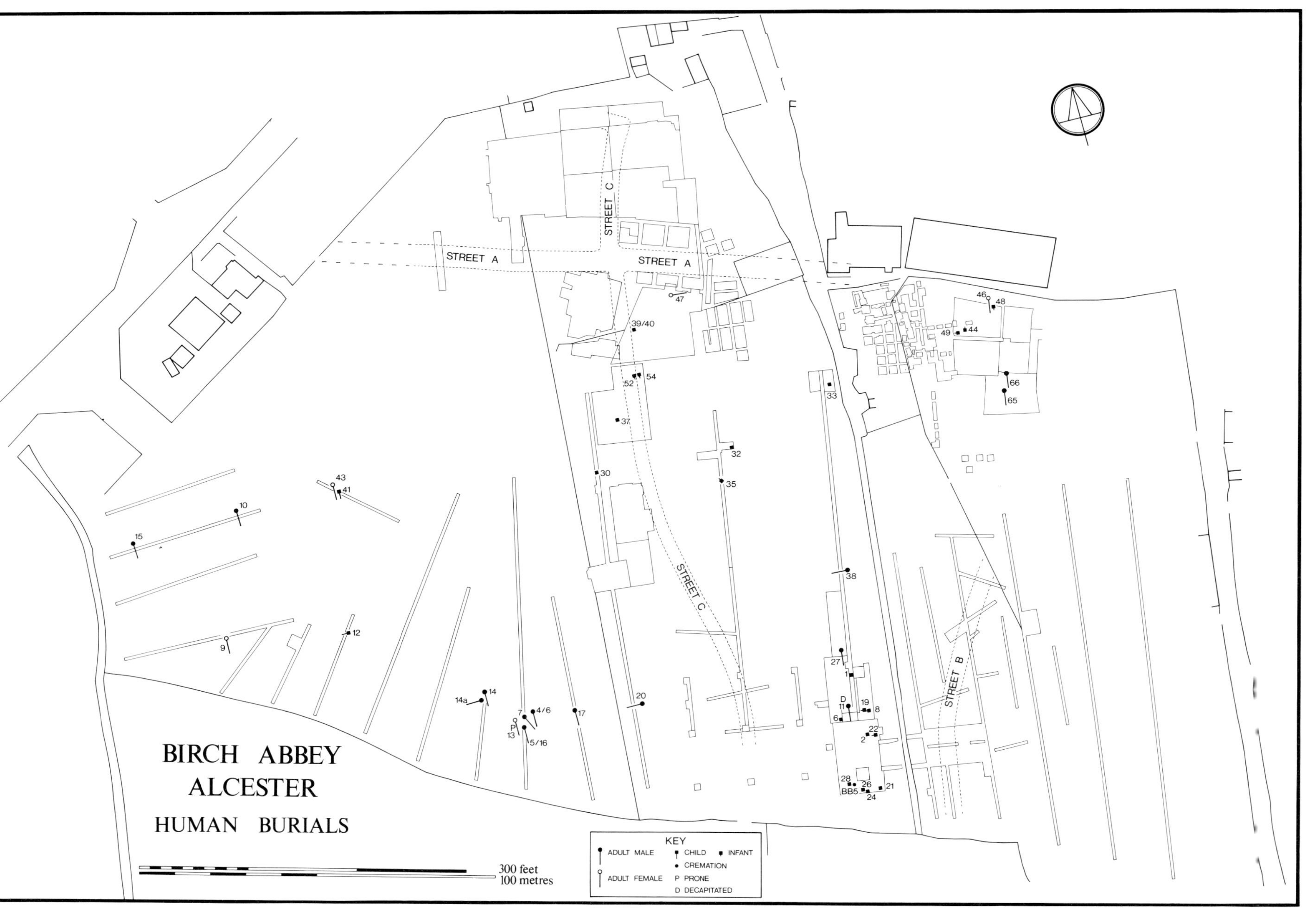

Figure 107 Birch Abbey, location of human burials

146

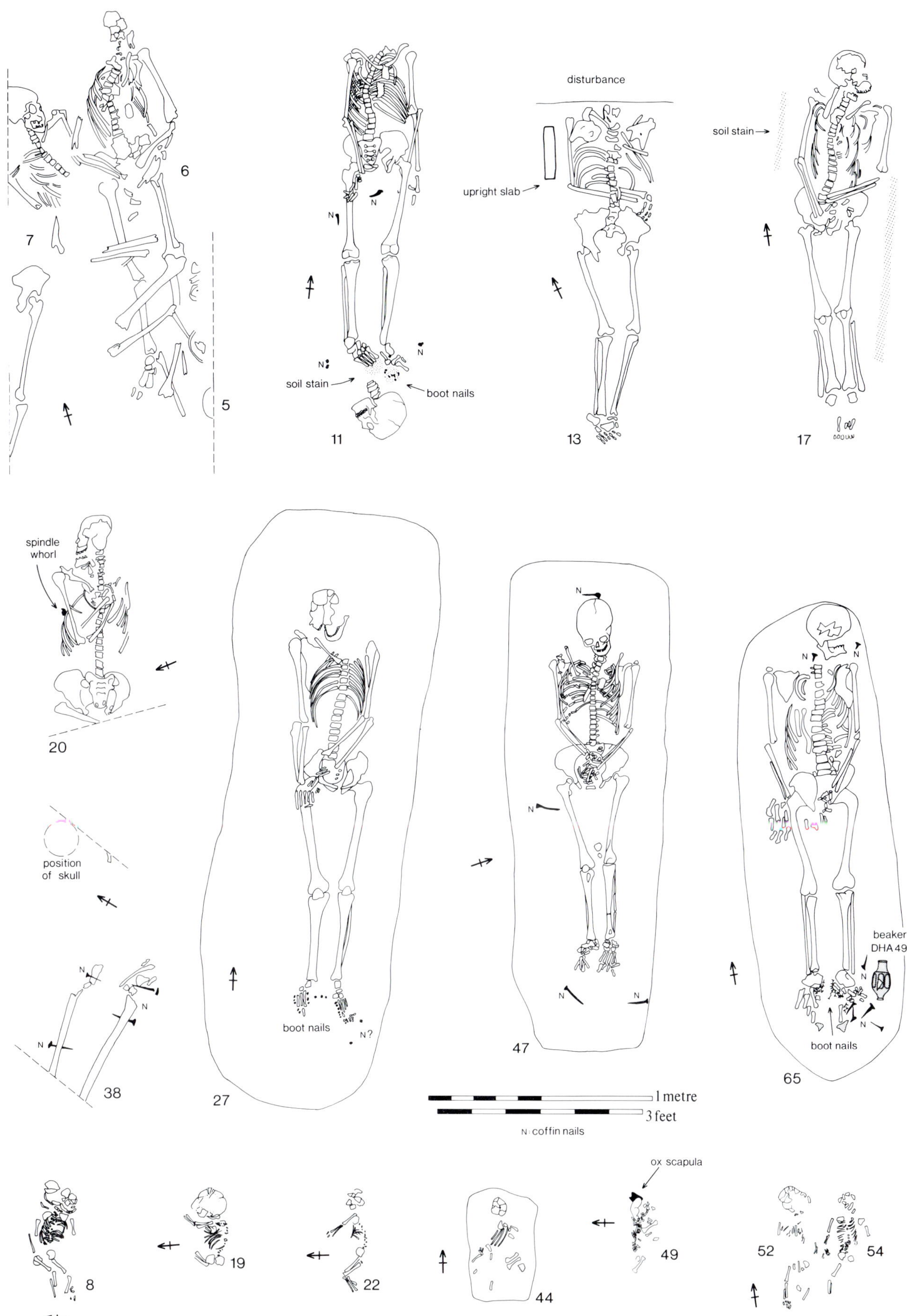

Figure 108   Birch Abbey, plans of the better-preserved skeletons

Buildings: summary description of types *Christine Mahany*

The building types on the Birch Abbey site could be broadly divided into five groups (figs 109–11):

A Native-type huts and enclosures.
B Timber buildings with horizontal sleeper beams.
C Timber buildings with post-in-trench construction.
D Timber buildings with individual postholes.
E Buildings incorporating stone foundations.
F Other buildings, not considered above.

There follow general descriptions of the building types (by Christine Mahany) and a separate discussion (by Paul Booth) with some overlap but different emphasis. Detailed descriptions occur under individual sites, as do descriptions of very fragmentary structures which are not dealt with in this section. Measurements are given, in the case of timber buildings, from posthole to posthole, or from centre-slot to centre-slot. As most timber buildings are somewhat irregular in plan, measurements are approximate, and the reader is referred to the illustrations, which all contain scales. Measurements of stone structures are internal.

It will be clear from an examination of the general plan of each site that any attempt to disentangle the complex sequence of buildings on a site is fraught with difficulties. On the whole the stratigraphy is shallow; and even uniform layers are patchy, and discontinuous. More reliable is the evidence for postholes cutting one another, or other features, but many are included in a particular building on the basis of alignment, or another element in a plan. Dating evidence is minimal. Nevertheless, in spite of these obvious problems, it has proved possible to produce a number of plans of a wide range of building types, many without obvious parallels elsewhere. No attempt has been made to assign functions to structures where no evidence exists for this. Most buildings could have been used for a variety of purposes, both agricultural and urban. As the Birch Abbey sites lie in a peripheral and suburban relationship to what is otherwise known of Roman Alcester, it is not clear whether they should be seen as the town encroaching upon the countryside, or vice versa. The presence of late Roman stone buildings widely separated from each other appears to give a picture, at least at this stage, of the suburban villa, much as might be found in the outskirts of a modern town.

The buildings at Alcester Birch Abbey range in date from the mid- to late 1st century to the late 4th. Native-type huts, as expected, are early, from the late 1st century to the early Antonine period. The divisions B to F are necessarily crude, since many buildings which are predominantly of one type also show traces of other kinds of construction within the

same structure. Nevertheless it has been thought necessary to make some attempt at classification.

Buildings with horizontal sleeper beams, sometimes combined with individual postholes, are found from the early 2nd (perhaps earlier) to the early 4th century. Post-in-trench construction is more short-lived, being found in Birch Abbey from the 2nd to the mid-3rd century. Buildings with individual postholes are found from the late 2nd to the 4th century. Buildings with stone foundations do not come in until at least the late 3rd century, and continue through to the late 4th.

Group A native-type huts and enclosures (fig 109)

There were three representatives of this group at Alcester, on sites E and F. (See also pp 158–9 for a discussion of this type.)

Structure EA

On site E, structure EA was a native-type circular hut, some 12m in diameter consisting of a post-trench in which some stakeholes were found, and occasional larger postholes. The entrance was to the east and was 1.8m wide. Part of the interior was subdivided by straight slots to form a sub-triangular inner room, perhaps a sleeping area. Inside the entrance were a number of irregular shallow pits, possibly postholes, but they were not necessarily roof supports. A rash of very small stakeholes in the western area of the interior could not be assigned a function. There was an approximately central hearth.

Dating: Neronian–Trajanic.

Structure EB

Structure EA was rebuilt on a slightly larger scale (structure EB). The diameter was some 13.4m. The entrance, still to the east, was defined by a larger gap in the circular trench than before (and by two postholes slightly inside it, perhaps forming the jambs of a door 2.7m wide). This structure was not subdivided into rooms, but contained instead a number of somewhat banana-shaped pits, containing ash, and a central hearth. There were no internal roof-supports. Outside the post-trench, to the south-east, was a shallow gully, probably a drip-trench for an overhanging roof.

Dating: Hadrianic–Antonine.

Site F, phase III enclosure

An enclosure, shaped like a parallelogram, defined an area 20.9m × 20.9m, with opposed entrances and the trenches terminating in echelon. Little evidence was found of timbers within the trenches, which were, however, steep-sided with a U-shaped base, as if to contain posts. Nor were there any internal features, except an irregular line of small stakeholes within the north section of the east wall. The accuracy with which the enclosure was laid out might suggest a ritual function.

Dating: Neronian–Trajanic.

Group B timber buildings with horizontal sleeper beams (fig 109)

Examples of this type were found on sites A, D, F, and G, though some were in a fragmentary form, as a result of incomplete excavation or later disturbance. (See also pp 159–60 for a discussion of this type.)

Structure DA

On site D, fragmentary traces survived of a building, structure DA, which in part consisted of horizontal timbers, with uprights at intervals. It had been much disturbed by later building on the site, but appeared to consist of a rectangular structure aligned north–south, with a western corridor and main structure. Evidence for internal room divisions survived at the north end, but the southern part of the building was suggested only by small and ill-defined postholes, which may or may not have been part of the structure, since there was no direct stratigraphical relationship.

Dating: 1st century to early Antonine.

Structure GB

On site G, structure GB, a slight and fragmentary structure, was found. It consisted of a porch-like arrangement of slots (with door-posts) leading to a rectangular structure of which only the north wall survived.

Dating: mid- to late 3rd century.

Structure AA

Site A. This rather incomplete structure was the only one excavated at Alcester where conditions favoured the preservation of evidence for a timber floor, supported on joists. The construction appeared to be much like that of the large timber huts that construction companies used on site before the invention of Portakabins, with the floors constructed of independent sections. Large joists, lying directly on the ground, were interspersed with smaller ones. The sections may not have had any relationship with the superstructure, merely providing a level base for a large floor area. Occasionally the building was anchored by upright posts, and a trapezoidal area in the presumed centre of the building defined by slots and postholes may have been related to a lantern-like arrangement in the roof for air, light, or to let out smoke from a brazier.

The building was evidently a workshop associated with the working of leather, particularly for shoes, and was provided with an underfloor rubbish pit (pit F). Its relationship to the structures fronting street B (site C) was unclear.

Dating: 3rd century.

Structure FC

Site F. This structure is difficult to interpret. It covered a more or less rectangular area some 23.4m × 10.8m, and consisted of a discontinuous outside wall with occasional postholes within the slots. The east side wall, in particular, is ambiguous and its complex appearance may be the result of rebuilding, to widen or narrow the building. Indeed the building may have been of two phases, but in spite of careful excavation the stratigraphy did not provide firm evidence to suggest that the various slots which compose it were not contemporary. Possible entrances may be postulated in the east wall, and at the east end of the north end wall. The southern end of the building was represented in excavation by a continuation of the west side wall southwards. The interior of the structure was subdivided by cross-walls into rectangular rooms of almost equal size, apparently intercommunicating at the west end, as the slots of the partition walls terminated before their junction with the west wall. It is difficult to be sure how such a building could be roofed, if indeed it had a roof, and was not merely, for example, a series of pens for animals. There appear to be two alternatives: a) that the roof ridge was longitudinal to the rectangle and supported on the side walls, or b) that a series of transverse ridges was supported on the room divisions. There was no evidence for the structure's function.

Dating: late 3rd to early 4th century.

Group C timber buildings with post-in-trench construction (fig 110)

Examples of this type were found on sites E, F, and G. (See also pp 159–60 for a discussion of this type.)

Structure EC

Site E. This was a slightly built but quite large hall-like building, situated beside and broadside on to a street. The main structure was composed of a rectangle 16.7m × 6.8m, of which the side walls were represented by a continuous trench, within which very small postholes could occasionally be discerned. The south end wall was similarly constructed, but at each of its ends were southward facing projections, suggesting buttressing. The north wall, however, was composed of individual postholes, perhaps representing a portico. Annexed to the south end wall was a subsidiary square room, containing a hearth. There was a possible further continuation to the south. A continuation southwards of the west side wall, after an interruption, was not matched by a corresponding extension of the east side wall, and is therefore difficult to relate to the rest of the plan. Internally the building was subdivided into rooms by partition walls. A slot lying outside the building to the west, and parallel with its side walls, although not containing postholes, should probably be related to it and may represent a corridor or verandah. There was no evidence for function, but the building's position adjacent to a street may suggest that it could have been a shop, perhaps with living accommodation.

Dating: late 2nd century?

Structures FA, FB, ED–EJ

There were several examples on sites E and F of small square structures, some of which, particularly EH and EI, had well-defined post-in-trench construction; in others, the remains were so slight or shallow that posts were not discovered, but they may have existed originally. The essential characteristics of these small structures were the presence of slightly rounded corners to the trenches, and where complete, the presence of a single entrance adjacent to a corner. In some cases there was a suggestion that the buildings were enclosed within an outer structure, possibly a fence. It is not known if the structures were roofed or not. Professor Sir Ian Richmond, on visiting the site, likened the buildings to Continental cigarette or newspaper kiosks, and suggested that they may have been small booths, perhaps connected with a market. Equally they could have been pens for small animals such as chickens or ducks.

Dating: early 3rd century.

Structure GA

This was a fragmentary structure measuring 4.8m by at least 13m, dating to the late 2nd to mid-3rd century (see fig 89).

Group D timber buildings with individual postholes (fig 110)

Examples of this type were found on sites D, E, F, G, and H. (See also pp 160–2 for a discussion of this type.)

Structure HA

An incomplete rectangular structure was found in trench H II, consisting of irregular postholes mostly in pits, some cutting earlier rubbish pits; some postholes showed signs of having been recut. The building measured about 12m × 7m at maximum. The east wall was represented by an approximately linear arrangement of large and small posts. The building was subdivided into one small and one large room by a cross-wall, where the postholes were set into earlier pits. Traces of a cobble surface were found within the structure. It is probable that this structure was of more than one phase, but the absence of stratigraphy makes it impossible to assign individual postholes to a particular phase. The overall plan seems to have persisted through any rebuilding.

Dating: Antonine to 3rd century on.

Structure EK

Structure EK was a rectangular building 12.9m × 7m, of five bays. The west end wall was incomplete as a result of later disturbance. The entrance was at the east fronting street C. There is no evidence that building EK was an aisled structure, and the postholes found probably represent the outside walls.

Dating: late 3rd century.

Structure EL

South of structure EK was another posthole building (EL), of more irregular form, and with an incomplete north wall. It measured 10m by approximately 2.8m.

Dating: late 3rd century.

Structure ELA

A somewhat similar structure to the south (structure ELA) lacked evidence for a north wall, and did not have traces of shallow slots between the posts. It represented a rebuilding of structure EL described above.

Dating: late 3rd century.

Structure EM

Structure EM was similar to the possible aisled buildings found on site D, with the difference that traces remained of a shallow slot joining some of the postholes, perhaps indicating the presence of an outside wall. In this case, therefore, it appears that the building was not aisled, but that the roof was supported on posts, in five bays, and that between the posts the walls were formed of lesser timbers deriving at the base from a shallow foundation. These timbers could have been horizontal or vertical plankwork. The building measured 9m × 3.5m.

Dating: late 3rd century.

Site D, trench D1. Examples of individual posthole buildings spanned phases IV–VI, in the form of barn-like structures which may or may not have been aisled. The posts for which evidence survived, in the form of postholes within stone-packed postpits, may have formed internal arcades, the external walls of the building having left no, or ambiguous, evidence. This is quite probable if the external walls were of slight construction, as would be natural in a building where the main thrust of the roof would be taken on the aisle posts. Alternatively the surviving postholes may have themselves represented the external walls.

Structure DB

The phase IV building (structure DB) was of six or seven bays, with a somewhat irregular south wall of smaller posts set fairly close together. There was a possible porch in the west and a small annexe in the south-east corner. The western line of posts was fragmentary in survival. The length of the building was at least 16.3m, and the width of the nave 6m.

Dating: late 3rd century.

Structure DC

The phase IV structure was rebuilt in phase V (structure DC). Here the postpits were larger, subrectangular, set closer together, and represented perhaps four bays. The surviving length was 6.1m, and the width 4.8m. Two large iron-working hearths were at the south end, one just inside, and one just outside the building. Outside, to the south, was a large pit containing iron-working waste and rubbish.

Dating: early 4th century.

Structure DCA

In phase VI the phase V building was extended southwards by two bays to form a structure (structure DCA) 10.6m long, by the addition of four extra postholes set rather further apart from each other than those further north, to give a bay length here of 2.7m as opposed to 1.3m. The effect was to enclose the southern iron-working hearth within the building at its south end. Some stone rubble outside the east and west walls may have been the remains of stone foundation trenches, indicating that the building was an aisled structure, but the material was too fragmentary and dispersed to allow a firm conclusion on this point.

Dating: 4th century.

Structure DD

In trench D II another posthole building was discovered in phase VIII. This had a slightly tapered plan, the surviving ends of the building being slightly less wide than the centre. The postholes also tended to diminish in size towards the ends. In this structure there was no differentiation between the posts and the postpits, though it must be assumed that what chiefly survived were the pits. The building had six surviving bays, with a length of 13m and a width at

the centre of about 4m. It had been constructed over the metalling of the disused street C.

Dating: late 4th century.

Structures FG and PA

On sites E, P I, P III, P VI, and F, just north of street A, a double line of postholes was found abutting the ditch to the north of the street. These were incompletely excavated, and may have represented buildings fronting the street, or a double fence line. The postholes were regularly spaced, forming a series of 2.7m square bays. There was little room for a side wall between the southernmost line and the street to form an aisled structure, but this cannot be ruled out.

Dating: 4th century.

Structure FD

On site F, a rectilinear timber building of some complexity was found. Essentially it was a rectangular building measuring 11m × 8.5m, divided into two rooms, the smaller to the north. The west wall continued north and south of the structure, and the east wall continued by two postholes to the south of the main structure. These extensions may have indicated that building FD was part of a much larger building of which other traces did not survive, or it may be that the western and eastern extensions merely indicated the position of property boundaries, such as a fence. In any case the central part of the structure was rebuilt on a similar plan, and then enclosed within a stone wall in phase XI (see 'Structures FE and FF', p 152). An alternative explanation of this structure sees the northern 'aisle' possibly as a free-standing building similar to EL, followed by a range of rooms around the enclosure walls (see 'Sites E, F, J, and P, phases X–XII', p 88 and below).

Dating: 4th century.

Group E buildings with stone foundations (fig 111)

Examples of this type were found by Mr (now Professor) Richard Tomlinson, east and west of site D; by the late H V Hughes, west of site G; and on site G itself. Few details are available of Tomlinson's and Hughes' excavations (see fig 4 for location; fig 11 for plans of these sites).

In addition, a stone structure on Site F is considered here. (See also pp 162–3 for a discussion of this type.)

Tomlinson's western building

Tomlinson's western building (fig 11), like that excavated in Priory Road in 1962, had a timber-built predecessor, possibly of late 1st-century date, of uncertain form, with both postholes and slots present. The stone building itself was of more than one phase. It was perhaps constructed in the later 3rd century and subsequently underwent considerable internal alterations, presumably at some time in the 4th century. It may have been overlain by a late Roman posthole structure.

Tomlinson's eastern building

The remains of Tomlinson's eastern building were more fragmentary (fig 11). It had ranges of rooms north and south of a courtyard which was open to the west. The eastern ends of the ranges were joined by a wall, although there was no evidence for further rooms along the east side of the building.

Hughes' building

The building on Hughes' site T (fig 11) was built with its short axis to the main road but not well aligned on it. It seems to have been in origin an aisled structure, to the east of which were added a corridor and small projecting wings.

All three buildings were situated end on to Street A. All had foundations of small stone rubble and could be paralleled in any late Roman town site. What is perhaps less typical is their rather dispersed plan, with large spaces between them. Some of the timber buildings described could have been ancillary structures, but it is not possible to demonstrate this positively, in the absence of precise dating evidence.
Dating: late 3rd to 4th century.

Structure FE

On Site F (phase XI) an earlier free-standing timber building (structure FD, described above) was enclosed within a stone perimeter wall (structure FE). Alternatively, the building could now be interpreted as a courtyard building with a central space surrounded by buildings on three sides perhaps with a corridor on the north side of the courtyard. However, the postholes so closely follow the plan of their predecessors that it is perhaps more sensible to envisage a continuation of the existing plan of a rectangular building, now within a perimeter wall. This wall measured 18.3m × 18.6m internally. (See also 'Sites E, F, J, and P, phase XI', p 88 where the idea of a courtyard building is further investigated.)
Dating: mid- to late 4th century.

Structures FE and FF

In phase XII the stone enclosure wall, structure FE, described above still stood but without its interior timber building. The postholes had been replaced by a metalled surface, and the only other internal feature was an internal L-shaped stone foundation in the south-east corner (structure FF). Although the perimeter wall was of slight construction, the L-shaped foundation was very substantial, and must have supported a structure of considerable weight, perhaps a recessed monumental entrance.
Dating: mid- to late 4th century.

Group F other buildings, not covered in previous groups (fig 111)

Examples were found on site G.

Structure GC

A very curious structure was erected on site G in phase IV consisting of walls represented by foundation or robbing trenches forming the west, north, and east sides. The wall trenches on the west side incorporated a small annexe and had vertical sides and flat bottoms, some containing fragments of painted wall plaster. The northern and eastern sides were much shallower with rounded profiles in section. The south wall was composed of groups of vertical postholes, some set into individual pits, perhaps supporting horizontal planking. These post-groups continued around the internal face of the western annexe, and appeared to be an integral part of its construction. Two similar postgroups were found within the northern foundation trench, probably indicating the position of an entrance. Some internal postholes may or may not have been structural or even associated with the building. The whole was placed within an enclosure represented by a semi-circular ditch to the north and west, and by an east–west gully with an entrance, to the south. The series of buildings erected on this site on approximately the same ground plan defies interpretation, and the writer has found no parallels for this combination of widely diverse building techniques within the same building.
Dating: early 4th century.

Structures GE and GF

Structure GE (phase VI) was incomplete, but included a row of five substantial predominantly squared postholes, packed with large lias blocks forming the west wall of a rectangular structure some 9m × 8m. The postholes were linked by a discontinuous foundation trench which was structurally earlier, but which may have been incorporated into the final construction. A further possible foundation trench lay to the west of the southern pair of postholes. The north wall was represented by groups of large lias blocks which may have formerly contained posts which had been replaced by stone packing. A shallow stone-filled trench joined the three eastern pits. Two further pits and stone groups continued the line of the eastern wall to the south. To the north was a small annexe of approximately rectangular shape represented by postholes with stone packings, of much slighter construction than the main building.

Structure GE after the demolition of GF

The northern annexe disappeared in phases VII–IX, although the northern end of the main structure persisted. In these later phases a timber-lined tank or reservoir was placed outside the west wall.

Dating: late 4th century.

It is difficult to imagine how any of the structures on site G could be roofed effectively, and the combination of strong foundations around the west, north, and east sides, and the absence of evidence for the south side, is a grave bar to interpretation. Nevertheless the phase VI structure, in particular, is interesting if only because of its uniqueness.

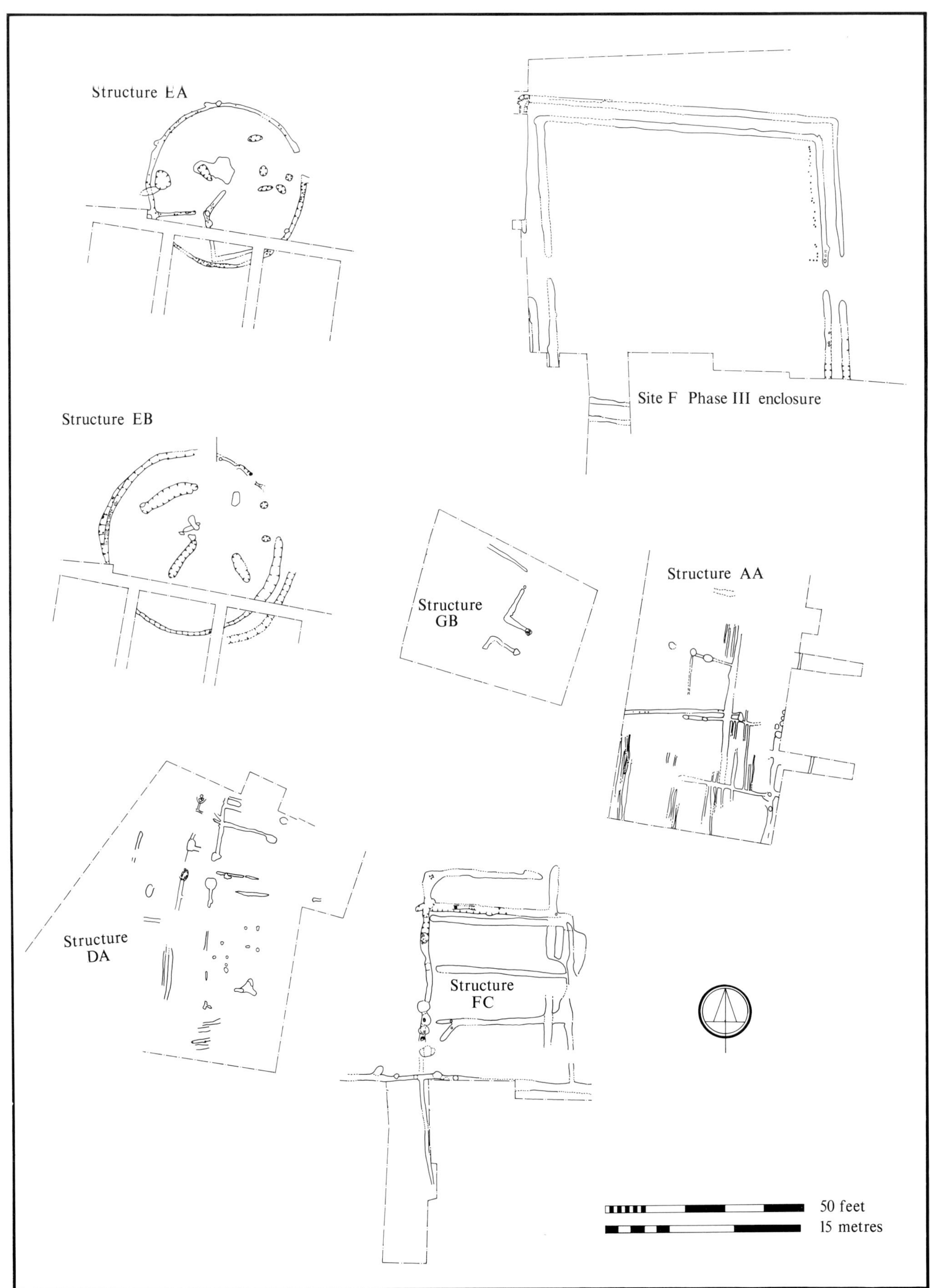

Figure 109 Building types: groups A and B

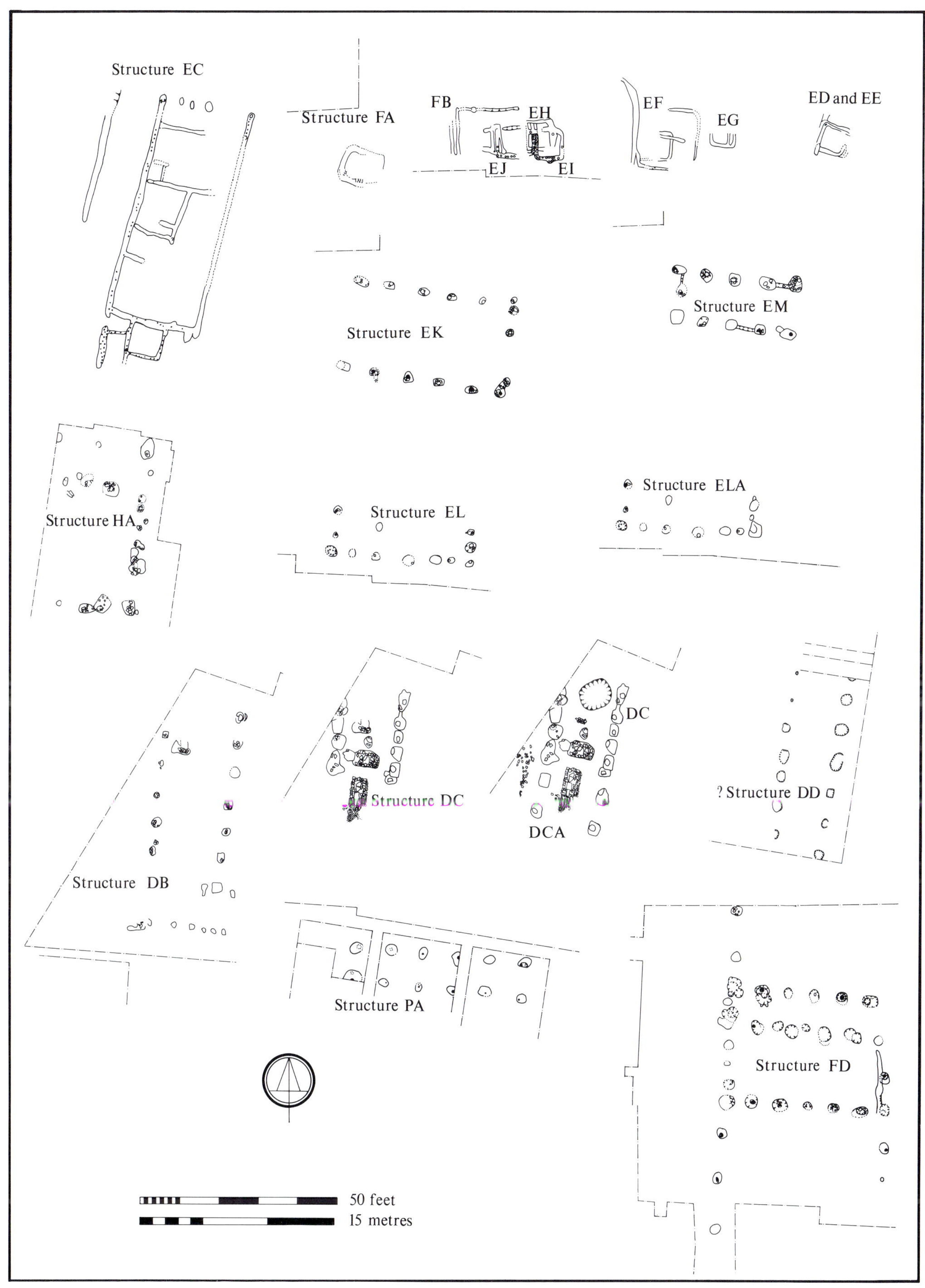

Figure 110   Building types: groups C and D

155

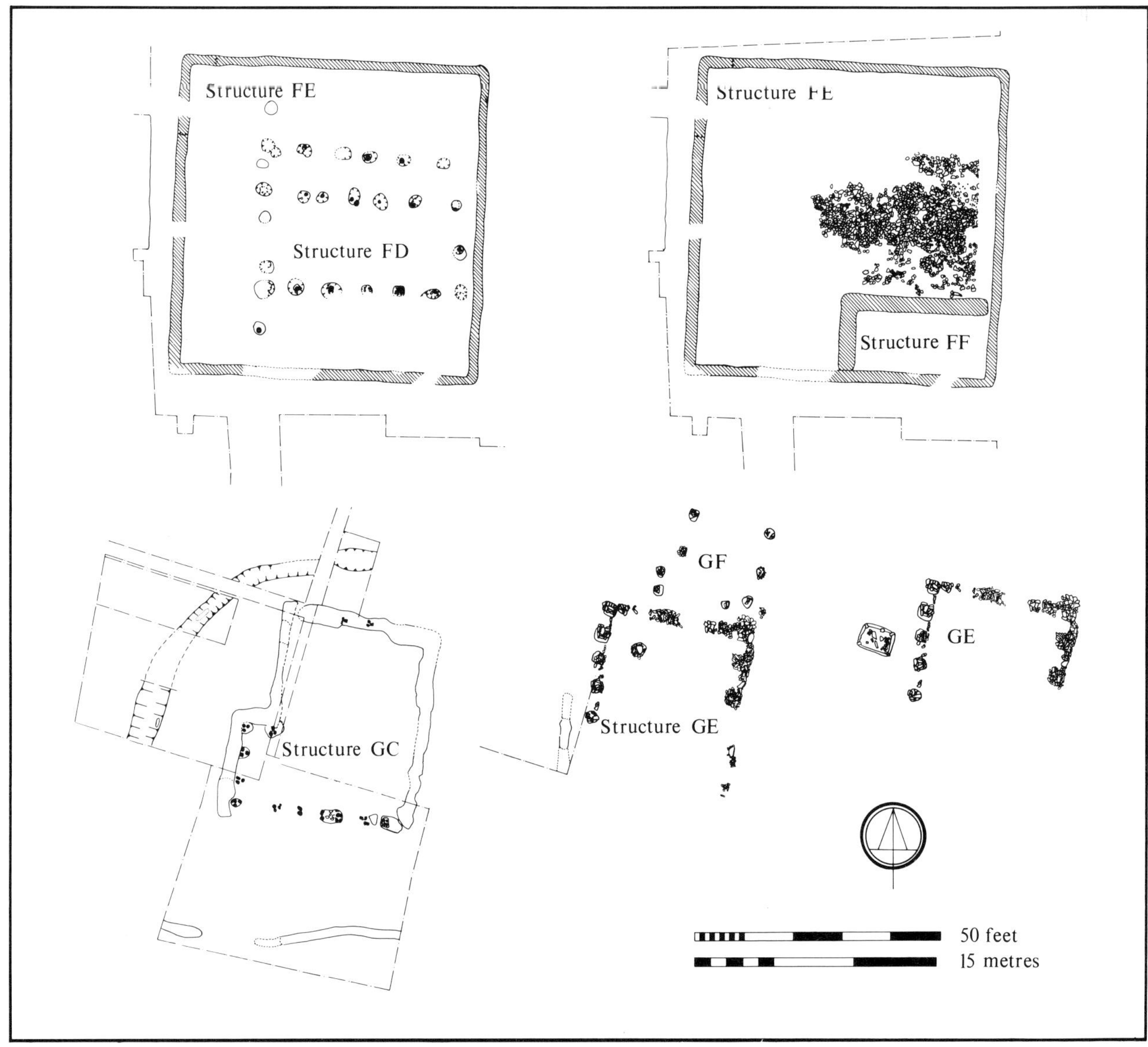

Figure 111 Building types: groups E and F

Buildings: discussion *Paul Booth*

The range of structural evidence from Birch Abbey and other parts of the town is very diverse. Birch Abbey produced a wide variety of buildings, with evidence of sufficient quantity and quality that some trends in the development of building types and construction methods can begin to be discerned. Early structures, drawing on both native Iron Age and more Romanized traditions, used a variety of sleeper beam and post- or stake-in-trench construction techniques. Some of these techniques persisted into the 4th century, but the dominant timber construction type in the later 3rd and the 4th century was the posthole building. In the later 4th century there may have been more diversity of construction types.

Broadly speaking there was also a trend for some early timber buildings to be replaced in the 3rd–4th centuries by structures either stone-built or based on stone cills, but this was by no means a universal occurrence, and a feature of the sites excavated in Birch Abbey is the variety of building types which were in use simultaneously. In the later Roman period these included stone-based and entirely timber-built structures.

Possible public/official buildings

There is little direct evidence for the function of many of the Birch Abbey buildings. Many may have combined two or more of a range of domestic, commercial, industrial, or agricultural functions; no public buildings were identified. The one exception may have been the double parallelogram feature in site F, in any case strictly an enclosure rather than a building, which may perhaps have had a religious function. Apart from this there is no suggestion that any of the Birch Abbey buildings had a public or official purpose. Such buildings probably did exist in Alcester, however, and two possible sites are discussed here.

The first of these lay east of Bleachfield Street on the north side of the main east–west road through the town. A substantial stone-built structure, investigated by Davis over a period of years and partly re-excavated by Hughes in the late 1950s (see above, p 152; **5** and **17** on fig 3), may have been the same as that located in the south-western corner of site L, where stone walls and robber trenches were roughly on and at right-angles to a west-north-west to east-south-east alignment. It is clear from trenches L VIII and L XI that there were two distinct periods of stone building, as seemed to be implied by the comments of Hughes (1958, 16) and suggested by the notes of Davis who recorded two successive concrete floors. The relationship of the various elements remains uncertain, however. The walls in site L trenches VIII and XI are on slightly different alignments. While they could belong to the same structure, they may have been of different phases within it. There was certainly a hypocaust in trench VIII and the depth of deposits in trench XI suggests that there was also one there, the two being situated almost 15m apart. Davis also recorded two hypocausts, both presumably further west, and the ?flue or *praefurnium* found by Hughes (*ibid*, 16) may have been the same as or related to one of these. The locations and orientations of the earlier excavations are not sufficiently precise to allow correlation with the evidence from site L, but it must be more than coincidence that structures of very similar type are found immediately adjacent. Whether the hypocausts belonged to ordinary heated rooms or to part of a bath suite is unknown.

The dating is also unclear. The later features in site L are mainly assigned to the 4th century, and in trench L VIII all the structural features are thought to have postdated a ditch which was filled in the 2nd century (fig 103). The primary structure in trench XI, however, distinguished by masonry of good quality, does not seem to be closely dated and could perhaps have been earlier than the other features in the south end of site L. Evidence from Davis' excavation suggested a possible 2nd-century date for at least one of the concrete floors which he found, but the reliability of this date is uncertain. It is tentatively suggested, however, that it may have been broadly correct and that part of the site was occupied at this time by a substantial structure with probably more than one hypocaust. Features of this structure include the use of circular *pilae* and perhaps also of stamped tiles. Three of the latter, bearing a stamp TCD, unique to Alcester (Booth 1980, 5), are known from this site and its immediate environs, and even though none was securely stratified their association with the site must be significant. The only other example of this stamp is from a site *c* 1km south of the town, discovered in fieldwalking in 1989. Stamped tiles are perhaps more likely to have occurred in a 2nd-century context than later. While on the present limited evidence several interpretations of this site are possible, it seems that the earliest stone structure, perhaps of 2nd-century date, was unusually well built and had one or more heated rooms. In the absence of contemporary evidence from Alcester and similar settlements in the region for well-appointed town houses of 2nd-century date it may be more likely that this was a public or official structure (cf Smith 1987, 15). In view of the location beside one of the main roads through the town a *mansio* with an integral bath suite seems the most reasonable possibility, though other possibilities include an independent bath building, and not all *mansiones* necessarily had main road frontage locations (eg Chelmsford and Godmanchester). The later building on the site could have been a reconstructed form of the original structure, perhaps covering a larger area, or it may simply have been another stone-founded house comparable to those excavated further west in Birch Abbey. The point cannot be proved without careful re-excavation.

Further north, immediately outside the south-western corner of the defended area, lay other unusual buildings with a possible official function (Booth 1985). The earliest of these is little known, having been encountered only in deep holes in the course of salvage recording at Coulters Garage in 1979 (**61** on fig 3). The bases of waterlogged posts suggested the presence of a timber building, perhaps a granary of standard military type, of possible later 2nd-century date. This was associated with substantial deposits of carbonized grain and chaff. These poorly understood features were succeeded *c* AD 300 on a slightly different alignment by a very large stone building with walls *c* 1m thick. It was *c* 11.5m wide and at least 40m long, being divided by cross walls into a series of at least ten rooms each *c* 9.5m × 3m internally. The building is without precise parallel in Britain but it is most likely to have been used for storage. While there is no direct evidence, such a building could have been used for the *annona militaris*. The scale of the construction and its location in a part of the town away from dense domestic settlement certainly suggests that this was not a private granary. The existence of facilities for the collection of the *annona* in Britain has been widely predicted (eg Rivet 1975, 112) but hitherto likely examples of such facilities have been scarce, though they include an aisled building adjacent to the *mansio* at Godmanchester (Goodburn 1976, 334). It is just possible that the underlying timber structure at Coulters Garage could have preceded the stone one in function as well as location, though this cannot be proven. The timber building was probably constructed before the earthwork defences and lay some 40m outside their line, perhaps at the edge of still-marshy ground. The latter, however, was filled in before the construction of the stone building. This was demolished in turn to make way for the construction of the late Roman town wall, which passed immediately north of the north end of the building. The date of the demolition and robbing of the building has been discussed in detail above. There is no evidence for later structures on the same site assuming the probable function of their predecessors.

Other buildings

Group A native-type huts and enclosures

The division of the Birch Abbey buildings by construction type has already been outlined above (see 'Buildings: summary description of types', p 148). Of the categories described some are more easily defined than others. The group A buildings, native-type huts

and enclosures, incorporate two different construction types (fig 109). The round houses EA and EB were principally of stake-in-trench construction, with occasional larger posts in the wall line, certainly of the earlier structure EA. Part of a possibly comparable structure *c* 8m in diameter (and thus rather smaller than the Birch Abbey examples) was located in excavations at 1–5 Bleachfield Street (**57** on fig 3). This structure was dated to the early 2nd century, but insufficient of it lay within the excavated area to determine with certainty if it was a building or simply a circular enclosure (Booth forthcoming). The former seems more likely, despite the apparent absence of floor surfaces. This structure was defined by a curving slot, but there was no evidence for stakeholes in the base of the slot.

Buildings of this type occur elsewhere in Roman towns, for example at Godmanchester, where such buildings were common (Green 1975, 196), and at Baldock (Stead & Rigby 1986, 36–8). At Godmanchester they did not outlast the 1st century AD; the date of the Baldock examples is uncertain, though one of them could have survived into the 2nd century. Round houses have even been found in 'suburban or peripheral areas' at cities such as Lincoln and London (Perring 1987, 149). More locally, at the major settlement of Tiddington, the Iron Age round house tradition also persisted alongside rectilinear timber structures into the early 2nd century (N Palmer pers comm). There are also sites where the type is probably not a direct survival of Iron Age times, such as Ringstead (Northants), *Vindolanda*, (Bidwell, 1985, 25–31) and Thistleton (P Irving pers comm). Perhaps the Alcester example should be seen in this context.

The double-quadrilateral enclosure in site F was considered with the group A structures principally because of its early date (figs 67, 68, 109). In terms of constructional type it probably belongs with the group C (post-in-trench) structures. Postholes were found in the slot on each side of the inner entrance, and it may be assumed that vertical timbers were set along the entire length of both slots even though the evidence for this did not survive. A striking parallel for this enclosure, although with differences of detail, was found at 6 Birch Abbey in 1983 (Cracknell 1985a, 26–7; **81** on fig 3). Here two slots on a comparable east–west alignment extended some 12m across the site, neither end being located. The slots were some 1.90–1.95m apart (centre to centre) and *c* 0.30m and 0.35m across with comparable depths. They were roughly straight-sided and flat-bottomed and were thought to have held horizontal timbers. The corresponding slots in site F were *c* 0.50m wide and up to 0.50m deep, with U-shaped profiles. They were *c* 1.50m apart (centre to centre).

The differences of detail between the two sites may mean that they do not represent the same sort of phenomenon, but the overall character of the two groups of features is very similar. It seems unlikely, in fact, that the slots at 6 Birch Abbey would have contained horizontal timbers. There would have been little point in laying timbers in the trenches if these were only intended to carry fences or palisades.

There is no other evidence from 6 Birch Abbey to suggest that the slots formed part of a building, unless it was a covered walkway, which is improbable. The slots here are therefore probably best interpreted as part of one side of another fenced or palisaded enclosure like the one in site F.

The dates of the two enclosures are similar, though they could be considered as successive. The 6 Birch Abbey slots were stratigraphically the earliest features on the site and may be assigned to the 1st century. The site F enclosure was not stratigraphically primary and was tentatively dated to the Neronian–Trajanic period. It is considered to have been in use in phases III and IV in this area, but there seems to be no good reason why it should not have remained in use in phase V as well, in which case it may have survived until the late 2nd century. The function of both the possible enclosures is uncertain, but superficially the carefully planned layout in site F has a religious character. A comparable layout, in stone, occurs at the temple complex and settlement site at Nettleton, Wilts, where building XI consisted of a double square with external dimensions of 21.9m. The two walls were just 0.9m apart. The building was interpreted as a 'hostel' (Wedlake 1982, 17, fig 2), but this is scarcely credible. Equally, the size of the structure is such that it is most unlikely to have been roofed, despite a superficial similarity to temples of Romano-Celtic type. An enclosed, but unroofed, shrine may be a possible explanation for both this and the Alcester structures. If the function of both enclosures was the same, and particularly if it was a specialized, perhaps religious one, it is less likely that they were in use simultaneously. The site F enclosure may then be seen as replacing a comparable site at 6 Birch Abbey. A possible context for the change of site of this establishment would be the designation of a large area at the northern end of Birch Abbey as an open market space (see above), requiring relocation of some activities elsewhere. The slots at 6 Birch Abbey were sealed by gravel surfaces which covered the site for much of the Roman period.

Groups B and C timber buildings with horizontal sleeper beams and those with post-in-trench construction

Beam slot buildings (group B) form the most problematical group of structures on the site (fig 109). None of the buildings assigned to this group has a complete plan. The more complex examples (particularly structures AA and DA) were imperfectly preserved and may have had more than one phase. The latter was probably also true of structure FC. In all these cases it was not possible to distinguish between the phases represented, and the reconstruction of the plans was thereby also rendered impossible. Even where the evidence for layout was relatively clear, as with structure FC, it was difficult to interpret this in structural terms. For example there is no reason to suppose that the southernmost east–west slot FI 190/220 was not an integral part of the structure (fig 73), yet it makes a nonsense of the otherwise relatively coherent plan, with the result that it is unlikely that FC could have been a single building. Special pleading would be required to distinguish between structural elements and features such as fences using the same construction method (as eg in the successor structure FD on the same site and in structure GG in site G). The suggestion that FC could represent a series of animal pens may be the most reasonable explanation.

In several examples of beam slot construction the technique was combined with others, particularly the use of vertical posts, found in structures AA, FC, GB, and DA. In any case the evidence for floor joists in structure AA may suggest that this was a rather different type of building from the other examples. A late 4th-century building at 1–5 Bleachfield Street was thought to be of comparable type, with the difference that the floor joists were raised above ground level on a rubble platform (see below, p 161).

The sleeper beam and post-in-trench construction types (groups B and C) may be seen as related (figs 109, 110). The date range assigned to both groups is wide. It extended through the 2nd and 3rd centuries and two beam slot buildings were assigned to the 4th century. These were building FC, of late 3rd- to early 4th-century date, and structure GH, thought to be late 4th century.

The use of the beam slot construction technique is known from elsewhere in Alcester. Part of a structure based on substantial horizontal timbers was excavated at Lloyd's Bank in 1975 (**55** on fig 3). This was not closely dated, but is unlikely to have been earlier than the 3rd century. Beam slot buildings also occurred within the defended area, both at Tibbet's Close (**83** on fig 3) and Gas House Lane (**93** on fig 3). In both cases a 3rd-century or later date is certain. This evidence is therefore consistent with that from Birch Abbey in suggesting that the beam slot construction technique covered a fairly wide chronological range, though how far its use extended into the 4th century remains unclear. At Tibbet's Close the beam slot building, probably of 3rd-century date, was replaced by a posthole structure. This sequence has been noted elsewhere, for example at Neatham (Millett & Graham 1986, 19), though here the change may have occurred somewhat earlier (*ibid*, 24). Within Birch Abbey itself structure DA, of 1st-century to early Antonine date, preceded a sequence of posthole buildings, and in sites F and G beam slot buildings were both predated and postdated by posthole buildings.

The functional range of the beam slot buildings was apparently quite wide. It included the specialist possible leather workshop AA (fig 17). Building DA was the first of a sequence of structures, the later ones of which also had an industrial function, but DA itself may have been a purely domestic building (figs 43, 109). Other buildings of this type, occurring particularly in site G, were thought to have possible agricultural connections.

The post-in-trench construction group (group C), like group B, is heterogeneous in terms of building plans. Building EC is arguably the only coherent structure in both groups B and C. It is one of very few buildings of classic 'strip' plan, embellished with a portico at its front but basically consisting of a small 'front' room and a larger back room with subdivisions and small additions, one housing a hearth, at the rear. A curious feature of this building is that its facade faced north, away from the line of street A. It may have fronted onto the large open market space to the north.

The small buildings ED–EJ etc were also concentrated exclusively in the vicinity or on the actual edge of the postulated market area, and their possible relevance for this area has already been mentioned. Comparable structures at 6 Birch Abbey (**81** on fig 3), also on the edge of the gravelled area, apparently employed post-and-slot construction techniques; they were therefore analogous but not exactly identical to the sites E and F examples. Like the beam slot building at Tibbet's Close (**83** on fig 3), the posts and slots at 6 Birch Abbey were replaced by structures entirely of posthole construction, but of comparable, irregular form and size, and presumably similar function, to their predecessors. A similar development ensued in site J, on the southern edge of the market area.

Group D timber buildings with individual postholes

Buildings largely or entirely based on earthfast posts (group D) were the most common structural type, although several of the examples listed above represented reconstructions of one building in successive phases (fig 110). The Birch Abbey examples of this construction type were concentrated mainly in sites D, E, and F but the distribution of the type was in fact universal, with structure CWC, in site C phase VI, being the best example from the southern part of the excavated area (see fig 19). With one exception, all the examples from Birch Abbey are thought to date from the later 3rd to 4th centuries. The exception was building HA in trench H II, to which an Antonine to early 3rd-century date was assigned. Two of the stone buildings excavated by Tomlinson, that in Priory Road (**12** on fig 3) and the westerly of his Birch Abbey buildings (**30** on fig 3), appeared to have predecessors of posthole construction, though little can be said about their plans. These structures may both have been of comparable date to building HA, since a later 3rd- to 4th-century date is likely for their stone successors.

The group D buildings fall into two principal groups, those which form coherent, self-contained rectangular buildings, and those which comprise less well-defined structures. The majority of the buildings were represented by simple rectangular arrangements of postholes (though in some examples evidence for one or more sides was lacking). They ranged in size from *c* 6m × 5m (structure DC) to perhaps *c* 18m × 6m (structure CWC). Apart from these extremes, dimensions were generally within the range *c* 10–15m × 4–7m. There was usually little suggestion of major internal divisions, though evid-

ence for possible transverse partitions was noted in structures HA, DC, and DCA. There was equally no certain evidence that any of these buildings was aisled, although it remains a possibility that some were. Structures of this order of size and simple type must have been common in Roman settlements. At Brampton, Norfolk, two adjacent posthole buildings, *c* 5.5m × 9m and 5.7m × 8.7m, of late 2nd- to 3rd-century date, had their narrow axes to the street frontage in exactly the same way as structures EK, EL, ELA, and EM (Green 1977, 44–7).

The most problematical of these buildings, and the only one with possible evidence for a substantial aisle, was structure FD (figs 74, 75, 76, 110, 111). This, exceptionally, consisted of three parallel rows of posts instead of two, which may indicate a building with a single aisle on the north side of the main room or nave. This building would have been unusually wide, however, and the evidence for more than one phase of postholes in the northern 'arcade' may indicate that there were separate structures here which had overlapped, though it is not easy to distinguish the individual plans. One difficulty with this building, as with some of the other structures of this type, is the apparent irregularity of the pairing of what must have been the principal structural members. In structure FD the closest correspondence of alignment and spacing, with one exception, was between the posts of the northern and southern walls, perhaps suggesting that the intermediate row of posts was somehow of secondary importance. The problematical exception, however, is that the post at the north-east corner was apparently missing, so that the south wall was of six bays but the north wall was only five bays long.

An alternative explanation for these buildings might be that the original structure consisted of two rows of posts, of very similar size and form to structures EL, ELA, and EM (figs 71–2, 110) in the position of the northern 'aisle', followed by a structure incorporating three ranges inside the north, west, and south walls of the stone enclosure. (The latter structure is discussed below under 'Group E buildings incorporating stone foundations', p 162.)

This interpretation, however, does not explain the close correlation between the posts of building FD and the slots of building FC below. The continuity between FC and FD is striking. The irregularity of both, however, is such that it may be more likely that they represented a series of small fenced enclosures, with the fences in some cases renewed several times. They were replaced by the enclosure wall FE and three rows of posts within the wall and parallel to it. These posts perpetuated some of the alignment of FC.

A rather different manifestation of posthole construction occurred in the final phase in sites F and P (structures FG and PA; figs 79, 110). These consisted of pairs of parallel postholes some 2.5–3m apart aligned roughly east–west along the northern edge of street A. Their extent in both sites is unknown. In site P, six pairs of posts were located, but the series could have extended to both east and west. Whether they formed narrow structures or a series of free-standing squares is unknown, but the regularity of the layout is such that the former seems more likely. A close parallel for this kind of building exists at Neatham (Hants), where a structure just over 3m wide and at least 13m long, interpreted perhaps as a row of shops, was aligned alongside the Silchester–Chichester road probably in the 3rd century (Millett & Graham 1986, 16–18, fig 15). At Birch Abbey there is no direct evidence for the function of these structures, but they seem to have been separated from street A by a ditch which would presumably have restricted access from the street. Surfaces to the north may indicate an extension of the open 'market' area at this time, and the structures may have been approached from that direction, though it is unlikely that an expansion of market facilities was required at this time (this phase being assigned to the second half of the 4th century at least).

Several groups of postholes did not seem to indicate structures of recognizable type. These included the posthole arrangements found in site J in phase VIII (fig 72). Such arrangements were essentially irregular and may have belonged to small, frequently rebuilt structures of what may be considered the 'market-stall' type, paralleled at 6 Birch Abbey in the 1983 excavations (**81** on fig 3) and replacing earlier equally irregular constructions of post-and-slot technique. Repeated reconstruction is the principal reason why the plans of these structures are so difficult to discern. Elsewhere, structures EL and ELA, both poorly defined on their north sides, may possibly have been of comparable type. Further groups of postholes may not have belonged to either type of building. A line of postholes between structure EM and the more haphazard groupings to the north just described may have related to the latter but could also have served as a fence line (fig 72). The evidence for structure GJ, occurring in a late phase (IX) in site G, consisted largely of a row of postholes which could perhaps as well be considered a fence-line as part of a building (fig 98).

Late Roman posthole buildings occur quite widely in Alcester. A building at Tibbet's Close (Cracknell 1985a, 14; **83** on fig 3), within the defences, has already been referred to. Unfortunately the plan of this structure was not completely recovered. The same was true of a similar building at 1–5 Bleachfield Street (**57** on fig 3), with a minimum length of 6.5m (it was probably rather longer). This building, which was probably rebuilt at least once, partly overlaid a stone building which seems to have been demolished *c* AD 350. It was in turn replaced by a later timber building of a different construction type (Booth forthcoming). A similar sequence, in which a posthole structure replaced a stone-built one in the late Roman period, may also have occurred in the westerly of the buildings excavated by Tomlinson in Birch Abbey (**30** on fig 3). There can be no doubt that the posthole construction method was one of the standard late Roman building types in Alcester.

Structural aspects of the posthole buildings are problematical. In some cases there was reasonable correspondence between the pairs of posts, and in such instances it may be supposed that these sup-

ported not only wall plates but also roof trusses. In more cases, however, the alignment of the structural posts was very imprecise and it may be less likely that these buildings carried a heavy roof structure. Since very few of the buildings had a large roof span, substantial roof constructions are unlikely to have been necessary. The limited evidence for partitions and aisles has already been referred to. There is equally limited evidence for floor surfaces within the buildings of this type although in some cases already existing gravel surfaces could have served as floors, and in other cases gravel disturbed by the excavation of postholes may have been spread as floor material.

The likely range of functions among the group D structures is as diverse as their locations. Structures DB, DC, and DCA all contained evidence for metalworking; in the last two buildings this was sufficiently extensive to suggest that metalworking was the principal activity. Indeed the amount of space occupied by hearths and related features was such as to leave little or no room for other activities. These buildings may therefore be seen as workshops. They occupied successively a central location at the crossroads of streets A and C, but whether they constituted a self-contained unit is less certain. The absence of a well-defined property boundary on the east side of the buildings might suggest that they were associated with the stone building excavated by Tomlinson a few metres further east.

Most of the posthole structures had street frontage locations, but this does not necessarily elucidate their function. EK, EL, ELA, and EM were all aligned with their narrow axes to street C (figs 71, 72). Structure FD, on the same alignment, stood further back from the frontage. There is no direct functional evidence for any of these buildings. It has already been suggested that EL and ELA had physical affinities with the 'market' structures further north and they may therefore have had a comparable function. Nevertheless, these and EK and EM could all have been domestic buildings, as was suggested for the late 4th-century posthole buildings at 1–5 Bleachfield Street (above), which probably replaced a building which combined domestic with other functions.

Further south, building CWC, like EK, EL, and EM, was also aligned with its narrow axis on street C (figs 19, 29). This (and its northerly neighbour CWB) may have been a 'strip' building of classic type. Its overall dimensions (perhaps *c* 18m × 6m) and what little is known of its plan are consistent with a building of this type. The fact that most of the interior of the building was not available for excavation makes any assessment of its function impossible.

The smaller, irregular posthole structures along the edge of the suggested open market space at the northern margin of the Birch Abbey excavations are assumed to have had a commercial function associated with the market area. The narrow building(s) alongside the north side of street A may have served a similar purpose. In contrast, posthole buildings in site G, structures GG and ?GJ (as well as the intervening beam slot structure GH), were considered to be possible agricultural buildings, perhaps for housing livestock.

A variant on the theme of posthole construction saw the use of stone bases to support the posts at or just above ground level. This technique does not seem to have been common at Birch Abbey, but did occur in site D, where two structures, DE and DF, were each represented by a single row of bases in phase IX (the remainder of these buildings lying outside the excavated area) (figs 53, 60). Parts of structure GE, also of 4th-century date, may have been built in the same way (fig 94). There is no clear comparable evidence from elsewhere in Alcester, but post base construction was found at the nearby settlement of Tiddington from the ?2nd century onwards, though it seems to have been most common in the 4th century (Palmer 1982, 12, 14). Post bases were widely used to support the arcade posts of aisled buildings which were otherwise of stone construction. This type of use is exemplified at Alcester in the building excavated by Hughes in his site T (**28** on fig 3), and also at Tiddington (Palmer 1982, 14).

Other timber building types found elsewhere in Alcester included a good example of a rubble platform construction of very late Roman date at 1–5 Bleachfield Street (building I; **57** on fig 3). The use of rubble platforms in this way was intended to raise a timber construction above ground level. In this instance the building was thought to have rested entirely on joists placed on the rubble. Other possible examples of this type of construction occurred at 1–5 Bleachfield Street, but were much less well defined than building I. No other examples of this type are known in the town, but preservation on this site was good since it did not seem to have been affected by post-Roman agricultural activities. Buildings of this type might have existed further south in Birch Abbey but have been damaged in the post-Roman period.

Group E buildings incorporating stone foundations

The Birch Abbey buildings with stone construction require little comment, particularly since there are no complete building plans from elsewhere in the town to provide comparable data. The use of stone foundations and walls does not necessarily mean that the superstructures of buildings so provided were also of stone. The evidence does not survive to allow certainty on this point, the term 'stone building' is therefore used to indicate the presence of stone foundations without prejudice to the possible nature of the superstructure.

From the work of Davis and others it is clear that stone buildings were common in the later Roman period. Leaving aside the 'public' buildings and those occurring within the Birch Abbey excavations the existence of some five stone-built structures within the defences can be postulated, with perhaps a further dozen in the extramural area. These may be only a small proportion of the original total. At present there is little indication of any uniformity of plan. The building excavated by Hughes was clearly

of aisled type, to which an east-facing corridor and wings were added. That this sequence of development follows a rural pattern was recognized by Todd (1970, 121). The form of the buildings excavated by Tomlinson was, however, rather different (fig 11). The building west of street C is difficult to understand without detailed analysis of its structural sequence (work which is proposed), but it clearly was not at any time an aisled structure, despite extensive internal alterations. The building east of street C seems to have consisted of two groups of rooms on each side of a courtyard. The fact that the latter was open to the west may support the suggestion that there was a connection between this building and the timber industrial buildings in site D.

The most completely excavated stone buildings elsewhere in the extramural settlement are those found at 1–5 Bleachfield Street (Booth forthcoming; **57** on fig 3). The first of these (building V) was built partly in stone but had one room constructed entirely in timber. It dated perhaps from as early as the mid-2nd century. It was enlarged later, in a construction programme which included a new western wall, considerably thicker than the earlier walls, defining a narrow room/passage on the western side of the building. This situation was paralleled in Tomlinson's westerly building, which also had an unusually substantial west wall defining narrow rooms along the west side. If this similarity is more than coincidental its significance is unknown. building V remained in use until the mid-4th century. A later building at 1–5 Bleachfield Street, constructed after the mid-3rd century, was entirely of stone (building VI). Unfortunately its plan is very incomplete, but it is likely to have consisted of at least three rooms with a wide entrance passage at one end. This building may have been largely, if not entirely, agricultural in function, while building V probably combined domestic and industrial/agricultural functions.

A possible agricultural function was suggested for the small stone building GD at the northern edge of site G (fig 92). This building was probably about 5.5m wide. The position of the edge of street A north of site G is not precisely known, but if GD had fronted onto the street it is likely to have been some 6m long. This building was constructed in the early 4th century and robbed in the later part of the century. Its significance is unclear, particularly as it contrasted markedly with the other buildings in site G and seems to have been isolated from other structures. Its relationship to the other site G buildings fronting on the main street is also uncertain; it was separated from structure GC to the south by a fairly substantial ditch but was not segregated from features to the west. A cobbled surface to the west of the building also existed within it. Further evidence for the occurrence of the same layers on both sides of the walls may have indicated that the building was not roofed. The problem of the occurrence of identical deposits inside and outside the building was also encountered in building VI at 1–5 Bleachfield Street Here an agricultural function was also suggested, but could not be specifically demonstrated.

Further west, on the north side of street A were the stone structures FE and FF (figs 76–8, 111). FE was in essence a square enclosure. It may have been built around an irregular, aisled, post-built structure (FD), which would be unique in Roman Alcester. The structural continuity from the underlying beam slot building FC supports this reconstruction, but this argument would be less compelling if the 'aisle' were in fact a free-standing building in its first phase (as suggested above), or if, as is perhaps more likely, both FC and most of the posts assigned to FD represented successive fenced enclosures. The alternative interpretation, however, suggests that the latest posts in the area belonged to a structure associated with the stone wall. Three rows of posts can be discerned, consistently situated with their centres some 5m from the north, south, and east enclosure walls. The rows of posts may have supported constructions the outer edges of which were carried on the enclosure wall. On the basis of this interpretation the entrance to the enclosure/building was probably from the east, into a courtyard area between ranges of rooms on three sides. This too, like the suggested building FD, would be an unusual structure and would effectively turn the initial interpretation of the building plan of FD inside out. Neither explanation is completely satisfactory.

In the following phase (XII; see fig 77) part of the enclosed area was surfaced. The timber constructions were either partly or completely demolished and a room measuring *c* 8.4m × 3.6m internally built in the south-eastern corner of the enclosure wall. The foundation of this room was so substantial that it is most unlikely to have carried a timber superstructure.

There is unfortunately no evidence for the function of these buildings in either phase, though it is perhaps conceivable that the whole complex could have represented the enclosed nucleus of a farm. The establishment of the enclosure wall as a principal feature may indicate, however, that security, perhaps allied to a specific function, was an important consideration.

The final buildings to be discussed are the successive and related structures GC and GE, apparently of 4th-century date. Both of these exhibit peculiarities of construction technique and plan which make interpretation very difficult. Structure GC seems to have been primarily built of stone but with the south wall of timber (fig 92). A combination of stone and timber construction techniques was used at 1–5 Bleachfield Street building V, but there one well-defined room was in timber, possibly carried on horizontal beams resting on large sandstone blocks, so it does not offer a precise parallel for the Birch Abbey building.

The absence of clearly identified internal features makes reconstruction very difficult. The plan makes the use of two roof ridges likely; these could have been parallel or at right-angles, but in either case the absence of internal posts continuing the line of G IA **93** and **100** eastwards is problematical. Such posts, however, could have been set at ground level, leaving little or no trace. The internal postholes which are known form no recognizable pattern. The doorway is not without problems for a hearth lay immediately inside it. This may indicate that the entrance and the hearth belonged to different phases of the building, or possibly that the two groups of posts in the north wall do not indicate a door position, although this remains the most likely possibility. A possible alternative or additional door position can be discerned in the south timber wall just west of the centre line where, uniquely, two pairs of posts occur, contrasting with the more usual grouping of posts elsewhere in the building in clusters of three or four.

The reason for the combination of timber and stone construction remains unknown, but as many of the posts were up to 0.20–0.25m across the timber elements might have been capable of supporting a tiled roof. The relative absence of tile may be explained by its reuse elsewhere after the demolition of the building. It seems unlikely that a building which may have had plastered stone walls (though the stone walls may have been no more than cills) would not have had a tiled roof, but other materials could have been used.

The superstructure of the later building, structure GE, may have been entirely timber-built (figs 94, 111). Its plan, however, is less certain than that of GC, particularly at the south end, where the evidence, which may in any case have been fairly superficial, was poorly preserved. Some internal details, such as the position of a hearth, closely mirrored those in the preceding phase, but evidence for internal partitions was extremely tenuous. Departures from the overall layout of structure GC included the removal of the enclosure ditch which had separated that structure from the rest of site G, and the addition of a subsidiary structure GF to the north side of GE.

GE and GF were at one time in contemporary use. Although structure GF would appear partly to have blocked the northern entrances to GE, this is not really an obstacle to this interpretation. There would presumably have been some means of communication between the two buildings (though this need not have been as wide as the gap between G IV 9A and 10A). Also, if structure GE was essentially domestic in purpose, there would have been no need for two large entrances in its north side and the gaps may have had a different significance. In any case an entrance could still have existed in the north wall of GE, west of GF; alternatively the main entrance to GE could have been in the south wall.

The excavations in the context of the Roman town *Paul Booth*

Introduction

The excavations provide a wealth of data for the development of the south-western part of the Roman town — hereafter referred to (for convenience) as Birch Abbey — along with lesser amounts of information about the rest of the urban area. The Birch Abbey area was, however, at no time central to the settlement as a whole (figs 2–4). In this section of the report, therefore, it is proposed to set the evidence of the excavations in the overall context of the Roman town, drawing on the evidence of the early excavations summarized above and on more recent work. This section is concerned principally with the physical characteristics of the town and considers its origins, the major elements of the settlement and their effects on its growth, and also some of the individual components. The building types are discussed above (see 'Buildings: discussion', p 157). In these areas it both draws on and supersedes earlier surveys (Booth 1980; Booth & Cracknell 1986). In the following discussion, work in progress is not usually referenced, and references to interim publications are only given when these contain particularly important information.

Summary of the development of the Roman town

The town probably developed from a civilian settlement which may have grown up around a fort in the Bleachfield Street area. This settlement expanded considerably through the 2nd century AD, developing a network of irregular streets, most of which branched off a principal east–west road. Earthwork defences, erected perhaps at the end of the 2nd century, enclosed an area in the northern part of the settlement which had been little occupied hitherto. This area saw increased activity in the later Roman period, and the defences were reconstructed, in part on a different alignment, in the later 4th century, but extramural occupation continued to thrive. The extramural area, occupied by a wide variety of timber and stone-built structures, also seems to have contained a large, open surfaced area, thought to be a market place, and perhaps public or official buildings. The latter were a possible *mansio* on the east–west road and, in the northern part of the area, a large store building, built about AD 300, which perhaps replaced a timber granary on the same site. The overall extent of the occupied area may have been as much as *c* 33ha (*c* 81 acres). It is unlikely, however, that all this area was occupied simultaneously and some parts of the town, particularly towards the north-west, may have been less densely settled than others.

A ditch ran through the southern part of the extramural area but did not exactly mark its limits. It was clearly not a defensive feature, and was relatively short-lived. The southern and western sides of the extramural area were defined in places by inhumation cemeteries, of which two have evidence suggesting a regular layout. Less clearly organized areas of burials occurred in Birch Abbey, and scattered inhumations are known from a variety of locations in the town. A few cremation burials are also known, but there is as yet no evidence for early Roman cemeteries.

Origins of the Roman town

The Roman settlement is thought to have originated in the context of early Roman military activity in the west Midlands. There is very little evidence for pre-Roman occupation at Alcester. A small quantity of Iron Age pottery was found at Tibbet's Close in 1983, associated with postholes and a pit (**83** on fig 3; Cracknell 1985a, 13, 18), and elsewhere sherds of hand-made pottery of Iron Age type have occasionally been found, but none apparently in a pre-Roman context. Sherds of late Iron Age or early Roman 'Belgic-type' fabrics also occur infrequently. Just over 1km south of the town, at Oversley Castle, the location of a possible Iron Age defended site of some 7ha may have influenced the siting of Roman military garrisons (see below). The date of this site remains uncertain, however.

There are two foci of Roman military activity at Alcester; one, suggested primarily by artefactual evidence, in the Bleachfield Street area of the town, and the second 400m south of the river, at Lower Oversley Lodge. At the latter site aerial photography (eg Webster 1981, pl 11) has revealed a large part of a fort of *c* 1.6ha. This had some early morphological characteristics. On the basis of these and of the location of the fort, which was in a tactically strong position on high ground overlooking the river crossings of the later town and within 0.5km of the possible Iron Age defended site, the fort may be tentatively assigned to a date in the late AD 40s. It has been suggested that it was one of a chain of outpost forts in advance of the so-called 'Fosse Way frontier' (Webster 1958, 49–55; Frere 1987, 59).

The Lower Oversley Lodge fort is likely to have been superseded rapidly as the Roman army consolidated its grip on the west Midlands, and it is to this secondary military context that a later fort in the Bleachfield Street area may be assigned. Such a fort would have had more immediate access to the road network and to the crossing points of roads over the river Arrow. The existence of this fort is attested by a growing body of military metalwork, by coins, and by considerable quantities of Neronian samian ware (Booth in prep). No military features of this period have been identified with certainty, but they may have existed at the Baromix factory (**47, 64, 95** on fig 3) and at 64 Bleachfield Street (**73** on fig 3). Possible military features at the latter site were aligned on an east–west axis (Booth 1983, 11–12). The suggested date range of this fort is in the Neronian to early Flavian period.

The Birch Abbey excavations shed no direct light on the question of the town's origins, lying south and west of the likely location of the Neronian–Flavian fort (though the north-east corner of site G was only some 50m from 64 Bleachfield Street (**73** on fig 3)). They might, however, have been expected to produce evidence for the expanding civilian settlement associated with the fort which, on the model of Webster (1966, 32) and Frere (1975, 5), should have provided the nucleus for the later civilian town, although Smith (1987, 8) has pointed out the relative scarcity of the physical evidence for such settlements. There was only limited evidence of late 1st-century activity in sites E, F, and J although the samian ware suggests pre-Flavian occupation. If, therefore, the fort is correctly located in the Bleachfield Street area, associated settlement to the west was probably of limited extent. Its extent in other directions is less certain. At 1–5 Bleachfield Street (**57** on fig 3) occupation of early Flavian date was thought to belong to civilian settlement perhaps still contemporary with military activity further south (Booth forthcoming), but the earliest deposits on this site were not extensively examined so this point remains uncertain. The alignment of features here was approximately north-west to south-east, in contrast to the east–west orientation seen at 64 Bleachfield Street some 160m to the south (**73** on fig 3). At Lloyd's Bank, *c* 70m east of 1–5 Bleachfield Street, pottery and other finds include pre-Flavian material, and some of these artefacts may be associated with early features, the general alignment of which reflects that at 1–5 Bleachfield Street. The significance of these features remains unclear, however. In addition to this possible *vicus* area to the north of the putative fort, the area around the southern end of Bleachfield Street, which remains archaeologically little known, could also have been occupied by settlement contemporary with the fort. A Flavian pit, unfortunately not more closely dated, was found during excavation of foundation trenches on the east side of Bleachfield Street next to no 66 (**90** on fig 3; Cracknell & Ferguson 1985, 131).

On evacuation by the military, the fort was presumably completely demolished and its defences levelled, although at Godmanchester, for example, this seems not to have been done completely (Rankov 1982, 363). Civilian occupation of the fort site itself was not necessarily immediate, however. At 64 Bleachfield Street (**73** on fig 3) the early possible military features were sealed by a layer of sandy loam which accumulated over a long period of time, perhaps up to the mid-2nd century, before a road was laid across it. There was thus no occupation on this site for perhaps as much as *c* 70 years (Booth 1983, 12). A similar situation could have prevailed elsewhere over the site of the former fort, the development of which may have proceeded piecemeal. Evidence for a hiatus between the military phase and the development of civilian settlement has been noted elsewhere, for example at Ilchester (Leach 1982, 7).

Major road alignments

A crucial question for the understanding of the development of the settlement in the 1st century is that of the influence of the possible Neronian–Flavian fort on the road network of the town. The principal Roman roads in Alcester were the north–south aligned Ryknild Street and an east–west road which, having crossed the Fosse Way at Ettington and the river Avon at Stratford, ran through the southern part of the town at Alcester where it was street A in the Birch Abbey excavations (figs 1–2). West of Alcester the route of this road towards Droitwich seems to have been along the line of Cold Comfort Lane, producing a staggered junction with Ryknild Street in the western part of the town. This presumably suggests that the two lengths of road, east of the town between Stratford and Alcester, and west from Alcester to Droitwich, were laid out at different times.

There are distinct differences between the two main roads. Ryknild Street is generally considered to have been an early military road in origin (eg Webster 1958, 63). Its course lies through the western extremity of the Roman town and may be presumed to have predated the settlement. Northwards from a point within the settlement its precise route is clear (Booth 1982a, 138), but south of here, and particularly in the area of the crossing of the river Arrow, there is less certainty. Running south of the river from Oversley Mill, the apparent line of Ryknild Street is perpetuated as a track and bridleway, but work on the line of the Alcester southern bypass in 1989 produced evidence of a Roman road some 150m east of the accepted route, with associated occupation debris. Surface evidence from further south suggests that this road line perhaps diverged from the traditional route of Ryknild Street at a point just over 1km south of the river and headed directly for the southern part of the Roman town. This new road line ties in very closely with a coin hoard found south of the river Arrow in 1967 (Carson 1969), which can now be seen as having been concealed close to the line of the road.

An additional complication in this area is that the accepted line of Ryknild Street cuts the eastern side of the possible Iron Age defended site at Oversley Castle, at which point the road is in a deep hollow way, presumably of medieval origin. It is perhaps unlikely that the Roman road would have been cut through upstanding earthworks when a diversion of a few metres would have carried it to the east of them.

Plate 12 Aerial view of the fields to the south of Stratford Road, looking south-west. The south end of Bleachfield Street and the corner of the housing estate built following the 1964–6 excavations can be seen at top right; the river is marked by the line of trees in front of the caravan park and sewage works. The main features visible are ditch A, the road system, and a series of enclosure ditches at right-angles to street A. (Copyright A Baker)

The truth of the matter is, however, uncertain without definite dating for the earthworks (now visible mainly from the air). Although an Iron Age date is likely (Hingley 1989, 141–3), they have also been considered to form an outer enclosure for the medieval Oversley Castle or a roadway to it (Chatwin 1936). If this was the case a medieval (or later) date would also apply to the road which can be seen to cut them. One possible interpretation of the evidence is that the line of Ryknild Street always followed the route indicated by the most recent work on the Alcester bypass, in which case traffic would have had to negotiate several junctions in the town before re-emerging on the main road to the west and north. The road cutting the Oversley Castle earthworks

would then be seen as entirely of medieval date heading for Oversley Mill on the river Arrow. Alternatively, and perhaps more likely, the newly discovered road line may be seen as a diversion of Ryknild Street, carrying traffic into the heart of the Roman town, replacing the original line of Ryknild Street which was laid out with quite different priorities in mind. Whether or not the early line of Ryknild Street cut the possible Iron Age site remains uncertain, but it may have done, and this would provide the rationale for the route of the later medieval road to Oversley Mill, which conveniently followed an existing roadway, albeit one perhaps little used after the early Roman period. This would explain why the course of Ryknild Street is apparently so well defined south of the river but quite invisible immediately north of it.

The Neronian fort was apparently sited some distance to the east of the early line of Ryknild Street, though it probably postdated the construction of the road (direct evidence for the date of the latter at Alcester is lacking). Had the valley bottom fort been in existence before Ryknild Street was built there is no good reason why the road should not then have run directly to the fort itself. The relationship of the fort to the main east–west road is less certain, but the siting of the fort away from Ryknild Street may indicate that by this time an association with the east–west trackway (as it presumably then was) was more important. The evidence from excavations in Birch Abbey and elsewhere suggests that the first surface of this road probably cannot be dated before the early 2nd century at the earliest, and in some places the primary road surface was thought to be of 4th-century date. This date, however, cannot be applied to the road as a whole but must reflect an extremely localized situation. It must be assumed that the east–west road was in existence for some considerable time before the construction of its earliest dated surface. Indeed it seems that the Flavian structures in Birch Abbey site F were aligned on it and that it was therefore an integral element of the settlement plan from the very beginning. It is possible that the road from Stratford was aligned on the east gate of the Neronian fort (assuming that the fort had a north–south to east–west alignment) or it may have passed just to the south of the fort. If the former, then Birch Abbey site G must have lain very close to the likely position of the west side of the fort; if the latter, site G may have been outside its south-west corner. The situation in which the layout of roads within a settlement was conditioned by their relationship to an earlier fort is paralleled elsewhere, most obviously at Great Chesterford, where a road junction in the centre of the town lay immediately outside the south gate of the Roman fort (Rodwell 1972, 290–2).

There is one outstanding problem relating to the east–west road. This is in the evidence from Hughes' site E (**26** on fig 3) that to the east of Bleachfield Street the road was built over, and perforce its use discontinued, at a date which was unspecified but not necessarily very late in the Roman period (Hughes 1958, 15–16; see also 'State of knowledge in 1964', p 8). It is hard to see why the principal thoroughfare through the town should have been built over in this way. While it can be shown that at Hughes' site T, west of Bleachfield Street (**28** on fig 3), what he thought was a comparable phenomenon was in fact a marginal infringement on the road by the building on this site, the description in the case of his site E is apparently unambiguous. The problem is only likely to be resolved by re-excavation of the site, but Hughes' suggestion that the possible road in Swan Street represented the rerouted east–west road can surely be discounted. If the east–west road really was blocked by building any realignment is likely to have been on a much more limited scale, involving local detours rather than a radical rethinking of the main elements of the street system.

The maintenance of one or both of the main roads outside the town in the first half of the 4th century is implied by the occurrence of the milestone of Constantine I reused in a foundation in Birch Abbey site G.

Roads within the town

The street network within the town was irregular and there is no suggestion of a formal layout (fig 2, plate 12). Within the area of the Birch Abbey excavations there was evidence for two roads in addition to the east–west street A. Both streets B and C followed irregular routes south of street A. Street C is evidenced in sites D and E, respectively south and north of street A, in the earliest phases of these areas, though it was not surfaced at this time. Street B was similarly in existence in phase I in site C. At the southern end of the occupied area, beyond the extent of the Birch Abbey excavations, aerial photographs show a junction of what are almost certainly streets B and C, both clearly surfaced (presumably with gravel). Street C approaches from the north and turns eastwards through an almost complete right-angle to cross the line of street B. The latter can be traced for a further 20–30m south of the junction before terminating, apparently fairly abruptly, in what is now rough pasture. At the point of the junction, street B is clearly the more substantial of the two roads (a point also suggested by evidence from within the Birch Abbey excavations). Its extent north of site C is, however, uncertain. It is not even clear that the street was located in the trenches at the northern end of site C. It seems likely, however, that it would have extended at least as far north as the line of street A, presumably to the east of site G.

A major element of the street layout must have been a road which linked the extensive extramural settlement area around Birch Abbey and Bleachfield Street with the defended part of the Roman town which lay to the north. Topographical considerations suggest that the choice of entry point of such a road into the defended area must have been restricted, probably to a line close to that of the present High Street at its southern end. Little is known of such a road but it may have been the one located north of street A at the Baromix factory in Bleachfield Street (**47** on fig 3). This road was on an approximately north–south alignment and had been constructed 'by early in the 2nd century' (Taylor 1969, 21). An alignment closer to north-west to south-east was observed by structures further north at 1–5 Bleachfield Street (Booth forthcoming; **57** on fig 3) and at Lloyd's Bank (Evans & Booth 1975; **55** on fig 3). These sites probably lay respectively west and east of the line of the road leading into the defended area. An early form of this road, unsurfaced, may have existed briefly in the eastern part of 1–5 Bleachfield Street, but if this was the case it must have been replaced subsequently by a road further east beyond the excavated area. To the south the road presumably ran as far as street A and may possibly have connected with street B, but if the alignments suggested above were consistently maintained, this would not have been the case (see fig 2).

Within the defences nothing is known of the street layout, but the limited evidence for recently recorded structures (eg Cracknell 1985a, 14–15; 1985b) suggests a fairly uniform alignment, roughly north-west to south-east, approximately consistent with that of 1–5 Bleachfield Street and Lloyd's Bank and presumably reflecting the alignment of the main street leading into the enclosed area. There is at present no indication of a road leaving the defended area in a northerly or (more likely) a north-easterly direction, though unless such a road had existed the defended area would have been very much a backwater of occupation, a situation apparently unparalleled in Romano-British towns. The existence of a road running north-east along the north bank of the river Alne may therefore be indicated, but is at present completely unevidenced on the ground.

In the south-eastern part of the town, at 64 Bleachfield Street (**73** on fig 3), a minor east–west road, parallel to street A and perhaps some 15m north of it, was constructed perhaps about the mid-2nd century but may have been out of use by the end of the century (Booth 1983, 15–17). Most of the evidence for minor roads in this part of the town comes, however, from aerial photography. To the east of Bleachfield Street and running north from street A a curvilinear street makes a T-junction with a similarly irregular street. At its eastern end the latter street was bounded by ditches on both sides, but between this point and the central section aligned south-east to north-west it appears as a dark mark on the aerial photographs, suggesting that at some time a length of the street was dug out and removed, presumably for its gravel content. A rather straighter and arguably more important street ran south-west from street A towards the south end of Bleachfield Street. An aerial photograph showing this street (and the two just described, as well as street A) is reproduced in plate 12. Limited excavation took place at the north end of this street in 1970 in advance of flood barrier construction. Here it was some 4.2m wide. The date of its earliest surface is unknown, but it was resurfaced in the 4th century (Taylor 1970; **48** on fig 3). This south-westerly street is important because it may have linked up with the suggested easterly line of Ryknild Street to the south of the town (see p 165) and would therefore have been a principal route through the town, particularly in the later Roman period. An alternative possibility is that Ryknild Street connected with street B to the west of Bleachfield Street; on present evidence this seems less likely.

A further minor street, known only from geophysical survey, ran south-eastwards from the junction of the south-west road with street A. This street may have served as access to the cemetery at the bend of the river Arrow, and possibly, via a ford in this area, to the stone quarries of probable Roman date at Primrose Hill, only some 500m south-east of the cemetery.

One possible street remains to be mentioned. This is the one identified by Hughes in Swan Street (see 'State of knowledge', p 10 and microfiche), which might have run along the line of Seggs Lane, perhaps to link up with the Roman road to Droitwich along the line of Cold Comfort Lane. The evidence for this street is slight and capable of alternative interpretations.

The overall street plan is of Burnham's group III, of 'developed' linear and road junction sites, with analogies at places such as Kenchester and Waternewton. Such sites are considered to show 'spontaneous internal street growth to meet the socio-economic needs of the local community' (Burnham 1987, 163–5). Street plans of this kind can be assumed to be dynamic rather than static, and the evidence from Alcester is certainly consistent with this. Dates for the earliest appearance of all the streets are not known, but there is no suggestion that the layout was determined in a single operation which then fixed the street plan of the settlement until the end of the Roman period. Evidence from the Baromix site (**47** on fig 3) shows that street frontages could be realigned, and the street at 64 Bleachfield Street (**73** on fig 3) was presumably constructed after the main elements of the layout were in place, only to fall out of use within about 50 years or perhaps even less. Even the main east–west street may have been partly realigned.

Not all streets were surfaced from the outset. The evidence from Birch Abbey suggests that to the south of street A trackways were in existence on or close to the line of streets C and B by the late 1st century. Street B may have been surfaced by the end of the 2nd century, but street C was apparently not surfaced until the 4th century. Repairs to and replacement of road surfaces could have been very localized, so extrapolation from individual sections can be dangerous.

Property boundaries and settlement layout

The influence of the possible early military establishment on the plan of the Roman town is as yet very uncertain. Possible military features at 64 Bleachfield Street (**73** on fig 3) were aligned east–west, but some 1st-century alignments elsewhere (particularly at 1–5 Bleachfield Street to the north; **57** on fig 3) were rather different. Of the two main roads, Ryknild Street was early in date and was probably peripheral to the settlement for much of the Roman period. It therefore had little influence on the development of the settlement pattern. The east–west main road through the town (street A) was much more important. It must have been a very early, if not primary, feature, and structures in Birch Abbey and elsewhere were aligned on it, with varying degrees of precision, from the later 1st century onwards. These alignments may have been less rigid in the later Roman period, for example the building excavated in Birch Abbey by Hughes (his site T) was only loosely at right-angles to street A. Further east the street may have been built over, but the significance of this remains unclear. Again, alignments on the street in this area may have been less precise in the later Roman period. The primary stone structure in trench L XI was more nearly parallel to the line of street A than the possibly later features in the same part of site L, but even this does not seem to have been precisely aligned (the part of the structure identified was, however, some 18–25m from the likely frontage and may not necessarily have related to it). Of more relevance in terms of alignments and layout may have been the two phases of ditch on the same site, which seem to have been aligned very closely parallel to the street and perhaps lay some 26m north of its edge. This ditch may indicate the rear boundary line of properties aligned on the east–west street. Evidence for a comparable layout of properties is surprisingly lacking further west in Birch Abbey, despite the extensive nature of the excavations there. In Sites E, F, and J the position of street C was indicated in an early phase by ditches running more or less at right-angles to the line of street A (fig 65). To the north of this area a ditch (ditch B; see fig 67) lay some 38m north of the eventual position of the ditch on the north side of street A (fig 79). The latter ditch was assigned to phase XIII, whereas ditch B and possibly related features were thought to be of phases III and IV. The two ditches were not, however, exactly parallel and any superficial similarity between their alignments may have been fortuitous.

There was little suggestion in this part of Birch Abbey of boundary features laid out at right-angles to street A. A fence line on the north side of trench F I may have divided off a plot with maximum dimensions of *c* 31m north–south × 26m east–west in the north-west corner of streets A and C, but this seems to have been a short-lived feature (fig 72). South of street A it is suggested that the buildings in site D and the adjacent stone structure to the east may have been part of the same property. There would therefore have been no need for a boundary between them. However, even in cases where it is likely that adjacent buildings belonged to different properties, there is not always clear evidence on the ground that this was the case (Smith 1987, 25–9). At Scole, in Norfolk, Smith (*ibid*) suggests that gravelled lanes roughly at right-angles to a major road served to demarcate properties. The significance of ditches on the same general alignment preceding one of these lanes is not clear (Rogerson 1977, 103–5), but if the principle is accepted this could have been one of the functions of the northern part of street C at Birch Abbey.

The clearest evidence for carefully laid out boundaries presumably indicating individual properties can be seen on aerial photographs of the south-eastern part of the settlement. Ditches aligned at right-angles to the east–west road (street A) can be seen on both sides of the road defining rectangular plots of unequal width. None of these is clearly defined at the rear, but on the south side of the road a possible ditch line, parallel to it at a distance of approximately 30m, is faintly visible. To the north, the rear of the plots may have been defined by a minor lane with ditches along each side, which ran roughly parallel to the east–west road at that point.

Other evidence for property divisions comes largely from the southern part of Birch Abbey, away from the main street frontages. Here a group of irregular enclosures, perhaps closes or paddocks, was laid out to the west of the trackway preceding street C. It is not known if these were individually owned plots or if the divisions were simply intended to facilitate control of livestock. Other agricultural or horticultural uses might be conjectured, however, and the ditch system seems to have been relatively short-lived. The area was later devoted to pit digging and was partly occupied by buildings. This development seems to represent a genuine expansion of the occupied area. Further south, in sites AA and C, there was evidence for boundaries approximately at right-angles to streets C and B, but there was no indication of the size of the plots defined by these features (see fig 14).

Most of the excavated structures in the southern part of the Roman town were related to streets or lay close to a known street line. Elsewhere there are buildings whose relationship to the street network is less certain. These included the buildings at the north end of Site L. Buildings at Lloyd's Bank (**55** on fig 3) and 1–5 Bleachfield Street (**57** on fig 3) probably lay at right-angles to a street between them from which access to these sites would have been gained. Further west, however, the situation is less clear. A building partly examined in 1975 at Acorn House, on the west side of Evesham Street, was probably at least 75m from both the main roads in the town, and no minor streets are known in this area (Cracknell 1985a; **56** on fig 3). The building in Priory Road (**12** on fig 3) may have been close to a Roman street if it is accepted that one lay beneath the line of Seggs Lane, but if not, this, and certainly the structures to the north-east at Coulters Garage (**61** on fig 3), were situated well away from any known street line. There were presumably many more minor lanes and streets, some perhaps unsurfaced, than are known at present. In some cases these may have served solely as access points for specific buildings.

Major east–west ditch

A major east–west ditch (ditch A) ran across the southern edge of the settlement (figs 7, 16, 32, 34, 37, 85). It extended at least from the western edge of the Birch Abbey area as far as street B (fig 2), and what was probably its continuation can be seen in aerial photographs in the field to the east of Bleachfield Street, running towards the bend of the river Arrow where the river turns sharply southward (plate 12). The cemetery which existed at this point (see 'Birch Abbey burials' above, p 144) may have lain entirely to the south of this ditch, or could have overlapped it. West of the cemetery, the aerial photographs indicate two separate ditch alignments. These are so close together that they are likely to represent successive versions of the same feature. The course of the ditch on both sides of Bleachfield Street was slightly sinuous. Between street B and Bleachfield Street it was not located and it did not appear on aerial photographs although it did appear on photographs of the area to the east. However, this does not rule out the possibility of it being present in some form.

The ditch may have been a boundary marker along the southern edge of the town and the presence of burials along its line may support this interpretation. Even though the burials were later than the supposed date of the ditch, it is likely that the ditch was still visible. Its size would indicate that it was not a mere property boundary. The presence of buildings in sites AA and C south of the ditch might be thought to militate against the boundary thesis but the buildings fronted onto street B and this could be interpreted as ribbon development. The location of a noxious industry away from the main settlement might also have been a factor.

There are several problems with this interpretation. These include the fact that features in sites AA and C were separated by the ditch from the rest of the settlement, and the fact that the ditch only seems to have been in use for a short period of time in the 3rd century, whereas elsewhere, for example also in site AA, other boundary features were retained through successive phases.

The physical character of the ditch is of interest. It was in places quite substantial, up to 3m wide and 2m deep. West of Bleachfield Street it adhered (with one exception) quite closely to a contour at about 38.5–39.0m above OD and had a bank on its southern (downhill) side. None of these characteristics seems consistent with a boundary feature. The ditch was too small to have had any possible defensive function, but was larger than was required for a simple boundary, and had it been intended to keep animals in pasture (to the south) out of the occupied area the bank would surely have lain to the north of the ditch.

It is noticeable that the most westerly point at which the ditch is known lies close to the point where the Spittle Brook turns southward to run down to the river Arrow. It is possible that the ditch was linked to Spittle Brook and carried water from it eastwards across the south side of the town. The bank on the south side of the ditch would have helped retain the water in such a channel. In site AA the bank was reinforced with posts which extended over an area up to 5m wide, suggesting that some kind of structure had been based upon it at this point. The presence of a heavy millstone, 0.65m in diameter, in the nearby trench A XIV might imply the existence of a mill, for which ditch A could have served as a millstream.

This alternative interpretation of ditch A is not without problems. The principal objections are, first, that the ditch may have terminated at street B though this was not certainly the case. Second, the drop over the 500m length of the leet was only *c* 0.5m (based on modern ground levels). Third, the bottom of the ditch rises about 1.07m (3ft 6in) between trenches B VI and B III, when it should have been level or dropping. The problems of the levels and lack of a significant overall fall indicate that even if the feature had been intended as a mill leet it may not have functioned effectively as such. This in turn could explain why it was only a short-lived feature.

Whatever the interpretation, the fact that the ditch was only in existence for a short period makes its importance in the townscape difficult to assess. It probably had no long-term effect on the layout of the settlement.

Defences

The relationship of the defended area to the rest of the settlement remains problematical. Alcester is unusual in the context of Romano-British town studies in that its extramural settlement area is much better known than the occupation within the defences. This is largely because the existence of the medieval and modern town centre, precisely overlying the Roman defended area, has precluded large-scale archaeological examination. Development within this area has been piecemeal and, until the 1980s, on a small scale. Until recently, therefore, evidence for this area comprised the results of limited work on the defences and of Davis' excavations in the 1920s (see above, p 9). Recent work by Cracknell (in 1983, 1986, and 1989) has considerably added to our knowledge of the defences themselves and of activity within them (sites **83, 88, 93** on fig 3; Cracknell 1985a, 1985b, forthcoming).

The earliest defences consisted of a bank, variously constructed of clay and gravel, with at one point a suggestion of a timber revetment of its front face. The bank has now been located at several places, on the north-west side close to the western corner (**60** on fig 3) and at the corner itself (the Gateway supermarket site; **88** on fig 3); on the south-east side just to the north of Gas House Lane (**93** on fig 3); and on the north-east side, where possible traces were found in site M (**43** on fig 3). The exact line of the circuit is still far from certain in the central stretch of its east side and on the north and north-west sides. The location of the north-west corner, in particular, is quite unknown.

At Gas House Lane, where it was most clearly seen, the bank was relatively insubstantial, being only some 5m wide. On the south-west and south-east sides of the circuit the bank was fronted by a wide, shallow hollow. This does not seem to have been a ditch in the normal sense, since there is little indication that it was dug out and its contents used to form the bank. At the Gateway supermarket site (**88** on fig 3), on the western corner of the defences, it was thought that the hollow was natural in origin, perhaps enhanced to serve as a defensive feature (Cracknell forthcoming). In both cases the lower part of the hollows may well have held water, particularly in winter.

There is no precise dating evidence associated with this defensive circuit. Only in the north-eastern sector, at site M, were there features sealed beneath what may have been the first rampart. Their contents suggested a 2nd-century date, but this remains to be proved. At the Gateway supermarket site most of the pottery in the infill of the 'hollow' in front of the defences was of 4th-century date. A construction date in the later 2nd century is possible on analogy with defences at other major settlements, but cannot be assumed to be certain.

The location of the earthwork defences is of considerable interest. The defences clearly owed their siting to topographical considerations. By the time they were constructed, for the sake of argument in the later 2nd century, the settlement had about reached its maximum extent, with the probable exception of the buildings in sites AA and C in Birch Abbey, which are thought to have been of 3rd-century date. The occupied area probably extended from the river Arrow in the east to Ryknild Street in the west. It was clearly impractical to enclose the whole of this area within defences, and presumably to defend only part of it would have been fraught with difficulties, although such a course must have been followed in many other settlements at this time. In these circumstances the adjacent gravel 'island' to the north presented itself as a reasonable alternative, with the advantage of natural defences in the form of the river to its north and east and the marsh to the west.

While the logic of the selection of this area for defence is reasonably clear, what is much less certain is the extent to which the area was already occupied at the time the defences were constructed. At present most of the evidence for structures within the defences dates to the 3rd century and later. It is therefore possible that widespread occupation of this area did not commence until after the earthwork had been constructed. Alternatively, the evidence for 3rd-century structures might suggest that the defences themselves were perhaps of 3rd-century date, though this seems less likely.

One peculiar feature of the ?2nd-century rampart is the apparent absence of a proper ditch. This was presumably because of the unsuitability of the adjacent ground for excavation of such a feature. The very unsuitability of this ground provided an appropriate defensive alternative to a conventional ditch. The only problem arising from the absence of a normal ditch was that there was no ready source of material for the rampart, which would therefore have to have been scraped together from the vicinity of the bank. This may explain the apparently small size of the rampart; a bank only *c* 5m wide (see above, p 170) cannot have stood much more than about 2m in height. It would have presented a more substantial obstacle had it had a timber revetment at the front, but the only good evidence for this is confined to a single site at the western corner of the defences, where special circumstances might have prevailed. One striking aspect of the bank, if it was constructed as suggested above, is the almost total absence of artefactual material within it. Assuming that the constituent materials were gathered locally, this supports the suggestion that the earthwork defences were built on a substantially unoccupied site.

One obvious result (assuming the relative dating of defences and internal structures to be correct) of the siting of the defences was to bring about a gradual shift in the settlement pattern of the town. Once enclosed, the northern part of the town became a favoured location for building, with intensive activity in the 3rd and 4th centuries. The area was apparently not, however, entirely occupied by late Roman structures, nor did its development result in a large-scale abandonment of the settlement to the south, including Birch Abbey. There is some evidence for limited contraction of the extramural area in the northern part of site L, which seems not to have been occupied after the 3rd century. This was perhaps also the case in the north-western part of the settlement, north of Seggs Lane and west of Priory Road, though the evidence for occupation of any date is scanty here, primarily because of a lack of excavation. This change — the abandonment of some small areas — seems to have occurred largely on the periphery of the settlement, leaving the core unaffected.

The late Roman defences are rather better understood than the early ones. First located in site M in 1965 (figs 105–6) and subsequently observed east of Malt Mill Lane (S J Taylor pers comm; **51** on fig 3), they have also been found at Gas House Lane (**93** on fig 3) and the Gateway supermarket site (**88** on fig 3), as well as being possibly located north of the latter site, in a drainage hole to the north of Bull's Head Yard (**58** on fig 3).

These defences took the form of a wall some 3.5–4.1m thick, backed by a rampart. Work at the Gateway supermarket site in 1986 amplified the evidence available from site M. The wall was based on a substructure of oak piles, around which were packed stone blocks, clay, and gravel. On this were set longitudinal and transverse horizontal timbers, also with packing material placed around them, and it was on this platform that the wall itself was constructed (Cracknell forthcoming). At no site does any of the wall itself survive, and at site M even the foundation material had been robbed, but at all the known locations the piles have been observed, either as voids, as at site M, or as waterlogged timbers as at Gas House Lane and, more particularly, at the Gateway supermarket site, where they were relatively well preserved.

The wall was backed by a bank which at site M and at Gas House Lane was *c* 9m wide and had a cross-sectional area of *c* 8sq m. The evidence from site M was particularly important in demonstrating beyond all possible doubt that the wall and bank were contemporary, the bank at this point overlying part of the foundation trench for the wall, which had been cut too wide. In this case, of course, the bank cannot have been formed directly from the upcast of the foundation trench, since this would have to have been moved a second time to fill the gap between the rear of the wall as constructed and the edge of the foundation trench as excavated. The size of the bank is also such that it cannot have been built solely of material derived from the construction trench of the wall, even though this feature was wider than elsewhere. It is very unlikely that a ditch would have been excavated fronting the wall at site M if this was not done elsewhere.

The Gateway supermarket site (**88** on fig 3) produced evidence for the hitherto unsuspected presence of an external tower added to the wall. The foundation trench for the tower was slightly trapezoidal in plan, being 6.2m wide against the wall face and 5.4m wide at the front of the tower. The depth was also 5.4m. The shape of the tower itself is unknown. The construction technique of the foundations for the tower was exactly the same as that for the wall, with piling and horizontal timbers. The tower was clearly structurally subsequent to the wall, a small ridge of clay having been left between the excavations for the two foundations. Analysis of the timber piles, which in the case of the tower were of alder, showed that these may have been felled some seven years after the oak used in the town wall. The wood retained its bark and was presumably unseasoned. If so this is important in demonstrating that the construction of the wall and tower(s) was probably part of the same overall programme of defensive works, but that the towers were added to the scheme at a late stage. It is possible that the gap between the two dates indicates the length of time taken to construct the wall.

There was no evidence of a ditch or ditches associated with the stone wall phase of the defences, presumably for the same reasons as applied to the earthwork defences. At the Coulters Garage site (**61** on fig 3) there was no sign of a ditch cutting the large stone building which extended up to *c* 40m away from the wall. Such a feature may therefore be assumed to have been absent.

There is fairly consistent evidence for the date of the stone wall and associated features although there was no useful dating evidence from site M. At the Gateway supermarket site the wall passed within *c* 0.1m of a very large stone building (**61** on fig 3) which was clearly demolished to make way for the construction of the wall, the stone from the building presumably being reused in the wall itself. A deposit associated with the robbing of this building contained a coin of Valentinian I dated AD 364–7 (Booth 1985, 83–4). This coin probably, but unfortunately not certainly, provides a *terminus post quem* for the destruction of the building and the construction of the wall. Only five coins were recovered from the site. Two, of Tetricus I and II, were found within the robber trenches of the stone building, but are irrelevant since the building was probably not constructed until the end of the 3rd century. The coin of Valentinian came from the line of a robber trench, either from the very top of the robber trench itself or from the base of an immediately overlying spread of robbed material, indistinguishable from the contents of the robber trench. The spread must have been almost exactly contemporary with the robber trench but could, of course, have been contaminated by later material. The remaining two coins were from the upper part of this layer. They were a third radiate and a siliqua of Julian (360–3). While there is no reason to suppose that the latter coin and the coin of Valentinian were intrusive, they do not date the robbing of the stone building quite as securely as could be wished. Equally, while they

suggest a *terminus post quem* for the construction of the wall, they do not prove it. If the suggestion is followed, however, the likely date for the wall would be very close to the traditional 'historical context' of the refurbishment of British defences by Count Theodosius (eg Frere 1987, 248), although this has been rejected by Casey (1983, 123).

Unfortunately, while it was possible to demonstrate the chronological difference between the timber piles of the tower and the wall, neither feature produced posts which were sufficiently large to produce an absolute dendrochronological date.

The late wall defined a polygonal area, two angles of which were located at the Gateway supermarket site (**88** on fig 3). In contrast it seems that the earthwork circuit was rounded at the western corner (Cracknell 1985b, 124, fig 1). The wall enclosed a slightly larger area than the earthwork defences, perhaps *c* 8.5ha (*c* 20.8 acres). This places it in the middle rank of enclosed settlements of this type in terms of the size of the defended area, comparable to sites such as Irchester, Kenchester and ?Worcester (Crickmore 1984, table 4; Burnham 1987, 184).

At site M, in the north-eastern sector, the earthwork and stone wall circuits may have been on the same alignment, but elsewhere they diverged. At Gas House Lane the wall lay some 15m south of the early rampart, and at the Gateway supermarket site and probably along much of the western side there was a space of about 35m between the two defensive lines. There is no evidence, however, for structures or other features in the area between the two circuits. Late 4th-century pottery has been found in deposits overlying the bank associated with the stone wall, but this may indicate nothing more than dumping of rubbish.

It is unclear why the defended area should have been enlarged, particularly since this involved siting the 4th-century wall on very poor, wet ground on the western side of the town. Perhaps it was intended to leave an open, defended space for use in emergency circumstances. In the rather earlier '*burgi*' situated along Watling Street, for example, there is little evidence for the presence of late Roman structures postdating the construction of their defensive circuits and it may be that space was left for the temporary accommodation of military units (Webster 1967, 42; for their ?late 3rd-century to early 4th-century date see Webster 1974, 56–7). Unless provision of this or a similar kind was being made at Alcester it is hard to see why the stone wall should have been realigned. At present the status of the earthwork defences after the construction of the wall is unclear, though they were obviously not completely levelled.

The late Roman town wall at Mildenhall, like Alcester, followed a different line from that of the earlier defensive circuit, but it is uncertain by what amount the defended area was enlarged. The dates of the walls at Alcester and Mildenhall may have been closely comparable. Realignment of successive circuits was relatively common, particularly at the *civitas* capitals and other major cities, which often had a longer defensive sequence than the small towns.

Cemeteries

The cemeteries of Roman Alcester are poorly known, with information coming principally from the work of Davis (see 'Birch Abbey burials', p 144). At present, cremation burials are known from eight disparate locations within and around the town. In each case they are individual burials and none need necessarily indicate an early cemetery, the locations of which remain unknown. The most unusual of these cremations was a casket burial, containing a coin of Vespasian, from 79 Priory Road (Booth 1982b; **69** on fig 3).

While it is impossible even to guess where the early Roman cemetery lay, the location of the later inhumation cemeteries is reasonably certain. It is less clear, however, which of the recorded burial locations represent formally laid out cemeteries and which indicate the more haphazard use of vacant areas at a time when the laws which governed disposal of the dead were less strictly observed than before. The site excavated in 1925 by Davis in Folley Field, west of the town (**7** on fig 3), with evidence for some rough stone-lined cists and consistently aligned burials, must fall in the former category. A coffin of oolitic limestone, uncovered south of this site in 1866, probably also derived from this cemetery, as did the burials briefly noted by Hughes in advance of housing construction to the west of Evesham Street, some of which were also contained in stone cists (Hughes 1962; **29** on fig 3). These burials probably belonged to the principal late Roman cemetery of the town, which may have extended almost up to the western side of Ryknild Street. At Hughes' site C a probable timber structure lay to the west of this road, which may indicate that an occupied zone separated the road from the cemetery (Hughes 1958, 12; **15** on fig 3).

The burials located at the bend of the river Arrow on the south-east side of the town (**82** on fig 3) may also have belonged to a formal cemetery since, on limited evidence, they seem to have been closely spaced and uniformly aligned. A necklace of jet beads is reported to have been found in this area.

Elsewhere, burials occur less consistently. Those found by Davis beside the old Stratford Road (**9** on fig 3) seem not to have been closely grouped, and while their peripheral location might suggest that they belonged to a normally positioned cemetery this is not necessarily the case. Whatever their status, however, it is very likely that they indicated the margin of the area of Roman settlement. The burials found in Birch Abbey (fig 107), although quite widespread, also seem to have been relatively dispersed, with the exception of a cluster in trench B III (although this impression may be the result of the limited extent of excavation in this area). It is possible that the burials in this south-west part of the Birch Abbey area did belong to a more formal cemetery, perhaps even an easterly extension of the one centred west of Ryknild Street, but the evidence is slight. It is uncertain whether or not these burials occupied an area which had always lain outside the built-up part of the town, but this is possible. There

would therefore probably have been little objection to turning this space over to burials.

Individual late Roman inhumations occur at sites throughout the town. One was apparently sealed within the bank associated with the town wall at Gas House Lane (**93** on fig 3) and others were found just outside the wall at the Gateway supermarket site (**88** on fig 3) and the adjacent Coulters Garage site (Booth 1985, 84; **61** on fig 3). Most burials of this kind were not accompanied by grave goods and while there was a tendency for them to be aligned roughly north–south, this was not an invariable rule. While few burials are thus intrinsically datable, some can be related to stratigraphic sequences. The burials associated with or close to the town wall, for example, are probably all contemporary with or later than its construction, for which a date in the 360s seems likely. Other burials occurring individually within the town seem generally to date at least to the second half of the 4th century, which is no more than would be expected.

Possible market area

An important element in the layout of the town seems to have been an extensive, open-surfaced area located around the northern part of Birch Abbey. Evidence for this was perhaps found by Hughes at Linby House (site G, Hughes 1958, 17; **19** on fig 3) and certainly in the same area at 6 Birch Abbey by Cracknell in 1983 (Cracknell 1985a, 25–38; **81** on fig 3). At 'The Bell', at the north end of Birch Abbey on the east side (**78** on fig 3), surfaces were also located, with a pit containing slag perhaps indicating their northern limit. West of Birch Abbey successive surfaces were excavated by Taylor in 1972 (Taylor 1972; **49** on fig 3) and further west again, in Evesham Street, have been observed at no 30 (**70** on fig 3) and between nos 32 and 34 (Cracknell 1985a; **80** on fig 3). In all cases, except for Hughes' observation of stone flags at Linby House, the surfaces were of gravel or cobbles. In the case of the site to the west of Birch Abbey, up to twelve layers of cobbles were recorded (Taylor 1972).

The consistent absence of evidence for other activity in this part of the Roman town suggests that the assumption that the different surfaces may all be part of a more widespread feature is probably justified. On present evidence the minimum dimensions of the open area are *c* 90m east–west and *c* 60m north–south, though there is, of course, no certainty that the surfaced area was rectangular. The southern limit of the area may have been roughly along the northern edge of Birch Abbey sites E, F, and J, but it is possible that a gravel surface which occurred on the east side of street C in site E in phase VI (3rd century; fig 70) was analogous with the surfaces further north. A series of small 'booth' structures was assigned to this phase in both sites E and F. These are paralleled by similar insubstantial constructions which occurred in several phases at 6 Birch Abbey. Since these make no sense in terms of conventional structures for domestic or any other purposes, it may be that they should indeed be seen as temporary market buildings, perhaps sited around the east and south edges of the large open space.

The surfaces at 6 Birch Abbey postdated features of 1st-century date (see below), and those west of Birch Abbey overlaid two brooches and a coin of Claudian date (Taylor 1972). The latter might suggest that the surface was in existence, at least in part, well before the end of the 1st century, but this cannot be certain. There can be no doubt, however, that the open area was established by the early 2nd century. Street C must have provided an access to the area from the south, despite the evidence that it was periodically diverted through a right-angle to the west at the north end of site F (see figs 67, 68, 72). Features and structures in site J on the north side of the diversion in phase VIII may have related to the area to the north of them. There were presumably other access points from different parts of the town.

One further feature relating to the surfaced area merits attention. At 6 Birch Abbey (**81** on fig 3) there was a setting for a very large post, 0.50m across, at the west end of the site (Cracknell 1985a, 30). This was not obviously part of a structure although related features could have lain further west, beyond the edge of the excavated area. Such a post could have been a very prominent feature. While analogies such as maypoles and flagpoles are probably inappropriate, a single, free-standing post, as this seems to have been, could certainly have had some symbolic or religious significance. A similar feature, in an overtly religious context, was a free-standing post some 0.60m wide contained in a large pit at the sanctuary site of Wood Lane End, Hemel Hempstead (Herts). The date of this feature is not known (Neal 1984, 205–6). The possibility of a religious context has also been considered for a free-standing pole found at Witham, Essex (D Priddy pers comm).

The most likely interpretation of the open space seems to be that it was a market area. These are indeed to be expected (Burnham 1987, 180) in settlements such as Alcester where marketing of many kinds of produce and commodities must have been an important function. Parallels from other small towns are, however, rare. The creation of a central rectangular space some 67m × 30m at Godmanchester in the 3rd century is one example (Green 1975, 204), but the best parallel seems to be at Dorchester-on-Thames where an extensive gravelled area may have been maintained throughout the Roman period (Frere 1984b, 98–100). In this respect it parallels the Alcester market area, if such it was, which probably remained a major feature of the townscape throughout much of the Roman period. In the small towns such markets could have been the counterpart of facilities often thought to have been located in the *fora* of the major cities (Wacher 1975, 60). It is possible, however, that, as has been suggested for *fora* in the cities (Mackreth 1987, 135), less mundane functions such as official rituals may also have been an important part of the role in town life played by such an obviously focal feature. In this context, the presence at Alcester of the large free-standing post should be remembered, and the possible religious associations of the late 1st/2nd-century double-quadrilateral enclosure just to the south of the market area in site F may also be of relevance.

General conclusions

The summary by Todd (1970, 120–4) of buildings in Romano-British small towns concentrated, largely as a result of the nature of the evidence available at the time, on stone-built structures of more-or-less recognizable Romanized type. These often had rural parallels, and aisled and corridor buildings, among others, were considered characteristic. The building in Hughes' site T (**28** on fig 3) conforms to this pattern, and some of the Birch Abbey posthole structures could have been of aisled type, but the overall variety of timber and stone construction types is wider than this. More recent surveys by Perring (1987), confined to evidence from the large towns/cities, and particularly that by Burnham (1988), emphasize the diversity of structural types to be found in the major settlements of Roman Britain. Burnham has assembled a useful body of comparanda for the Alcester evidence.

Although it is not true at Alcester, the range of stone buildings in small towns and other settlements is still often much better understood than the variety of timber structures, largely because of the difficulties of identifying the latter in excavation. (Compare, for example, the stone buildings illustrated by Leech (1982, 30, fig 20) with the timber buildings from Alcester.) In those places where timber buildings have been examined, such as Godmanchester (Green 1975, 195–6), Baldock (Stead & Rigby 1986, 33–42), and Neatham (Millett & Graham 1986), the plans of the buildings are sometimes ill-defined. In settlements such as Wanborough they may be extremely ephemeral (eg Wacher 1975). Certain types of building at Alcester, particularly the group B and some of the group C structures, are very difficult to interpret and as yet add little to our overall understanding of urban structures, except to emphasize that these could be complex in plan and probably quite sophisticated in construction.

Excavations at Tiddington, an extensive settlement 13km east of Alcester where stone buildings were extremely rare, have produced a comparable variety of timber structures which complement the Alcester evidence (Palmer 1982; 1983). Elsewhere in Roman Warwickshire excavated structures are scarce. Among the larger settlements only *Tripontium* has been extensively examined, in a rescue/salvage context. Here it is extremely difficult to identify building plans and there is only one fairly clear example, a simple rectangular possible beam slot structure some 19m × 7m with an entrance to the north-west (Cameron & Lucas 1966, fig 5). At Stretton-on-Fosse, a rural settlement in south Warwickshire, the plans of one stone and several timber structures were incomplete but these buildings seem to have been essentially small (the largest was probably *c* 8m × 5m), with one or at most two rooms. Posthole or post-in-trench construction was favoured

(Gardner, Haldon & Malam 1980, 7–9). These buildings contrast in character with those from Alcester in their size and in the apparently haphazard nature of their layout in relation to the site as a whole.

It remains true, however, that throughout the Roman period some of the buildings in Alcester were of simple plan and unsophisticated construction. Problems arise because it has not usually been possible to define the function of such buildings or to identify a clear distinction between domestic and other structures. Domestic buildings at the upper end of the scale are relatively easy to identify, being of substantial construction (often in part of stone) and having features such as painted wall plaster. Wall plaster was associated with Hughes' building in his site T (**28** on fig 3; fig 11) and probably with both the buildings excavated by Tomlinson in Birch Abbey. It also occurs in connection with most of the buildings examined by Davis, and large quantities were found in a building excavated by Taylor in 1973 in advance of flood barrier construction south of the Stratford Road (**50** on fig 3). More was found by Cracknell in salvage recording at a site in Bleachfield Street on the line of the main east–west road (**90** on fig 3; Cracknell & Ferguson 1985, 129). Wall plaster was also found in building V at 1–5 Bleachfield Street. Its association is therefore generally with stone buildings, and its presence in structures GC and GE is relatively unusual. It is possible, however, that at least some of the plaster found in site G may have derived from the adjacent building in Hughes' site T, as is thought to have been the case with some of the other finds in the area. Plaster in the postholes and foundation trenches of both structures GC and GE should have been placed there in the construction process and therefore has no relevance for the buildings themselves although in some cases it was difficult to distinguish between construction and destruction contexts. Plaster in the destruction layer of building GC may, however, have come from the building itself and plaster in the foundation trenches of GE could also have derived from the earlier building GC. Nevertheless, there is no *a priori* reason why buildings constructed entirely or partly of timber should not have had plastered and painted walls, and a beam slot building from Gas House Lane (of ?3rd-century date; **93** on fig 3) may have been so decorated. Such cases were, however, rare.

Not all the inhabitants of domestic buildings necessarily had the resources or the inclination to decorate their homes in a Romanized way, so the problem of what proportion of the more modest timber structures had a domestic function is at present indeterminable. In the Birch Abbey quarter of the Roman town there is little evidence for heavy pressure on the space available for building. This is indicated by the fairly low density of structures and by their plans. The relative paucity of strip buildings has already been referred to. Such buildings indicate, among other things, that street frontage sites were at a premium, a situation which may have been generally more true in Romano-British towns in the 1st and 2nd centuries than later (Perring 1987, 152). Their existence in Alcester presumably reflects the spread of the building type rather than pressure on development space. Although the evidence for the 3rd and 4th centuries is better than that for the early Roman period, it is nevertheless clear that the street A frontages in Birch Abbey were no more densely built up in the 1st and 2nd centuries than later. Whether the situation was different elsewhere in the town is not clear. The close juxtaposition of structures CWB and CWC on the street B frontage in site C, and the sequence of buildings on the south-west road examined by Taylor (Taylor 1970; **48** on fig 3) may indicate greater densities of buildings in some places than others, not always necessarily in central locations. Much more work would be needed, however, to establish the pattern and significance of any real concentrations of buildings.

Nevertheless, the picture which emerges, primarily from Birch Abbey but also from elsewhere in the town, is of a pattern of buildings and properties which were aligned with varying degrees of precision on the streets of the settlement and closely but by no means densely packed. While the density of buildings was not necessarily much greater than in some rural sites the close relationship of the buildings to the street layout contrasts with that found in rural sites such as Catsgore where such a relationship was perhaps less important (eg Leech 1982, 37). It is possible, however, to see at least parts of the Birch Abbey area as being relatively peripheral to the town as a whole and thus unrepresentative in terms of the overall settlement density, particularly perhaps in the early stages of the growth of the town. The occupied area expanded considerably in the 2nd century and at the southern end of Birch Abbey buildings were apparently being constructed on new sites as late as the 3rd century. The plan of later Roman Alcester appears to develop, on a reduced scale, some of the features of the major towns at this time in terms of the amount of space within which individual buildings were placed, the relative (but not absolute) scale of some of the buildings themselves, and the gradual change in construction techniques from timber to stone. The latter trend was ultimately reversed, with the replacement of stone buildings by timber ones, a change which perhaps began in some places as early as the mid-4th century. This change was also seen in some of the major towns, most spectacularly on the Baths Basilica site at Wroxeter.

Bibliography

Bidwell, P T, 1985 *The Roman fort of Vindolanda at Chesterholm, Northumberland*, HMBCE Archaeol Rep 1

Birss, R S, 1985 Worked bone and shale, *in* J Dool *et al*, Roman Derby: excavations 1968–1983, *Derbyshire Archaeol J*, **105**, 144–6

Booth, P M, 1978 [Bull's Head Yard peat] Alcester, Warwickshire, *West Midlands Archaeol News Sheet*, **21**, 79

—— 1980 *Roman Alcester*, Warwickshire Museum, Warwick

—— 1982a Recent work on Ryknild Street at Alcester, *Trans Birmingham Warwickshire Archaeol Soc*, **92**, 1982 (1988), 136–44

—— 1982b Roman features at 79 Priory Road, Alcester, 1981, *Trans Birmingham Warwickshire Archaeol Soc*, **92**, 1982 (1988), 144–8

—— 1983 Excavations at 64 Bleachfield Street, Alcester, Warwickshire, 1981, *Trans Birmingham Warwickshire Archaeol Soc*, **93**, 1983–4 (1989), 9–32

—— 1985 Roman storebuildings at Alcester, *Trans Birmingham Warwickshire Archaeol Soc*, **94**, 1985–6 (1990), 63–106

—— forthcoming Excavations at 1–5 Bleachfield Street, Alcester, *CBA Res Rep*

—— in prep The origins of Roman Alcester

Booth, P M & Cracknell, S, 1986 Alcester, from prehistory to the Norman conquest, *in* E Savile (ed), *Alcester: a history*, Alcester and District Local History Society, Studley, 5–25

Booth, P M & Grieg, J, 1977 Alcester — Bull's Head Yard, SP089574, *West Midlands Archaeol News Sheet*, **20**, 69

Burnham, B C, 1987 The morphology of Romano-British 'small towns', *Archaeol J*, **144**, 156–90

—— 1988 A survey of building types in Romano-British 'small towns', *J Brit Archaeol Association*, **141**, 35–59

Buxton, D, 1921 The discovery of a Roman coffin at Lower Slaughter, Gloucestershire, *Antiq J*, **1**, 340

Cameron, H & Lucas, J, 1966 Tripontium: first interim report on excavations by the Rugby Archaeological Society at Cave's Inn, near Rugby, *Trans Birmingham Warwickshire Archaeol Soc*, **83**, 1966–7 (1969), 130–79

Carson, R A G, 1969 Alcester (Warwickshire) find of Roman *antoniniani* and *sestertii*, *Numismatic Chronicle*, (7th series) **9**, 123–8

Casey, J, 1983 Imperial campaigns and 4th-century defences in Britain, *in* J Maloney & B Hobley (eds), *Roman urban defences in the west*, CBA Res Rep **51**, 121–4

Chatwin, P B, 1936 Oversley Castle, Alcester, *Trans Birmingham Warwickshire Archaeol Soc*, **60**, 1936 (1940), 145–6

Cracknell, S, 1985a Roman Alcester: recent archaeological excavations, *Trans Birmingham Warwickshire Archaeol Soc*, **94**, 1985–6 (1990), 1–62

—— 1985b 27 High Street, Alcester: a watching brief, August 1987, *Trans Birmingham Warwickshire Archaeol Soc*, **94**, 1985–6 (1990), 124–6

—— forthcoming *Roman Alcester: defences and defended area*, CBA Res Rep

Cracknell, S & Ferguson, R, 1985 The Builder's Yard site, Bleachfield Street, Alcester, 1987: salvage recording, *Trans Birmingham Warwickshire Archaeol Soc*, **94**, 1985–6 (1990), 126–32

Crickmore, J, 1984 *Romano-British urban defences*, BAR **126**

Davis, B, unpublished notes Notes and Diary relating to archaeological investigations in Alcester in the 1920s and 1930s

Dugdale, W, 1656 *The Antiquities of Warwickshire*, London

Evans, E & Booth, P, 1975 Lloyd's Bank gardens, Alcester, Warks [interim report], *West Midlands Archaeol News Sheet*, **18**, 49

Evans, J forthcoming Roman pottery, *in* S Cracknell (ed), *Roman Alcester: defences and defended area*, CBA Res Rep

Frere, S S, 1975 The origin of small towns, *in* W Rodwell & T Rowley (eds), *Small towns of Roman Britain*, BAR **15**, 4–7

—— 1984a British urban defences in earthwork, *Britannia*, **15**, 63–74

—— 1984b Excavations at Dorchester on Thames, 1963, *Archaeol J*, **141**, 91–174

—— 1986 Foreword, *in* M Millett & D Graham, *Excavations on the Romano-British small town at Neatham, Hampshire 1969–1979*, Hampshire Field Club Monogr 3, xv–xvi

—— 1987 *Britannia*, 3rd edn, London

Gardner, P J, Haldon, R & Malam, J, 1980 Prehistoric, Roman and medieval settlement at Stretton-on-Fosse: excavations and salvage 1971–6, *Trans Birmingham Warwickshire Archaeol Soc*, **90**, 1980 (1982), 1–35

Goodburn, R, 1976 Warwickshire: Alcester, *Britannia*, **7**, 331

—— 1978 Roman Britain in 1977, *Britannia*, **9**, 439–40

—— 1979 Roman Britain in 1978, *Britannia*, **10**, 299

Green, C, 1977 *Excavations in the Roman kiln field at Brampton, 1973–4, East Anglian Archaeol*, **5**, 31–95

Green, H J M, 1975 Godmanchester, *in* W Rodwell & T Rowley (eds), *Small towns of Roman Britain, BAR* **15**, 183–210

Green, M J, 1976 *The religions of civilian Roman Britain, BAR* **24**

Gwinnett, A J, 1954 *A history of Alcester*, privately printed, Alcester

Harman, M, Molleson, T I & Price, J L, 1981 Burials, bodies and beheadings in Romano-British and Anglo-Saxon cemeteries, *Bull Brit Mus (Natur Hist)*, **35 (3)**, 159–68

Haverfield, F, 1904 Romano-British Warwickshire, *The Victoria History of the Counties of England, Warwickshire*, vol 1, 223–49

Hingley, R, 1989 Iron Age settlement and society in central and southern Warwickshire, *in* A Gibson (ed), *Midlands prehistory, BAR* **204**, 122–57

Hughes, H V, 1958 Recent work at Roman Alcester, *Trans Birmingham Warwickshire Archaeol Soc*, **76**, 1958 (1960), 10–18

—— 1959 Recent work at Roman Alcester II, *Trans Birmingham Warwickshire Archaeol Soc*, **77**, 1959 (1961), 27–32

—— 1960 Roman Alcester, *West Midlands Archaeol News Sheet*, **3**, 3

—— 1961 Roman Alcester, *West Midlands Archaeol News Sheet*, **4**, 3

—— 1962 Roman Alcester, *West Midlands Archaeol News Sheet*, **5**, 4

—— 1963 Alcester, Warks, *West Midlands Archaeol News Sheet*, **6**, 4

—— 1964 Alcester, *West Midlands Archaeol News Sheet* **7**, 5

—— 1965 Alcester [interim report], *West Midlands Archaeol News Sheet*, **8**, 5

Lapidge, M, 1977 The medieval hagiography of St Ecgwine, Vale of Evesham Historical Society Research Papers 6, 77–94

Leach, P, 1982 *Ilchester*, vol. I, *Excavations 1974–1975, Western Archaeol Trust Monogr* **3**

Leech, R, 1982 *Excavations at Catsgore 1970–1973, Western Archaeol Trust Monogr* **2**

Mackreth, D F, 1987 Roman public buildings, *in* J Schofield & R Leech, *Urban archaeology in Britain, CBA Res Rep* **61**, 133–46

Maloney, J & Hobley, B (eds), 1983 *Roman urban defences in the west, CBA Res Rep* **51**

Meaney, A, 1964 *A gazetteer of early Anglo-Saxon burial sites*, London

Millett, M & Graham, D, 1986 *Excavations on the Romano-British small town at Neatham, Hampshire 1969–1979, Hampshire Field Club Monogr* **3**

Morris, P, 1979 *Agricultural buildings in Roman Britain, BAR* **70**

Neal, D S, 1984 A sanctuary at Wood Lane End, Hemel Hempstead, *Britannia*, **15**, 193–215

Osborne, P, 1971 An insect fauna from the Roman site at Alcester, Warwickshire, *Britannia*, **2**, 156–65

Palmer, N, 1982 *Roman Stratford: excavations at Tiddington 1980–81*, Warwickshire Museum, Warwick

—— 1983 Tiddington Roman settlement, *West Midlands Archaeol*, **26**, 36–46

Perring, D, 1987 Domestic buildings in Roman towns, *in* J Schofield & R Leech, *Urban archaeology in Britain, CBA Res Rep* **61**, 147–55

Place, U, 1964 Alcester [interim report], *West Midlands Archaeol News Sheet*, **7**, 3

—— 1965 Alcester [interim report], *West Midlands Archaeol News Sheet*, **8**, 10

Rankov, N B, 1982 Roman Britain in 1981, *Britannia*, **13**, 328–95

Rivet, A L F, 1975 Summing up: the classification of minor towns and related settlements, *in* W Rodwell and T Rowley (eds), *Small towns of Roman Britain, BAR* **15**, 111–14

Rodwell, W, 1972 The Roman fort at Great Chesterford, Essex, *Britannia*, **3**, 290–3

Rodwell, W & Rowley, T (eds), 1975 *Small towns of Roman Britain, BAR* **15**

Rogerson, A, 1977 *Excavations at Scole, 1973, East Anglian Archaeol*, **5**, 97–224

Ross, A, 1968 Shafts, pits, wells — sanctuaries of the Belgic Britons? *in* J M Coles & D D A Simpson (eds), *Studies in ancient Europe: essays presented to Stuart Piggott*, 255–85

Royce, D, 1883 Finds near Stow-on-the-Wold, *Trans Bristol Gloucestershire Archaeol Soc*, **7**, 76

Seaby, W A, 1945 A Roman building at Alcester, Warwickshire, *Trans Birmingham Warwickshire Archaeol Soc*, **66**, 1945–6 (1950), 35–48

—— 1951 Alcester and other Roman settlement sites of the West Midlands, *The Archaeological News Letter*, **3(7)**, 119–20

Schofield, J, & Leech, R, 1987 *Urban archaeology in Britain, CBA Res Rep* **61**

Smith, R F, 1987 *Roadside settlements in lowland Roman Britain, BAR* **157**

Stead, I M & Rigby, V, 1986 *Baldock, the excavation of a Roman and pre-Roman settlement 1968–72, Britannia Monogr Ser* **7**

Taylor, S J, 1969 Alcester, Warks, Nos 27–33 Bleachfield Street, *West Midlands Archaeol News Sheet*, **12**, 21–2

—— 1970 Bleachfield Street, Alcester, Warks, *West Midlands Archaeol News Sheet*, **13**, 38–9

—— 1972 Birch Abbey, Alcester, Warks, *West Midlands Archaeol News Sheet*, **15**, 14

—— 1973 Summary report on excavations at Alcester, 18th June to 1st August 1973, *West Midlands Archaeol News Sheet*, **16**, 22

Todd, M, 1970 The small towns of Roman Britain, *Britannia*, **1**, 114–30

Tomlinson, R A, 1964 Alcester, *West Midlands Archaeol News Sheet*, **7**, 5

Bibliography

—— 1965 Alcester [interim report], *West Midlands Archaeol News Sheet*, **8**, 5

Wacher, J, 1966a Earthwork defences of the second century, *in* J Wacher (ed), *The civitas capitals of Roman Britain*, Leicester, 60–9

—— (ed), 1966b *The civitas capitals of Roman Britain*, Leicester

—— 1975 *The towns of Roman Britain*, London

Webster, G A, 1958 The Roman military advance under Ostorius Scapula, *Archaeol J*, **115**, 1958 (1960), 49–98

—— 1966 Fort and town in early Roman Britain, in J Wacher (ed), *The civitas capitals of Roman Britain*, Leicester, 31–45

—— 1967 A Roman system of fortified posts along Watling Street, Britain, in *Roman frontier studies 1967* (1971), Tel Aviv

—— 1974 The West Midlands in the Roman period; a brief survey, *Trans Birmingham Warwickshire Archaeol Soc*, **86**, 49–58

—— 1981 *Rome against Caratacus*, London

Wedlake, W J, 1982 *The excavation of the shrine of Apollo at Nettleton, Wiltshire, 1956–1971*, Res Rep Comm Soc Antiq London 40

Wilson, D R (ed), 1966 Roman Britain in 1965, I, sites explored, *J Roman Stud*, **56**, 206

—— 1971 Warwickshire: Alcester, *Britannia*, **2**, 262

Wright, R P, 1966 Roman Britain in 1965, II, Inscriptions, *J Roman Stud,* **56**, 224

Young, C J, 1977 *Oxfordshire Roman pottery*, *BAR* **43**

Index *by Lesley Adkins*

Main page references are given in bold. Entries which are shown in italics are page numbers on which figures, tables and/or plates occur. As most of this report refers to Roman features and finds, there is no separate entry for Roman or Romano-British. The microfiche has not been indexed: full references to the microfiche are given throughout the text. References to Part 2 refer to the index in the accompanying volume.